WEBS
OF
SMOKE

1 *Papauer ſativum album.*
White garden Poppie.

WEBS
OF
SMOKE

SMUGGLERS, WARLORDS, SPIES, AND THE HISTORY OF THE INTERNATIONAL DRUG TRADE

Kathryn Meyer
and
Terry Parssinen

ROWMAN & LITTLEFIELD PUBLISHERS, INC.
Lanham • Boulder • New York • Oxford

ROWMAN & LITTLEFIELD PUBLISHERS, INC.

Published in the United States of America
by Rowman & Littlefield Publishers, Inc.
4720 Boston Way, Lanham, Maryland 20706

12 Hid's Copse Road
Cumnor Hill, Oxford OX2 9JJ, England

British Library Cataloguing in Publication Information Available

Library of Congress Cataloging-in-Publication Data

Meyer, Kathryn.
    Webs of smoke : smugglers, warlords, spies, and the history of the
international drug trade / Kathryn Meyer and Terry Parssinen.
        p.   cm. — (State and society in East Asia)
    Includes bibliographical references and index.
    ISBN 0-8476-9016-4 (cloth : alk. paper).
    1. Drug traffic—History.   2. Narcotics, Control of—History.
I. Parssinen, Terry M.   II. Title.   III. Series.
HV5801.M45   1998
363.45'09—dc21   98-23716
                                                                CIP

Design by Deborah Clark

Frontispiece: Woodcut for John Gerard, *The Herball or General Historie of Plantes*
(London, 1633). Rare Book Collection, David Bishop Skillman Library,
Lafayette College.

Calligraphy: Zhongguo Huafa Dazidian [Dictionary of Chinese Writing Styles]
Taibei, Taiwan: Taiwan Datong Huaju Yinhang, 1976.

Printed in the United States of America

∞ ™ The paper used in this publication meets the minimum requirements of
American National Standard for Information Sciences—Permanence of Paper
for Printed Library Materials, ANSI Z39.48–1984.

To our parents,

Helen Meyer and the late John Meyer

and

June and Ollie Parssinen

CONTENTS

ILLUSTRATIONS

TABLES

MAPS

FOREWORD

JACK BLUM

The public debate over drug use and drug law enforcement policy is frustrating for those of us who have studied the issue in depth. Invariably the debate over drugs—in the political arena, on the talk show circuit, and in the press—is highly emotional. Extremes command center stage. One group wants narcotics legalized, whereas another wants ever stronger punishment and ever longer jail terms for both dealers and addicts. The African-American community sees a genocidal plot. Nativists see a foreign assault on the United States. Yet this river of words is only rarely related to reality. Most of the proposed solutions are related to the politics of the proposers—not to the way the drug business in fact operates.

Law enforcement agency rhetoric and government statistics are tailored to support budget requests and political needs. Very little "data" relating to the drug problem can be taken at face value. At the 1996 meeting of the American Society of Criminology researchers effectively challenged the validity of government-sponsored statistics on drug use among those arrested. The statistical data set was a creation of the Reagan administration, which was then in the process of hyping the drug problem to make political capital. The Park Service justifies a portion of its budget for its rangers by assigning them to fight drug use in the national park system. The Park Service "drug" budget is then folded into the larger budget of the "war on drugs."

The impact of drugs on users, on their families, and on society as a whole is all too real. Drugs have destroyed promising careers, have impoverished families, and have turned neighborhoods into war zones in which rival gangs fight over markets and market share with automatic weapons. This is not an isolated American phenomenon. In some countries the damage has become a national crisis. Pakistan, for example, has 3 million heroin addicts in a population of a little more than 100 million. The addicts are among its best educated and most promising young men. Wherever it appears, the problem cannot be ignored or wished away—it demands governmental involvement.

This book makes an important contribution to the drug debate by presenting the history of the modern narcotics traffic and its parallel law enforcement efforts in a fully textured and balanced way. It probes motives and examines structures, following trafficking organizations from their creation to their demise. The search for understanding and solutions must begin with this history, which shows that the problem is perennial and cannot be solved by winning a war. It is part of the human condition and is likely to remain so. The challenge for policy makers is to keep the problem small and manageable and to limit the damage to society.

Above all, the players in the drug business are flexible. Their behavior shifts to take advantage of the profit opportunities of the moment. They exploit weakness wherever they find it. They make themselves into a target that moves. When one market is closed, they find another. When one smuggling method is detected, they try something else.

Politicians and bureaucrats who work the drug issue can be equally flexible and opportunistic. The story of Harry Anslinger and his role in the American counternarcotics effort is highly instructive in this regard. Anslinger built a career and a bureaucratic empire by promoting the drug threat. As I see it, for the last thirty years the "war on drugs" and the "tough on crime" sloganeering in elections has frequently been just as opportunistic. In an environment in which outright racism is unacceptable, the drug problem provides useful code words for those who wish to avoid being identified as racist in today's American political debate.

The drug trade is run by a constantly changing and shifting group of individuals and organizations, whose power waxes and wanes, shifting from group to group and from country to country. The traffickers exploit the gaps in the international and national legal systems. They are good at bribing governments and government officials and even better at using the artificial boundaries of the nation-state to block the efforts of law enforcement agencies. They use the offshore banking and financial system to hide their money.

This book will convince the reader that the drug trade is not the product of a global conspiracy. There is no central command and control and no master plan to destroy any population or group. The trade is there to serve market demand and make money for the traffickers. It is a business, albeit an illegal one. Strategies to disable it should focus on its commercial weaknesses.

Read on and join the ranks of those who appreciate just how complicated a problem drug trafficking and use really is.

PREFACE

ON POPPIES

Then Helen, daughter of Zeus, turned to new thoughts. Presently she cast a drug into the wine whereof they drank, a drug to lull all pain and anger, and bring forgetfulness of every sorrow.

Homer, *Odyssey*[1]

Even the missionary reformers who traveled through China preaching against the evils of opium had to stop every so often to marvel at the splendor of a poppy field in bloom. *Papaver somniferum* is a magnificent flower whose gaudy petals, whether white, orange, or purple, seem all the more glorious because of their brief display. After a day of bloom, the petals fall, revealing a capsule that oozes a white latex when scored with a small knife. The latex darkens on contact with the air and hardens into a gummy paste that can be scraped, balled, and sold as raw opium.

A reader might come away from this text with the impression that opium is Chinese in origin. Nothing could be further from the truth. The opium poppy is native to Asia Minor and was known in the ancient world. Sumerians called it the plant of joy. References to it appear in the works of Homer and Hesiod, and it was noted in the pharmacology of Hippocrates and Dioscorides of Anazarbus. As folk medicine, poppy capsules, stems, and seeds were boiled into a tea to relieve stomach complaints, diarrhea, sleeplessness, and, of course, melancholy. John Gerard, the English herbalist, recommended "the heads of Poppie boiled in water with sugar to a sirrup causeth sleepe, and is good against rheumes and catarrhes." He also noted that "it leaveth behind it oftentimes a mischiefe worse than the disease it selfe."[2] Medicinal use of laudanum, which is a tincture of opium, continued in England and America through the early twentieth century.

British history is tied to the opium trade, yet it was not Europeans who introduced poppies to Asia. Opium traveled east with the Muslim traders who preceded the Europeans by centuries. It appears in Chinese medical texts in the eighth century A.D. In China, as in Europe, it was boiled and used primarily as a medicine. A medical text from 1578 calls it *a fu yong* after the Arabic *afyoun*, which later became the modern Chinese *yapian* or Japanese *ahen*.

Opium was taken as tea until the discovery of the New World brought tobacco to the Asian coast. Combining opium with tobacco introduced a new, more potent method of ingestion and allowed for the separation of its recreational use from its medicinal role. The full opium smoking ritual with all its accoutrements—lamp, pipe, and bowl—developed almost immediately thereafter. Opium is not lit and smoked like tobacco. Rather, a ball of opium paste is placed on a pin, which is then heated over a lamp. The resulting vapor is inhaled through the pipe. The development of this opium smoking ritual, so associated with the Chinese, happened along the South China coast, where Dutch and Portuguese sailors mingled with Chinese.

The British contribution to poppy proliferation was the commercialization of opium. As the British East India Company extended its control through the Asian subcontinent in the 1700s, it increased its revenues by licensing opium farms in the area around Patna in Bihar and around Benares in Uttar Pradesh. Seeds were given to *ryots*, who were government-licensed farmers. They planted in November, harvested in February or March, and sold their product to agents of the company (and later of the Crown). The opium was then auctioned through Calcutta to private traders commanding speedy and elegant opium clippers. By the 1820s, this developed into an efficient system of product standardization and delivery that brought to the China coast an increasing volume of high-quality opium. It triggered a fiscal and social crisis in that nation.

Opium is a good cash crop from a peasant's point of view. The opium poppy will grow in any climate below latitude fifty-six degrees to the equator. It flourishes in well-drained, fertile soil, which produces the highest morphine content; yet poor soils will also sustain the poppy. Poppy seeds can be sown in the fall in warmer climates, or in the early spring. They germinate in cold weather. The young shoots need to be thinned, but the young leaves can be eaten. The harvest is over by late spring, permitting a second food crop in many areas.

The poppies bloom in middle to late spring. The flowers blossom and drop their petals over the course of a day or two, leaving behind a green seed bulb, or capsule. After a few days the capsule takes on a whitish hue. At this critical moment opium farming becomes a labor-intensive operation. The farmer must go through his field making small incisions along each capsule about two millimeters deep. The latex oozes from the cuts and is allowed to sit overnight and harden. In the morning the residue is collected, balled, and wrapped. This is the raw opium, which is sold to the processor. It is then boiled in water, filtered, and boiled a second time. It then becomes the gum that can be used for smoking.

Opium produces its effect through the action of its primary alkaloid, morphine, on the nervous system. Poppies also carry other alkaloids—thebaine, codeine, papaverine, narcotine, and narcacine. Morphine content averages around 10 percent in the poppy but varies according to soil and climate conditions. When it is smoked or taken as tea, opium contains a mixture of elements other than morphine that provide buffers to the body. Opium smokers in China at the turn of the century preferred the opium from Patna. The morphine content was in fact lower, but the resulting experience was more pleasant. Indeed, Bihar to this day produces medical-grade morphine, preferred because its opium has a higher content of narcotine, which counteracts opium's tendency to produce constipation and sleep.

We have come across many references in the documents to casual users of opium—social smokers who do not have a daily habitual craving for the drug. We do not find the same kind of references in the case of those who substituted opium's derivatives when smoking opium became illegal and therefore dangerous. Morphine, first isolated in 1806 by a German pharmacist, Friedrich Sertürner became more versatile once the hypodermic syringe came into use in the 1850s. Heroin, introduced in 1898, was a further refinement of morphine with greatly increased potency. These "white drugs" were the choice of poor addicts in China during the early years of our century whenever smoking opium became scarce. They were smoked, vaporized and inhaled through tinfoil, taken as pills (red pills or gold pills, which could be either swallowed or smoked) or injected. Those who could afford opium and could smoke in safety favored the pipe, the lamp, and the opium couch. It was when this luxury became hard to procure that our story begins.[3]

N O T E S

1. Homer, *Odyssey of Homer,* S. H. Butcher and A. Lang, trans. (New York: Modern Library, n.d.), 51.
2. John Gerard, *The Herball or Generall History of Plantes* (London: Adam Islip, Joice Norton, and Richard Whitakers, 1633).
3. Information about poppies can be found in U.S. Treasury Department, Bureau of Narcotics, *The Opium Poppy and Other Poppies* (Washington, D.C.: Government Printing Office, 1944); John Scarborough, "The Opium Poppy in Hellenistic and Roman Medicine," in *Drugs and Narcotics in History,* ed. Roy Porter and Mikulas Tiech (Cambridge: Cambridge University Press, 1995), 4–23; Herbert A. Giles, *Some Truths About Opium Smoking* (Cambridge: W. Heffer, 1923), presents a lot of information about opium in China as he argues for its legalization; Daniel M. Perrine, *The Chemistry of Mind-Altering Drugs: History, Pharmacology, and Cultural Context* (Washington D.C.: American Chemical Society, 1996); the novel by Gay Courter, *Flowers in the Blood* (New York: Dutton, 1990), includes detailed descriptions of the British opium operation in India, as does the preface to Peter Ward Fay's *The Opium War, 1840–1842* (Chapel Hill: University of North Carolina Press, 1975). Alvin Moscow, *Merchants of Heroin: An In-Depth Portrayal of Business in the Underworld* (New York: Dial, 1968), gives a detailed description of opium growing and processing in Turkey. For a descriptive catalogue of all drugs, see Andrew Weil and Winifred Rosen, *From Chocolate to Morphine: Everything you Need to Know about Mind-Altering Drugs* (Boston: Houghton Mifflin, 1993). Michael Pollan recently described his experience growing the legally questionable poppy in "Opium Made Easy: One Gardener's Encounter with the War on Drugs," *Harper's,* 294 (April 1997), 35–58. The following Web sites also have a wealth of information about poppies: <www.hort.purdue.edu/newcrop/duke-energy/papaver-somniferum> and "The Vaults of Erowid," <www.erowid.com/herbs/poppy/poppy.shtml>.

ACKNOWLEDGMENTS

We are grateful to the following institutions and persons, without whose assistance we could not have written this book.

For research funding and support: the National Endowment for the Humanities; Lafayette College junior faculty leave program; the Center for Chinese Studies at the University of California, Berkeley; Temple University Faculty Research Fund; University of Maryland Office of the Dean of Undergraduate Studies; and the Dana Faculty Research Fund of the University of Tampa.

For referring us to sources and assisting us in archives: Annie K. Chang, Alison Altstatt, and Jeff Kapellas, all of the Center for Chinese Studies Library at the University of California, Berkeley, gave valuable advice and important leads and kept Kathryn well fed and cheerful through a critical year of research; Mark Haller of Temple University gave us some important references to smuggling from Cuba in the 1920s; and William O. Walker III of Florida International University made us aware of the existence of the State Department name files of international narcotics traffickers. Kathryn was warned that, as a woman writing about the military, she would have difficulties doing research in Japan. However, this did not prove to be the case, as many Japanese colleagues provided generous assistance. In particular, Kathryn wishes to acknowledge Imura Tetsuo, Professor of Humanities, Niigata University, Niigata, Japan, whose encyclopedic knowledge of Japanese military and colonial archives in Japan and the United States helped her locate the documents to piece together the Japanese side of the story and Tanaka Harumi of the Japanese National Defense Academy, Yokosuka, Japan, who provided her with valuable criticism and encouragement.

For reading and criticizing the manuscript in whole or in part: David Courtwright of the University of North Florida; David Musto of Yale University; Alan Block of Penn State University; Frederic Wakeman Jr. of the Institute of East Asian Studies of the University of California, Berkeley; Jonathan Marshall of the *San Francisco Chronicle*; Andy Solomon of the University of Tampa; Mark Haller and Allen Davis of Temple University; Corinne Lyman of Ohio Wesleyan University; William O. Walker III of Florida International University; Elizabeth Perry of Harvard University; and William Miles of the Department of Chemistry, Lafayette College, who helped us understand some of the technical aspects of narcotics processing.

For encouragement and sustenance: Peter and Barbara Ilias, for providing Terry with housing during research in London; Yoko Maeda, for providing Kathryn with housing during research in Tokyo; Betsy Meyer, Sarah Meyer, and Scott MacKay for providing room, board, and encouragement in Washington D.C.; Higashihara Fumikaze for cheering us on and running last minute errands in Tokyo; Diana Boxer; and especially Carol Parssinen.

INTRODUCTION

MEN IN THE SHADOWS

The facts show how weak human laws are against human passions.

Canton [Guangzhou] Register,
November 8, 1827[1]

Drug dealers are entrepreneurs engaged in a high-risk, high-profit enterprise. From a businessman's perspective, narcotics are an ideal commodity. Relative to their weight and bulk, their value is considerable. Produced in countries where peasant labor is cheap, they can be sold readily on markets that seem to need little in formal development or advertising. They can sustain an enormous price markup. The world appetite for drugs is expanding and appears to be virtually limitless.

THE NARCOTICS BUSINESS

Drug dealers, like their legitimate counterparts, have logistical business problems. They have to recruit, train, and retain loyal subordinates. They need to ensure their source of supply and to control their markets. They must decide where to bank and how to invest their profits. They worry about competition, as well as the reliability of their associates. Beyond this, because their business is illegal, they face additional concerns.

They must consider the use of violence and the effective expenditure of bribe money. And, of course, they take risks that ordinary businessmen do not, such as incarceration and death. These worries are perhaps the most distinguishing feature of their business.

Traffickers as entrepreneurs operate in a challenging environment of laws deliberately created to adversely affect their trade. Such regulations make their businesses vulnerable in four critical areas. First, the fields in which poppies or coca grow and the factories in which they are refined are ready targets for police action, leading to frequent disruption of supply. Second, the process of delivery includes the crossing of guarded borders. Third, banking their profits in the ordinary manner opens them up to scrutiny that they would rather avoid. Lastly, enforcement of their mostly verbal contracts poses a problem. When wronged, they cannot turn to the courts for justice. Thus supply, delivery, finance, and contractual enforcement are critically altered by legal constraints on their business.

Such constraints, however, were not always the major challenge faced by narcotics dealers. From 1858 until the opening years of the twentieth century, traders in opium and opiates went about their business freely, amassing profits that they reinvested in other commodities and enterprises. When they organized, it was to form merchant associations. They enjoyed the social status that their wealth allowed them. Many of the great trading houses with ties to the China coast owe a debt to the opium trade: Jardine, Matheson, and Company, the Sassoons, and Butterfield, Swire and Company. Many reputable European pharmaceutical companies produced morphine and heroin in massive quantities: Hoffman La Roche, Merck, and Bayer. Until 1906 they did so without subterfuge; their only restrictions were tariff schedules.

After 1906, however, the business climate began to shift. In that year the Chinese empire, with the active support of both British and American governments, issued regulations designed to rid its territory of opium use within ten years. Such a sudden change in one nation's legal code disrupted the normal flow of business. China was the world's leading market for narcotic drugs. The negotiations leading to the Chinese anti-opium edict of 1906 marked the beginning of an international effort that would find concrete form in League of Nations narcotics control efforts in the 1920s and 1930s. As the trade moved underground, traffickers who remained in the business had to reorganize their operations in the four critical areas of supply, delivery, finance, and contract enforcement if they were to keep their customers satisfied.

Until the Communist revolution of 1949, those customers mostly lived in China. In the early twentieth century, smaller markets developed in North America and Egypt, but these were dwarfed by China. For instance, Colonel (later General) Joseph W. Stilwell, serving as an American military attaché in China in 1935, estimated that 20 percent of China's population of 400 million was addicted to opiates. Of these, 90 percent (72 million) used opium. The other 10 percent (8 million) used morphine or heroin.[2]

By contrast, Harry Anslinger, the head of the U.S. Federal Bureau of Narcotics, estimated the number of American addicts in 1931 to fall between 120,000 and 140,000. By 1938, the American rate of addiction had fallen to less than .2 percent. T. W. Russell Pasha, conscientious Director of the Egyptian Central Narcotics Intelligence Bureau, estimated that in 1929 Egypt had about 250,000 regular users of heroin. Although the precision of these figures is open to question, as order-of-magnitude estimates they are useful. The maximum number of American and Egyptian heroin addicts amounts to less than 5 percent of the Chinese morphine and heroin addicts. Assuming that another 400,000 heroin addicts may have been scattered around the world, Chinese addicts still accounted for about 90 percent of the total. This is in addition to an estimated 72 million opium smokers. Furthermore, these calculations were made thirty years after the first prohibition went into effect.[3]

EFFORTS TO RESTRICT NARCOTICS

The multinational restriction of narcotics began in 1906, when the Chinese government, with the blessings of Great Britain and America, began programs to eliminate the habit at home. From its first laws and decrees grew an international network of legal arrangements to contain the traffic. The United States initiated the first narcotics convention, convened at Shanghai in 1909, to discuss the problems of opium smoking throughout the Far East. Follow-up conferences at The Hague in 1911–12, 1913, and 1914 resulted in more substantial agreements that became the basis for League of Nations initiatives that followed the end of World War I.[4]

In 1921, the League of Nations created the Advisory Committee on Traffic in Opium and Other Dangerous Drugs, commonly known as the Opium Advisory Committee. Between 1925 and 1936 it produced plans to control narcotics at their source. One such arrangement was the creation, in 1925, of a certificate system to track the international movement of narcotic drugs. Thereafter importers had to secure a certificate from the appropriate government official attesting that each of their consignments would be used only for medical or scientific purposes. Again, in 1931, a conference formulated an agreement aimed at reducing the world's supply of manufactured drugs to a level equaling the estimated requirement for medical uses. The framers hoped that this arrangement would eliminate the excessive production of opiates that was being diverted into the illicit traffic.[5]

In addition to formulating conventions, the Opium Advisory Committee did valuable work in less visible ways. It gathered and disseminated information about seizures of illicit drugs, their origin, and the names and nationalities of traffickers. This sharing of information allowed the League to pinpoint hot spots in the drug traffic and to bring political pressure to bear on offending nations, albeit with varying degrees of success. The statistics cited above are but one small sample of the data made available by this intelligence system.

DRUG TRAFFICKERS' EFFORTS TO ADAPT

Our study analyzes the changing structure of the international narcotics business that the League of Nations system sought to eliminate. The establishment of legal and enforcement barriers created a new climate. From 1907 through the 1930s the methods of delivering drugs to consumers changed drastically, with traffickers reacting to prohibitionary legislation and enforcement policies as problems to be solved. They created secret delivery systems and opened new sources of supply. Legitimate and traditional businessmen were gradually supplanted by illicit entrepreneurs and criminal gangs.

Criminal organizations specializing in vice already existed. They brought their special skills and experience in illicit markets into the arena being vacated by the legitimate companies that had developed the drug market. However, what transpired after 1906 was not simply a case of organized crime stepping into the narcotics business.[6] The changing enterprise forced traffickers to reach accommodations with men in power. Although this had often occurred in vice markets in the past, the nature and profitability of the drug trade intensified the need for such arrangements. A drug trafficker could create opportunities for a politician, and vice versa. On the most primitive level, traffickers offered politicians a share of the profits in return for protection. But that was only the first step. By the 1930s, men with political connections dominated the drug traffic in Asia. These men moved beyond mere bribery to become political actors in their own right. The larger and more successful became involved in arms procurement and espionage as well as narcotics trafficking. Some even managed, like their predecessors, to acquire social status in the legitimate world.[7] Sympathetic politicians could offer much more than mere protection. They could smooth over a variety of business difficulties. Dealings between traffickers and politicians evolved into complex, multifaceted relationships.

It is no coincidence that narcotics traffickers thrive in areas of political tension and instability. Individual politicians may enter into transactions with traffickers for personal enrichment. But enduring relationships must be grounded in something more substantial than personal greed. Successful traffickers find situations in which politicians, who might be uneasy about such relationships under normal conditions, are willing to compromise their scruples in order to serve larger political goals. In such a climate, traffickers can offer politicians substantial rewards. Traffickers have vast sums of money, of course, but they also have access to secrets. In addition, their smugglers' skills at moving drugs can be just as easily applied to arms or money. The most successful traffickers become entrepreneurs who thrive in conditions of disorder in which politicians with strategic agendas need their support.

The key to this relationship lies in the four vulnerable points of the trafficking enterprise: supply, delivery, investment, and enforcement. Supply is the most cumbersome operation. Narcotic drugs must be cultivated, harvested, and processed. Sympathetic politicians can help create the time and space required for the operation. Delivery is the most dangerous undertaking. A trafficker's success lies in his ability to penetrate barriers. At the point of entry contraband becomes vulnerable to government interception or to hijacking by other thieves. This is all the more true of goods with the value of narcotics. Borders are places where traffickers forge working relationships with political or military figures who provide protection for their operations.[8]

Finance is the most delicate business arrangement. The profits from narcotic sales have often underwritten legitimate enterprises. Moving money from the underworld to open financial ventures means crossing a second kind of barrier. As early as the 1930s bank accounts and money transfers began to pose a special danger to traffickers, unless government or military officials rendered investment risk-free. Enforcement is the most brutal aspect of the trade. When it is not handled discreetly, it brings unwanted public scrutiny to the business. Government or military officials can be helpful in disciplining errant business associates or eliminating rival operations, often under the guise of antinarcotics campaigns.

This study concentrates on the development of the increasingly illicit narcotics business between 1907 and 1949. It focuses on traffickers as illicit entrepreneurs adapting to problems of supply, delivery, investment, and enforcement during the years when East Asia dominated the traffic. It is a global study, yet it describes similar business problems encountered by traffickers from diverse cultures. The book is divided into ten chapters, each focusing on a specific time, place, and set of personalities. Some of the chapters overlap, and some of the characters leave the narrative only to reappear later. The subject of the book is not any one character but the structure of the illicit narcotics industry itself. It is an enterprise that is very much with us today.

ORIGINS OF THE OPIUM TRADE

Earlier in this century opium smoking was considered a Chinese vice that would take root elsewhere as Chinese communities formed around the world. International trafficking laws were put into place as much to keep the evil from spreading as to cure China. Yet the habit, although deeply rooted in China by the beginning of this century, was not indigenous. When the Chinese government banned opium in 1906, it was returning to an earlier prohibition that it had surrendered only by force. Smoking opium first came to Chinese shores in foreign merchant vessels, primarily those flying British and American flags. Ironically, these were the same countries that later encouraged the twentieth-century restrictions.

China's first attempt to ban opium use began in the early 1700s, and culminated in the Opium War of 1840–42. In spite of the exotic setting—South China in the days of the tea clippers, swashbuckling British merchant-adventurers, and imperial Chinese bureaucrats with their robes and rituals—certain patterns exist at the center of the tale that reappear wherever drugs, money, and politicians come together.

The story of the Opium War originates in Europe. Although opium was used in Asia prior to Western penetration, it was with the coming of the West that its full commercial potential was realized. In the seventeenth century Portuguese, Spanish, and Dutch merchant-adventurers were searching for wealth in the Far Eastern trade. These were the first nations whose mariners got to the Spice Islands in the South Seas and

progressed along the China coast. These daring men came as merchants, pirates, empire builders, or missionaries; many followed careers
that defied easy classification. They met a hostile climate, many losing
their lives to dysentery, cholera, and malaria. Others adapted and survived. It was in the search for medicinal protection against the ravages
of such diseases that opium came into use.

Opium's other charms soon became evident as well. It was first used
for purely recreational purposes mixed with another addictive substance
introduced from the New World: tobacco. It was an easy step to take
from the tobacco mixture to make a processed paste that, when held by
a pin and heated over a lamp, produces a narcotic vapor that can be
inhaled through a pipe. Opium use not only induces a pleasurable
dreamlike state but entails intricate rituals of use, such as preparing the
opium ball, holding it on the pin over the heat of the lamp so that it will
vaporize but not burn, and inhaling the smoke through the pipe in a
single, lung-expanding gulp. It involves equipment that can be beauti-
fully crafted and with use takes on the character of the user: pipes,
lamps, and the couch on which the smoker enjoys his reverie. Opium
smoking became an expression of refinement and wealth.[9]

The Chinese empire of the seventeenth and eighteenth centuries
could afford its luxuries. The stability that resulted from the Manchu
invasion of 1644 gave rise to an economic vitality whose richness can be
witnessed in the luxury of the palace itself. Manchurian emperors became active patrons of Chinese arts and scholarship. Financial well-
being created the self-confidence that allowed the Qianlong emperor in
1793 to respond with disdain to a formal request by King George III to
open trade. "The productions of our Empire are manifold, and in great
abundance," he said, "nor do we stand in the least Need of the Produce
of other Countries."[10]

Behind the emperor's words lay more than mere boasting. He was
reiterating for British petitioners a principle that had become encoded
into law: International commerce was not essential to the empire. Indeed, foreign merchants had proven by their actions over time that they
were little better than the pirates and brigands that plagued the coast.
The dynastic reaction to the arrival of European merchants had been to
close China's port cities to trade in 1757. As a small concession to those
who sought Chinese products, the emperor designated the city of
Guangzhou as the singular port for foreign trade. He created a trade
monopoly, the Cohong, where a set number of Chinese merchant
houses purchased the privilege of engaging in foreign commerce. Com-

mercial regulations limited the trading season to the spring. Laws restricted the lives and activities of those foreigners allowed into the city: They could not leave a designated enclave, the island of Shamen; they could not bring women with them; they could not learn Chinese (although some did); and they could not communicate directly with the government but had to rely on their Chinese trading partners to forward any requests or complaints to the authorities.

At the time of these first encounters, European trade was equally monopolistic. The British East India Company, for instance, capitalized half by government monies and half by private stockholders, limited the right to trade between England and the Far East to only licensed company merchants. Much the same was true of their continental counterparts. These companies often engaged in private commerce while carrying out governmental functions. It was the armies attached to the British East India Company, for instance, that carved out the beginnings of the empire. The Battle of Plassey of 1757, a decisive engagement that ensured British domination over northern India, was fought largely by the company's army, as were the battles against the French for preeminence on the subcontinent.[11]

Once established as the regents of Northern India, the company needed revenue to function. Its agents found this in the opium fields in the area under their control around the city of Patna. They took control of the poppy crop and its revenues, growing it by license and selling it at regular auctions in Calcutta. They understood the nature of the commodity they were handling. To assuage their consciences, they maintained some control over the drug by selling only a limited amount at a high price. They nodded to their Chinese counterparts by engaging only in the production of opium. The dirty work of smuggling was left to private traders; the company divorced itself from responsibility for the drug once it left Calcutta. Nevertheless, the revenue from opium sales made its way into company accounts. Under the pressure of competition from Malwa opium grown near Bombay, the company increased its own production and eventually established control over the output of the princely states as well.

The eighteenth century was an age of mercantilist sensibilities. Both European and Chinese governments worried about their national store of silver and gold. Under Guangzhou trade regulations, foreign merchants worked at a disadvantage. Because China bought little from abroad, all merchants paid for Chinese products with precious metal. As British merchants attempted to slake the growing national thirst for tea with the popular Chinese product, British silver flowed into Chinese coffers. Enterprising merchants found their way around this commercial difficulty through opium. A triangle traffic developed in which opium smuggling yielded the silver later used to buy tea legally, which was then shipped to London.

Thus, far from being an indigenous Chinese problem, opium came to that country with foreign trade and against the mandates of the legal codes. The official reaction to opium was regulation. It was restricted to the medicinal tariff schedule in 1729. Laws of increasing severity were enacted against its import over the next hundred years, all to little effect. Opium smuggling continued. Not only did it prove to be profitable to the merchants involved but the situation created by the smugglers on the China coast became the key to implementing a larger national policy. As the East India Company valued its good name and did not directly engage in the trade, it sold the drug to private traders. These country traders, as they were called, weakened the company monopoly by carrying legal goods as well. At the same time smuggled opium pioneered British commerce inside the closed Chinese border. The growing popularity of opium in spite of regulation convinced British merchants of the boundless China market, and it was these men who became champions of free trade.

In the early days, when opium use was limited to the South China coastal area, Beijing authorities did not consider it a crisis. By 1813 they realized how widespread the habit had become when it was discovered inside the palace walls. In 1832, Qing dynasty soldiers, hampered by their opium addiction, performed poorly when putting down a rebellion in southern Guangdong. Such evidence of unchecked opium use revitalized the anti-opium crusade. When a new emperor, Daoguang, came to the throne in 1820, he made the cause his own. He resolved to end the problem. Two conditions that arose in the early years of his reign steeled his determination even further.

The first was a financial crisis. The copper price of silver, which formed the basis of the internal monetary system, inflated. Peasants, who paid taxes quoted in silver, lived most of their economic lives through copper transactions. This meant a de facto tax increase for them, causing hardship in the countryside and leading to dangerous signs of rural unrest. Imperial advisers were convinced that the cause was the drain of silver "into the sea." In other words, the Guangzhou trade balance, which had formerly been a source of silver for the empire, shifted by the 1820s because more opium was being bought than tea was being sold.

The silver flow was reversed, and economic unrest in the countryside came in the wake of this disruption.

The second was the joint effort of British opium traders and the new industrialists to bring new ideas of political economy and laissez-faire to the China coast by attacking both the East India Company and the Guangzhou trade system. The British East India Company was dispatched with relative ease, a process completed in 1834. The Chinese trade system, being outside of British sovereignty, was not so easily manipulated, but that did not stop the British from taking action. Once the British East India Company dispersed, government officials performed the functions once handled by the select committee. From 1834 on, British officials appeared in South China waters demanding that China open Guangzhou and allow a British consul to represent British merchants in that port. From the British perspective, these demands were merely a request to rationalize trade.

With the alarming increase of opium use inside the empire, it is not surprising that Chinese bureaucrats considered British consuls to be untrustworthy fellows in league with opium traffickers. They saw the British petitions as self-serving and coercive. In the second half of the decade Chinese bureaucrats debated ways to handle the opium problem, which had taken on an increased urgency. In 1836, certain Chinese officials proposed legalization of opium in China, using arguments that sound surprisingly modern. They nearly convinced the Daoguang emperor to change course. Almost, but not quite. In the end a second group of officials arguing for tough punishments for opium law violators (using arguments that are also strikingly modern) carried the day. Their most famous representative was Lin Zexu. Regarded still as a national hero, Lin carried out such a severe campaign against opium that the traffic momentarily came to a halt. He also brought his country into a war against the British empire.

For the British navy the war was no more than a skirmish; for China it was a humiliating defeat. It destroyed the career of Lin Zexu, who went into exile even before termination of hostilities. It concluded with the Treaty of Nanjing, signed August 29, 1842, which failed to mention opium in the text. Although it remained technically illegal, the opium trade resumed with vigor, finally to be legalized in China in 1858. The first treaty also included a provision for *extraterritoriality:* the right for British subjects in China to be judged by their own consuls and tried under their own legal system. Events during the tense years leading up to the war and through the conflict itself brought graphic demonstrations of the rigors of Chinese law. British negotiators insisted on inserting the extraterritoriality clause into the treaty, claiming that British law was more humane, impartial, and rational than Chinese law. The privilege, later granted to other foreign powers, created enforcement-free safety zones used by traffickers when drugs once again became illegal in twentieth-century China.

Scholars who have written about the Opium War have searched for the causes of the conflict. Some have emphasized the obvious cultural clash. Others have seen it as an inevitable consequence of the rise of Western industrialization and the ensuing search for markets. These explanations look beyond opium, taking the drug as the spark but not the tinder and treating it as an exotic accompaniment to the larger forces in the world.[12] Yet opium has a peculiar nature that adds an essential element to the tale. It was, after all, a war about a substance that continued to divide China from Western powers well into the twentieth century.

The political regulation of addictive substances is never simple. Their use or restriction take on the colorations of the wider political context. Nor does this happen only in a symbolic sense. In the events leading to and following the Opium War, narcotics became wedded to larger issues because the men who engineered their delivery became powerful agents for others with larger agendas. The men who moved drugs through the shadows became enmeshed in the political process. If this was true in the nineteenth century, it was even more so in the first four decades of the twentieth, when the growing illegality of narcotics demanded that traffickers forge alliances with political figures. Inevitably, distinctions blurred and identities melded. Some traffickers with political connections became political actors; some politicians became drug traffickers. These men worked in the shadows because the bright light of public scrutiny would have endangered their business dealings and political machinations.

The international legal structures that gave shape to modern narcotics control in the 1920s and 1930s were small successes of the League of Nations, an organization that is usually remembered for its failures. The League did not curb militarist aggression in Europe and East Asia. Its member states could neither understand nor come to terms with the Soviet Union and the new fascist states of Italy, Germany, and Japan. They failed to comprehend the national aspirations of the colonial and semicolonial areas, of which China was one. Yet the moral crusade against narcotic drug use in China was one in which the League's member states and responsible Chinese leaders could cooperate. Unfortunately, the central government of China was weak. During these years China remained in a state of endemic civil war and on the verge of military invasion. (China's internal affairs were so enmeshed in international politics that its major cities kept foreign affairs officers on their municipal staffs.) It was in this hothouse, created by China's disintegration and the League's successes, that gangsters and politicians molded the modern international narcotics trafficking industry. The symbiotic relationship between trafficker and politician that has become the dominant feature of the contemporary drug trade has its roots in Asia in the early twentieth century. The men in the shadows succeeded because they structured their careers with webs of smoke at the point where profits and power converge.

NOTES

1. *Canton (Guangshou) Register,* November 23, 1827.
2. Joseph Stilwell, "Political Issues and Problems—The Narcotic Situation" [hereafter Stilwell Report], box 7205, 893.114NARCOTICS/1547, 1935, State Department, Record Group 59, United States National Archives, Washington, D.C. [hereafter RG 59], 3.
3. Treasury Department, *Traffic in Opium and Other Dangerous Drugs* (Washington, D.C.: Government Printing Office, 1931); Treasury Department, *Traffic in Opium and Other Dangerous Drugs* (Washington, D.C.: Government Printing Office, 1938); Egyptian Government, C.N.I.B. "Annual Report for 1929," Registry files, R3165/13298, League of Nations Archives [hereafter LON].
4. Bertil Renborg, *International Drug Control* (New York: Kraus Reprint, 1972). See also David Musto, *The American Disease* (New Haven, Conn.: Yale University Press, 1973); Arnold Taylor, *American Diplomacy and the Narcotics Traffic, 1900–39* (Durham, N.C.: Duke University Press, 1973).
5. Britain had begun unilaterally enforcing a certificate system covering exports of manufactured drugs to Japan as early as 1917. Terry Parssinen, *Secret Passions, Secret Remedies: Narcotic Drugs in British Society, 1820–1930* (Philadelphia: Institute for Study of Human Issues, 1983), 149–52.
6. Joe Bonanno, father of the Brooklyn, New York, crime family, describes the change that took place as some members of what he called the Sicilian tradition became Americanized and went into narcotics. In his autobiography, *A Man of Honor* (New York: Simon and Schuster, 1983), he laments the new system in which the tradition became a syndicate, the fathers of families became bosses, and the values of the members began to place wealth before loyalty and honor. He blames Charles "Lucky" Luciano and his cohorts from Manhattan for the change.
7. The problem of defining organized crime is no simple task, nor can the two

words be casually thrown together on the page. As Howard Abadinsky points out in the introduction to *Organized Crime* (Boston: Allyn and Bacon, 1981), each of the states in our union has its own different legal definition. Donald R. Cressey has called it a business organization supplying illicit goods and services. Alan Block and William Chambliss, whose approach provides a definition closer to our own in *Organizing Crime* (New York: Elsevier, 1981), understand it as the rational choice of criminals given the contradictions of our age. Yan Jingyao in *Zhongguo de Fanzui Wenti Yu Shehui Biangai de Guanxi* [Crime in relation to social change in China] (Peking: Peking University Press, 1986) describes Chinese crime as being organized in such a way that takes into itself the basic fabric of the society, the family communalism of the Confucian culture.

8. Patricia Adler, in *Wheeling and Dealing: An Ethnography of an Upper Level Drug Dealing Community* (New York: Columbia University Press, 1989), 33, describes the border phenomenon as a double funnel. In other words, the supply and distribution networks involve many people at the points of origins and sales, but the danger involved in crossing borders pushes the process into the hands of a few, highly capitalized individuals. Therefore organization charts of the traffic would look like two funnels standing end to end.

9. Jonathan D Spence, "Opium Smoking in Ch'ing China," in *Conflict and Control in Late Imperial China,* ed. Frederic Wakeman Jr. and Carolyn Grant, (Berkeley: University of California Press, 1975), 143–73.

10. The letter as sent to the king is in H. B. Morse, *The Chronicles of the East India Company Trading to China, 1635–1834* (London: Oxford University Press, 1926), 2:247–54.

11. Brian Gardner, *The East India Company: A History* (London: Granada, 1971); Michael Greenberg, *British Trade and the Opening of China, 1800–1842* (Cambridge: Cambridge University Press, 1951); David Edward Owen, *British Opium Policy in India and China* (Hamden, Conn.: Archon Books, 1968).

12. Peter Ward Fay, *The Opium War, 1840–1842* (Chapel Hill: University of North Carolina Press, 1975); Brian Ingles, *The Opium War* (London: Hodder and Stoughton, 1976); Chung Tan, *China and the Brave New World* (Bombay: Allied Publishers, 1975); Jack Beeching, *The Chinese Opium Wars* (London: Hutcheson of London, 1975); Owen, *British Opium Policy in India and China*; Greenberg, *British Trade and the Opening of China.*

CHAPTER ONE

BUREAUCRATS

1 9 0 7 – 1 9 3 6

I must have your financial assistance, owing to heavy expenses incurred in protecting myself against the same fate that overtook Mr. Tiewe. In other words I must PAY FREELY to get the goods FREE OF CONTROL.

H. M. F. Humphrey, narcotics trafficker[1]

The Palais des Nations was built to last forever. This structure, home of the League of Nations, was the symbolic phoenix rising from the ashes of the Great War. Its permanence, expressed in massive stone, was an architectural statement of a human hope. The long hallways, the soaring ceilings, the white marble, the brass trimmings all seemed calculated to overwhelm the building's inhabitants, as if to remind them of the insignificance of cantankerous individuals in the face of mankind's brotherhood. To underscore the message, the building was decorated with murals ponderously emphasizing unity. Black children and white children, red mothers and bronze mothers all played and worked harmoniously, at least on the walls of the Palais des Nations.[2]

The grounds too were calculated to soothe. Set on a bluff overlooking magnificent Lake Geneva and dotted with ageless pine trees, the serene estate invited diplomats to walk among the cool greenery, to set aside their conflicts, to make peace. Even the winners of the First World War, Britain and France, had sacrificed half a generation of young men on the battlefields of the western front. The experience convinced leaders of the 1920s to pursue world peace through collective security. The architecture of the building housing the offices of the League of Nations reflected that dedication.

The Palais des Nations was built to encourage men to talk rather than fight. Dark-suited diplomats trod its hallways softly and spoke to one another in measured tones. They had a delicate mission: to kindle and nourish the spirit of international cooperation on matters of mutual interest and, above all, to keep the peace. So important was harmony and so threatening was discord that diplomats at the League of Nations were even more tactful and accommodating than their colleagues elsewhere. A serious argument at the Palais des Nations would not only embarrass the individuals involved, and their respective countries, but it would also undermine the ideal of international harmony on which the League was founded. Although the consequence of such caution—an unwillingness to engage aggressors—would in the 1930s result in the League's complete inability to deal with the ambitions of Japan and Italy, in 1926 the dream of collective security remained alive. If intelligent men could meet together and reason things out, problems could be amicably solved.[3]

This spirit of friendly cooperation was so pervasive in Geneva that when an exchange between diplomats at a plenary session of the Opium Advisory Committee on May 31, 1926, became a heated argument, it drew genuinely shocked notice. Under discussion at the time was the large illicit traffic in Persian-grown opium from the port of Bushire on the Persian Gulf to the Far East. In a period of only ten months, over 500 tons of opium had moved along this route, although the entire annual world requirement of opium for all legitimate purposes was estimated at only 300 tons. The bulk of this Persian opium would be off-loaded along the China coast and smuggled onto the mainland, to be sold and consumed as smoking opium or manufactured into heroin.[4]

CONFLICTS OVER THE CONTROL OF ILLICIT DRUGS

Sir Malcolm Delevingne, a permanent undersecretary in the Home Office, an expert on the control of narcotic drugs and an original member of the League's Opium Advisory Committee, represented the British government during the meeting. Delevingne explained how, under new regulations enacted by his government, any British ship leaving Bushire with opium had to obtain a document from the British consul certifying that the drug was intended for a legitimate dealer. Delevingne was confident that this step would immediately halt the involvement of British shippers in the illicit opium traffic from Persia. However, since most of the opium exported from Bushire was carried on ships of Japanese registry, the committee asked to hear what controls the Japanese would impose. Mr. Sugimura Yotaro, the Japanese representative, replied cryptically that Japan possessed no consular agent in Bushire.

If Sugimura hoped that his lame excuse would mollify the tenacious Delevingne, he was badly mistaken. Sir Malcolm's temper erupted. His remarks came perilously close to crossing the line between diplomatic inquiry and outright accusation. He said that he had listened with profound disappointment to the statements made by the Japanese representative. The evasion of regulations by that country had been known for a long time. The British government had been making friendly representations to its Japanese counterpart on the matter as far back as September 1923, asking it to adopt measures of control equivalent to the ones that the British government itself was about to enforce at the time. The British government had supplied, at the request of the Japanese government, evidence of Japanese vessels engaged in the traffic. Yet three years later no definite reply had been received from the Japanese government regarding the requests, and nothing appeared to have been done by the Japanese authorities.

Not only had the Japanese been remiss in the past about drug control, but, protests notwithstanding, they seemed no more interested in 1926. Although Sir Malcolm granted that measures along British lines were perhaps not possible because the Japanese lacked a consul at Bushire, he nevertheless expressed astonishment upon learning that the Japanese government was able to exercise no authority and had no jurisdiction over its own ships after they left Japanese waters.[5] He could hardly believe there was no way the Japanese government could discipline the owners of vessels engaged in the illicit opium traffic.

Sugimura refused either to admit guilt or to promise action. Instead he appealed to the committee, asking it to help the Japanese government in drafting laws or legislation that would be effective in suppressing the traffic. At present, Sugimura argued, Japanese law made it impossible for the government to interfere with the commerce of Japanese-registered ships, especially if they were leased to foreigners. He noted that his government wanted badly to suppress the opium smugglers, since "they were prejudicial not only to Japanese honour but to Japanese interests."[6]

Sir John Campbell, representing India, found Sugimura's defense ludicrous. It was, after all, a well-established principle of international law that a ship flying the flag of any country was regarded as forming a portion of the soil of that country. As such, it would be subject to that nation's laws.[7] In the face of these intimations of Japanese duplicity, Sugimura insisted that his government had been guilty of nothing more than naiveté. In reply to Sir John, he reiterated that Japan needed help in drafting appropriate legislation. Delevingne responded with considerable sarcasm. If the Japanese government, after having considered the matter for more than two years, had been unable to find any way of dealing with the subject, he did not see how Sugimura could expect the committee, in the course of a short session, to do so.[8]

Sir Malcolm stopped short of accusing the Japanese of hypocrisy, but he clearly implied it. He said that the Japanese government had a moral responsibility to halt the drug traffic. Sugimura happily agreed, no doubt relieved to elevate the discussion to the aerie realm of moral principle and out of the embarrassing morass of practical failing. Lest the committee hope for too much too soon, Sugimura concluded by reminding them that foreigners could charter Japanese vessels, complicating the situation for his government.[9]

With Sir Malcolm still fuming, the meeting adjourned. On that one afternoon in May 1926, he had been moved to real anger. The result had made for most undiplomatic diplomacy. It was not the first time that the Opium Advisory Committee had been engulfed in rancor, nor would it be the last. By now Delevingne was growing accustomed to being at the center of such storms. His brief exchange with Sugimura encapsulated some of the issues for which he had struggled, as well as some of the frustrations that he had encountered.

The illicit trade in drugs had grown enormously during and after the First World War. Thus, in 1921, the League of Nations established the Advisory Committee on Traffic in Opium and Other Dangerous Drugs, more commonly known as the Opium Advisory Committee, to try and bring this traffic under control. It was, like the League itself, an expression of the postwar faith in collective security; like the League, it was severely limited by its lack of legal authority. The committee could gather information, draw up guidelines, and make suggestions, but ultimately it was up to individual governments to enact narcotics laws and to enforce them. Some governments, like Turkey, a major opium producer, refused to cooperate at all. The Turks reasoned that although it was unfortunate if Europeans, Americans, or Chinese misused opium, the Turkish peasant who profited from poppy crops should not be made to suffer economic losses. Other governments, among which Japan was an example, formally adhered to League policy but, in fact, refused to crack down on their citizens who were engaged in the illicit traffic. Sir Malcolm believed that the Japanese could be shamed into adopting a more vigilant posture if they were constantly forced to answer charges of lax enforcement. Thus his heated exchange with Sugimura.[10]

Sir Malcolm Delevingne, like many policy makers in our own age, considered that the key to narcotics control lay in curbing supply. Growers of crops like opium and coca, as well as manufacturers of such drugs as morphine, heroin, and cocaine, produced much more than could conceivably be used for legitimate medical purposes. The excess was diverted by smugglers into the illicit traffic, ending up in the veins or the lungs of addicts. Delevingne eventually convinced his colleagues on the Opium Advisory Committee that growers and manufacturers must be forced to cut back production to designated levels. To achieve this, individual governments had to agree to monitor carefully the worldwide commerce in drugs. If this were accomplished, he believed, the illicit traffic would disappear. The members of the Opium Advisory Committee assumed the manufacture of drugs like heroin, morphine, and cocaine to be so complicated that smugglers would be incapable of producing their own. If overproduction were ended and diversion were curbed, they reasoned, smugglers would go out of business and the illicit drug traffic would wither and die.[11]

Yet Delevingne's attack sounded like hypocrisy to Sugimura's ears. The Japanese government was well aware of the role British merchants had played in commercializing the opium traffic less than a century earlier. Japanese officials also realized the financial contribution that the opium monopoly made to the several colonial budgets. In their own defense, Japanese officials described their state-run narcotics operation as having been developed from the British model into a masterpiece of public health legislation designed to care for and cure Chinese addicts under their jurisdiction. They could further speculate that the British government's reversal on the international opium question was based on the decline in revenues derived from the Indian opium monopoly in the face of Chinese competition.

Such speculation was not groundless. The British government had

not always been such an ardent advocate of international narcotics control. In the 1880s, when British missionary groups began to organize
public opinion against their own government's involvement in the
trade, their appeals were met with official apology and defense of such
commerce. Representatives of the government, like Earl Percy, defended the traffic in the House of Commons in 1906, using many of
the same arguments the Turkish government would use in the 1920s.
Nevertheless, in the opening years of the twentieth century the political
climate was such in England that the government began to shift its
stance.[12]

One manifestation of the change was the beginning of a turnabout
in British relations with the Chinese government on the question of
Chinese opium prohibition. In Calcutta, in September 1905, during negotiations on a different matter, British diplomats suggested to Tang
Shaoyi, the Chinese representative, that if China would undertake
opium eradication, the British government would back it up by reducing, and finally ending, Indian opium sales to China. Tang Shaoyi was
an important member of the imperial government during the last years
of dynastic rule. American educated, he was an advocate of constitutional reform and modernization. His career survived the collapse of the
Qing dynasty in 1911. He became something of an elder statesman, and
he held various posts during the early years of republican China. Ironically, his career ended abruptly in 1942, when as a Chinese official serving the Japanese occupation government in Shanghai, he was labeled a
traitor and was assassinated by a hit squad organized by Dai Li and
funded with opium monopoly revenues. In 1905, both Tang and his
government, which had legalized opium under duress in 1858 after losing two wars, were most receptive to the possibility of British assistance
in opium prohibition.[13]

U.S. MEDIATION EFFORTS

British cooperation with Chinese efforts to restrict opium use did not
signal a complete or immediate about-face in their attitudes to the traffic. When the first international conference on opium met in Shanghai
in 1909, the details for ending the India-China opium trade were still
being worked out in Beijing. It was the American government that took
the lead in bringing world representatives together to address the problems caused by opium. A sullen British delegation came to Shanghai

reluctantly, like school bullies called before the headmaster to answer for a long list of transgressions.[14]

The American government arranged the Shanghai Opium Commission for several reasons. First, Americans saw themselves as the leading moral entrepreneurs in China. Their Protestant missionaries, scattered throughout the country, were powerful shapers of the American view of China. They were resolutely opposed to the use of opium: A soul could not be won for Christ if the body that it inhabited were addicted to opium. Although a few Americans had participated in the opium trade, they were not so clearly identified with the traffic as were the British. Indeed, many God-fearing Yankee traders scrupulously refused to deal in opium, no matter what profits they had to forgo. Nor had the Americans participated in the carving up of China by European countries and Japan into spheres of economic influence. Americans had rejected trade concessions in favor of an "open door" policy toward China. This genuine Yankee concern about the political, economic, and moral well-being of China took the form of opposition to the international opium trade, in which the Chinese were the leading victims.

A second reason for American desire for the conference, one that formed a flip side of altruistic missionary concern, was the hope of huge profits to be made if a grateful Chinese government and people spurned their European predators and instead dealt exclusively with American businessmen. At the turn of the century China loomed large in both the American press and political circles as a market for the products of a bountiful and productive land. In the minds of American businessmen the China market was a basket of wants waiting to be filled. Thus moral reformers and business entrepreneurs both had high hopes for China: Millions of souls would be won while billions of products would be sold. An international conference against opium smoking would be a small American investment that might pay substantial dividends in the future.[15]

The Americans harbored yet another concern about opium. In the wake of the Spanish-American War (1898), America had appropriated a number of former Spanish colonies, including the Philippines. As was the case throughout Southeast Asia, the Philippines had a significant minority of Chinese, five thousand of whom were opium smokers. Spain, like all the other European countries that had colonies in the Far East, sold opium through a government monopoly, the profits of which accrued to the colonial government. At the time, Europeans were either realistic or cynical enough not to be troubled by such arrangements. Americans, however, were too righteous to accept such monies.

In 1903, President Teddy Roosevelt appointed a commission to look into the matter. Under the leadership of the Episcopal bishop Charles H. Brent, the body recommended that the opium monopoly be phased out and that opium smokers be given assistance to overcome their addiction. The commissioners quickly realized, however, that if they suppressed the legal trade in smoking opium in the Philippines, the void would be filled by illicit traffickers from nearby countries. The commission concluded that an international agreement to end the opium traffic throughout the Far East would be necessary if the problem in the Philippines was to be solved. All of these hopes, dreams, and practical considerations motivated the American government to convene, at the formal request of the Chinese government, the Shanghai Commission of 1909 in order to explore ways of suppressing the traffic in opium.

The Shanghai Commission, although dominated by China, Britain, and America, was attended by ten other powers, including Japan and all those European countries having colonies in the Far East. Little of substance was accomplished. The Americans and the Chinese pressed for a total and immediate ban on opium trafficking, but the other conferees were considerably more cautious. There were, after all, profitable monopolies at stake. Among the various resolutions that the conferees considered was one calling for a suppression of the illicit opium trade. It passed. But such idealistic resolutions cost nothing, and the opium trade remained untouched.

The American delegation, led by Bishop Brent, came out of the Shanghai Commission frustrated by its innocuous resolutions, angry at British foot-dragging, and determined to secure more substantial controls on the opium traffic. Almost immediately Bishop Brent began to lobby for a second opium conference. The British government indicated that it would attend only if the agenda included a discussion of manufactured drugs, like morphine and cocaine, partially to divert attention from the notorious India-China opium trade. Brent readily agreed. Thus a second opium conference convened in The Hague in December 1911. The agenda expanded to include worldwide control of all narcotic drugs.

THE HAGUE CONFERENCE

The Hague conference produced a document, "International Opium Convention," which was signed by all the participants on January 23,

1912, and then circulated to their home governments for ratification. Again, no concrete steps were taken within the text to suppress the opium trade. Every government was left to police the traffic as it saw fit. But these conferees did recognize the dangers of unregulated manufacture and trade of morphine and cocaine. The "contracting powers" agreed to restrict the trade and consumption of drugs "to medical and legitimate uses." They agreed to prohibit the export of dangerous drugs to other countries except when the importer had been issued a license by the authorities in the importing country. And finally, they agreed to apply these regulations to all preparations containing more than .2 percent morphine or more than .1 percent of either heroin or cocaine. At the insistence of the German representatives, the Opium Convention would not come into force until all the signatories' governments had ratified it. But in 1914 war intervened before the ratification process was complete. International drug control remained in limbo for the next five years. Yet it was not forgotten. When the Paris Peace Conference opened in 1919, the Opium Convention came to the negotiating table as unfinished business.

The peacemakers at Versailles decided to urge all sovereign states that had not done so to ratify the Opium Convention. Using the spirit of international cooperation that was a legacy of the war, they charged the newly created League of Nations to oversee its enforcement. Thus The Hague conference of 1911 had far-reaching effects. It led national governments that had previously ignored the narcotics problem to enact regulatory drug legislation. America's Harrison Act (1914), which brought narcotic drugs under federal control, and Britain's Dangerous Drugs Act (1920) were both passed in response to the commitments each country made to the Opium Convention. It also created a model for the "certificate system," by which the legal traffic in drugs was controlled by government agencies certifying that shipments of drugs had a legitimate destination. Finally, it led to the creation of a permanent body, the Opium Advisory Committee of the League of Nations, to monitor the world's drug traffic.[16]

History occasionally witnesses unexpected reversals. The course of the antidrug crusade was one of these. Americans had been the leading force behind the two initial opium conferences, cajoling and prodding other countries into taking the first steps toward international narcotics control. Yet after the First World War the U.S. Senate refused to ratify the Versailles Treaty. Thus America did not become a member of the League of Nations and the Opium Advisory Committee, which was the outcome of two decades of American initiative, included no Americans. Meanwhile Great Britain, which had been, in 1909, the international delinquent on drug control, in 1920 became its leading advocate. To a considerable extent, this dramatic reversal was due to the efforts of Sir Malcolm Delevingne.

SIR MALCOLM DELEVINGNE

British history has served up a number of colorful rogues, brilliant statesmen, and noble generals. But it has also been shaped by a vast army of men and women who went about their work so unobtrusively that, after they died, few people remembered that they had ever lived. Sir Malcolm Delevingne was such a man. He is generally not reckoned to be a notable historical presence of the early twentieth century. He was a bureaucrat and as such passed through life quietly. When he died in 1950, he did not leave wife, children, great property, or even many good stories behind him. Yet Delevingne accomplished much and aspired to accomplish even more.

By the standards of the British civil service, his career was successful but not extraordinary.[17] Born in 1868 to a businessman's family in the respectable London suburb of Ealing, Delevingne attended a good public school (City of London) and took first-class honors in classics at Trinity College, Oxford. In 1892 he passed into the civil service and stayed in the Home Office for his entire career. He became an expert on workers' safety in factories and mines, and he initiated many useful reforms. To the end of his life he was in demand to sit on various boards and commissions because of his vast experience and expertise.

Delevingne was also the prime architect of narcotics policy in Britain between 1913 and 1926, when its foundations were laid. He became the country's expert by default in 1913, when an interdepartmental committee of bureaucrats, created to formulate British narcotics policy but bored by the task, handed it to him. He wrote a stopgap wartime narcotics law in 1916, and he prodded the government to introduce permanent legislation, conforming to the Opium Convention, after the First World War. His preeminence on the subject was acknowledged, even by his rivals. When civil servants of the newly created Ministry of Health tried to wrest control of the narcotics issue from the Home Office in 1920, they had to admit defeat because, as their chief admitted, "they had no one who could match Delevingne in tenacity or understanding."[18]

Delevingne also pushed for international narcotics control. It was at his insistence that the issue was incorporated into the Treaty of Versailles. After it had been accepted by the League of Nations, Delevingne suggested that responsibility for it be vested in a specialized body, which became the Opium Advisory Committee. After the committee's creation he became its most forceful personality. According to one colleague, he had "a sharp brain in a very small body."

Passionate on the subject of narcotics control, he "was often very irritable at meetings, since he did not suffer fools gladly." Even on the rare instances when his views did not prevail, his presence was felt. During the 1931 League of Nations Conference on the Limitation of Drug Production, the conferees rejected a draft proposal that he had authored. Piqued, Delevingne refused to participate. But he could not bring himself to stay away altogether, so he came to meetings and ostentatiously read a newspaper. When the chairman asked him if he could help them clarify a muddled issue, he snapped, "Certainly not." The Canadian delegate, Colonel Sharman, said in a stage whisper, "Sir Malcolm, your attitude would be much more convincing if you did not read your London *Times* upside down."

Delevingne was a fervent Christian. Although the outward display of his faith was modulated by the restraint befitting an upper-middle-class English civil servant, he was nonetheless a believer. His religious convictions guided the issues that he chose to make the focus of his life's work—workers' safety and drug addiction. His life was not filled with dramatic moments. It was the slow pilgrimage of one who believed that the human condition could be ameliorated and that he was, in fact, responsible for accomplishing that. It is a curiously nineteenth-century idea that Delevingne sought to realize during his tenure in the twentieth century.

Christian though he might be, Delevingne was also a realist, whose limited sense of what was possible was shaped by three decades of guerilla warfare in the thickets of the civil service. Improvement, if it came at all, he believed, came in small doses. In 1922, the most significant problem of international narcotics control facing Britain and the Opium Advisory Committee was the diversion of drugs that had been manufactured by legitimate pharmaceutical firms into the illicit international narcotics traffic.

DRUG SMUGGLING

Much of the smuggling of narcotic drugs in the early 1920s was freelancing by merchant seamen. A sailor on a European freighter might buy a half kilo of cocaine at a waterfront bar in Hamburg, where it was readily available and very cheap, stow it until the ship docked in London or New York and sell it there for two or three times its purchase price. The risks were small. But occasionally the local police or customs authorities would seize a shipment and report it to the League of Nations. The League's Opium Advisory Committee kept a detailed record of such seizures because they hoped to trace illicit drugs back to their source. If, for example, they discovered that a substantial amount of cocaine seized in London had come from a single factory in Germany, they could infer a connection between smuggler and manufacturer that German authorities might wish to investigate. As long as drugs were carried by anonymous seamen and other small fry, the committee was more interested in stopping the flow of drugs at its source than in tracking down individual smugglers. The Humphrey case changed that.

European morphine, and later heroin, had trickled into China since the 1880s. This flow became a torrent after 1913, when the shortage of smoking opium forced many addicts to turn to morphine or heroin as a substitute. British, as well as German, Swiss, and French, manufacturers sent huge amounts of morphine and heroin to the China market until 1920. In that year the passage of the Dangerous Drugs Act, as well as the adoption of the certificate system, made it illegal for British drug manufacturers to sell to known smugglers. Enormous profits were lost. For example, in 1916, the London firm of T. Whiffen & Sons had grossed £469,000 on sales of 650,000 ounces of morphine, virtually all of which was destined for the China market. By 1922, in the wake of the Dangerous Drugs Act, Whiffen's morphine revenues had plummeted to £21,000 on sales of only 53,000 ounces. Not surprisingly, Whiffen found the temptation to maintain links to the underground drug network irresistible.[19]

The laws created new barriers, which produced more sophisticated smugglers. The obstacles did not simply lie in getting the drug into China as before, but getting it out of Europe. The task required infinitely greater organization and capital than had previously been the case. The trial of H. M. F. Humphrey in 1923 revealed to Delevingne and his colleagues on the committee that they were encountering a smuggler far more resourceful than the simple merchant seamen. Humphrey's downfall began with an arrest made in the Crown Colony of Hong Kong. On October 11, 1922, Hong Kong authorities detained one Tieu Yiu Kim, a Japanese subject, in illegal possession of 2,500 ounces of cocaine and 2,400 ounces of heroin. More to the point, he was also carrying documents showing that Humphrey, a thirty-two-year-old businessman, was delivering illegal morphine to Tong Say Brothers, Tieu Yiu Kim's employers.[20]

Authorities immediately alerted Sir Malcolm, the senior Home Office official in charge of drugs, about the case. He arranged to have Humphrey's mail opened. An outgoing letter to Loo Benn Tan, the managing director of Tong Say Brothers, revealed the scale of his smuggling activities. In spite of Tieu's recent arrest, Humphrey hoped that they could continue doing business. (Obviously Humphrey did not suspect that Tieu had been carrying the implicating documents at the time of his arrest.) He reminded Mr. Loo that "the [drug] Manufacturers are personal friends [of mine]."[21]

Humphrey proposed a deal in which they would buy 50,000 ounces of morphine at 16s. an ounce—£40,000. Humphrey promised to come out personally with the parcel to see its safe delivery. He was sure that they could easily sell this quantity in China at 48s., which would raise £79,000, even if the goods were sold at this cheap figure. He speculated that they might even get as much as 200s. per ounce. Humphrey concluded with a plea for front money to buy the drugs and to bribe officials. In reference to Mr. Tieu's unfortunate fate in Hong Kong, he requested financial assistance to protect himself. "I must pay freely," he said, "to get the goods free of control."[22]

The deal never came off. Unknown to Humphrey, Sir Malcolm had him under surveillance. In January 1923, he ordered the police to arrest Humphrey and search his flat. The search turned up correspondence which indicated that Humphrey was in business with two other Englishmen, F. L. Baker and A. L. Baxter, in an elaborate scheme to move drugs to the Far East. Their Chinese customers preferred British morphine. Humphrey, always the accommodating businessman, tried to please them. When he could not buy British morphine, he hired a Berlin printer to forge labels of British pharmaceutical manufacturers, which he applied to containers of lower-quality morphine. But Humphrey was able to buy genuine British morphine manufactured by T. Whiffen and Sons from several European drug dealers. One of these was John Laurier, president of the British chamber of commerce in Paris. In 1922, Laurier bought 21,000 ounces of morphine from Whiffen, over 40 percent of the firm's total output that year, and nearly one-third of all the morphine imported into France. Only the most naive or conniving managing director of a pharmaceutical firm could fail to be suspicious of an order of that magnitude. Through an intermediary, Laurier sold the morphine to Humphrey and his associates. The British smugglers picked up the drugs in Basel, Switzerland, at the firm of Bubeck and Dolder, where they repacked it into innocent consignments, like chemicals or furniture, and shipped it to the Far East.[23]

The final link between European manufacturers and Chinese addicts was Japanese smugglers. Official controls were notoriously lax at Japanese-controlled colonies such as Formosa or other Japanese concessions on the Asian mainland. From these staging areas drugs were smuggled by Japanese into China. By the early 1920s, then, the route of illicit morphine into China was circuitous. In this case, it traveled from London to Paris to Basel to China. But the potential profits made it a worthwhile business. As Humphrey's letter indicated, by the time British morphine reached China, it sold for between three and twelve times its purchase price in England. Business on this scale required manpower, organization, and capital. Humphrey realized the advantages of size. Papers confiscated from the residence of his partner, A. L. Baxter, described plans for a syndicate that would include the three English smugglers, Dundas Simpson, and Joe Kahan of R. Fuller and Company, the Basel firm of Bubeck and Dolder, and one Macdonald, an American shipper and drug trafficker operating out of Freiburg-Baden. Thus Humphrey existed at the center of a nascent international narcotics smuggling ring. In 1923, this was a new form of organization, created by smugglers to thwart the first efforts by Britain and her allies to stop the international drug traffic.[24]

The results of the Humphrey case disappointed Delevingne. Humphrey received the maximum sentence of a £500 fine and six months' imprisonment that, the judge noted, was scarcely a deterrent to would-be smugglers. Baxter and Baker escaped and were soon dealing in narcotics from France. Although Delevingne communicated with the governments of France, Germany, Belgium, and Switzerland, detailing their citizens' involvement in the drug traffic, arrests were few and convictions were nil. Within a few months it was business as usual.

Delevingne and Humphrey existed symbiotically. Both were creations of the changed mood that led to international narcotics control. Delevingne, the Christian reformer and bureaucrat who wanted to alleviate human suffering, devoted his career to eradicating the narcotics traffic. Humphrey was the descendant, at least in spirit, of those eighteenth- and nineteenth-century English merchants who had made huge profits by selling opium to Chinese addicts. Morality was not their concern. For Humphrey, the existence of antinarcotics laws meant that the trade was a bit riskier but the profit margin was correspondingly greater. Delevingne, the hunter, ensnared Humphrey, the quarry. But Delevingne was slow to recognize and loath to admit that no matter how often he modified the barriers, the drug smugglers would adapt.

Nevertheless, the reformer achieved one satisfying result from the Humphrey case. The managing director of T. Whiffen and Sons was summoned to an interview with Sir Malcolm at the Home Office. Sir Malcolm asked some hard questions. How could the firm have carried on business with a person like John Laurier without investigating his connections and the ultimate destination of the drugs they sold him? Was Whiffen so intent on chasing profits that it winked at the illicit traffic? Sir Malcolm concluded that Whiffen had not technically broken the law and thus could not be criminally prosecuted. However, he judged that the firm had been so negligent that he revoked Whiffen's license to manufacture narcotic drugs. Thus T. Whiffen and Sons, hitherto the most prolific English producer of opiates, quite suddenly dropped out of the morphine business.[25]

Sir Malcolm learned two things from the Humphrey case. The relative ease with which the smugglers had been able to buy morphine strengthened his belief that manufacturers of narcotic drugs must be forced to cut back production to the small amounts necessary to supply the world's legitimate medical demand. He also became convinced that the sudden appearance of well-financed international smuggling rings made it more necessary than ever for agencies in affected countries to cooperate with one another in strictly enforcing drug regulations. Delevingne returned to the League of Nations determined to press vigorously for tightened controls on the international drug traffic.

THREE CONFERENCES

Delevingne, through the Opium Advisory Committee, became the driving force behind three international conferences on drug control held under the auspices of the League of Nations in 1925, 1931, and 1936. Each conference focused on a different aspect of the international traffic; each produced agreements that made it more difficult for smugglers like Humphrey to operate. To a considerable extent, the League's successes were his successes, and its failures were his failures.[26]

The first necessity, Delevingne believed, was to make certain that all countries adhered to the certificate system. In the early 1920s, the leaks in the legitimate drug traffic were created by countries like Switzerland, which did not fully accept the system, or Japan, which did not enforce it. Delevingne convinced the Opium Advisory Committee to make its first priority a conference to ensure worldwide compliance with the certificate system.

Britain had begun a primitive form of the system unilaterally in 1917, when it was brought to the government's attention that the massive amount of British morphine exported to Japan was destined for Chinese addicts. The British government refused to allow dealers in narcotic drugs to export to Japan unless they could produce a certificate from the Japanese government attesting that the importer was a respectable dealer, and that the drug was to be used only for legitimate medical purposes. As a result, exports of British morphine to Japan fell to almost nothing in 1919. Drug traffickers quickly discovered that they could beat this problem by shipping the drug to Japan via America, with which Britain had no arrangement.

Delevingne countered by entering into bilateral agreements with all the major countries—such as France and the United States—with which Britain had a commerce in narcotics. Although this finally took British manufacturers out of the drug traffic to the Far East, it still left manufacturers in the countries that did not adhere to the system free to participate, as before, without restrictions. In essence, the Far Eastern opiate business that was abandoned by British manufacturers was picked up by continental firms. Delevingne reasoned that international control of the drug traffic would only be effective if all of the major drug-producing countries agreed to adhere to the certificate system. Thus the acceptance of the certificate system was the major item of business, as well as the major accomplishment, of the Geneva Opium conference of 1925. It meant that no narcotic drugs could be sold internationally unless the exporter could produce a certificate from the importer, signed by an official of a government agency of the importing country, attesting to the drug's legitimate destination and use.

When the agreement was finally ratified, its effects were dramatic. It became clear that much of the world's production of morphine, heroin, and cocaine had been going into the illicit traffic. When the leaks were plugged, world production of narcotic drugs dropped sharply.

An interesting sidelight of the 1925 conference was the behavior of the American delegation. Although the United States was not a member of the League, Americans had been invited to participate in the Geneva conference because of their long-standing interest in the problem. The American delegation argued that the root of the narcotics problem was

TABLE I.I
Exports of Dangerous Drugs, 1928–1932

Year	Morphine (kg)		Heroin (kg)		Cocaine (kg)	
	A	B	A	B	A	B
1928	6,840	132	6,531	58	3,213	17
1929	5,902	154	842	9	2,276	5
1930	2,567	51	490	396	1,771	18
1931	1,723	199	326	32	1,415	36
1932	1,516	244	290	21	1,314	102

A: Total exports of principal exporting countries (Germany, United Kingdom, France, Japan, Netherlands, and Switzerland).
B: Total exports of other exporting countries.
Source: OAC, "Draft Report to the Council on the Work of the Eighteenth Session, held at Geneva from May 18th to June 2nd 1934," LON Pub. No. O.C. 1562, 7.

the overproduction of raw opium, and they introduced a resolution calling for opium-producing countries to reduce their supply drastically. When this resolution was defeated, the Americans, along with the Chinese delegation, withdrew in anger. America never became a signatory to the 1925 Opium Convention. Delevingne knew that the Americans were right. He had held their position privately for many years. But he also knew that such a resolution was far too advanced to be passed by the conference in 1925. Simply put, too many countries had too much invested in opium to give it up overnight. Patience was needed, he believed, and the Americans had precious little of that where narcotics were concerned.

After the 1925 Opium Convention was signed, Delevingne kept the pressure on. He wheedled, complained, and twisted arms. At the 1927 meeting of the Opium Advisory Committee he introduced a resolution expressing alarm at the continued leakage of narcotic drugs from legitimate sources. He called for greater vigilance, asking government agencies to take care to issue licenses only to persons of impeccable reputation. Despite some minor cavils and a few changes, Delevingne's resolution passed. By the late 1920s, Delevingne had convinced his colleagues on the committee that the next major task was to limit production of manufactured drugs—morphine, heroin, and cocaine. If the certificate system had made it difficult for smugglers to obtain supplies by diversion, limitation would cut them off entirely.

Thus the 1931 League of Nations Conference on narcotic drugs was dedicated to limiting production of manufactured drugs. This time the proceedings did not go entirely to Delevingne's liking. His committee proposed a limitation in which existing drug manufacturers would retain their current market share, whereas total production would be scaled down to equal the worldwide legitimate medical demand. No other manufacturers would be allowed to produce narcotic drugs. The conferees rejected this proposal, pointing out that it gave a perpetual monopoly to the handful of European and Japanese manufacturers presently in business. Eventually the conference came up with a limitation scheme geared to the domestic and export market of each country. If Norway, for example, had an annual medical need for fifty kilograms of morphine, a Norwegian firm could set up in business and produce that much. Delevingne disliked the idea, since he thought that it would be more difficult to monitor and control the production of many smaller manufacturers than a few larger ones. Nevertheless, he was willing to give in, and he did get an agreement on limitation.

By the early 1930s, then, traffickers faced a crisis of supply. In order to maintain their businesses as their sources dried up, smugglers became manufacturers. Illicit drug factories began to turn up in unusual places. Bulgaria, for example, became the heroin capital of the world for a short time. Bulgarian-manufactured heroin turned up in Europe, Egypt, and America. Meanwhile, in China, Shanghai became a center of illicit heroin manufacture. Because the city was divided into large extraterritorial sections administered by foreign countries, the Chinese could exert very little police control. Vice of all kinds flourished, run by the Red and Green gangs. In Manchuria and in Tianjin Japanese chemists perfected their product, making it available at a competitive price.

Other heroin factories were discovered in Greece, France, Italy, and America. Their existence disproved the Opium Advisory Committee's assumption that the manufacture of drugs was so complex that it could not be undertaken by mere criminals. Thus it was only for a few years in the early 1930s, while clandestine factories were being set up and competent chemists were being recruited, that there was a temporary shortage of opiates on the illicit market. But this supply shortage soon passed. By 1934 underground factories were pumping enormous amounts of morphine, cocaine, and heroin into the illicit drug traffic. Police closed scores of them every year, but to no avail. The demand for narcotic drugs was so great and the traffic was so profitable that new factories appeared continuously. The sources of supply changed from legitimate pharmaceutical companies to illicit manufacturers, but the international drug traffic continued to thrive.

The League conference of 1936 focused on law enforcement issues such as extradition of drug smugglers and cooperation among national agencies. This reflected the changes in the illicit traffic. Where the Opium Advisory Committee had first concentrated its efforts on cutting off the diversion of legitimate pharmaceuticals into the illicit traffic, it now turned to stopping the traffickers themselves. Although a number of important steps were taken at the 1936 conference, war intervened before they could come into effect. Once again, international narcotics control remained an issue of unfinished business for the postwar peace conference. The United Nations succeeded the League of Nations as the primary international agency concerned with narcotics control.

Sir Malcolm Delevingne retired from the British civil service in 1932 after an exemplary forty-year career. He stayed on at the Opium Advisory Committee for two more years.[27] In 1934, when he finally gave it up, Sir Malcolm must have evaluated his accomplishments with some ambivalence. More than any other single individual, he had been responsible for the international agreements on narcotics control between the wars. Certainly that was a formidable achievement. But his great hope, of eradicating the illicit narcotics traffic entirely, had eluded him. All that he had done was to sever the links between the legitimate drug manufacturers and the illicit traffickers. Indirectly, he was responsible for the creation of clandestine drug factories in the 1930s. That was a failure, perhaps of policy, certainly of imagination.

In his waning years, Delevingne retired to his home in the dowdy London suburb of West Kensington. He tended roses and served on the governing board of Dr. Barnardo's Homes, a philanthropic organization that provided for orphans, until his death in 1950 at the age of eighty-two. The great accomplishment of Sir Malcolm Delevingne and the Opium Advisory Committee was to produce a series of agreements that gradually transformed the international narcotics traffic from a licit to an illicit industry. Legal barricades to the traffic sprang up, first in China and then in the rest of the world. These barriers were not sufficient to eradicate the traffic, as Delevingne had hoped, but they did create new realities. In order to carry on their business activities safely, drug traffickers needed political protection. In some places, especially the Far East, they formed alliances with politicians, which resulted in a rationalized narcotics business consolidated in a few hands. In other places, such as America and Europe, increasingly strict laws and enforcement policies put drug traffickers at greater risk, which did not halt the trade but made it less stable and more fragmented.

NOTES

1. "Delevingne on Humphrey Case," Records of the British Foreign Office [hereafter FO], Public Records Office [hereafter PRO], London, England.
2. The Palais des Nations, Geneva, Switzerland, today houses several agencies of the United Nations as well as the League of Nations archives.
3. In the general histories of the League of Nations, drug control rates only brief mention: F. P. Walters, *A History of the League of Nations* (London: Oxford University Press, 1969), 183–86; Elmer Bendiner, *A Time for Angels: The Tragicomic History of the League of Nations* (New York: Knopf, 1975), 171, 402; F. S. Northedge, *The League of Nations: Its Life and Times, 1920–1946* (New York: Holmes and Meier, 1956), 183–84.
4. Advisory Committee on Traffic in Opium and Other Dangerous Drugs [hereafter OAC], "Minutes of the Eighth Session, held at Geneva from May 26th to June 8th, 1926," LON, C.393.M.136.1926.XI, 57–58, 65–67.
5. "Minutes of the Eighth Session," 65.
6. "Minutes of the Eighth Session," 65.
7. "Minutes of the Eighth Session," 66.
8. "Minutes of the Eighth Session," 66.
9. "Minutes of the Eighth Session," 67.
10. The idea for the OAC came from the British government, specifically from Malcolm Delevingne. "Memorandum Respecting Traffic in Opium," 1920; PRO, FO 371/5308/233, 238–41.
11. OAC, "Report to Council . . . 1927," LON, C.521.M.179.XI, 7.
12. For a detailed description of the British movement to prohibit narcotics, see D. Bruce Johnson, "Righteousness before Revenue: The Forgotten Moral Crusade against the Indo-Chinese Opium Trade," *Journal of Drug Issues*, Fall 1975: 304–26; Terry Parssinen, *Secret Passions, Secret Remedies*, 129–43.
13. *North China Herald*, February 8, 1907; Sir Alexander Hosie, *On the Trail of the Opium Poppy* (London: George Philip, 1914), 2:191; Thomas Reins, "Reform, Nationalism, and Internationalism: The Opium Suppression Movement in China and the Anglo-American Influence, 1900–1908," *Modern Asian Studies* 25 (February 1991): 101–42.
14. There are several books that tell the story of twentieth-century efforts to enforce international drug control: Kettil Bruun, Lynn Pan, and Ingemar Rexed, *The Gentlemen's Club: International Control of Drugs and Alcohol* (Chicago: University of Chicago Press, 1975); Peter D. Lowes, *The Genesis of International Narcotics Control* (Geneva: Droz, 1966); Musto, *American Disease*; Renborg, *International Drug Control*; and Arnold Taylor, *American Diplomacy and the Narcotics Traffic* (Durham, N. C.: Duke University Press, 1973); H. Richard Friman, *Narco Diplomacy, Exporting the U.S. War on Drugs* (Ithaca, N.Y.: Cornell University Press, 1996).
15. The classic statement of the China market sentiment is Albert J. Beveridge, "March of the Flag," in *The Meaning of the Times* (Indianapolis: Bobbs-Merrill, 1908), 47–57. A modern reading can be found in Thomas McCormick, *China Market: American Quest for Informal Empire, 1893–1901* (Chicago: Quadrangle Books, 1967).
16. Musto, *American Disease*, 49–65.

17. Biographical data about Delevingne is sparse. The details come from the following sources: *Who Was Who, 1941–1950*, 304; *Dictionary of National Biography, 1941–1950*, 207–8; and Bertil A. Renborg, "The Grand Old Men of the League of Nations," *Bulletin on Narcotics* 16, no. 4 (October 1964): 1–11.

18. PRO, Ministry of Health 58/51, quoted in Parssinen, *Secret Passions, Secret Remedies*, 136.

19. Parssinen, *Secret Passions, Secret Remedies*, 153–54.

20. The Home Office files on the Humphrey case are still closed. In 1923, however, Malcolm Delevingne of the Home Office sent a series of letters to the Foreign Office, setting out the facts revealed by the investigation and trying to enlist the Foreign Office's cooperation in urging European governments to crack down on their subjects involved in the illicit drug traffic. These are contained in "Delevingne on Humphrey Case," PRO, FO 371/9247/24–50; PRO, FO 371/9248/127–40.

21. "Humphrey Case," PRO, FO 371/9247/24.

22. "Humphrey Case," PRO, FO 371/9247/24.

23. "Humphrey Case," PRO, FO 371/9247/26.

24. "Humphrey Case," PRO, FO 371/9248/26–28.

25. "Humphrey Case," PRO, FO 371/9248/49–50.

26. The secondary sources for the following account are listed above in note 7. The League generated many documents relating to its attempt to control the international drug traffic. Following are the most relevant: OAC, "Report . . . 1921," LON, C.28.1921.XI.; OAC, "Minutes of the Eighth Session . . . 1926," LON, C.393.M.136.XI; "Records of the Conference for the Limitation of the Manufacture of Narcotic Drugs . . . 1931," LON, C.509.M.214.1931.XI; "An Analysis of the International Trade in Morphine, Diacetylmorphine and Cocaine for the Years 1925–1929," March 12, 1931, LON, C.587.M.228.1930.XI; "Analogies between the Problem of the Traffic in Narcotic Drugs and That of the Trade in and Manufacture of Arms," LON, May 4, 1933, IX.Disarmament. 1933.IX.4.LON; OAC, "Studies and Documents Regarding the Working of the System of Import Certificates and Export Authorisations," LON, November 2, 1935, XI.Opium and Other Dangerous Drugs.1935.XI.11; "Records of the Conference for the Suppression of the Illicit Traffic in Dangerous Drugs, 1936," LON, C.341.M.216.1936.XI; and "Pre-War Production and Distribution of Narcotic Drugs and Their Raw Materials," 1944, LON, C.24.M.24.1944.XI. In addition to these special reports and studies, the OAC issued reports of its annual (occasionally semi-annual) meetings. These are too numerous to list individually but, for example, see OAC, "Report . . . 16th Session . . . April 15–May 4, 1932," LON, C.385M.193.1933.XI.

27. Delevingne to Ekstrand, October 4, 1932, LON, R3168/6450.

CHAPTER TWO

MERCHANTS

1 9 0 6 – 1 9 1 9

Opium has been made a test case of the sincerity of the Republic,
accentuated by the recollection that where the Manchus were
succeeding the Republicans had hitherto notoriously failed.

"The Opium Crisis," *North China Herald*, December 28, 1912[1]

During the hot, stormy Shanghai summer of 1906 one chronic problem caused by the opium trade seemed at last to have been settled.
Unsightly antique ships, relics of the early days of the port, had been
obstructing river traffic since the time of the bloody Taiping Rebellion
in the 1850s. Their owners finally agreed to move the boats to moorage
on the Pudong side of the river closer to the customs house, whose dis-
tinctive clock tower still is the landmark of the city. Angry residents concerned with the smooth operation of the harbor had called these obstacles "monstrosities resembling a child's toy ark" or "conspicuous
nuisances with a vitality exceeding that of a cat." They were the opium
hulks, stationary vessels that had been anchored in the upper harbor so
long that they had grown into composite jerry-built floating warehouses.[2]

The opium hulks were dangerous to the traffic in the harbor, at the
time the world's busiest. Shanghai was first and foremost a commercial

center. Obstacles to the smooth operation of the harbor were serious cause for concern. One professional pilot who knew the waters of the China coast wrote to the *North China Herald*, the English-language paper of the commercial and predominately British elite, complaining in technical detail about the danger posed by such grave hindrances. He suggested that they remained in the way only because of certain powerful vested interests. There was no need for the relics to be where they were, he wrote, because facilities for bonding opium in customs warehouses on shore were newly available. Yet long habit made native opium buyers prefer to purchase the drug offshore, at least according to the owners of the opium hulks, men who ran the large opium hongs—companies like Jardine Matheson, Cawasjee Pallanjee, Sassoon, and Isaac Ezra. These vested interests included some of the wealthiest men in Shanghai.[3]

In only a few years' time the proximity of opium and the customs house would become unthinkable because the enterprise would soon become illegal. During the course of a ten-year reform that began in 1906, the business of opium sales would have to move from the mainstream of Shanghai finance to underground. This would cause the legal traders to scramble to adjust. Most would branch into other businesses; indeed, most already had moved their profits into diversified trade and real estate. They also would find it necessary to band together during the last few years of their trade to protect their reputations from increasingly harsh public criticism. More than their good names, they would need each other to reap the last legal profits from attacks on all sides: smugglers, the Chinese government, and the British foreign service.

SHANGHAI: FOREIGN TRADE CENTER

In Shanghai's busy port in 1906 the floating warehouses, like the drug itself, had become a part of the Chinese landscape. People smoked opium in licensed public opium dens, often called divans, many of which were luxurious and lively public meeting places. It could also be purchased for private consumption from opium shops. Taxed by the authorities, opium was a good source of revenue.[4] Such arrangements were true of the Chinese-administered city as well as the foreign settlements.

Shanghai was a city of districts. Extraterritoriality, a treaty privilege won through opium, had created a city that was a patchwork quilt of jurisdictions. The Chinese city, administered by the *Daotai* (later called

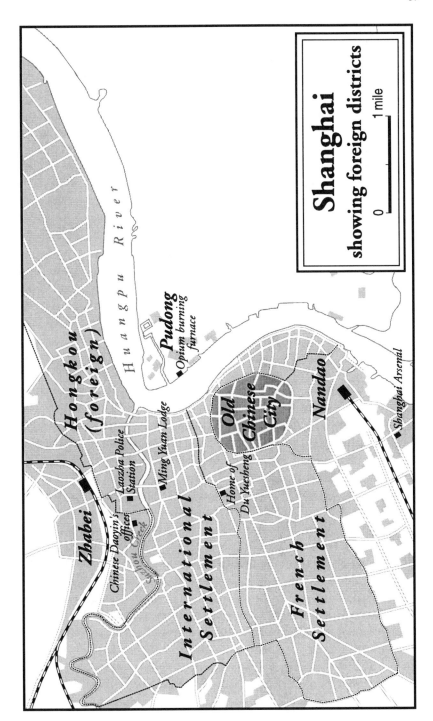

Shanghai
showing foreign districts

0   1 mile

Huangpu River

Hongkou (foreign)

Pudong
■ *Opium burning furnace*

□

■ *Ming Yuan Lodge*

Laozha Police Station

■

Chinese Daoyin's offices ■

Suzhou Creek

Zhabei

■

Old Chinese City

Nandao

■

■ *Shanghai Arsenal*

■ *Home of Du Yuesheng*

International Settlement

French Settlement

Daoyin), an official appointed from the capital, included the largest territory and the poorest. The International Settlement was the financial center. It was governed by the Municipal Council, nine men elected by the wealthiest foreign taxpayers (called the ratepayers) in the area. Among these men was one Edward Ezra, a Persian Jew by birth, a British subject by naturalization, and an opium trader by profession. Ezra's wealth had afforded him a substantial social position in the community. Next to this "Model Settlement," as it liked to call itself, was the smaller French Settlement, location of the most desirable residential neighborhoods, which had a separate French ruling council.

Each administration had its own police force; crossing jurisdictions in chase of criminals was nearly impossible. Foreign nationals were tried by their own consuls. The United States and Great Britain established formal courts for China. There was also the Mixed Court with both Chinese and foreign assessors to hear the many cases involving parties from different nations. Because the nature of the city gave municipal affairs the complexity of international diplomacy, the Chinese stationed a foreign affairs officer there as well.

This hodgepodge of jurisdictions, administrations, and languages fronted on the Huangpu River, which provided the city with its harbor. Along the river ran the Bund, a paved trafficway that was the address of the most prestigious banks, companies, clubs, and the customs—all housed in modern Western buildings. Across the river from these fortresses of treaty port power lay the docks and warehouses, and beyond these, the vast slums of Pudong. The river itself was actually a branch of the Yangzi River delta. It was this access to the South China waterways that made the city so attractive to the early traders. With its decent harbor and proximity to the tea- and silk-producing areas, it had superseded the old port of Guangzhou within a few years of the signing of the Treaty of Nanjing. By the early twentieth century, Shanghai handled half of China's foreign trade.[5]

As Shanghai grew and the number of treaty ports increased from the original five of 1842 to over forty by 1906, the relative importance of the opium traffic declined. Once opium became legal after 1858, Chinese merchants joined the trade while opium poppies flourished in Chinese fields. By 1906 the most productive opium-growing provinces were those in the southwest, Sichuan, Guizhou, and Yunnan, bordering what today has become the world's Golden Triangle. Other provinces also had some acreage given over to poppy cultivation. Nevertheless, the size of the native crop remained limited because opium smokers preferred Indian opium over the native variety. Smokers considered the product from Patna the champagne of opiums.

At the turn of the century opium had become part of the social landscape in China, whereas the number of habitual smokers seems to have stabilized. The findings of the British Royal Commission on Opium of 1893–94 attested to both facts. In 1902 American consular reports from around the country showed similar results. Writing from Shandong province, the American consul claimed that opium consumption was not so widespread as in the south. Still, business deals in the area would only be considered closed after opium was smoked. Those who were not given to using the drug might take a puff or two, just to be sociable. Further south in Xiamen (Amoy) all households kept opium on hand. Again, those who did not use the drug themselves felt compelled to offer it to guests. At the same time the amount of opium imported and the number of shops opened seemed to indicate that the habit was not spreading.[6]

REFORM EFFORTS

The addictive nature of opium had provoked reformers since the earliest days of the trade. By the early twentieth century these voices began to have their effect in political circles. For the Chinese the motive for control was clear. Prohibition was their government's original policy; opium was a constant reminder of successive military defeats, international humiliation, and national sovereignty violated by unequal treaties. Western missionary groups found the drug an embarrassing impediment to winning Chinese converts. For the foreign merchant community, the hideous opium hulks were a graphic reminder of the origins of the treaties that favored their trade. In Shanghai men like Arnold Foster, a thirty-year veteran of China missions, and the American missionary Hampden DuBose, president of the Anti-Opium League, organized protests among foreigners and Chinese alike and kept the moral aspect of the problem alive among the foreign community. These reformers worked with prominent Chinese and with their counterparts in the United Kingdom and the United States. Indeed, the organizations of church groups like the Society of Friends and the Anti-Opium Missionary Society of London had been actively pamphleteering governments since the 1880s.[7]

In the first decade of the twentieth century these private anti-opium activities created an audience receptive to opium control in official circles in both the United States and Great Britain. In England, anti-opium forces gained a significant political voice through the Liberal Party victory in the parliamentary election of 1906. Soon thereafter legislation to limit the Indian opium monopoly began to appear. In 1905 the American government began initiating discussions to end international trafficking in narcotics that would lead to the first international opium convention in Shanghai in 1909.[8]

If China was to enforce anti-opium legislation, the active involvement of Great Britain was the one key to success. Early in the century British diplomats indicated their interest in just such a project. Tang Shaoyi, the American-educated Chinese diplomat sent to Calcutta to discuss British involvement in Tibet, privately received the information that Great Britain would be willing to forgo the profitable Indian exports of opium to China if China could reduce demand for the drug. In 1905, Wang Daxie, minister to Great Britain, formally petitioned the Chinese government to include opium eradication in governmental reforms that were in progress at the time. The next year British authorities formally made China an offer. If the Chinese could demonstrate a willingness to end opium use in their kingdom, the British government would begin gradual reduction of Indian exports to China.[9]

The debate about opium was interwoven with concerns about revenues. Once the proposal to end the traffic began to take serious shape, the British government had to consider possible substitutes for the huge Indian opium returns. After all, the colonial budget relied on those monies. At the same time, the British government was not willing to end such lucrative exports without sincere Chinese efforts to eradicate opium use. Such a move would merely shift huge profits from the Indian exchequer to that of the Chinese. As things stood in 1906, experts estimated that the Chinese government realized £830,000 per year on opium revenues. At the time Chinese opium was taxed in transit between provinces through an internal tariff mechanism known as the *likin*, whereas foreign opium paid a hefty duty. Therefore British negotiators offered a gradual program reducing opium exports from India by one-tenth annually, beginning with a three-year trial period.[10]

The Chinese government readily agreed to the proposition. On September 20, 1906, the Guangxu emperor issued an edict stating his desire that opium cultivation, sales, and use should end in ten years. This was followed by specific regulations issued in November, which were made even more stringent in April 1907. Calling opium the cause of China's poverty and weakness, the regulations aimed at curing the population within ten years. All addicts were to come forward and receive permits to purchase opium for a limited time. Those over sixty would be treated more leniently than younger addicts, for fear that sudden withdrawal would kill them. Addicted officials were admonished to go through a cure immediately. Should they voluntarily admit to opium use, they would be granted a leave of absence to undergo a cure. Otherwise they were assured of harsh treatment. The April regulations began restricting Chinese poppy cultivation.[11]

In response to Chinese enthusiasm for reform, Sir John Jordan, His Majesty's Minister to Beijing, worked out an agreement with the Chinese Foreign Affairs Bureau in which China's Indian imports would be reduced by 10 percent a year beginning with 1908. The starting figure for Indian imports was 51,000 chests, a number derived by taking the average imports from India between 1901 and 1905. The British side agreed to abide by this arrangement for a trial period of three years.[12]

The arrangement met with misgivings in some circles. Those who knew China well doubted the drug could be eradicated. For one thing, the habit was entrenched in Chinese society and opium is not easily put aside. More important, the turn of the century saw the Chinese government in a state of decay. Administered by venal gentry-bureaucrats, many of whom smoked opium themselves, and defended by a fragmented armed service crippled by a series of stunning military defeats, the body politic of China did not show signs of the vigor required to turn around the vices of its subjects. In the countryside banditry was rife. Revolution was in the air. How could such a nation cure an addicted population?

Thus the energy with which the Chinese government and the public at large undertook the anti-opium campaign came as a surprise. Anti-opium fervor gripped the nation. For instance, in Ningbo, a commercial town and one of the original ports opened to foreign trade, Chinese held a rally at which they proclaimed it the duty of loyal and patriotic Chinese to end opium use. People discussed taking up a subscription to replace their government's lost revenue and to show their own sincerity. In Fuzhou members of an anti-opium society took it upon themselves to close opium dens. Responding to their fervor, local officials designated May 12 as the last day such shops could remain open. After that date vigilance groups patrolled the streets to ensure that all dens remained closed. Students rallied with anti-opium banners and appeals to patriotism. By 1910 all shops in Fuzhou closed, bringing protests from foreign

opium merchants who demanded a place to sell their declining allot-
ments.[13]

In Shanghai, Duan Fang, the viceroy of Jiangsu and Zhejiang provinces, closed all opium dens in the Chinese city on June 22. No one
assumed this would be an easy task, as Shanghai and its environs remained one of the best markets for opium. Throughout the two months
preceding the closing date, Duan contacted local groups to enlist their
support. He authorized merchant and student exercise clubs to patrol
and help maintain order lest suddenly deprived addicts create disturbances or formally closed dens secretly continue business. Private
groups also contributed funds to establish a center at the temple of the
city god to train the employees of the old dens for other callings. An
agency, established by Lin Zengji, private merchant, opened at the fire
god temple where used opium pipes and lamps were purchased for destruction. The owners of the dens that closed early received silver
medals.[14]

Duan Fang also contacted the authorities of the foreign settlements
asking for their assistance. He advised them to ready themselves for the
possibility of disturbances by thugs caused by the changed situation in
the Chinese city. Settlement police and the volunteer force went on
alert. This was especially the case after anonymous posters appeared
through the city urging patriotic Chinese to attack the opium hulks anchored in the river.[15]

All Chinese appeals to end opium smoking included strong nationalistic language. The notion that opium smoking was a foreign-born evil
lurked just below the discussion of abolition, adding to the tension that
made passing and enforcing legislation in the divided jurisdiction all
that more difficult.

RESISTANCE TO REFORM

The Chinese administration in Shanghai asked for the active cooperation of foreign municipalities in the battle to end opium use. Hoping to
close all public dens in the city at once they requested foreign authorities to join in the ban. The strategy created rifts in the foreign community. Some residents were as strongly opposed to opium as the Chinese
reformers. As one foreign writer put it, "the moral ball is in the court of
the Model Settlement." Over a thousand licensed opium dens in the
International Settlement provided revenue to the local government and
a market for those who owned the opium hulks. The Municipal Council

was not willing to close the dens merely to follow the Chinese city. Yet with the Chinese so vigorously attacking the trade, Settlement reluctance to join in the movement was hard to defend. The Municipal Council resorted to twists of logic such as claiming that keeping Settlement dens open provided a goad to the Chinese to actually carry out their program. More opportunistically, they hinted that they might close Settlement dens in exchange for additional territory.[16]

Thus the century-old opium debate heated up. There were those who defended opium use per se. One writer stated that the drug was a mere stimulant, not the drastic chemical monster as reported by the alarmists. Some argued that opium was not as harmful as alcohol. These people claimed that opium use, however detrimental it may be to the addict, is not so damaging to society as a whole. Unlike spirits, it led its victims to lethargy rather than violence. Herbert Giles lent his distinguished name to this argument. As a veteran of Britain's consular service in China, a compiler of a prestigious Chinese dictionary and a noted Cambridge scholar, his voice carried weight and conviction.[17]

Such arguments strengthened the Shanghai Municipal Council's reluctance to close businesses whose operators had, until the recent debate, assumed they were no more morally blameworthy than owners of the local British pub. Although the arguments fell into many categories from moral to strategic, the council's main concern was to maintain the wealth on which Shanghai was based and to preserve the treaty privileges that defined their businesses and their lives. This central concern would become clearer during the second phase of the anti-opium campaign.[18]

On the other side of the debate stood the many missionary societies in China, some of the local foreign merchants, and a large number of the Chinese taxpayers, who could not vote but did pay a substantial portion of the municipal taxes. By fall 1907 the British and American diplomatic corps had joined their side by pressuring the Municipal Council to stop issuing new licenses for opium dens and prepare to revoke those already in existence. Pressure mounted; the Council relented. In 1908 the Council presented a scheme to the voting (foreign) ratepayers by which they would gradually phase out all opium dens over two years, closing one quarter of the establishments each six months by lot. In April the plan passed readily; in July the first lot of 359 dens closed.[19]

CHINA'S SUCCESS

There was disbelief among old China hands that the initial flurry of activity could be sustained over time with significant results. Thus it was with surprise that over the next three years foreign travelers throughout the interior of China reported increasing success of prohibition measures. Typical was the following news from Hunan. "I am amazed at the effect of the proclamations. I fully expected they would be mere paper. . . . A young man thinks twice today before he begins to smoke."[20] Other correspondents gave less optimistic accounts. Conflicting claims of success and failure of opium suppression caused the British government to undertake a systematic survey. In 1910, Sir Alexander Hosie completed a province-by-province study including a personal tour of the principal opium-growing areas. Although he noted that the accomplishments of the opium eradication campaign in the provinces were mixed, he concluded that the result was generally positive. Two of the most surprisingly successful provinces were Shandong and Yunnan. He recommended that Great Britain take stronger action to encourage the Chinese government in its obviously sincere and difficult task.[21]

That Yunnan should be included is especially ironic. Located as it is in the remote border region, it was then and continues to be to this day a center for poppy cultivation and smuggling. The province contains a diverse ethnic population along with the Han Chinese. Many of the mountain tribes grew and used opium long before the rest of China, perhaps learning of it through early contacts with Muslim traders from the Middle East. Yunnan is located on the border with Vietnam, in those days colonial French Indochina, and an area that provided a good market for its produce. Although Chinese-grown opium was considered to be inferior to foreign varieties, opium from Yunnan province was prized. Yet reports up to the year 1911 (and even after the revolution to 1915) declared the Yunnan eradication policies to have been successful thanks to the efforts of an enthusiastic governor, Xi Liang.[22]

China's unexpected success created pressure on both sides of the initial treaty to do more. In May 1911, Britain and China reached a new accord that restated the goal of ending all opium sales by 1917. It further provided that all Indian opium imports would terminate immediately to any individual province following proof that poppies no longer grew in the area. From the time of the agreement all Indian opium certified for China would be marked so as to avoid such common frauds as selling opium to Singapore and transshipping it to China. Both governments agreed to allow inspectors inside their borders, with British teams to certify that Chinese provinces produced no poppies and Chinese inspectors to oversee Indian opium exports to China. This agreement was a tribute to the success of the campaign.[23]

Why did the campaign work? Observers at the time gave several reasons. Foreigners took the self-serving attitude that it was through their initiative that China would be weaned away from its vice. Although it was true that China could not have made the moves that it did without foreign cooperation, this was because the government's hands were tied by treaties foisted upon them when they tried and failed to control the traffic in the first place. The Chinese could not make a move without foreign consent. In the end, even with international support, the treaties proved to be insurmountable obstacles to long-term success.[24]

A second reason for success given time and again was the strong anti-opium stance taken by what was called Chinese public opinion. This clearly referred to the students, gentry, and merchants of the urban areas, those groups who were coming to the political awakening that would be given voice in the October Revolution of 1911. This Chinese public opinion was clearly on the side of the prohibition. The papers of the times reported meetings of anti-opium groups and public bonfires where opium paraphernalia was burned amid speeches. For these reformers opium represented the disintegration of central authority in the face of foreign power. We have already seen the dramatic patriotic language that accompanied the opium campaign. Fueled by these emotions, events were about to take a dramatic turn.

In October 1911 came the first Chinese revolution. A republican form of government replaced the Qing monarchy at the beginning of 1912. During the chaos of the sporadic fighting that accompanied the transition and the uncertain administration during the first months of 1912, opium suppression efforts stalled. Even as the revolution progressed, foreign powers with opium interests met at The Hague in December 1911 and came up with an opium protocol designed to begin the process of international regulation of narcotic drugs. The republican government for survival's sake renewed all treaty arrangements, including the May 1911 opium limitation agreement, upon assuming power.

What was the new republic? The original revolutionaries vaguely envisioned a republican government with a legislature. As their uprising spread they appointed Sun Yat-sen to be the provisional president of the new nation. Once successful, they turned their revolutionary alliance into a party, the *Guomindang*, hoping to substitute the ballot box for rebellion. Yet they could not have completed the uprising without the help of General Yuan Shikai and the modern Chinese army under his command. Yuan Shikai had been a power broker during the Qing dynasty. He maintained this power from his position as commander and creator of the *Beiyang* Army, a Western-style modern army that he commanded for the Manchu rulers. Although not noted for a high level of personal integrity, he was much opposed to opium and had been active in the beginnings of the anti-opium campaign. In 1909 he was forced into retirement because of internal conflicts; nevertheless, his army remained loyal to him. At the time of the revolution he nominally backed the crumbling dynasty while he privately negotiated with the rebels. Yuan's support was critical to success. As a reward for his backing Sun Yat-sen agreed to hand over to him the coveted presidential position. Yet once a real constitution came into being, the framers made the position weak by balancing it against a cabinet with a strong premier.

This structure set off power struggles between army and civilian republicans that might have been resolved earlier except for the weakness of both factions. Initially Yuan's position was the stronger one. He controlled the army and placed military governors loyal to him in charge of each province. He took steps to consolidate his own power by assassination, by curtailment of the original constitution, and, in 1913, by outlawing the *Guomindang*. By late 1915 he began the process of making himself emperor of China, an absurd project that he had to give up in spring 1916. After Yuan Shikai died in June 1916, all the factions came back together to try to recreate the old order. It was a doomed project. By 1917, the country split into north and south as generals transformed local power bases into autonomous regions. The early republic had the cohesion and dynamics of a lava lamp.[25]

Yet in the first years of republican government opium eradication continued apace after only a brief pause, despite chaotic conditions. In May 1912 Sun Yat-sen wrote an open letter of appeal to the British government and public asking for support in stamping out the opium evil from the new republic. He suggested that it would be hard to eliminate native cultivation without also prohibiting the trade and sale of opium. This could not be accomplished so long as the existing treaties allowed limited foreign imports. In short, he requested an immediate rather than a progressive end to the British Indian opium trade. Under the standing agreement private consumption of opium would continue for five more years, hampering eradication efforts.[26]

In the wake of the revolution, discussions about opium increasingly focused on treaty rights and privileges. One goal of the new republic was the abolition of extraterritoriality, returning settlement areas to Chinese administration and tariffs. Opium led directly to discussions of the treat-

ies. We have already seen how Chinese progress in closing down dens
became ammunition for attacking the International Settlement. This
kind of argument would intensify when set against a larger debate about
treaty revision. Further, as the price of opium rose and full-scale smuggling fed the Shanghai market, the number of jurisdictions in the city
made policing the traffic impossible. Yet because foreigners clung to the
treaties, refusing to create a workable system that would return jurisdiction to China, smugglers and corrupt officials were forming symbiotic
relationships that would become the standard worldwide.[27]

In 1912, while revolutionaries and generals hashed out the details of
a new parliament, the work of opium eradication resumed, this time
with revolutionary zeal. Reports of poppy eradication once again came
from the interior in summer 1912. Sometimes the republican officials,
finding poppies replanted, allowed the first crop to pass with fines and
dire warnings. Other officials proved to be less forgiving, and reports of
executions and outright battles between police and peasants came to
the ears of the foreign observers. Hunan, for instance, had done a good
job of eradication before the revolution. But poppies had reappeared,
and a complete moratorium on opium use went into effect in July. After-
ward examples were made of offenders such as when a gentry family was
fined $800 for smoking. After October, when a new proclamation made
death the penalty for growing opium, two farmers were shot in public.
In Changsha provisions were made for anonymous denunciation of
smokers, and those who sought help voluntarily were sent to Red Cross
hospitals.[28]

Reform progressed at a time when the young republic desperately
needed funds. Soldiers went unpaid, foreign loans had to be met, and
new loans were being negotiated. Elimination of the opium revenue was
a sacrifice. Yet the new government had to demonstrate its ability to
control its territory. Opium eradication would be a true indicator of
effective power because the Manchus had been internationally recognized for their successful program.[29]

Often the provinces outdid the central government in rigor and enthusiasm, which generally brought them into violations of foreign treaties. For instance, in cases where enthusiastic officials burned opium in
public bonfires, if they included foreign opium, then treaty questions
came into play. Just such a case occurred in September 1912 at an opium
burning in Anhui province. On this occasion Sir Everard Fraser, the
consul general at Shanghai who personally disliked the opium traffic,
had to make a formal protest against the event. He was encouraged to

be firm or else give up the British stand in the Far East. In the fall of 1912 many areas of Young China began arbitrarily closing their provinces to foreign opium. Zhejiang was one of these errant states, and a sensitive one since it was close to the port and had always been a strong market for Indian opium.[30]

POPPIES AND PEASANTS

The anti-opium campaign was popular among the officials and intellectuals of the time but not among the peasants, who could make a good income by planting poppies. The land given over to the crop could be used again, since poppies were planted in November, sprouted in early winter and bloomed in April. Soon thereafter they were harvested. In the early days of the poppy eradication campaign, those inspecting for poppies learned that their trips had to be made in spring, when the plant was in flower, or their optimistic reports were worthless. Although in the initial years of the campaign, peasants often voluntarily abandoned opium growing, there were ways to conceal the plants. If inspections were made early during the growing cycle, they might cover the young sprouts with dirt until the inspector left the area. Poppy plants could be interplanted with melons and beans to hide the telltale flowers in the spring. Peasants never planted opium near the roads.[31]

After the success of the Manchu phase of opium suppression, the price of opium rose, creating unexpected windfall profits for some and temptations for others. Chinese peasants were the first to yield to the attractions of a quick return and the most easily foiled in their schemes. The revolution interrupted local administration just at the time when the price of opium was increasing. Occurring in October, it coincided with planting season; poppies reappeared in the fields immediately. When authority began to return to the countryside, making itself known through renewed opium bans, peasants did not so docilely adhere to the policy a second time. Reports surfaced of battles waged between farmers and deputies sent to enforce the renewed laws, especially in the southwest areas of Yunnan, Guizhou, and Sichuan.[32]

Peasants were not the only ones to respond to the increase in opium prices. International Settlement revenues also increased from the disruption in opium supply. The earliest regulations came in the Settlement only after heated debate and did not prohibit smoking per se, merely public indulgence. In 1909 the last of the Settlement opium dens—public emporiums, often ornately decorated, in which customers gathered to smoke on divans, using equipment provided by the establishment and served up by beautiful and available women—closed. Meanwhile retail shops selling opium for private consumption continued their business. After 1910 the number of these licensed shops grew, as did the income that the settlement received from them. By 1914 there were so many of these establishments along Fuzhou Road that citizens complained about the garish signs, rising crime, and the questionable clientele the area was attracting.[33]

The critics of the Settlement did not come solely from the native governing class. Within the foreign community there was a large faction opposed to opium. Men such as Archibald Little and Edward Waite Thwing petitioned strongly against the Settlement's opium policy. One resident inquired if the council was not perhaps self-serving rather than public minded in its quest for revenue. He pointed out that two bankers and one opium dealer were included among the nine men running the affairs of local government. Little, being himself a ratepayer, brought the issue to a vote in 1915 by demanding that all such shops be closed immediately.[34]

Confrontation between the two factions came to a head in winter 1915, as residents looked forward to the upcoming ratepayers meeting, a ritual in which the elite few who could vote in municipal elections exercised their franchise. Before the meeting Little proposed an amendment that would close all opium shops in the settlement by the end of the year. The Municipal Council itself, under orders from the British Foreign Office to close the shops, put forward its own program to close the shops gradually, by lottery over the two years remaining of the time limit. The Council resorted to several tricks to pass their program, including a measure buried deep inside a general budget proposal. When the vote came, the Council's program passed. The next month all the licensed opium shops submitted to a lottery and the unfortunate one-quarter among them closed their doors.[35]

Those who benefited most from the end of the legal traffic were the opium hongs. These firms, the vested interests clinging to their opium hulks at the century's outset, greeted the end of their business with one last orgy of speculation. Indeed, the opium bans made their product so valuable that they had to move it out of the opium hulks and into protected godowns in 1910. In 1911, when Indian opium bound for China became earmarked and thus drastically limited, the hongs ceased selling any of it at all. They bought up all that they could and stockpiled it. The price of opium became erratic. It soared from Tls 1,600 per chest in May

1911 to Tls 4,000 in September, a month before the revolution. Once the fighting broke out, inland traffic ground to a halt and the price crashed. By summer 1912 a chest of foreign opium sold for Tls 2,000 and faced competition from the native drug planted by peasants taking advantage of internal anarchy and high prices. It did not stay low for long. By 1914, the price rose again to as much as Tls 7,000 per chest.[36]

Nevertheless, the opium traders claimed hardship. The revolution had caught them unawares, they claimed. Trade with the interior ceased. For six months they had not been able to sell their opium at any price; when market conditions settled back to normal, they had a huge surplus of Indian opium on their hands. Financial consternation went beyond their own small circle. While they had waited for trade to revive, foreign banks had loaned them Tls 26,000,000 on future sales. The banks could not be repaid. Clearly, in the debate over opium in the Settlement, there was more at stake than the fortunes of a few opium hongs. One writer estimated that £4,000,000. of the business of the port was directly or indirectly linked to opium. Such practical considerations must have lurked just beneath the surface when the ratepayers weighed moral reform against financial pragmatism and delivered the vote that they did.[37]

SURPLUS OPIUM

These foreign opium traders came out of the revolutionary period with large stocks of opium on hand that had to be sold by 1917. They were not inclined to take a charitable view of any calls from Sun Yat-sen or others to end Indian exports early. In April 1915 the opium merchants formed the Shanghai Opium Combine, a union to protect their interests. Edward Ezra became their president.

The Ezra family did well in the opium trade. They were Persian Jews whose wealth bought them status in money-oriented Shanghai. They belonged to the best clubs. Ned Ezra, the father, argued theology in the pages of the local paper; they supported the local synagogue. They also speculated in real estate; in 1915 Edward Ezra sold a choice property to the U.S. government for the American consulate. He also served on the Shanghai Municipal Council. During the many debates over municipal opium policy, he received harsh criticism for his obvious conflict of interest. Yet he was reelected time and again. It was not until 1919 that he was forced to retire from public life. His downfall came, not from opium, but from a gambling scheme of his brother's to benefit from a baseball tournament. When Judah Ezra was found to have paid the favorite team to lose, he was thrown out of the prestigious Shanghai Race Club. The next year an embarrassed Edward Ezra declined to stand for election.[38]

The Opium Combine formed first to handle the problems caused by the large surplus of stocks in Shanghai. Chinese patriots continued to argue that all Indian opium should be banned. Some suggested using what was left of the Boxer Indemnity[39] to buy up the opium stock and have it destroyed. For the Opium Combine, the situation seemed critical. The British government was not necessarily on their side. In 1914, provincial inspections resumed. When declared free of poppies, a province would be released from treaty obligations to buy foreign opium. Faced with criticism, uncertain official agendas, and erratic sales, the combine entered into private negotiations with the Chinese government. Representatives from the Chinese side contracted to allow sales of Indian opium stocks in the three southern provinces of Guangdong, Jiangxi, and Jiangsu. For each chest the Combine agreed to pay a surcharge of $3,500 per chest. This solution also met with protest because the province of Jiangxi was at the point of being declared opium free by the British government and so being cut off from such imports.[40]

The program was not successful, however. The combine found that their opium did not sell at the high price they had expected. There was too much competition from smugglers, and the provinces involved were not stable. When the uprising against Yuan Shikai began in 1916, their product became even harder to sell. The combine found, in the end, it was smugglers who did the worst damage to their trade. They became unlikely champions of the Chinese opium laws. Who better than opium traders to find illicit opium? Detectives hired by the Opium Combine began bringing violators to the Mixed Court on charges of selling or transporting Persian or Yunnan opium in contravention of Chinese law and in competition with their own stock. They provided a roster of experts, both foreign and Chinese, who could identify the origins of opium by the way it burned and the color of the ash. One of these experts was Edward Ezra.[41]

EVENTS IN YUNNAN PROVINCE

Smuggled opium came from Persia or, increasingly, from the Yunnan and Guizhou areas. As mentioned above, these provinces had been successful in their pre-revolutionary poppy eradication campaigns. But the

1911 revolt coincided with poppy planting season. The lapse of central control, combined with higher prices, brought forth new crops. After the revolution, Yunnan came under the control of Cai E and Tang Jiyao, both military reformers whose ardent republicanism had made the remote province a center for the uprising. From 1911 through 1915 these men tried to end poppy growing in the area again. Yet their attention was turned elsewhere because of the political uncertainty of the times. Their successes in opium control were spotty at best. Yunnan and Guizhou provinces saw some of the worst fighting between opium inspectors and peasants.[42]

Yunnan is an area that lends itself to the illegal traffic. It is remote from the centers of authority and blessed with a rugged, mountainous landscape beloved of poppy growers. It is an area of diverse ethnic groups located on China's southern border. From 1912 on Yunnan smugglers began to adapt to the new market. They developed routes to get their product to urban centers. Overland they shipped opium by mule; local tinsmiths prospered from the sudden demand for special containers for fitting opium into mule collars. The drug could also be smuggled into French Indochina to the south where it would be transshipped by sea from Haiphong to Hong Kong or Shanghai.[43]

In the early 1910s Yunnan also became a center for military leaders opposed to Yuan Shikai. Many political figures, including Sun Yat-sen (after the first glow of revolution died), opposed Yuan's dictatorial ambitions. But without military support such a position was difficult to maintain. Between 1911 and 1916, when Yuan Shihkai died, there were two movements against him. The first came in 1913 after Yuan's agents assassinated a popular *Guomindang* candidate for president. This short-lived second revolution provided the excuse for Yuan to suspend the constitution and outlaw the *Guomindang*, Sun's political party. In summer 1915, Yuan decided to become emperor of China. This move alienated even military men close to him. In the fall of that year Generals Cai E and Tang Jiyao of Yunnan province seceded from the central government in protest. The remote province suddenly became the center of national armed resistance to Yuan. Several prominent civil leaders retreated there and helped to create the National Protection Army, which received good wishes and financial contributions of other patriots elsewhere in China.[44]

The commemoration photograph of the leaders of the National Protection Army suggests no connection between the reformers and drug dealing. The picture shows thirteen distinguished men in a formal Chinese garden. The group includes generals in polished uniforms, several with decidedly scholarly faces that betray their gentry upbringing. There are two members of the national parliament disbanded by Yuan Shikai in 1914. These men led the movement against Yuan's imperial scheme at great personal risk and sacrifice. Yet within two months of the successful uprising, three of the men were brought to trial in Shanghai on opium smuggling charges. They saw their names dragged into the papers under the headline "Yunnan Opium Scandal." In their journey from patriot to smuggler they were participating in the creation of the new-style opium enterprise.[45]

The uprising began late in December 1915. However, even before the fighting began, rumors of the impending imperial scheme brought the Yunnan military group together to plan the uprising. These men were veterans of the 1913 revolt. They were professional military men, graduates of the Japanese military academy, who had served in the reformed Qing dynasty army even while they harbored ideas of revolution. Both Cai E and Tang Jiyao had scholarly backgrounds. They had passed the first round of the civil examinations, but shifted course and pursued military careers when they became convinced of the need for a republican government. As professional soldiers, they were the most likely to succeed in opposing the seasoned general Yuan Shikai. They considered their earlier failure against Yuan to be the result of poor financial backing and equipment. As these men analyzed their situation in the summer of 1915, they agreed that they needed better funding and arms.

They began raising money by draining the Yunnan provincial budget. They obtained loans from the provincial bank and received contributions from Shanghai businessmen sympathetic to the cause and from Chinese communities overseas. During the Yunnan uprising the Shanghai Municipal Police blotters filled with complaints by merchants about the strong-arm tactics used by groups such as the Iron and Blood Braves to raise money for the revolt. It is also during this period that reports of a Yunnan opium monopoly began to surface in the province.[46] At the same time a flood of Yunnan opium cascaded into Guangdong, competing with Indian opium and therefore destroying the scheme to sell the last of the Shanghai stocks owned by the Opium Combine in the southern provinces. Detectives hired by the combine and customs officials looked for the contraband from Yunnan. During the summer of 1916 their vigilance payed off in a spectacular arrest.[47]

In the face of strong opposition, Yuan Shikai gave up his imperial scheme in May 1916 and died in June 1916. In the summer of 1916, the

many factions that had united against Yuan came together in Beijing
hoping to revive the 1912 constitution in order to create political stability. Members of the old parliament who had taken refuge in Yunnan
and representatives of the Yunnan army traveled together to Beijing.
The Yunnan leadership expected to be instrumental in the creation of
a new, viable government. This group included H. E. Zhang Yaozeng,
minister of justice and *Guomindang* member who had gone to Yunnan
province when the fighting broke out, and several generals including
Tang Jiyu, the cousin and confidant of Tang Jiyao, and several aides.
The group left Yunnan June 23, traveling to Haiphong by train where
they caught a ship for Hong Kong then on to Shanghai.[48]

THE YUNNAN OPIUM CASE

Before leaving Yunnan, the delegates, along with Tang Jiyao and other
leaders of the uprising, met to plan their strategy for entering national
politics. The leadership vacuum created by Yuan Shikai's death made
them ambitious. Tang Jiyao hoped to capitalize on the visibility the war
brought him to move from an obscure position on the periphery of
China to national prominence. To this end, the men from Yunnan
planned to establish a partisan newspaper and publicity office in Shanghai. However, there was no money in the provincial coffers with which
to finance the proposed propaganda organs; even the delegates' passage
to Beijing was hard to cover. Thus they turned to opium.[49]

They acquired their supply from the local police who had confiscated
large amounts during the earlier eradication campaigns. They loaded it
into the trunks that would accompany the delegates on their journey
north. They took precautions for getting the contraband past Shanghai
customs. Before their departure, an official from Yunnan contacted the
Shanghai *Daoyin*, Zhou Jinzhen, asking him to arrange for their sixty
pieces of baggage to clear customs on a diplomatic pass, free of inspection. Nevertheless, news of a large shipment of opium leaving the province reached the British consul in Yunnanfu, who notified Shanghai
authorities.[50]

On Saturday, August 5, the delegates arrived in Shanghai on their
way to Beijing. They were met at the dock by the secretary from the
Daoyin's *yamen*, and their baggage cleared inspection. Men and trunks
were escorted to the Mengyuan Lodge, a native hotel on Hebei Road in
the International Settlement. However, the secret cargo in the luggage
was not easily hidden from the stevedores who unloaded the trunks.

Dock workers were part of the Green Gang. They informed Li Zhengwu, a salt merchant and Green Gang boss who had also served as a general in the 1911 revolution. Li informed the Opium Combine that sixty trunks of opium had entered the port, confirming British consular intelligence. Li's sense of civic duty was aroused by the failure of the Yunnan group to include the Shanghai gang in the deal.[51]

The combine detectives obtained the necessary warrants. Accompanied by the attorney M. G. D. Musso and officers from the Shanghai Municipal Police, they went to the hotel where they discovered four trunks filled with opium in the room of the Yunnan delegates' aides. They could arrest only the hapless assistants to the parliamentary party, as the officers and delegates themselves had left town. There were still fifty-six chests unaccounted for.[52]

The detectives traced twenty (or perhaps twenty-two) other trunks that had been taken to an address in the French Settlement by wheelbarrow and from there to a second address in the northern suburb of Zhabei by motor car. They learned that left alone with their cargo, one of the aides had turned to none other than Li Zhengwu for help in distributing the opium. Li obligingly arranged to move the bulk of the opium out of the Settlement. He carted most of the trunks to his home in the French Settlement and then transferred them to Zhabei, in Chinese territory, keeping fifteen aside for himself.[53]

Opium Combine detectives located the driver of the rented car who had handled the trunks. On the evening of August 9, they went with him, following the trail of the leather trunks. They brought along Chinese police, as it was Chinese jurisdiction, and Musso to handle legal complications. Their search ended at a house in Zhabei that belonged to the *Daoyin* of Shanghai, who had signed the customs passes allowing the trunks to enter the port in the first place. The *Daoyin*, Zhou Jinzhen, was not on the premises when the detectives arrived, but a nervous secretary showed them where twenty chests had recently been stored behind the *yamen*.

The boxes were opened, revealing opium, and immediately shipped to the Laozha police station back in the International Settlement. The procedure was highly questionable. The Chinese police fled from the investigation team as soon as they learned they were about to search the office of a man who was the senior official in their city. The move was made with a last-minute warrant signed by Xu Guoliang, the Chinese commissioner of police. Thirty-six chests in all remained unaccounted for, but information from the Shanghai underworld reached the Opium

Combine detectives indicating that indeed a large amount of Yunnan opium had recently come on the market.[54]

The case resulted in a highly publicized trial during which the names of ranking Shanghai city officials and Yunnan delegates were tarnished. At the final verdict, however, only the three unfortunate aides received sentences, while Li Zhengwu was fined 1,000 taels. Yet the other participants were affected indirectly. The minister of justice, Zhang Yaozeng, claimed from the first that he knew nothing of the sixty trunks or the affairs of his traveling mates, yet the disgrace of the scandal forced him to withdraw his name from the cabinet post. Zhou Jinzhen was soundly accused by the British assessor of the court although he remained in Chinese territory, refusing to appear before the International Settlement jurisdiction. He resigned from the post of *Daoyin* shortly after the case closed. Tang Jiyu and his fellow generals were all implicated in the bungled deal. They all stayed away from Shanghai for the duration of the trial.[55]

Xu Guoliang, the commissioner of police for Chinese Shanghai, also came close to losing his post. Throughout the case he received severe censure from the Chinese press for signing off on the search warrant so easily, thereby selling Chinese rights to try the Yunnan opium case to foreigners and further weakening Chinese sovereignty. The outcry became all the more intense when testimony of one defendant indicated that twenty-two trunks left the Mengyuan Lodge but only twenty arrived at the Laozha police station. "Was this the reason that Commissioner Xu was so willing to sign away Chinese rights to the case?" asked one commentator.[56]

Certainly the Yunnan opium case demonstrates the complexities, even the impossibility, of trying to enforce narcotics laws under conditions of extraterritoriality. More than this, it underscores important changes already taking place in the international opium market. As European reformers began imposing restrictions aimed at curtailing world production of opium, smugglers' supply and delivery arrangements became critical. The men involved in the Yunnan plot had one ingredient necessary to a successful narcotics operation: a secure supply. The coincidence of a nationalist military movement based in the fertile poppy growing area in Yunnan brought together elements that allowed the more enterprising and less scrupulous among them to turn a profit.

From beginning to end this bungled attempt to sell a private stock of opium was redolent of amateurism. In order to move their cargo through the Shanghai customs barrier the conspirators needed and ob-

Route traveled by the Yunnan patriots and their opium-laden baggage

tained the compliance of a government official. Unfortunately for their plans, Zhou Jinzhen was not powerful enough to handle the complexities of the Shanghai market. To be successful they had to square their plans with the Shanghai gangs, of which Li Zhengwu was a member. Opium smuggling was falling into the hands of organized crime groups who thrived because of police protection. One of the men involved in the developing underground Shanghai trade was Edward Ezra, head of the Opium Combine.

We can speculate that the Yunnan group was aware of this problem and was trying to solve it. On the evening of the arrests at the Mengyuan Lodge, one of the delegates, General Ye Xiangshi, was being entertained in style in Hangzhou by the military leaders of Zhejiang province. His hosts included men who would provide decisive support in the early 1920s to the most successful of the up-and-coming underground organizers, Du Yuesheng. In 1916, however, the Zhejiang warlords were only one of many competing opium smuggling operations.[57]

Shanghai reformers remained unaware of the scope of the new illicit industry. They remained fixated on the problem of disposing of the legal Shanghai opium stocks. The March 31, 1917, deadline for Indian imports was fast approaching, and the Opium Combine still had two godowns full of overpriced opium. They petitioned the government in Beijing to extend the deadline. The suggestion did not sit well with anti-opium forces, foreign and Chinese. For two years alternative solutions floated about, all of which involved government purchase of the stocks. But since no stable government secured a hold on the capital or the nation, these opium purchase plans came and went for a year and a half. At the dawn of 1918, the year designated by treaty for the elimination of opium from China, excess stocks still sat in the godowns of Shanghai. By June, a government syndicate finally reached an agreement to buy the stocks from the Opium Combine.[58]

The purchase did not meet with general approval. It brought formal protest from Chinese organizations and the Chinese parliament as well as the American and British governments. No one trusted the chests to arrive safely in Beijing. Meeting such strong disapproval, the government approved an alternative arrangement; the opium would be burnt publicly in Shanghai, where sophisticated opium burning facilities already existed.

This furnace, an architectural creation of the anti-opium campaign, stood on the Pudong wharfs, close to where the opium hulks once anchored. The furnace consisted of a long brick ovenlike structure with a chimney and two openings with shoots where opium balls and the discarded chests could be dumped. Burning opium was no easy matter. Initially coal fires had to be used. The first opium balls dumped down the shoot tended to turn to gel and resist the flames. Once ignited, however, they fueled each other and burned nicely, although periodic raking was required to keep the fire going.[59]

In January 1919, officials of the Chinese customs service, along with concerned Shanghai citizens of standing such as C. C. Nie and Y. H. Mo, welcomed Chinese government officials to oversee the process of burning. The Opium Combine chests that had caused such problems lay in storage in the godowns of Jardine Matheson and Sassoon. Those godowns had been sealed in November of the previous year. Amid much public ceremony, prominent community leaders entered the Jardine godown. Chest by chest the delegation inspected the opium, after which they resealed the chests, marked them, and ferried them over to the furnaces on the Pudong wharf, where they were burned. The inspection process took a week; only one chest contained balls that had been tampered with. It was obvious to everyone that the mischief had been done some ten years earlier when the chest had first arrived from India.[60]

It would be a fitting tribute to Lin Zexu to be able to say that the last opium was publicly inspected by Chinese representatives in the warehouses of the company founded by the man Lin had called the "Iron Headed Old Rat" and destroyed publicly just as he had done years earlier. However grand the spectacle and however prestigious the silver cups given out at a banquet when the job was done, the gesture was futile.

Even as the opium burned in Shanghai, poppy planting was on the increase in Yunnan and elsewhere in China. Opium use and sales continued in Shanghai and its environs, at the same time reports of morphine sales increased. The last years of the government's opium suppression campaign were rife with obvious corruption, stemming from the ever increasing need for revenues by all participants in the endemic Chinese civil war. Thus a campaign that for a brief moment showed remarkable success has since been forgotten. Yet it would be too easy to say, as many Europeans did, that the conflict between reform and needed government revenues was a Chinese characteristic. The British government too, while pursuing an anti-opium policy, had to face trade-offs between idealism and financial realities in regulating the opium monopolies in its Asian colonies.

NOTES

1. "The Opium Crisis," *North China Herald*, December 28, 1912.
2. "The Opium Hulks," *North China Herald*, November 5, 1902.
3. "The Opium Hulks," *North China Herald*, November 5, 1902; December 3, 1902; July 20, 1906.
4. Opium imports into China were legalized by the 1858 Treaty of Tianjin, thereafter being taxed at Tls 30 per *picul.* An additional Tls 80 per *picul likin* tax was added by the Zhefu [Chefoo] Convention of 1885.
5. Rhoads Murphy, *Shanghai: Key to Modern China* (Cambridge, Mass.: Harvard University Press, 1958).
6. From American consular reports reproduced in "Use of Opium in China," *North China Herald*, December 11, 1903. In Shanghai, the number of opium licenses dropped from 1,510 in 1897 to 1,226 in 1900. Imports of opium declined from 70,782 *piculs* in 1892 to 49,482 *piculs* in 1901; see also R. K. Newman, "Opium Smoking in Late Imperial China: A Reconsideration," *Modern Asian Studies* 29, no. 4 (1995): 765–94.
7. The letters from both men and others who agreed with them periodically appeared in the correspondence section of the *North China Herald*.
8. Owen, *British Opium Policy*, 333–35.
9. "The Anti-Opium Campaign," translated from the *Sinwenpao*, *North China Herald*, January 26, 1918; "T'ang Shao-yi: Speech to the Board of British-Asian Opium Societies," *The Friend of China* 26, no. 2 (April 1909): 34–39; Hosie, *On the Trail of the Opium Poppy*, 2:191.
10. Hosie, *On the Trail of the Opium Poppy*, 2:191.
11. "The Opium Edict," *North China Herald*, April 26, 1907.
12. The full text of both the edicts and the international agreements are reproduced in Sir Alexander Hosie, *On the Trail of the Opium Poppy*, 2: appendix 1.
13. "The Opium Rally," *North China Herald*, January 25, 1907; Mueller to Grey, January 26, 1910, FO 9392/6812, in Great Britain, Foreign Office, *The Opium Trade, 1910–1941* (Wilmington, Del.: Scholarly Resources, 1974).
14. "Shanghai Jinyan Shiyi 1–26" [The events of Shanghai's opium prohibition, pts. 1–26], *Shen Bao*, June–July 1907; "Opium," *North China Herald*, June 7, 1907; "Opium In the City," *North China Herald*, June 14, 1907; "Suppression of Opium," *North China Herald*, June 28, 1907.
15. "Shanghai Jinyan Shiyi Shiqi Hao" [Shanghai anti-opium events number 17], *Shen Bao*, June 23, 1906.
16. "Anti-Opium Campaign," *North China Herald*, July 5, 1907; "Opium Campaign," *North China Herald*, July 26, 1907; "Suppression of Opium Smoking," *North China Herald*, June 28, 1907.
17. Herbert Giles, "The Opium Edict and Alcohol in China," *Nineteenth Century* 370 (December 1907): 987–1002; "One Who Knows," letter to *North China Herald*, December 28, 1906; "Opium and Alcohol," *North China Herald*, January 10, 1908.
18. "Opium in the Settlement," *North China Herald*, March 6, 1908.
19. "Opium in the Settlement," *North China Herald*, March 6, 1908; "Opium Restrictions," *North China Herald*, July 4, 1908; "Opium in the Settlement," *North China Herald*, October 25, 1907.

20. "Opium in Hunan," *North China Herald*, March 13, 1908.

21. Hosie, *On the Trail of the Opium Poppy*, 2: appendix 2; "The Opium Regulation," *North China Herald*, May 31, 1907; "Opium in Hunan," *North China Herald*, March 13, 1908.

22. "Sir A. Hosie's Report," *North China Herald*, June 8, 1911; China: Inspector General of Customs, *Opium: Historical Notes or the Poppy in China* Special Series, no. 13 (Shanghai: Kelly and Walsh, 1889), 38. Xi Liang was followed in office by Li Jingxi, who continued the good work even though himself addicted to opium. Butler to Grey, February 9, 1910, FO 9392/9773, *The Opium Trade*.

23. "The Opium Agreement," *North China Herald*, May 20, 1911.

24. "The Opium Memorial," *North China Herald*, September 28, 1906.

25. Jerome Ch'en, *Yuan Shih-k'ai* (Stanford, Calif.: Stanford University Press, 1972); O. Edmund Clubb, *Twentieth Century China* (New York: Columbia University Press, 1964); Hsi-sheng Ch'i, *Warlord Politics in China, 1916–1928* (Stanford, Calif.: Stanford University Press, 1976).

26. "Opium and Republic," *North China Herald*, May 18, 1912.

27. The complicated police arrangements are well described in Frederic Wakeman Jr., *Policing Shanghai, 1927–1937* (Berkeley: University of California Press, 1995).

28. "Opium Prohibition," *North China Herald*, June 22, 1912; "Opium in Hunan," *North China Herald*, October 12, 1912.

29. "The Opium Crisis," *North China Herald*, December 28, 1912.

30. "The Anhui Opium Burning," *North China Herald*, October 12, 1912; Jordan to Grey, January 22, 1913, FO 10481/6308, *The Opium Trade*; Jordan to Grey, March 5, 1912, FO 10168/12644, *The Opium Trade*.

31. "The Opium Curse," *North China Herald*, May 13, 1911. Even before the revolution, angry peasants sometimes attacked opium officials; through 1912–13 reports are full of peasants' attempts to grow poppies among other crops and away from the roads, for instance, "Opium in Hunan," *North China Herald*, December 21, 1912.

32. "Opium in Szechuan," *North China Herald*, January 18, 1913; "Opium," *North China Herald*, April 28, 1912; "The Opium Question," *North China Herald*, July 23, 1913.

33. Reverend Arnold Foster, *Municipal Ethics* (Shanghai: Kelly and Walsh, 1914); "Opium and the Council," *North China Herald*, October 17, 1914; "Opium in Shanghai," *North China Herald*, November 15, 1914.

34. Henry V. S. Meyers, letter, *North China Herald*, January 9, 1915; "Opium in Shanghai," *North China Herald*, January 16, 1915.

35. "Today's Meeting," *North China Herald*, March 27, 1915; "Opium Licenses in Shanghai," *North China Herald*, July 3, 1915.

36. "The Opium Deadlock," *North China Herald*, July 6, 1912; "Last Stocks of Opium," *North China Herald*, October 31, 1914.

37. "The Opium Deadlock," *North China Herald*, July 6, 1912.

38. "The Baseball Scandal," *North China Herald*, August 24, 1918; August 9, 1918; August 31, 1918.

39. After the Boxer Rebellion of 1900, eight foreign powers whose nationals

had been attacked by the rebels received Tls 450 million in compensation, which was to be paid with interest through December 1940. The United States remitted part of its share of the indemnity in 1908 and all of it in 1924.

40. "The Opium Combine," *North China Herald*, September 2, 1916; September 23, 1916; "A Paralyzed Government," *North China Herald*, February 1, 1913; "An Opium Impasse," *North China Herald*, May 24 1913; "Opium and the Indemnity," *North China Herald*, July 19, 1913; "Chinese Press and Opium," *North China Herald*, July 3, 1915.

41. "An Opium Test Case," *North China Herald*, July 8, 1916.

42. "Opium in Yunnan," *North China Herald*, 1911–16 passim.

43. "Yunnan and Kweichou," *North China Herald*, April 12, 1913; "Opium in Szechuan," *North China Herald*, January 18, 1913; January 25, 1913. Opium moved easily over the rugged terrain, even without official connivance. Rice did not have such an agreeable marketability. A bumper crop of rice glutted the local market, and officials recommended producing rice wine as a solution. "Opium or Spirits," *North China Herald*, October 10, 1914.

44. Yu Enyang, *Yunnan Shouyi Yungho Gungho Shimo Ji* [Record of Yunnan righteous leadership in protecting the republic] (1917; reprint, Taibei: Wenhai Chubanshe, 1966); Li Zonghuang, *Yunnan Qiyi Xinshi* [The true history of the Yunnan uprising] (Taibei: Zhonguo Difang Zizhi Xuehui, 1946).

45. Yu, *Yunnan Shouyi*, frontispiece.

46. Yu, *Yunnan Shouyi*, 241–49, 113–15.

47. October 29, 1916, IO 670, Shanghai Municipal Police, Criminal Investigation Division [hereafter SMP CID]; July 15, 1916, IO 448 SMP CID contains a letter that is an example of pure extortion: "We wrote to you previously asking for contribution for the sake of the nation. However you were so stupid as to pay no attention to it. This resulted in action by several hotheaded members. We do not blame them. Yesterday the hotheaded members sent the Dare to Dies to your house and asked for a contribution of $10,000."

48. "Hong zhuan yishi zhi Da Situan" [The shocking opium smuggling case], *Minguo Ribao* [Republic daily], August 22, 1916.

49. Zhang Zaichuan, "Xuanhu Yishi de Tang San" [The emminent Tang San (Tang Jiyu)], *Panlong Wenshi Ziliao*, vol. 1, Kunming, Yunnan, 1986.

50. Zhang, "Xuanhu Yishi de Tang San."

51. Zhang, "Xuanhu Yishi de Tang San."

52. "Yunnan Opium Scandal," *North China Herald*, August 19, 1916.

53. Zhang, "Xuanhu Yishi de Tang San."

54. "Yunnan Opium Scandal," *North China Herald*, August 19, 1916; "Hongzhuan Yishi Yan Tuan, 10," *Minguo Ribao*, August 19, 1916.

55. "Mengyuan Lushe Chahu Situ An, 1–13" [Investigation and arrest in the Mengyuan Lodge opium smuggling case], *Minguo Ribao*, August 10–24, 1916; *North China Herald*, August 12, 1916; August 19, 1916; August 26, 1916.

56. "Situ Zashu" [Miscellaneous writings on the opium smuggling case], *Minguo Jihpao*, August 19, 1916.

57. "Mengyuan Lushe Chahu Situ An, 10," *Minguo Ribao*, August 19, 1916.

58. "The Opium Combine," *North China Herald*, June 15, 1918; "The Opium Deal," *North China Herald*, June 29, 1918.

59. "Opium to Burn," *North China Herald*, January 11, 1919; "Opium Burns at Pootung," *North China Herald*, January 18, 1919.

60. "Ershi Guodi Daibiao Huanying Jintu Weiyuan" [Twenty eminent national representatives welcome anti-opium committee members], *Minguo Ribao*, January 4, 1919; "Wanguo Jinyanhui Chengli Dahui Ji" [Record of the establishment of organization by the International Anti-Opium Association], pt. 2–4, *Minguo Ribao*, January 19–22, 1919; "End of the Opium Destruction," *North China Herald*, February 1, 1919.

CHAPTER THREE

MONOPOLIES

1920 – 1930

It seems better that the opium-smoking habit should be suppressed gradually by legalising smoking by confirmed addicts and by supplying such smokers with Government opium. This method only offers the possibilities of limiting individual consumption and preventing the spreading of the habit to more and more individuals.

League of Nations[1]

On June 2, 1924, eight high-ranking British civil servants representing the Home, Colonial, and Foreign Offices met to discuss a policy issue of pressing concern. In light of the stalled success of Chinese opium suppression and in the face of vocal world opinion for reform, what position should His Majesty's Government take at the League of Nations meeting on opium smoking to be held at the end of the year? The men in the room, and the politicians they served, were in an extremely uncomfortable spot. On the one hand, the British government through Sir Malcolm Delevingne, its representative to the League of Nations Opium Advisory Committee, had become one of the world's leading crusaders for stricter regulation of the international traffic in opium and narcotic drugs. On the other hand, opium smoking was per-

mitted in several British Far Eastern colonies, such as Hong Kong and
Malaya, which had substantial Chinese populations.

Indeed, in the colonial possessions of Britain and other European
nations, opium was sold by government monopolies and was often
smoked in monopoly-owned dens. The general revenue funds of the
colonial governments derived considerable profits from these enterprises. Thus the governments of Malaya and Hong Kong, as well as other
colonies, condoned and profited from an activity that the home government in London condemned. At this meeting, men at the highest level
of the very government that had commercialized the opium traffic a
century earlier confronted the contradiction between maintaining colonial revenues and suppressing an acknowledged social vice. British civil
servants were at least trying to deal with the dilemma; other European
governments lagged behind them.[2]

CIVIL SERVANTS DEBATE OPIUM POLICY

In response to American prodding, the League of Nations agreed to
convene an international convention on the international opium problem at Geneva in December 1924. The impending conference forced
His Majesty's Government to address the obvious hypocrisy of its own
colonial practices. Moreover, the British institutions had recently received unwanted publicity from America, an erstwhile ally. As Sir Malcolm bluntly put it, the government "was being continually pressed by
public opinion in the United States, which has the support of the American Government, to take immediate steps to reduce or to abolish opium
smoking in their Far Eastern territories."[3] It was to discuss and to resolve
this pressing issue of the empire's policy on opium smoking that the
civil servants met on June 2.

Sir Malcolm Delevingne, as a leading architect of the League of Nations' drug suppression policies, chaired the meeting. Since the British
government had already committed itself to the League's Opium Convention, which called for "the gradual and effective suppression of the
manufacture of smoking opium," it had no choice, according to Delevingne, but to institute a plan that would lead to prohibition.[4]

Mr. Fletcher of the Colonial Office strenuously opposed Delevingne
during the meeting. He asserted that the agitation against opium, being
mainly foreign, did not take into account what he saw as a lack of any
Chinese desire to abolish the habit. On the contrary, he stated, given
the recrudescence of opium growing and smoking in China itself, any

policy of prohibition would be fruitless, particularly in Hong Kong, which was "an integral part of China."[5]

Sir James Jamieson, an old Foreign Office Asia hand with thirty-eight years service in China, spoke next. Like Sir Malcolm Delevingne, he favored the absolute prohibition of opium smoking. In contrast to Fletcher, Sir James believed that public opinion in China, especially among the younger generation, was swinging decidedly against opium smoking. But regardless of Chinese practice, Sir James said, "we should go into this matter with clean hands." Britain could not continue to denounce blatant drug trafficking in French Indochina or Portuguese Macao while His Majesty's Government profited from opium monopolies in its own Far Eastern colonies.[6]

Fletcher pointed to the practical problems that would be caused by such a dramatic change of policy. He said that "the discontinuance of the Government monopoly would mean an increase of smuggling and consequently of the use of the drug."[7] Furthermore, suppressing opium smoking entirely in Hong Kong would simply lead to an increase in worse habits, such as the use of cocaine and heroin. Fletcher was supported by Mr. Pountney, of the government of Malaya and the Colonial Office, who cautioned that the prohibition of opium smoking in his colony would give rise to "grave disorders" among the Chinese population.[8]

The acrimonious debate wore on. Delevingne and Jamieson, arguing from the point of view of the Home Office and the Foreign Office, maintained that Britain must comply with the League of Nations and the Opium Convention and institute a plan to prohibit opium smoking in British colonies. Fletcher and Pountney, steeped with Colonial Office sensibilities, pointed out the practical impossibility of prohibition and the great disruption that it would cause in Malaya and Hong Kong.

Sir Malcolm then shifted the discussion to fiscal concerns. While the amount of revenue derived by the government of Hong Kong from its opium monopoly was relatively slight, Malaya counted on opium revenues to meet nearly half of its total budget. He said that this dependence on dirty money opened the British to strenuous criticism, especially from some Americans. Mr. Pountney countered that the lack of revenue alternatives made it quite impossible for the Malayan government to do away with the opium monopoly in the near future. The only way he saw to mollify world opinion was to make certain that the opium revenues "be devoted to medical services and education."[9] Sir Malcolm responded that this transparent ruse could also become a trap, for it would entrench the opium monopolies forever because the elimination of opium revenues would endanger those government services that were most necessary and most popular.[10]

As the long afternoon's debate wound down, Sir Gilbert Grindle of the Colonial Office reminded his colleagues of the Indian connection. Opium growing was a government monopoly in British India, a legacy of the age of imperial expansion when it had been so useful. Nearly all of the opium sold by the colonial monopolies in the Far East came from this Indian source. "If the British possessions were asked to suppress the smokers of opium, would the Indian Government be asked to prohibit the export of opium for smoking?" Grindle's question clearly implied that such would be the case. With government monopolies at either end of the supply pipeline, the question of opium suppression raised vexing moral, political, and financial questions at the heart of the British empire.[11]

EVOLUTION OF THE BRITISH POSITION

The opium policy debate of June 2, 1924, reflected conflicting and unyielding departmental priorities, with the Home Office and the Foreign Office favoring suppression in order to keep Britain in line with its principled global commitments. The Colonial Office argued for a continuation of the status quo on the basis of practical considerations.

Over the next few months, the struggle to define His Majesty's Government position became a bureaucratic dogfight, with each side trying to outmaneuver the other. In July, J. H. Thomas, the colonial secretary, drawing on position papers from colonial officials, elucidated Fletcher's earlier arguments in a detailed memorandum addressed to the cabinet. It concluded that the strong opinion of colonial governors and high ministry officials was that far more evil than good would result from trying to prohibit the practice of smoking opium among Chinese.[12]

Thomas pointed out that the British colonies were far more advanced than other European countries in instituting a system for controlling the opium trade. "What we want is to get other countries to go as far as we have gone and are prepared to go," he wrote. Until that happened, and until China effectively suppressed opium cultivation in its territories, Thomas suggested, Britain should not allow a few American enthusiasts to bully it into an uncomfortable position.

In the end, the policy victory went to the Colonial Office. After the cabinet discussed the issue, they agreed that the concerns of the Colonial Office had "much force." The prime minister decided that "although we wish to see an end of the [opium] traffic, we cannot ignore practical difficulties which Americans, in particular, must be made to understand."[13] Despite vehement opposition from representatives of the Home Office, the official British position on legalized opium smoking was a masterpiece of hypocrisy, which combined a commitment to high principle with a condition that rendered it useless:

> His Majesty's Government undertakes that opium smoking shall be abolished in British Far Eastern territories in which such smoking is temporarily authorised, within a period of not more than fifteen years from the date on which the effective execution of the measures taken by China to suppress the growth of the opium poppy has reached such a stage as to remove the danger of opium smuggling from China into these territories.[14]

In other words, His Majesty's Government agreed only to the gradual, not the immediate, suppression of opium smoking in its colonies, and then only in the unlikely event of effective Chinese suppression of opium cultivation and trafficking. In fact, given the renewal of opium growing in China in the 1920s, the British had committed to a continuation of the status quo.

The British debate in 1924, which pitted rival departments against one another, reveals a government caught in its own historical evolution. Government opium monopolies were improvements on their antecedent institutions, the "opium farms," which had replaced the free-trading days of the opium clippers. As British and other European powers acquired Far Eastern colonies in the course of the nineteenth century, they each faced the question of how best to handle Chinese opium smokers in their newly acquired territories. Often the Chinese were a distinct minority, as in the Netherlands East Indies or in the British colony of Borneo. But in other colonies, such as Portuguese Macao or British Hong Kong, the Chinese were the overwhelming majority. In any case, the nineteenth-century colonizing powers perceived opium smoking to be a question of social control and revenue production, not a moral issue. They bequeathed this sensibility to their twentieth-century counterparts.

In virtually all of the colonies, the European powers resorted to the same solution: "opium farms." "Farming" was, in fact, a means of collecting state revenue that had Western roots. Before the nineteenth century, European governments had often licensed private persons to collect taxes or other revenues due the state. In Asia, colonial governments farmed out the right to run an opium monopoly to the highest bidder or, more often, to a syndicate of bidders. The government received the revenue with only the minimal effort required to hold a bidding auction for the right to collect it.[15]

By 1910, however, as world opinion about opium smoking was changing, some governments searched for different solutions. Reform-minded Americans, as noted by the prime minister, were in the forefront of this movement, and they did, in fact, have some experience with colonial problems. In the wake of the Spanish-American War, the United States acquired the Philippines, its first and only direct colonial possession. With a population of some 25,000 Chinese opium smokers, the islands forced the issue on the American government. The Americans opted for a policy of complete prohibition. The policy was remarkably successful.[16]

OPIUM MONOPOLIES

Thus Americans, along with Chinese reformers, became the leading crusaders for the banning of opium smoking worldwide. European colonial governments were unwilling to go as far as the Americans, but they realized that they needed to respond to growing international pressure by asserting greater control over opium smoking. A necessary first step was to replace the opium farms with government monopolies. Between 1910 and 1919 all of the British Far Eastern colonies converted from farms to opium monopolies.[17] A similar process occurred in French, Dutch, and Portuguese possessions. By the early 1920s, opium farms had been universally replaced by opium monopolies.

But opium monopolies remained vulnerable to the criticisms that emanated from a changed public opinion about the drug. No matter that European governments that licensed and taxed alcohol were in much the same position. A combination of racial paternalism of whites toward the Chinese and a changed medical awareness of the dangers of drug addiction made opium smoking seem uniquely evil.

Still, governments could not easily eliminate opium monopolies. They generated revenues that were, in varying degrees, essential to the financial health of colonial governments. At the same time, they were perceived to be the only way to maintain order among Chinese opium smokers and to keep smuggling under control. In the 1920s, the colonial opium monopolies were morally anachronistic, yet for practical reasons European powers were reluctant to abolish them.

Although opium monopolies were an improvement over the unregulated system that previously existed, they were certainly open to criticism. British colonial opium policy came under attack from public organizations like the Edinburgh Anti-Opium Association, the Beijing Anti-Opium Association, and the International Missionary Council. All of these groups published pamphlets, wrote letters to editors, and planted parliamentary questions with their supporters in Westminster. Parliamentary questions were particularly embarrassing, since they forced His Majesty's Government to admit the extent to which colonial governments profited from the monopolies.[18]

American crusaders were strident and were well connected to their government. One such critic was Mrs. Hamilton Wright, whose attacks in print and at the League of Nations constantly vexed the British. In one typical letter, published in the *New York Times* in 1921, she compared the British campaign to suppress the international slave trade after 1815 to the British inactivity over opium: "The opium habit is worse than slavery. The drug should no longer be tolerated as a basis of revenue, an obsolete practice inherited from a primitive and unethical past." Mrs. Wright's letter prefigured the U.S. government's position on opium monopolies at the League of Nations conference in 1925: "It is not necessary or desirable," she wrote, "to pull down ruthlessly the financial structure of India or the colonies of the Far East, which at present rests upon this unwise source of revenue. But the principle of its eventual abolition must be accepted, and other means of raising revenue substituted."[19]

When the League of Nations convened its 1925 conference on opium smoking, the American delegation did indeed bring in a proposal to phase out all opium monopolies by reducing supplies by 10 percent per year.[20] The British government, acting on the policy set by the cabinet in spite of the objections of the Home and Foreign Offices, opposed any change in the status quo. Ironically, Sir Malcolm Delevingne, who had argued vigorously but unsuccessfully within government circles for a phasing out of the monopolies, had to defend the British position in Geneva. He argued against an American proposal that was virtually identical to his own.

Despite the crescendo of public opinion and the Americans' forceful arguments, the League of Nations conference on opium smoking changed nothing. The colonial governments, led by the British, stood pat. The Americans, who refused to compromise from their principled stance, stalked out of the conference when their proposals were not accepted. Thus, in the wake of the 1925 conference, colonial opium monopolies were unchanged.

With monopolies the order of the day, in 1929 the League of Nations appointed a Commission of Enquiry to visit colonial opium monopolies and draw up a comprehensive report. It yielded a wealth of information, which is displayed in the following tables.

The data contained in Table 3.1 should be taken for the order-of-magnitude speculations that they are. Yet they reveal some interesting points. The largest number of opium smokers—both legal and total—lived in the Netherlands Indies, although there were more total smokers in the eight British colonies than in the colonies of any other single power. In some colonies, such as the Netherlands Indies, or tiny Brunei, nearly all the smokers enjoyed their drug legally. In other colonies, such

TABLE 3.1
Estimated Numbers of Smokers

Territory	Number of Legal Smokers	Quantity of Opium Sold (kgs.)	Estimated Illicit Smokers	Estimated Licit and Illicit Smokers
Burma	13,219, plus 41,063 consumers other than smokers (eaters)	23,619 (raw opium)	45,000	100,000
Straits Settlements	39,503	43,200	30,000	73,000
Federated Malay States	52,402	43,600	—	53,000
Unfederated Malay States	Unknown, except for Johore (23,426)	25,130 (Johore 14,800)	—	50,000
Brunei	458	350	—	500
Sarawak	4,664	5,900	—	5,000
British North Borneo	5,087	3,700	—	5,100
Netherlands Indies	186,114	57,100	30,000	216,000
Siam	Unknown	61,000	20,000	110,000
French Indochina	Unknown	68,268	45,000	115,000
Kwang-Chow-Wan	Unknown	1927: 20,180	1927: 6,000	1927: 22,000
Hong Kong	Unknown	6,800	10,000*	10,000*
Macao	Unknown	12,356	87,000*	87,000*
Formosa	26,942	34,970	30,000	55,000
Kwantung Leased Territory	30,858	35,530	65,000*	65,000*

*Ten percent of the male Chinese population
Source: Commission of Enquiry into the Control of Opium, "Smuggling in the Far East. Report to Council," November 1930, LON, C.635.M.254.1930.XI, 20-1.

as the Straits Settlements or French Indochina, there were nearly as many illicit as licit consumers. Finally, the number of estimated opium smokers in all fifteen colonies totaled over a million.

As Table 3.2 indicates, the retail price of monopoly opium varied widely. Using a comparable measure and translating local currencies into Swiss francs, the price varied from 4.95SF per tahil in Kwang-Chow-Wan to 62.50SF per tahil in the Netherlands Indies. Nevertheless, the commission's report noted that high prices did not necessarily lead uniformly to lowered consumption. Well-to-do consumers were undeterred by high prices. "Smokers who did not wish to or could not pay the high Government prices obtained their supplies from illicit sources."[21] Thus smugglers, being adaptable businessmen, were best able to compete with high priced government monopolies, especially in those colonies, such as Hong Kong, that were adjacent or close to China. Any attempt to raise prices far above free market levels simply resulted in a shift of smokers from monopoly to illicit opium.

A completely regulated monopoly, according to the commission's re-

TABLE 3.2
Comparative Prices of Opium

Territory	Price per Tahil* in Swiss Francs	
	At Par	Actual Rate, October 2, 1930
Macao	7.56	3.90
Kwang-Chow-Wan	4.95	4.64
Kwantung Leased Territory	7.12–5.13	7.04–5.07
Formosa	10.32	10.20
Burma	14.50	14.31
Indochina	16.75	15.68
Sarawak	23.52	23.36
Hong Kong	—	24.18
Brunei	29.40	29.20
British North Borneo	29.40	29.20
Siam	34.35	32.25
Straits Settlements	36.75	36.50
Federated Malay States	36.75	36.50
Unfederated Malay States	36.75	36.50
Netherlands Indies	62.50	62.19

*Tahil: The Malay equivalent of the Chinese tael or ounce. 1 tael = 1.3333 oz. avdp.
Source: Commission of Enquiry into the Control of Opium, "Smuggling in the Far East. Report to Council," November 1930, LON, C.635.M.254.1930.XI, 42.

port, would have to include registering, licensing, and rationing individual smokers. Only with such complete control was it feasible to contemplate the gradual phasing out of monopolies, as old smokers either died off or were weaned from their habits and new smokers were prohibited from starting. The report noted, however, that in the Far Eastern territories, a myriad of problems kept the licensing and rationing of smokers out of general use. On the contrary, such a case was an exception.[22]

Finally, the report addressed the politically sensitive issue of opium-produced revenues.

As Table 3.3 indicates, the percentage of total government revenues derived from opium declined in nearly all colonies from 1920 to 1929. In the Straits Settlements and in Hong Kong, this decline was dramatic. Nonetheless, the amounts of money at stake were substantial. Therefore the report recommended that as much of the opium-derived revenue as possible should be dedicated to the campaign to cure addicts and to educate people against smoking. The report concluded that prohibition

TABLE 3.3
Comparative Statement of Opium Revenue

Territory	1920 Net Opium Revenue		1929 Net Opium Revenue	
	In Swiss Francs at the average rate of exchange of the year	*Percentage of net opium revenue to total revenue*	*In Swiss Francs at the average rate of exchange of the year*	*Percentage of net opium revenue to total revenue*
Burma	6,490,957	2.3	7,263,194	3.14
Straits Settlements	37,390,867	46.1	24,003,065	15.1
Federated Malay States	19,168,424	13.9	34,168,171	12.3
Johore	6,145,645	29.39	11,575,834	23
Kedah	4,121,728	34.55	5,702,751	26.78
Perlis	346,298	35.85	542,845	30.15
Kelantan	679,177	20	1,208,613	16.8
Trengganu	419,562	28.2	738,627	17.7
Brunei	64,445	16.76	195,344	19.51
Sarawak	1,846,180	17.86	2,208,133	13.9
British North Borneo	2,642,254	29.1	2,358,020	19.2
Netherlands Indies	73,979,977	12.99	71,584,204	6.35
Siam	34,031,195	23.09	38,591,339	15.81
Indochina	38,178,521	13.85	18,138,113	4.7
Hong Kong	10,326,078	27.8	4,779,060	9.06
Macao	7,322,410	45.49	1,281,482	22.16
Formosa	6,048,340	3.15	6,875,471	2.72
Kwantung Leased Territory	8,152,120	24.1	3,274,814	6.4

Source: Commission of Enquiry into the Control of Opium, "Smuggling in the Far East. Report to Council," November 1930, LON, C.635.M.254.1930.XI, 48–51.

was an impractical goal at present in light of the intractability of opium smoking in the colonies. It recommended gradual suppression through legalizing smoking by confirmed addicts and by supplying such smokers with government opium.[23]

Efforts to confront the question of gradual suppression showed that there were practices and problems shared by all opium monopolies. But, there were also important differences among them, and these differences determined the responses of each administration. The British Colonial Office, with responsibility for monopolies in eight colonies, was acutely aware of how these irregularities made it nearly impossible to establish a uniform, highly restrictive policy. In order to appreciate these issues, it is necessary to examine the problems and practices of the opium monopolies in four disparate colonies: Hong Kong, Malaya, French Indochina, and India.

HONG KONG

Geographically and culturally most closely tied to China among all the European Far Eastern colonies, Hong Kong had four hundred miles of coasts and borders between its territory and China, with over 10,000 persons passing through the frontier daily.[24] Over 95 percent of the population was Chinese, mostly from Canton, the province with the longest history of opium consumption. In the decade between 1907 and 1916, when prohibition of opium cultivation and smoking was effective throughout China, Hong Kong served as a staging area for smugglers who moved it into China. In the next decade, however, the situation turned around. Even as the anti-opium campaign in China fell apart, opium regulation became stricter in Hong Kong. The flow reversed, with China becoming the source for illicit opium that was consumed in Hong Kong. By 1924, Hong Kong officials claimed that illicit opium sales in the colony had grown to at least the size of legitimate sales through the government's monopoly. Thus for Hong Kong, the primary issue raised by the opium monopoly was its relationship to the illicit trade.

According to one estimate, from 20 to 25 percent of the population of Hong Kong—variously estimated from 650,000 to 1.3 million—were regular opium smokers. A frustrated colonial official compared opium smoking in China [and thus in Hong Kong] to betting in England, the one practice being as difficult to eradicate as the other.[25] Hong Kong officials looked at opium smoking primarily as a policing issue with many difficulties. With an opium-smoking population this large, and with access to Chinese opium so easy, they regarded prohibition as an unenforceable policy. Past experience documented that if the government made monopoly opium too expensive or too inconvenient for smokers, they would simply turn to the illicit market for supplies. For example, in 1912, when the government suppressed legal divans (opium dens), opium smoking moved to holes and corners.[26] In the early 1920s, the government of Hong Kong raised the price of monopoly opium to a figure equal to four times the price of illicit opium in an attempt to discourage consumption.[27] As a result, only the wealthy could afford it, and the poor were forced into the illegal market. Raising prices served only to swell the illegal market for opium.

What, then, were the policy options for Hong Kong? One was to dramatically lower monopoly opium prices, which would recapture the poorer smokers who were currently served by the illicit market. In fact, the governor of Hong Kong tried this in 1927 without first consulting the home government. Naturally, the move sparked a renewal of the opium debate by the interdepartmental committee back in London. Sir Gilbert Grindle of the Colonial Office defended the measure, pointing out that opium smoking was too widely accepted by the Chinese in Hong Kong ever to be completely suppressed. Law, in this case, would have to accommodate to social practice if it had any hope of being respected by the populace. He pointed out that if the law was to be enforced, the whole population would be in jail. As the government of the colony could not be asked to build new prisons, he saw no alternative but to approve the scheme of pricing the smugglers out of the market.[28]

Sir Malcolm Delevingne was furious. The unilateral move by the governor, by running directly counter to the policy of His Majesty's Government on which they had taken a stand at Geneva, placed the government in a serious difficulty.[29] Sir Malcolm, in a speech heavy with sarcasm, pointed out how little had been won by this policy change. He claimed there was nothing to show that there would be any ultimate gain as regards the restriction of opium consumption. The only result apparently would be that the field that had been opened up by the smugglers would be occupied by the government. He queried whether the Hong Kong government was simply seeking relief from the embarrassment of keeping people in prisons.[30]

Another policy option was to embrace prohibition but, in effect, not to prosecute it vigorously. Effective enforcement of anti-opium laws depended entirely upon a system of rewards paid to police officers and informants. If the government simply stopped paying rewards, the informants would not talk, and the police would quietly yield the playing field to the smugglers. The result would be a system that would be theoretically defensible at the League of Nations, since His Majesty's Government could point to the enactment of prohibition and the precipitous decline in opium prosecutions as a measure of its success. Yet the cost of such a policy would be to drive the entire opium trade underground, with a resulting loss of control and revenue for the government.[31]

The debate about the Hong Kong opium monopoly was not resolved because, in essence, it posed a dilemma that would be impossible to resolve. If His Majesty's Government forced Hong Kong to conform to the commitments that it had made in Geneva, colonial officials would be placed in the unenviable position of having to carry out a law that they believed was unenforceable. It would, they said, be like trying to prohibit the consumption of wine in Marseille while it was quite legal in the remainder of France. Yet if the Hong Kong opium monopoly were allowed to operate as local officials wished, it would make a mockery of the public stance taken by British officials at the League of Nations and elsewhere.

MALAYA

Colonial British Malaya included several distinct areas. The Straits Settlements, centered in Singapore, included a substantial Chinese majority; in both the Federated Malay States and the Unfederated Malay States the population was predominantly Malay with Chinese minorities. Because of its larger Chinese population, the magnitude of the opium smoking issue was much greater in the Straits Settlements than in the other parts of British Malaya.

Malaya's opium monopoly faced somewhat different problems from those of Hong Kong. Although illicit opium entered Malaya through the busy ports of Singapore and Penang, it was not so close to China that the black market made any sort of meaningful controls unthinkable. In contrast to Hong Kong, in 1924, a Malayan opium committee set out a plan to bring the traffic under tight control. They optimistically set themselves the eventual goal of phasing out opium use entirely. Their agenda included provisions to eliminate private retail shops and smoking "salons," and to replace them with a limited number of government-owned shops. They would then institute a system of registration and rationing of individual smokers, a move considered to be impractical in Hong Kong. They also established a reserve fund, to be accumulated by taking a small portion from each year's opium revenues, which would ease the eventual fiscal transition to a time when the government of Malaya would no longer receive monies from this tainted source.[32]

The plan looked much like that recommended by the Opium Commission. But before it could be fully implemented, Malaya produced an embarrassment for the home government. The Malayan economy was heavily dependent upon the export of tin and rubber. When the world market for these commodities went through a boom phase, the Malayan economy prospered, and an influx of Chinese laborers poured into the country, swelling the number of potential opium smokers. Indeed, it was common knowledge that many Chinese only became opium smokers after coming to Malaya. According to Sir John Anderson of the Colonial Office, "We were open to a very dangerous attack on the ground that we were creating new addicts. Chinese who are too poor to buy opium in China go to the Straits and earn wages which enable them to buy opium in Government shops."[33]

The rise and decline of opium use in colonial Malaya followed economic trends rather than regulation. Immediately after the First World War, and then again in 1924–28, world demand for tin and rubber surged, and a wave of prosperity washed over the colony. The second of these waves, coinciding with the implementation of the reforms and with the Opium Convention of 1925, produced a large increase in the amount of opium consumed through the government monopoly that, in turn, created embarrassments for British representatives in Geneva. Lord Cecil, as he contemplated his unenviable situation, complained that he would be able to convince nobody, not even an audience at home, that His Majesty's Government had done their best. "We were selling thirty per cent more opium than before, and in our own shops," he said. Who would believe that His Majesty's Government could not force the Malayan government to improve this state of affairs?[34]

In spite of this embarrassing rise in consumption in the mid-1920s, the British colonial government in Malaya was reasonably successful in controlling and reducing opium consumption, at least in the legal market. The government managed to reduce the number of retail shops and smoking salons to less than 20 percent of what it had been in the early 1920s; and it introduced registration in 1929 and rationing in 1934. Women and children were effectively barred from smoking establishments. As a result, the percentage of government revenue derived from opium continued to decline during the 1930s.[35] All signs pointed to a decline in opium consumption in Malaya in the 1930s although, once again, this was probably less a result of government policy than of the collapse of Chinese laborers' purchasing power because of the world depression.

In spite of a measure of success, certain problems remained. First, as government restrictions made it more difficult for smokers to obtain their opium through legal sources, the illicit market grew. Although Malayan government officials did not characterize their situation as "hopeless," as did their counterparts in Hong Kong, they conceded that any attempt to reduce consumption through an increase in the price of monopoly opium would simply lead to a flight of consumers into the illicit market.[36] Second, a government program to provide hospital cures for addicts was a failure. Chinese did not regard opium smoking as a disease for which they needed to be treated. They entered rehabilitation programs only during times of economic hardship, when opium supplies were nonexistent, or when they were unemployed. When prosperity returned, the clinics emptied as the "patients" now had jobs and the wherewithal to smoke. Finally, the Malayan monopoly, from the mid-1920s, became increasingly dependent upon Persia for its supply of opium, at the very time when Sir Malcolm Delevingne, at the League of Nations, was trying to organize a worldwide boycott of Persian opium.

FRENCH INDOCHINA

French Indochina lay outside of His Majesty's government's control. Nevertheless, in the early 1920s, the opium monopoly in this colony was of particular concern to British authorities who alleged that it became a conduit for Indian opium that reached the illicit market in Hong Kong. According to Sir Malcolm Delevingne, colonial officials in Indochina purchased Benares opium at the Calcutta auction only in quantities sufficient to supply registered opium smokers in their colony, thus complying with international regulations. However, they regularly sold 30 percent of this Indian opium, which was always considered the choicest, at a considerable profit, into the hands of illicit traffickers and replaced their Indian opium with the cheaper Chinese product purchased from nearby Yunnan province. Indian opium diverted in this way reached Hong Kong, where it was highly prized by well-to-do Chinese smokers, and added further to the mounting problems of Hong Kong officials.[37]

But this was not the only way that French officials in Indochina contributed to the swelling problem of illicit opium. The heaviest poppy cultivation anywhere in China occurred in the southwestern province of

Yunnan. Because of the province's remote location and mountainous topography, Yunnan opium was difficult to move by overland routes into the populous, high-consumption areas along the China coast. The most efficient route, that used by the cronies of the warlord Tang Jiyao in 1916, ran through adjacent northern Indochina, and then by sea from the port of Haiphong into the coastal cities of China.

British observers in Indochina were convinced that French officials quietly condoned this transit across their territory in order to maintain the profitability of their own opium monopoly. In 1929, for instance, F. G. Gordon, His Majesty's Consul in Saigon, accused the governor-general of Indochina himself of complicity with opium smuggling. He maintained that any concern with trafficking in the French colony originated in the rapidly decreasing revenue obtained therefrom in the north of the union due to competition from Yunnan opium. Thus the authorities viewed with favor the question of allowing Yunnan opium to transit in large quantities through Tonkin under special guard for shipment to North China. The step reduced the amount of opium available in Yunnan for smuggling into Tonkin for local consumption.[38]

In Paris, meanwhile, the French government denied any complicity of its colonial officials with illegal traffickers. M. Raymond Poincaré, the conservative premier of France, in a reply to the British Foreign Office, alleged that the major part of opium smuggling throughout the Far East, including French Indochina, was directed by a syndicate of traffickers headquartered in Hong Kong. Indochina, M. Poincaré reminded the British, had a much longer frontier than did Hong Kong, which made effective control of the opium trade even more difficult for French colonial officials. Poincaré reaffirmed his confidence in his colleagues: "The important struggle against this illicit commerce is being pursued by all means at the disposal of the Indo-Chinese administration."[39]

As long as the French denied any improprieties by their officials, British options remained limited. The British settled on a policy centered in a territory they controlled. They reduced the export of Indian opium to the Indochina opium monopoly. At the same time they tried to make French colonial officials account for the disposal of what they did send in a meaningful way.[40] However, these measures barely scratched the surface. As long as French politicians in Paris regarded international narcotics trafficking as a trivial issue, as they did throughout the 1920s, their colonies in the Far East, including Indochina, continued to be safe havens for illicit traffickers, and their opium monopolies continued to be sources of personal enrichment for colonial officials.

INDIA

India represented a special case among opium monopolies. Although it had its own population of opium consumers, in the early twentieth century India was best known as a producer of the drug.[41] From the 1780s through 1906, it was the source of supply for the enormous market of Chinese smokers. Indeed, this trade had grown along with the British Empire. Enterprising British subjects, such as Jardine, the Sassoons, and Edward Ezra in Shanghai, had done much to commercialize the opium.

Yet in the decade following the historic agreement between Great Britan and China in 1907, the amount of opium produced in British India declined precipitously. Whereas in 1902–3 colonial accounts record 10,227,867 pounds exported, by 1919–20 the amount had dropped to 1,876,114 pounds.[42] In the 1920s, opium production declined even further, as the government of India tried to act responsibly within the framework of the Opium Convention and succeeding League of Nations agreements.

It was legitimate, however, for India to supply Asian opium monopolies. India initially sold directly through registered agreements to gov-

TABLE 3.4
Opium Situation in British India, 1919–1929

Year	Acreage under Poppy Cultivation in British India	Value of Opium Exports in Rupees
1919	NA	34,216,390
1920	NA	32,835,830
1921	NA	31,630,584
1922	NA	29,636,088
1923	NA	34,412,829
1924	142,889	31,685,150
1925	135,194	25,998,025
1926	115,851	26,527,150
1927	72,617	33,648,000
1928	54,156	30,124,000
1929	48,854	27,112,000

Source: PRO, FO 371/10970/127; PRO, FO 371/139721/118.

ernment monopolies in all of the British colonies, as well as to Siam and
the Dutch East Indies. Other monopolies, including French Indochina,
purchased Indian opium at the public auctions that were held annually
in Calcutta.

By the early 1920s, however, the Indian monopoly moved to eliminate
auction sales because, as in the French case, it had little control over the
eventual disposal of the opium. In its place, the authorities substituted
direct purchase agreements with other monopolies, which gave it
greater leverage.[43] For example, after the First World War, the Portuguese colony of Macao, under the tolerant rule of corrupt colonial officials, became a safe haven for smugglers. British officials suspected the
Portuguese in Macao of reselling the Indian opium that they had purchased at auction onto the black market. The British Foreign Office
proposed, and the Indian government implemented, a plan that permitted Macao to buy British opium only through a direct sales agreement
with the Indian monopoly, and then in quantities so strictly limited that
none would be available for smuggling.[44] By 1924–25, when even this
measure did not stop the leakage through Macao, India ceased opium
sales to Macao altogether. In the following year it did the same to Japanese Formosa, which was also guilty of passing Indian opium into the
illicit traffic.[45]

Nevertheless, American anti-opium crusaders in the 1920s continued
to pummel the British government for the vestiges of its past sins in
the international drug traffic, particularly because production of opium
continued in India in spite of reduction measures. Yet by the late 1920s,
this criticism was largely unjustified. Although opium eating in India was
widespread, the practice, unlike smoking, was mostly harmless and, in
any case, it was sanctioned by local folk medicine. Opium exports from
British India had declined dramatically since the beginning of the century. When Indian officials suspected their customers of supplying the
black market, they responded by refusing to do business with them.

Britain had an easier time in getting India, its producer colony, to
adhere to League of Nations standards governing the international
opium traffic than in getting Hong Kong and Malaya, its consumer colonies, to conform to them. Yet there were several far-ranging and global
effects of this "clean hands" policy. Most noticeably, as Indian opium
gradually became scarce in the Far East, it was replaced by Persian and
Chinese opium, as well as by heroin and other more powerful forms of
the drug.

Thus in the 1920s Western colonial opium monopolies faced uneasy relationships with both their home governments as well as with League of Nations regulating agencies. This tendency is especially striking in Great Britain, whose officials were active in the international movement to control narcotic drugs. Yet European monopolies would become the model for the very people the reformers sought to help. Europeans had trouble balancing the desire for reform and the need for revenue on one hand, and the professional sensibilities of various bureaucracies on the other, during the years of relative peace and prosperity between the wars in Europe. How much more difficult it would be to perform such a feat as political tensions in Asia increased!

In the years that followed, Chinese warlords and later the *Guomindang* government duplicated this monopoly system as a financial source of revenue under the pressure of civil war. But the Chinese had no colonies. It was the Japanese who embraced the colonial monopoly, claiming to be following the British example. In Japanese hands the institution developed military applications.

NOTES

1. Commission of Enquiry into the Control of Opium, "Smuggling in the Far East. Report to Council," November 1930, LON, C.635.M254.1930.XI, 43.
2. Carl Trocki, *Opium and Empire: Chinese Society in Colonial Singapore, 1800–1910* (Ithaca, N.Y.: Cornell University Press, 1990), has demonstrated the substantial role that opium monopolies, called farms, played in developing the colonial economy in Malaya. He points out the irony that the beginning of the free trade empire was supported by monopoly. Table 3.3 in this chapter gives a concrete example of colonial opium finances.
3. "Note of a Conference Held at the Home Office on the 2nd of June 1924 to Consider What Recommendations Should Be Made as to the Policy to Be Adopted by His Majesty's Government at the Forthcoming International Conference on Opium Smoking in the Far East," PRO, FO 371/10324/29.
4. "Conference Held at the Home Office," 29–30.
5. "Conference Held at the Home Office," 30.
6. "Conference Held at the Home Office," 31.
7. "Conference Held at the Home Office," 32.
8. "Conference Held at the Home Office," 33.
9. "Conference Held at the Home Office," 35.
10. "Conference Held at the Home Office," 35–36.
11. "Conference Held at the Home Office," 36.
12. "Cabinet. Opium Policy. Memorandum by the Secretary of State for the Colonies," July 31, 1924, PRO, FO 371/10326/25. The Home Office equivalent is contained in "SECRET Draft Memorandum for Cabinet," November 1924, PRO, FO 371/10324/65–72. This was almost surely written by Sir Malcolm Delevingne.

13. Waterlow to Delevingne, August 1, 1924, PRO, FO 371/10325/145. Other documents relating to the debate are "Telegram from the Governor of Hong Kong to the Secretary of State for the Colonies," July 14, 1924, PRO, FO 371/10325/137–39; and Delevingne to Waterlow, August 2, 1924, PRO, FO 371/10326/386–87.

14. "Record of Proceedings at Inter-Departmental Conference . . . Forthcoming Opium Conference," January 16, 1925, PRO, FO 371/10966/79.

15. Trocki, *Opium and Empire*; Carl Trocki, "The Rise of Singapore's Great Opium Syndicate, 1840–86," *Journal of Southeast Asian Studies* 18, no. 1 (March 1987): 58–80.

16. Musto, *American Disease*, 26–28.

17. A British memorandum explained how this happened: "In 1907 a Commission was appointed by the Governor of the Straits Settlement [i.e., Singapore] to enquire into the extent to which excessive indulgence in the smoking of opium prevailed in the Colony and to consider what steps should be taken by the Government to minimise and eventually to eradicate the evils arising from the practice. The Committee . . . recommended that the 'Farming' system then in operation should be abolished and that a Government monopoly of the preparation and distribution of prepared opium should be substituted. This policy has been carried out in all the Far Eastern Colonies and Protectorates. The Opium Farms were abolished in the Straits Settlements and in the Protected Malay States of Johore, Kedah, and Perlis in 1910, in the Federated Malay States in 1911, in Brunei in 1913, in Hong Kong and the State of North Borneo in 1914 and in the more backward and remote State of Tranganu in 1917." "Opium Smoking in the Far Eastern Colonies and Protectorates [1925]," PRO, FO 371/10966/36. Also on the history of opium monopolies, see "Reference Conclusions of an Interdepartmental Conference held February 8, 1921," PRO, FO 371/6593/93–94; Sir L. Guillemard to Viscount Milner, November 30, 1920, PRO, FO 371/6593/107; and G. Grindle to Foreign Office, December 8, 1920, PRO, FO 371/5309/48–50.

18. See, for example, the PQ from Mr. Campbell, July 5, 1927, concerning the revenue realized from the Malayan monopolies. PRO, FO 371/12531/291.

19. "Extract from the *New York Times* of July 3, 1921," PRO, FO 371/6595/224–26. See also "Extract from the *New York World*, July 21, 1924," PRO, FO 371/10326/91–92.

20. "Geneva Opium Conference," December 19, 1924, PRO, FO 371/10966/5–11.

21. Commission of Enquiry into the Control of Opium, "Smuggling in the Far East. Report to Council," November 1930, LON, C.635.M.254.1930.XI, 43.

22. Commission of Enquiry, "Smuggling in the Far East," 44.

23. Commission of Enquiry, "Smuggling in the Far East," 53.

24. The best document on the background to the Hong Kong opium monopoly is "Report of the Opium Committee [of Hong Kong]," March 1, 1924, PRO, FO 371/10340/91. See also Lord Curzon to Wellington Koo, April 29, 1921, PRO, FO 371/6594/46; and R. E. Stubbs to Churchill, March 7, 1921, PRO, FO 371/6594/150.

25. "Report of Opium Committee," 1.

26. "Interdepartmental Opium Committee," October 31, 1927, PRO, FO 371/12526/314–15.

27. "Observations on Secret Cable of 9/1/28 from Secretary of State to the Governor of Hong Kong," PRO, FO 371/13254/203.

28. "Observations," 313.

29. "Observations," 316.

30. "Observations," 317.

31. "Observations," 205.

32. "Mr. Amery to Governor of the Straits Settlements," September 16, 1927, PRO, FO 371/12531/293–94.

33. "Record of an Inter-Departmental Committee held at the Foreign Office on November 25, 1926, to consider the recent Increase in the Consumption of Prepared Opium in Malaya," PRO, FO 371/11712/40. See Waterlow to Grindle, January 5, 1926, PRO, FO 371/11711/120, which also addresses the issue of the influx of Chinese into Malaya and the relationship between prosperity and opium smoking.

34. "Record of an Inter-Departmental Committee," PRO, FO 371/11712/40. For greater detail about the precise increases in opium consumption, see Amery to Governor, September 16, 1927, PRO, FO 371/12531/293–94.

35. "Memorandum," May 1937, PRO, FO 371/21045/28–32; and Blaxter to Talbot, May 1938, PRO, FO 371/22197/86–92.

36. "Memorandum," May 1937, PRO, FO 371/21045/28–32; and Blaxter to Talbot, May 1938, PRO, FO 371/22197/86–92, 90.

37. Delevingne to Foreign Office, July 2, 1924, PRO, FO 371/10338/176–78; and Governor-General of Hong Kong to Foreign Office, May 26, 1924, PRO, FO 371/10338/172.

38. F. G. Gorton, HM Consul, Saigon, to Governor-General of Hong Kong, December 22, 1924, PRO, FO 371/10967/160.

39. Poincaré to the Marquess of Crewe, March 27, 1924, PRO, FO 371/10338/160.

40. B. C. Newton, "Excerpt from Home Office paper on India-Indochina Opium Traffic," March 24, 1924, PRO, FO 371/10338/156–57; and Lord Birkenhead, India Office, to Governor-General of India, August 6, 1925, PRO, FO 371/10969/223.

41. Opium was eaten rather than smoked in India. The eating of opium was a part of medical practice and village folklore. Between 80 and 90 percent of all Indian babies were fed opium, and adults took it for real and imagined medical problems, including chronic pain and indigestion. Elderly men were allowed opium as one of the consolations of old age. As long as opium was ingested for medical rather than recreational purposes, authorities in British India strenuously rejected any need to curb its use. See National Christian Council of India, Burma, and Ceylon, Opium in India (Calcutta, 1924), 7–17; LON, R784/39840, and Government of India to Mr. Montagu, March 4, 1921, PRO, FO 371/6594/74–75.

42. Government of India to India Office, March 18, 1921, PRO, FO 371/6597/131.

43. Government of India to India Office, March 18, 1921, PRO FO 371/6597/
    68. There are copies of the sales agreements between the government of
    India and Far Eastern opium monopolies in PRO, FO 371/8002/88–155.
44. Marquess of Curzon to Carnagie (Lisbon), October 30, 1922, PRO, FO 371/
    8028/228.
45. PRO, FO 371/13972/118.

CHAPTER FOUR

NOUVEAUX RICHES

1895 – 1928

Hoshi really met with a bitter experience. If I had, through Hoshi's
introduction, gotten involved in the subsidized acreage program, what
percentage, what amount of income I might have received from the
Home Ministry. Today I would be a multi-millionaire. But, that money,
I suspect was money smuggled through collusion with officials. Getting
involved in the drama might have brought me into court as well. Knock
on wood. Knock on wood.

Nitanosa Otozo (Kawabata Otojiro)[1]

In May 1896, Kawabata Otojiro, a peasant youth from Osaka, barely
twenty-one years of age, appeared in the offices of the Japanese Home
Ministry in Tokyo with a petition. He asked permission to begin growing
opium in Japan. He was hardly a shady character with a dubious scheme.
Indeed, Kawabata was caught up in the patriotic excitement that accompanied his nation's first success in a modern conflict. In 1895, Japan
defeated China in a short, sharp war and acquired its first colony: the
island of Taiwan. Stories of the colonization process filled the various
news media, so that even a country boy like Kawabata knew of the peculiar problems his nation's army faced in trying to bring order to the
island.

Kawabata had heard the current talk about the Taiwan opium problem, including the arguments for and against establishing a colonial monopoly. He knew nothing about politics, but he understood plants. He knew that the white wild flowers that blossomed in his area each spring were descendants of poppy seeds scattered in Japan in the late sixteenth century by Portuguese merchant adventurers. Kawabata proposed to cultivate and improve these poppies to supply the colonial monopoly. Instead of being shown the door, he found his proposal forwarded to Goto Shimpei, who, as head of the Department of Public Health, would design Japan's colonial system. Early entry into the narcotics industry would allow Kawabata and others like him to join the ranks of Japan's *narikin*, or nouveaux riches, by the time of the First World War.

DRUG TRAFFICKING AND POLITICS

Perhaps nowhere is the connection between drug trafficking and politics as intimately woven as in the case of Japan. The fifty-year history of this hidden industry mirrors Japan's experience with industrial development in the modern age. Just as the leaders of Japan's modernization promoted industry for strategic reasons, allowing crucial businesses to be run by their friends under strong government protection, so they gave the narcotics traffic its substance and shape and provided encouragement for select entrepreneurs.

Japanese officials came to the opium traffic reluctantly, embracing it only as part of the established colonial world order of Asia. Simply stated, they regarded the opium traffic as part and parcel of the Western conquest of Asia. Their own status in the power structure of East Asia determined their attitudes to opium. In the mid-1800s, when they first came into contact with the West, and when they were vulnerable, they rejected opium. Once they became power brokers in the area themselves, their attitudes changed. The peasant Kawabata began his career in the midst of this transition.

It is a cherished myth of American history that before 1853, when Commodore Perry forced isolationist Japan to open its ports to foreign commerce, that nation remained ignorant of the outside world. Although Japanese authorities shunned foreign contacts, through the limited trade with authorized Dutch and Chinese merchants at Nagasaki, they knew something of foreign conditions. They knew, for instance, of the increasing sophistication of the Western naval vessels that occasionally entered Japanese waters. They were also aware of the illegal opium trade off the coast of China. And they learned of the Chinese defeat in the Opium War of 1839–42. Knowledge of such events only confirmed the wisdom of the closed-country policy that their predecessors had put in place in 1637. Japanese authorities believed that foreigners might talk peace, commerce, and religion, but their real goals were economic penetration and political domination.

Despite Japanese efforts to keep foreigners out, the number of Europeans in Asia continued to increase. In the mid-1800s, a growing faction among the *samurai*, or warrior class, favored military preparedness for a foreign invasion that seemed more certain each year. These *samurai* radicals used the Japanese emperor, at the time a weak figure, as a rallying symbol to elevate their cause above the petty feudal conflicts of the established *bakufu* system of the day. By the time Perry arrived in 1853, this faction was large enough to create havoc in the old order; and by 1868, new leaders emerged from this group. After what was, by world standards, a bloodless coup d'etat, they began the revolutionary work of creating a modern state based on a rigorous trade and a strong defense in order to preserve Japan's independence in a dangerous world.

JAPAN AND THE WEST

Although these leaders came to power with an incendiary slogan, Expel the Barbarian, they were eminently practical men who understood the immediate need to come to terms with the Europeans. They quickly negotiated commercial treaties with powerful Western nations, allowing trade in designated ports under certain conditions unfavorable to Japan. They did so not out of trust but to buy time to establish themselves at home and to learn the secrets of the West. In drafting the treaties, they yielded on many points, but they remained firm on one: Opium was forbidden to be sold or used on Japanese soil. Western citizens could trade with Japan exempt from the rigors of Japanese law, and they could preach the Christian gospel on Japanese soil, but the opium traffic was to remain in China.[2]

The slogan "Rich Country, Strong Army" well describes the policy pursued by these men, who came to be known as the Meiji oligarchs, after the Meiji emperor whom they both revered and controlled. They were determined men who were willing to dismantle the feudal order in which they had been reared and were ready to transplant institutions from the West in order to protect the modern nation they were creating. In the 1880s, men like Ito Hirobumi, creator of the constitution, under whose cabinet the first opium policy was drafted, and Yamagata Aritomo, father of the imperial army, which was the ultimate beneficiary of narcotics sales, had as their paramount goal the forging of a strong Japan. Their names resound with the same importance in Japan as do Washington and Jefferson in the United States.[3]

They borrowed selectively from the West. Parliamentary democracy was one institution they preferred to do without. Instead they created their own variant: a weak Diet that remained under their influence. After they died, it drifted in a rudderless fashion until equally determined generals seized control of the government in the 1930s.

Modern industry and commerce most interested the oligarchs, especially insofar as they had military applications. From 1868 into the 1880s the oligarchs established model factories, which were purchased from abroad and managed by foreigners while Japanese learned the jobs. Once the nascent industries became operative, the oligarchs sold the factories to friends and backers who had supported their cause during the difficult years of revolt. The names of these friends are perhaps not as well known to us as their organizations—Mitsui, Mitsubishi, Sumitomo—that prospered through the continued patronage of the oligarchs. The economy, led by these profitable companies, enriched the country and the government sufficiently to finance an impressive army and navy. Twenty years later the narcotics industry would follow the same pattern.

THE ACQUISITION OF TAIWAN

This industrial policy was spectacularly successful. By the turn of the century Japan seemed to have thrown off its feudal past. In the 1890s Japan joined the Western nations in creating the sine qua non of a great power: a strong military with an empire to protect. In 1895 the military defeat of China led to Japan's acquisition of its first colony, Taiwan. In 1905 Japan defeated Russia, receiving Dairen (pronounced Dalian in Chinese) as a concession territory, as well as significant economic interests in Manchuria (including the South Manchurian Railway) and in Korea. By 1910 Korea had become a formal colony. When the First World War erupted in 1914, Japan immediately joined on the side of the Allies and thus acquired the German interests in China's Shandong province. The policy of learning from the West, in colonial policy as in other spheres, paid off handsomely.

Imperial success forced Japan to reevaluate its opium policy. In 1895, the Japanese population had little experience with the drug. During the first thirty years of dynamic transition, Japanese focused their energies on the dramatic changes taking place at home. Some experimented with new ideas and products from the West; others worried about the loss of something essentially Japanese in the new society. There were those who opposed the power of the oligarchs, first through armed rebellion, and later through political organization. During these tumultuous years, opium remained a remote concern of both public and policy makers until the acquisition of Taiwan, which, unlike Japan, was a center of opium consumption.

Taiwan, the first Japanese colony, had been conquered many times. It was a late addition to the Chinese realm. Chinese settlers began to move to the island only around the time that the first Europeans began to appear in the southern ocean. The Chinese had to displace Dutch traders, who controlled the island from 1620 to 1662, before they could call it their own. Taiwan was, however, one of the first places in East Asia where opium was smoked. The drug was introduced by the Dutch, who initially used it to counter the symptoms of malaria. The Taiwanese soon discovered the pleasures of smoking, and opium use became well established there by the nineteenth century.

After 1895, as the Japanese army struggled to subdue a hostile population, the conquerors had to confront an opium habit that had been entrenched for more than two hundred years. Opium suddenly became a matter of intense debate in Japan.[4] Fearful that the Taiwanese habit could spread to the home islands if allowed to continue, Japanese, both in government and in the press, assumed they would extend their own strict opium prohibition into the new empire. Initially, only a handful of men advocated legalization of opium in Taiwan. Goto Shimpei was the most notable of this group.

Goto was a man who flourished during Japan's spectacular transition. Born during the last days of the old order to a poor *samurai* family, Goto embraced modernization, choosing to attend a Western-style medical school and later studying in Germany. He briefly practiced medicine and served as head of the Aichi Medical College in Nagoya. But Goto was politically ambitious, and he did not intend to remain for long in the obscure world of academic medicine. He made contacts with politicians by writing strongly worded articles on the benefits of a public health policy to a modern nation. Once he entered politics, he remained among the upper echelons of policy makers until his death in 1929.[5]

In 1895, Goto was the head of the Department of Public Health in the second cabinet of the oligarch, Ito Hirobumi. Just as Ito had created the constitution and Yamagata had created his victorious army, Goto had helped design the Japanese public health service. Thus when Goto advocated as a policy for Taiwan the legalization of opium as a prelude to gradual withdrawal from the drug, his voice carried weight. His arguments for allowing legal opium initially came from an informed medical concern for the well-being of opium addicts among the Taiwanese. Goto did not think it was possible for serious opium users to withdraw from their habits overnight without harming themselves. At first his proposal met with opposition. Even within his own organization, one Kato Takashi, a Board of Health bureaucrat, wrote against legalization. Yet Goto was not a man to change his stand easily and time was on his side.

The Japanese army began occupying Taiwan in May of 1895. Within six months, Mizuno Jun, the head of Taiwan Civilian Administration (and thus the man in charge of carrying out the newly imposed opium prohibitions) became an influential advocate of legalization. He urged ending opium restrictions both in the Diet and in the press, where, in turn, he was attacked as a public poisoner. Early in 1896, he countered these allegations by articulating what became known as the sake/opium antagonism theory. Mizuno explained that the Chinese use of opium was a physiological characteristic. Japanese, belonging to a sake-drinking race and by nature more active, would not be able to tolerate opium; the Chinese, more lethargic and docile, were naturally suited to the drug. This being the case, said Mizuno and others who adopted this theory, there was little danger that opium use would spread from Taiwan to Japan. (Just to make sure, early Taiwan opium laws established the death penalty for anyone selling opium to Japanese.)[6]

The sake/opium antagonism theory made legalization easier to accept at home, as did the position paper that appeared in 1896, predicting that it would take another two army divisions to bring Taiwan under control and enforce strict opium prohibition. The colonial operation was already more expensive than had been anticipated. When Goto issued a second proposal calling for gradual opium withdrawal, which in the interim would create a revenue-producing opium monopoly for the Japanese, it was quickly accepted.

Goto spoke to the concerns of the Meiji oligarchs and presented a concrete proposal for the rigorous control of supply and sales. He advocated a controlled system with police supervision of licensed opium dens and dealers, as well as medical examinations of registered addicts. He estimated that the income from the monopoly would reach ¥1,600,000, which he wanted to see used for public health programs and education of youth to keep them from acquiring the habit.[7]

In February 1896, the Japanese Home Ministry assigned Goto the task of putting his proposed monopoly into operation. He took on the title of colonial health adviser and sent Kato Takashi, the same bureaucrat who had initially opposed opium, to Taiwan. Kato's assignment was to learn the art of processing raw opium into smokers' prepared opium, an odd assignment for one so recently opposed to the habit. In order to run the monopoly, the Japanese government had to learn the secrets of opium processing. Kato arrived in Taibei (pronounced Taihoku in Japanese, it is the capital city of Taiwan) in April. He spent the summer intensely studying his subject, enjoying little sleep or recreation. By October he had mastered the secrets of opium preparation. The Taiwan opium monopoly began producing three grades of smoking-quality opium, packaged and sold under brand names designed to appeal to the Chinese ear.[8]

Goto Shimpei paid close attention to conditions in Taiwan. Two years after the opium monopoly had been instituted, he accepted the difficult assignment of going to Taiwan himself to apply his social policy to the island's population, which continued to resist Japanese pacification efforts. He saw, in Taiwan, a chance to advance politically by expanding his administrative experience beyond opium and public health into colonial affairs. While serving in the Department of Public Health, he had developed his own theory of social environment, which he called physiological perfection. He felt that the people of any nation had to be nurtured through beneficial public programs. The strength of a nation depended on the health of its population. As applied to Taiwan he extended these theories to become a system of biological control.[9]

THE TAIWAN OPIUM MONOPOLY

In March 1898, Goto Shimpei became the head of the Taiwan Civil Administration. He accompanied General Kodama Gentaro, who became the fourth governor-general of Taiwan. Dubbed by modern scholars as the Kodama/Goto *kombi* (combination), the two men worked well together. In Taiwan they created the foundation of Japanese colonial policy, a system that was exported to the Chinese mainland after the Russo-Japanese War in 1905, when the same two men shifted their attention to Manchuria.

When Kodama and Goto arrived in Taiwan, the situation was tense. For the first three years Japanese colonial policy had consisted of outright military suppression of Taiwanese dissidents. This met with little success. Although most urban centers were in Japanese hands, the mountainous countryside sheltered Taiwanese guerrillas. Kodama and Goto tempered tight military control with economic incentives to those who complied with Japanese administration. Taiwanese guerrillas who turned themselves in were rewarded with amnesty rather than execution. Although the Japanese system included a strong police and tolerated no dissent, there were rewards for those who helped the colonizers.

Yang Jichen was one such collaborator. In return for his support of the Japanese, which included providing detailed information about the resistance movement, Yang received a lucrative opium franchise.[10] Other well-placed collaborators also received franchises. Not only did these opium monopolies aid the pacification effort but they fit into Goto's larger plans.

At the core of Goto's colonial system was a set of government monopolies that soon covered the costs of occupation. Opium was the first and most controversial product, but the monopoly bureau expanded to include camphor, salt (1899), and tobacco (1905). By 1907, when resistance ended, Taiwan, once a drain on the Japanese budget, had become financially self-sufficient. The success of his policies earned Goto an appointment to the Japanese peerage.[11]

JAPANESE POPPIES

Goto Shimpei prided himself on having a scientific approach to social problems. He approached the issue of colonial control in his typical fashion, gathering data necessary to analyze the problem. In Taiwan, the Bureau for the Investigation of Traditional Customs studied all aspects of Chinese life, seeking information that would facilitate Goto's control. Later, in Manchuria, as president of the South Manchurian Railway Company, Goto established a similar research bureau, which did everything from population studies to economic planning. The research bureau became a standard feature of joint official/merchant ventures and played a role in service institutions created under war conditions in the late 1930s and 1940s. Goto created these research bureaus to facilitate colonial control. Yet they became instrumental to the Japanese narcotics industry as well.[12]

Once a monopoly existed, Taiwan authorities needed to procure a steady supply of raw opium. Satisfying this need became a problem the Japanese had to face for the duration of their empire. The constant need for raw opium became a shadowy counterpoint to the leitmotif of foreign resource dependence, which runs through Japan's modern industrial experience even to this day. From 1900 through the defeat in the Pacific war in 1945, the Taiwan opium monopoly tried to satisfy its customers' demand through a variety of procurement schemes.

At first the monopoly came by its supplies easily. Until 1911, when international restrictions began to affect supplies, the monopoly purchased opium as needed on the Hong Kong market. The best was Indian, acquired from the British opium monopoly; for lesser grades, Japanese bought Persian, Turkish, and Chinese opium. When the Hong Kong market closed after 1911, the monopoly had to resort to other methods.

Authorities experimented with different shippers at different times, but Mitsui Bussan remained the backbone of the overseas supply lines. During the 1910s and 1920s Japanese experimented with opening the supply to competing companies, but as international criticism increased and global tensions of the 1930s made supplies from Persia uncertain, Japan sought control of its own supply. Japan expanded economically into Manchuria and Mongolia, hoping to tap the resources of northern Chinese territories in order to develop a self-sufficient economic bloc. As part of this campaign, the Japanese began widespread opium plantings in areas that came under their control, with the goal of becoming independent of foreign suppliers. The ability to undertake this enterprise in the 1930s sprang from research into poppy cultivation initiated decades earlier by Goto Shimpei's Taiwan opium monopoly. Thus it was that on that day in May 1896, when young Kawabata Otojiro appeared in his offices petitioning to begin growing opium, he received a warm welcome from Goto Shimpei.

Once the government authorized his experiments, Kawabata found he had more sophisticated material at his disposal than the poor wild poppies of Osaka. He was permitted to procure seeds from India through certain Osaka medicine shops. Kawabata became one of a handful of farmers in the home islands licensed by the government to grow opium under strict control. Located predominantly in Osaka and nearby areas, these farmers continued their experimentation and produced their crops with varying degrees of encouragement from the government.[13]

Association with Goto Shimpei brought the young peasant a social

prestige he could not have otherwise achieved. He married into a neighboring family of high status that boasted three generations of doctors.
He took his wife's surname as his own and changed his given name to
one that had a more sophisticated ring to it. In a stroke he became
Nitanosa Otozo. Over the years he became such an expert on poppy
cultivation that he came to be known as the opium king, even in the
reports of American treasury agents. It was a title that he hated.

Nitanosa did not live the flamboyant life that one might expect of an
opium king. He was a family man concerned with his status and security,
one who shared the deep patriotic feelings of his age. He was a farmer
and maintained the rough manners of the countryside throughout his
life. Nonetheless, his connections with the government afforded him a
better income than most Japanese farmers enjoyed at the time. It also
brought him into influential industrial and political circles in the Osaka
area. He received numerous rewards and citations for his contribution
to the nation. Nitanosa owed his status to the continued support and
patronage of Goto Shimpei, a relationship that continued until Goto's
death in 1929. Nitanosa revered his patron and Goto returned the admi-
ration; Nitanosa's home displayed a large piece of Goto's calligraphy
among the family treasures. When Goto passed away, Nitanosa, a man
not known for emotional displays, openly wept.[14]

Nitanosa firmly believed there was an ethical foundation to his experiments. When periodic political scandals or international criticism
seemed to reveal that the opium monopoly had become a source of
smuggling and profit for some colonial officials, Nitanosa was shocked.
He had convinced himself that the work he was doing supplied an organization created to better the Chinese race by easing them off their
opium habit. He blamed the failure to achieve this goal on evil merchants and bureaucrats, not on the system itself.[15]

Thus for forty years Nitanosa and his colleagues worked with patriotic
fervor to improve the quality of Japanese poppies. Nitanosa occasionally
faced difficult times. During the first years of his experiment poor
weather decimated his crop. Yet he continued to study the qualities of
soil and climate that produced the finest poppies; and periodically he
and his colleagues prospered, such as in the years of the First World
War, when combat conditions cut off German supplies of morphine.
At that time Nitanosa increased the morphia content of his poppies,
becoming so expert that he could judge quality by the smell and color
of the blossom. He was so successful that some of his hybrid poppies had
a morphia content of 25 percent. (Indian poppies contained 6 percent

morphia and Persian poppies contained 12 percent morphia.) During the 1920s, when Japan yielded to international anti-opium pressures, support for Nitanosa waned, only to return in the 1930s when he made several trips through Manchuria to advise the Japanese army about its opium-growing operations.[16]

Success in Taiwan accelerated the careers not only of Nitanosa but also of Goto and Kodama. In 1900 Kodama left Taiwan to become minister of war. He remained in that position until war with Russia seemed certain in 1903, at which time he left for Manchuria as a vice commander on the general staff. When war broke out in February of 1904, Kodama was in the center of action. By the war's end a year later, Kodama was the ranking staff officer and as such he called upon Goto's help once again. They worked together a second time to extend the colonial system they had perfected in Taiwan into the newly acquired territories.[17]

These spoils included the leased area of Guandong, which they controlled outright; rights to the unfinished South Manchurian Railway, which was begun by the Russians; the right to mine areas along the South Manchurian Railway track; and the right to police territories designated as being under Japanese control. Even before the war's conclusion Goto had plans to make the South Manchurian Railway a central part of his colonial vision.

By 1906, Goto became the first president of the South Manchurian Railway Company. He modeled his company after the British East India Company, funding it half from government monies and half from private sources. He brought to the company institutions perfected in Taiwan, including police, monopolies, and a research bureau. The company not only expanded track mileage and improved rolling stock but took advantage of treaty stipulations to open and develop mines at several points along the track. When Korea became a Japanese colony in 1910, the railway provided a strategic link that made the northeast of China a Japanese power base strong enough to cause concern, not only for Chinese but for Western nations with interests in Asia.[18]

THE SOUTH MANCHURIAN RAILWAY

Transportation is critical to drug traffickers. Their profession requires that their crafts either be fast, like the cigarette boats of Miami, or inconspicuous, like the mule trains in the mountains of South China. Never have smugglers had such a perfect tool as the South Manchurian Rail-

way. Policed by sympathetic guards who worked closely with the Guandong army (as the Japanese army in Manchuria was called), it featured
modern equipment that was constantly upgraded and expanded. In the
1930s, the company's luxury train *Ajia* (the Asia) was the pinnacle of
railroad design and comfort; had Manchuria offered more in the way
of scenic attractions, it might have rivaled the *Orient Express*. Certainly
Japanese remember it with nostalgia.[19]

The South Manchurian Railway extended through an area that was
jurisdictionally vague, making it ideal ground for smuggling. It originated at the port of Dairen on the Guandong peninsula, a leased territory administered by the Guandong civil administration and dominated
by the Japanese army. It ran north toward Siberia and east to Korea
through territory that remained in Chinese hands until 1931. Nevertheless, the railroad itself and towns where the trains stopped were under
Japanese control. Japanese policed the railroad and regulated the route.
Japanese subjects, including Koreans and Taiwanese, were tried by Japanese consular courts. Manchuria became a hydra-headed administration
with three Japanese organs of control—consular personnel, the Guandong army, and the railroad—as well as Chinese authorities. [20]

Attached to the (Japanese) Guandong civil administration was the
Opium Monopoly Bureau, which was allegedly in business to remedy the
Chinese opium habit, just as it was in Taiwan. Had the policy of gradual
opium withdrawal remained only in Taiwan, perhaps the program would
have worked as planned. Taiwan, indeed, did see a reduction in smokers
over the course of thirty years of monopoly. But because the structure of
colonial administration was so much more complicated on the Chinese
mainland, leaks naturally occurred where jurisdictions merged.[21]

To meet this problem, in 1914 the Guandong authorities created a
Chinese benevolent association called the Kosai Zendo (Hongji Shan-
tang in Chinese). The ostensible purpose was to provide charity for Chinese living in Japanese-run areas. But it also had a branch responsible
for curtailing opium smoking. The Anti-Smoking Office of the Kosai
Zendo in fact became the medium for supplying opium to licensed
smokers along the railroad zone. It was staffed by Japanese who were
appointed by the head of the Guandong civil administration. Despite
its name, the Anti-Smoking Office became notorious as a purveyor of
narcotics throughout Manchuria.

CONTINUED JAPANESE EXPANSION

These mainland territories attracted opportunistic Japanese fortune
hunters to Manchuria. They gravitated to the cities, setting up busi-

nesses and creating Japanese enclaves along the railroad in Dairen, Mukden, Harbin, and Changchun. The vagueness of borders, the privilege of Japanese status, and profitable business ventures on the frontier drew thousands of Japanese adventurers and investors to the new land of opportunity where many of them became involved in the narcotics traffic.

From their power base in Northeast Asia, the Japanese pushed further into China. During the First World War, Japanese troops used the war against Germany as justification to occupy Shandong province. During and immediately after the war Japanese merchants extended their businesses through China while Japanese populations in cities like Tianjin and Shanghai expanded dramatically. After the Russian Revolution, the Japanese army moved into Siberia, where it remained until 1922. As remote as these places seem to us today, to the international powers present in early twentieth-century China they were points of strategic importance.

The Meiji oligarchs believed that the strength of their modern state would be based on the army, the bureaucracy, and the modern economy. In their quest to fashion a strong, centralized nation they were successful. And yet, as they opened the country to trade, the oligarchs were unable to filter out such Western ideas as democracy, which challenged their dominance. The oligarchs naturally made enemies who formed opposition political parties in the Diet. The years from 1912 to 1926, during which the emperor known to us as Taisho reigned, are called the age of Taisho democracy because of the intensity of political conflict. During these years the Meiji oligarchs began to die, leaving room at the top for a younger generation that rose to prominence through political parties. In this milieu of political intrigue, factional fighting, and scandal, opium quite naturally played an important role.

The Taisho era also experienced dramatic economic swings. The first few years of Taisho coincided with the First World War. In Japan the war, which proved disastrous for European economies, offered an opportunity to establish a significant economic presence in China. Whereas the economies of Japan's allies declined, its own soared. Thus the early Taisho age was marked not only by political parties maneuvering for more power but also by the rise of a class of nouveaux riches. These men, often of humble origins, supported the political parties and joined clubs like the *kojunsha*, where they made business contacts and engaged in political discussions. Many men made fortunes from the colonies. The Suzuki family, of the Kobe Suzuki Trading Company, for instance, owed its prosperity to profits made from the Taiwan camphor monopoly, an arrangement they negotiated through Goto Shimpei.[22]

HOSHI HAJIME AND MORPHINE

Hoshi Hajime was one of these successful entrepreneurs. In 1919, Hoshi cut a dashing figure in business circles. He was a member of prominent clubs and was on good terms with important political figures of the day. Yet he had come from a poor family. Like Goto and Nitanosa, he set out to take advantage of the times to better his lot in life. The course of his journey would lead him eventually to the narcotics trade.

In 1898, at the age of eighteen, Hoshi traveled on his own to New York City, where he wanted to study politics at Columbia University. Unable to afford the regular course, he audited classes while he worked at part-time jobs. He had a gregarious and energetic personality and he made a wide circle of friends among the Japanese in America, many of whom helped him in later years. Twelve years later, when he returned to Japan from his study abroad, he tried his hand at journalism, but the life did not appeal to him. Calling on his American experience, he borrowed money and went into the pharmaceutical business.

Hoshi did not set out to become a narcotics manufacturer. He began with an idea that merged profits and patriotism; like Nitanosa, he sought to make Japan self-sufficient. When he had been in America, Hoshi had not had enough money to allow him frequent visits to the doctor. He had treated his various ills with patent medicines available over the counter. On his return to Japan, Hoshi noticed that German firms dominated the Japanese patent medicine market. He used his borrowed funds to found the Hoshi Pharmaceutical Company, hiring chemists to produce a line of patent medicines for Japan. His first success was Ichthyol, an unguent made from coal tar, and the company later became known for a popular stomach remedy. But even as these products became successful and his advertising signs lined railroad tracks in the countryside, Hoshi looked to expand his product line.[23]

Hoshi liked the role of entrepreneur. He brought to his business an open style that he had picked up in America. He treated his employees in a familiar fashion, defying the rigidly hierarchical structure of most Japanese companies. He became an American advocate. Hoshi translated Herbert Hoover's *American Individualism* into Japanese, and in 1919 his newspaper ads featured a picture of the Statue of Liberty. He supported practical scientific research through his company and through philanthropy. On a return visit to the United States he met Thomas Edison, which, he later recounted, was the highlight of his life. His Hoshi Pharmaceutical Building, seven stories of concrete and glass, would not look out of place in the Tokyo of today, but it was considered quite modern in the Kyobashi area in 1920. The building had a showroom on the first floor along with an American-style cafeteria and an ice cream parlor.[24]

Like his building, Hoshi had an open, smiling manner about him that made him stand out among his more serious countrymen. He was tall and always fashionably dressed, with neatly groomed hair and silver-rimmed glasses. Yet in spite of his good looks and outgoing personality, he resisted the temptations that Japanese society might have afforded a man in his position. He neither smoked tobacco nor drank alcohol. He put off marriage until he was over forty and events had forced him out of the morphine business. When well-meaning friends pushed him on the subject, he declined their offers to arrange a suitable match by claiming that living with a husband who was always at work would not be ideal for a young bride. He had little time or energy to offer a family. He spurned the luxuries that his money might have bought. When police came to search his residence at the time of his 1924 trial for opium smuggling, they went to the wrong house, not believing that the president of such a well-known company would live in such a simple style.

Hoshi did have an incredible capacity for work. He could often be found in his office late at night, poring over his business papers and drinking strong black tea. He was always on the lookout for new opportunities and for contacts with people who could help him. It was this insatiable ambition that caused him to push his company beyond the narrow confines of patent medicines, and it was Hoshi's political contacts that led to his downfall.

Once his patent medicine lines began to prosper, Hoshi began to consider marketing opium alkaloids. He made this choice because, once again, he saw that his country was completely dependent on German-made morphine. Hoshi liked to combine patriotism with an economic venture. He also knew that if his new venture were to thrive, he would need political assistance negotiating around the government control of opiates. Fortunately, upon his return from America, before he had settled on a career in business, he had worked for two months with Goto Shimpei, who had appreciated Hoshi's frank and open manner. Goto provided Hoshi with the proper introductions to the Taiwan Opium Monopoly.

Hoshi, however, did not rely on connections alone. In 1913, he approached the opium monopoly with a well-researched and well-argued proposal that illustrated his understanding of the fundamental importance of supply. He pointed out the benefits of Japan's becoming self-sufficient in such an important medical commodity as morphine. He then argued that the Taiwan monopoly itself could become more efficient by substituting morphine for the smoking opium it supplied to registered smokers. He demonstrated that money could be saved by switching from Indian opium, which contained only 6 percent morphia, to Persian and Turkish poppies, which sold at much the same cost but had a morphia content close to 12 percent. Although smokers preferred the gentler Indian opium, chemistry made the Persian variety more profitable.[25]

Hoshi presented his proposal in May 1914. His timing coincided with two changes in the international climate that made his recommendation welcome. By 1914, the Taiwan monopoly was beginning to feel the effects of international anti-opium conventions. As supplies from British India grew increasingly inaccessible, Taiwan authorities were forced to consider alternative sources. Furthermore, the outbreak of war in Europe disrupted the flow of German morphine that had previously supplied Japanese demand. Hoshi won the concession.

Because opium and morphine were Taiwan monopolies, Hoshi was initially ordered to set up his operation in that jurisdiction. Although he did establish a factory and a branch office in Taibei, the tropical climate and problems of theft with a Chinese staff enabled him to convince the authorities to move the bulk of his morphine production to Japan.[26]

Morphine made Hoshi a rich man. Wartime inflation made him even richer. Between the years 1914 and 1918, when Hoshi had the exclusive morphine franchise, he produced 20,000 pounds of morphine a year. During that time the world price of morphine rose from ¥500–600 to ¥1,000 per pound. Wealth brought Hoshi into influential circles. He joined the *Kojunsha*, and he helped to form the Poppy Cultivation Promotion Association. In this latter organization he met and befriended Nitanosa Otozo, whom he visited frequently. During the war, concern over opium supply moved the government to support domestic poppy programs. At the same time planting programs began in Korea. Colonial officials passed out seeds to designated Korean farmers who were paid for their produce on a sliding scale that rewarded high morphia-yielding crops. Nitanosa went to inspect the Korean fields but found the conditions poor. Korean poppies never produced the potency that Nitanosa or Hoshi desired.[27]

Morphine was not the end of Hoshi's pharmaceutical exploits. Once his company had mastered the technique of extracting morphine, he turned to cocaine. Hoshi contacted a friend from his American days who worked for a trading company with business ties in South America. This friend arranged to supply Hoshi's chemists with one kilo of coca leaves from Peru. In the process he mentioned to Hoshi that another drug company was conducting the same experiments. Hoshi made inquiries and learned that Sankyo Pharmaceutical, a major competitor, had tried and failed repeatedly to isolate cocaine from the coca leaves. Hoshi's informant advised him to give up his quest; cocaine seemed to be too much trouble for too little reward. To be sure, there was little demand for cocaine in Japan or in China. However, as we know from the testimony of Mr. Gibson, a British sailor who earned extra cash by moving drugs through his ports of call, there was a substantial clandestine market for cocaine in India. Hoshi's chemists soon learned the technique for processing cocaine and Hoshi, ever mindful of supply of raw materials, invested in coca fields in Peru.[28]

While Hoshi's chemists worked on cocaine, they also experimented with quinine. Hoshi learned that he could procure the bark of the cinchona tree, the source of quinine, from the Dutch East Indies, where plantations supplied a European buyers' cartel. Hoshi dashed off a letter of inquiry to the Japanese embassy in Batavia inquiring about the availability of supplies. In response, he received a summons from the Board of Health.

Hoshi was nervous about bureaucrats, but when he arrived at the Board of Health offices, he found that affairs had worked to his favor. Dutch East Indian plantations, unable to ship their harvests to Europe because of submarine warfare, found themselves with warehouses full of suddenly valueless cinchona on hand. Plantation owners agreed to sell their produce at good prices to the Japanese government, which in turn offered attractive terms to Hoshi. He was offered a five-year monopoly on the sale of quinine, which he would sell at a fixed price for the first three years. He was required to buy three hundred tons of bark on the spot, although he was given letters of credit from the Bank of Taiwan to facilitate the sale. Hoshi accepted the offer.

However, no sooner had he begun to make preparations for production of quinine than Hoshi discovered that he would be sharing his monopoly. First he learned that his right to ship the cinchona bark had

been transferred to Mitsui Bussan. Hoshi was furious because he had
wanted the Bank of Taiwan bank credits that came with the chore. Hoshi
then learned that the Naikoku Pharmaceutical Company had been receiving money from the Board of Health to experiment with quinine.[29]

In his own recollection of the incident Hoshi fumed against the
treachery of bureaucrats and, in a typically American manner, the use-
lessness of government subsidies. He claimed that Naikoku's product
was inferior and that the formation of the company, which seemed to
appear out of nowhere, was suspicious. (Sankyo merged with Naikoku
in 1920. Sankyo products, unlike Hoshi's, are still very much in evidence
on Japanese pharmacy shelves.) In spite of his denunciation of government intervention, we must remember that Hoshi had benefited from
the cooperation and encouragement of certain bureaucrats, especially
those in Taiwan. These government connections pulled him into the
whirl of Japanese political battles raging during the heady days of Taisho
politics. They would take their toll on Hoshi and his enterprise.[30]

In the 1910s, Japanese politics was in transition from the innovative
but tightfisted control of the early Meiji bureaucrats ultimately to the
militarist rule of the 1930s. In between there was a period of fifteen years
in which men from the political parties held significant power in the
Diet and cabinet. Champions of people's rights were vocal and visibly
eclipsing the military in public esteem. Numerous parties formed, reformed, and disappeared, as well as many cliques, clubs, and study
groups. The Taisho years (1912–26) seemed to be a new age, and the
democratization of Japanese political life appeared to be possible. Some
oligarchs were aging (Yamagata died in 1922) and some were already
dead (Ito died by a Korean assassin's bullet in 1909 as he conducted an
inspection tour of his own colonial creations in Manchuria). As nature
took its course, political scandals further weakened the prestige of the
aging oligarchs.[31]

The opposition members of the Japanese Diet could neither make
policy nor choose the prime minister and cabinet. But they could harass
the government, and they did so effectively. Adding their support to
activists in the Diet were the disenfranchised Japanese citizens who demonstrated in the streets, demanding universal manhood suffrage (which
was not granted until 1925) and protesting high prices. The Taisho emperor reigned over a turbulent age, which often featured fisticuffs on
the floor of the Diet. Such was the raucous political environment of
Taisho democracy in which Hoshi operated. As a supporter of one of
the political parties, Hoshi was a participant in the bruising political

process. As a result, his monopoly on Taiwan morphine came under attack.

Hoshi's ordeal began during the cabinet of General Terauchi Masatake (October 1916–September 1918), who was a Yamagata protégé. It continued during the cabinet of Hara Kei. In September 1918, Hara, president of the *Seiyukai* (the largest of the parties) became the first party member to be asked to form a cabinet. Hara's tenure lasted until his death at the hands of an assassin in 1921. The *Seiyukai* continued in power until 1924. Hoshi fully supported the party.

During these years Goto Shimpei moved through Taisho politics like a fish through water. A bureaucrat who only briefly belonged to any party, Goto's name still seemed to be present whenever parties reformed or cabinets dissolved. He served on several cabinets himself and worked well with *Seiyukai* members. Hoshi believed that the early attacks on his monopoly were really directed against Goto, but he felt that Goto, ever the political creature, did not give him full support in his troubles.

Opposition members of the Diet led attacks on Hoshi. In the first attack, which came in 1917, a diet member called for an end to Hoshi's monopoly on morphine production. Hoshi claimed that during these attacks, money from a rival drug company (implying Naikoku) reached both Diet members and certain officials in the responsible government bureau, especially the Board of Health. Hoshi's defenders came from the Taiwan Governance Office and the Taiwan Monopoly Bureau.

In the face of these attacks Hoshi proved to be adaptable. He bowed to the inevitable and did not openly protest when forced to share his franchise with the Naikoku and Dai Nihon pharmaceutical companies. Hoshi even managed to win a concession during this restructuring. Before the reorganization, Hoshi had to buy raw opium from the Taiwan government at a fixed price. After reorganization, the three licensed companies were permitted to buy fixed quantities of opium on the open market. The Board of Health accepted that granting Hoshi this request would reduce the profits of the Taiwan Monopoly Board. Even in defeat Hoshi had salvaged a victory. In the wake of reorganization, Hoshi assumed that his problems were behind him and that he had made the best of a bad experience. He was wrong.

HOSHI'S DOWNFALL

Once Hara Kei became prime minister the attacks on Hoshi began again. Hoshi was a strong supporter of the *Seiyukai*, and perhaps that alone sealed his fate. Nevertheless, early in 1920, during the forty-first Diet session, questions were once again raised about Hoshi's links to Taiwan officials. This time Tsuchiya Kenzaburo of the opposition published a list of Hoshi's shareholders, which seemed to demonstrate close ties between the company and the Taiwan government. Hoshi held the majority of stock, with 3,572 shares in his name. Certain Taiwan officials privately held twenty shares, and a charitable club organized by the wives of Taiwan officials held the remaining 3,200 shares. The implication that Hoshi and the Taiwan colonial government were growing rich together was hard to miss. Hoshi's friend and supporter, Kaku Sagataro, had to spend many hours testifying before Diet committees before the matter died.[32]

Hoshi's eventual downfall came about because of his concerns about supply and his understanding of the additional income that could derive from such ventures. In 1917, when he took over opium procurement responsibilities from Mitsui, he immediately began looking for the best opportunities and the easiest routes. He tried with some success to buy Persian opium in small packets through the mail, but he kept searching for simpler methods. In 1919, at the war's end, the price of raw opium dropped. Hoshi, seeing an opportunity in such a market, met with Kaku Sagataro, Goto Shimpei's protégé who was at that time the head of the Taiwan Monopoly Bureau. The two men agreed to buy a large supply of opium from the Middle East. Although Hoshi was restricted in the amount of opium he could bring into Japan in one year, he found a legal loophole that allowed him to store opium in bonded customs warehouses, where his goods would technically not clear customs until such time as he needed them. Thus he could take advantage of a buyers' market that he assumed would not last. In 1920, he bought 2,000 chests of Turkish opium through the R. L. Fuller Drug Company of New York and stored them in Yokohama.

Suddenly and unexpectedly in the summer of 1921, all customs warehouses received an urgent message to clear their opium stores immediately. Hoshi had to dispose of his Yokohama opium at once. The timing of the order created a problem for Hoshi, since he had hoped to wait for a rise in the world price. He inquired at the Ministry of Home Affairs to see if they could alter the decision. He learned that a British consul in Kobe had seen bonded opium being moved out of a warehouse illegally one night. The consul had protested to the Japanese government and the Japanese government had responded by demanding a housecleaning of all bonded warehouses.

Hoshi's plans collided with the times. The Japanese statesmen who forged foreign policy during the later Taisho period argued that Japan should integrate into the community of nations by joining the new international organizations rather than pursuing a unilateral policy in Asia. Japan signed the Versailles Treaty, joined the League of Nations, and participated in the Washington Disarmament Conference of 1921. In keeping with this spirit of international cooperation, Japanese representatives joined in the narcotics control discussions just beginning in Geneva. Kaku Sagataro represented Japan at the League's Opium Advisory Committee during the 1920s, arguing sanctimoniously about the efficiency of the Taiwan opium control system and producing statistics showing the decline in addicts on the island over the years. Given the broader political goals of the government and its sensitivity to international reaction to wrongdoing, British accusations of illicit smuggling from Japanese territory provoked an instant reaction.

Hoshi had to move fast. He asked for help from a friend, Sekito Shinji, an American-educated businessman who owned a shipping company in Yokohama. Sekito immediately began to ship Hoshi's opium from Yokohama to Siberia. On his second run, while his ship was docked at Otaru in Hokkaido, it was searched by harbor police and the opium was impounded. Hoshi's name appeared in the newspapers again. He claimed the shipment was in order, showing that the opium was going to Vladivostok and had proper documents from the government there (that is, from the Merkulov government, which was fighting the Bolsheviks and was supported by the presence of the Japanese army). At the same time Hoshi began transferring even larger amounts of opium to Jilong, the port just north of Taibei, Taiwan. Hoshi explained that the entire maneuver was legal and that it made good business sense.[33]

Nitanosa Otozo expressed shock when he heard of Hoshi's problems. "Such a gentleman. How can this be true?" Hoshi attributed his tribulations to the vengeance of a jealous world toward the successful pioneering entrepreneur. He claimed that he was attacked domestically by unscrupulous business rivals and hostile bureaucrats, and internationally by callous functionaries of the British empire, which changed its own opium trade policy only when Japan and Hoshi began to offer stiff competition. (Blaming enemies was Hoshi's characteristic reaction to adversity. He once stood for election as a *Seiyukai* candidate in his hometown of Fukuoka. When he lost, he blamed his defeat on the bribes of the opposing party.[34])

As the Otaru incident faded from the news without causing Hoshi any

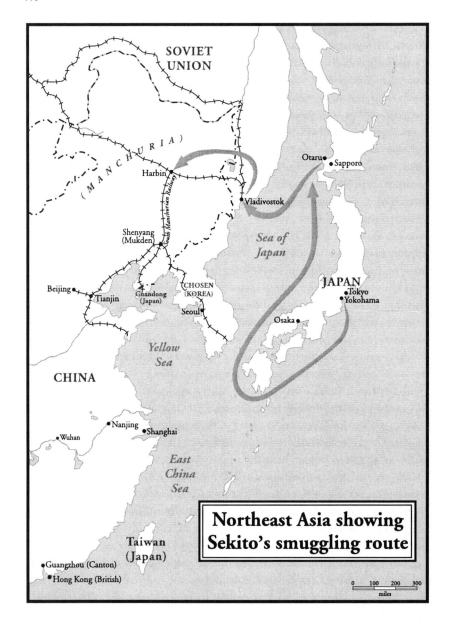

Northeast Asia showing Sekito's smuggling route

severe damage, he seemed once again to have survived. He optimistically turned his energies to a new project, developing air conditioning for factories. Early in 1925, as he was in the midst of raising capital for this venture, the opium problem surfaced once again. In June of 1924, the *Seiyukai* government folded. An opposition party, the *Kenseikai*, formed a new cabinet. At that time Kato Komei, a bitter enemy of Goto Shimpei, became prime minister and immediately began to change personnel in the Taiwan Opium Monopoly. In 1925, the new staff resurrected the evidence from the Otaru incident and brought charges against Hoshi. In May of that year, Tokyo police searched Hoshi's residence and office, and he was taken to the police station in handcuffs for questioning. Later he was indicted and forced to stand trial in Taiwan, where he was found guilty and fined.

Hoshi, like drug traffickers of our own time, could afford the best available legal counsel. He hired legal stars of the day to defend him, who appealed the conviction and got the sentence reversed. Nevertheless the damage was done. In the course of his trials, Hoshi lost his opium franchise, incurred massive expenses, and abandoned his air-conditioning project. After the mid-1920s, Hoshi's name reappears in Japanese records as one of several morphine suppliers, but his dominance in the narcotics business waned. He retreated to the lucrative, but less controversial, quinine, and perhaps cocaine, trades. He never abandoned his Latin American enterprises. In fact, he died on January 19, 1951, while traveling to his properties in Peru.[35]

Hoshi needed political connections to become the pioneering businessman that he was. Having become entangled in politics, he was exposed to the shifting fortunes of his backers. Yet he had to maintain connections to the government as best he could because in the new international climate only suppliers with such arrangements could survive. Hoshi had the added luxury of being openly attached to a licit monopoly with one backer who was a Japanese government representative to the League of Nations. This allowed him to play the role of gentleman, while it eased the obstacles to delivery. His opium and morphine reached the illicit market in China. Clandestine sales of opium that had government clearance could be extremely profitable and could easily be done before passing into Japan and onto the official record.

Hoshi's venture into quinine becomes less innocent when we recall how protective he was of the shipping rights and the banking arrangements that went with it. (One observer suggested that cocaine also was coming from Java.) It was profitable enough that it attracted the interest of his competitors. In May 1920, the Sankyo Pharmaceutical Company opened a branch in Taiwan. In September of the same year, Sankyo merged with Naikoku Pharmaceutical, Hoshi's competitor. After Hoshi went bankrupt in 1925, Mitsui once again became the opium supplier for the Japanese government, a concession that lasted to the end of the Pacific War. Mitsui is a major stockholder of Sankyo Pharmaceutical.[36]

Revelations about opium trading were part and parcel of factional strife in the age of Taisho democracy. Goto Shimpei, who created the colonial system and its opium monopoly with the best intentions, knew that the system was leaking at the seams. In 1916, he used that knowledge to discredit a cabinet in which Kato Komei, his enemy, served as foreign minister. Goto published and circulated a report listing dubious activities of the Japanese army in China, including its connections to drug dealers. A year later, when the Terauchi cabinet came to power and Goto, himself, held a portfolio, he went to considerable expense to buy up all the suddenly embarrassing pamphlets.[37]

Incidents of factional conflict allow us glimpses of a part of the Japanese colonial structure that most authorities tried to keep hidden. Publicly, apologists for the opium monopoly stressed its successes and the benevolence of the system. People like Kaku Sagataro built a career on it, rising from head of the Taiwan monopoly, to head of the Taiwan civil administration, and finally to Japan's representative at Geneva.[38] But the opium scandal and ensuing revelations demonstrated a darker reality.

The establishment of Japanese opium monopolies on the Chinese mainland made certain men with good political connections wealthy. In this early stage the monopolies enriched a few well-established entrepreneurs, while allowing the Japanese government to claim that they were intended to benefit Chinese addicts. This dual aspect of opium monopolies gave the profitable trade a humanitarian guise. Politicians in Tokyo could feign ignorance of abuses in the system and profess outrage whenever its true nature surfaced during periodic scandals. Indeed, their representatives at Geneva pointed proudly to the Taiwan monopoly's success in registering addicts and lowering their numbers over the years.

Despite this dissembling behavior, the unvarnished truth was that Japanese politicians and entrepreneurs cooperated to nurture an infant industry that delivered narcotic drugs into the lungs and veins of millions of addicted Chinese. In the 1920s, as the Japanese military and the civilian governments clashed over basic policies at home and abroad, the profits of this traffic would prove useful in financing Japanese adventurers and extending Japanese power. At the same time, the success of these Japanese entrepreneurs, combined with stricter enforcement of League of Nations guidelines in Europe, eventually drove European pharmaceutical manufacturers out of the lucrative Chinese market.

NOTES

1. Nitanosa Nakaba, *Senso to Nihon Ahen Shi: Ahen O Nitanosa Otozo no Shogai* [War and the history of opium in Japan: the life and times of Nitanosa Otozo, the opium king] (Tokyo: Subaru Shobo, 1977), 77–78.
2. The first commercial treaty signed with the United States in 1857 prohibited opium. The policy was reiterated in the new treaties redrawn in April 1868, after the Meiji Restoration. Okura Sho [Ministry of Finance], *Meiji Taisho Zaisei Shi* [Financial history of the Meiji and Taisho years, 1868–1925] *Gaichi Zaisei* [Overseas finances] (Tokyo: Keizai Orai Sha, 1958) 19:826.
3. The best general history of the Meiji Restoration is W. G. Beasley, *The Meiji Restoration* (Stanford, Calif.: Stanford University Press, 1972).
4. Ryu Meishu, *Taiwan Tochi to Ahen Mondai* [Control of Taiwan and the opium problem] (Tokyo: Yamakawa, 1983), 5–10.
5. Kitaoka Shinichi, *Goto Shimpei: Gaiko to Bijyon* [Goto Shimpei: foreign policy and vision] (Tokyo: Chuo Koron Sha, 1988).
6. Ryu, *Taiwan Tochi to Ahen Mondai,* 46–47.
7. Ryu, *Taiwan Tochi to Ahen Mondai,* 50–54.
8. Ryu, *Taiwan Tochi to Ahen Mondai,* 74–83.
9. Kitaoka, *Goto Shimpei,* 20–25.
10. Ryu, *Taiwan Tochi to Ahen Mondai,* 100–03.
11. Okura Sho, *Meiji Taisho Zaisei Shi,* 19:507.
12. Kitaoka, *Goto Shimpei*; Many of the essays in Ramon H. Meyers and Mark R. Peatie, *The Japanese Colonial Experience* (Princeton: Princeton University Press, 1984), mention Goto and his ideas as applied by the Japanese in the administration of its empire.
13. Nitanosa Nakaba, *Senso to Nihon Ahen* , 1–23.
14. Nitanosa, *Senso to Ahen,* 124–35.
15. Nitanosa, *Senso to Ahen,* 133–35.
16. Minami Mantetsu Kabushiki Kaisha, Keizai Chosakai, Daigobu [Manchuria railway economic investigation bureau, section five], *Chosen Ahen Mayaku Seido Chosa Hokoku* [Report on an investigation of opium and narcotics in Korea], mimeographed report, 1932. Reports of Nitanosa's success with increasing the morphia content of poppies vary. This report claims that the average Korean poppies yielded a morphia content of 10 percent.
17. Harada Katsumasa, *Mantetsu* [The South Manchuria Railway] (Tokyo: Iwanami Shoten, 1981), 2–49.
18. For a description of the bureaucratic operations of the South Manchuria Railway, see Joshua A. Fogel, trans., *A Life along the South Manchurian Railway: The Memoirs of Ito Takeo* (Armonk, N.Y.: Sharpe, 1988).
19. Akimoto Shunkichi, *Manchurian Scene* (Tokyo: Taisho Eibunsha, 1933) is an

apologist for Japanese control of Manchukuo but describes travels through the new nation on the train.

20. Shimada Toshihiko, *Kantogun: Zai Man Rikugun no Dokuso* [The Kuantung army: the independent actions of the army in Manchuria] (Tokyo: Chuo Koronsha, 1965), 14–15.

21. John Jennings, *The Opium Empire: Japanese Imperialism and Drug Trafficking in Asia, 1895–1945* (Westport, Conn.: Praeger, 1997), details the successes of the Japanese monopolies.

22. Imai Seiichi, *Taisho Demokurashi* [Taisho democracy] *Nihon no Rekishi* [Japanese History], (Tokyo: Chuko Bunku, 1974), 23: 87–91.

23. Hoshi Shinichi, *Jinmin wa Yowashi; Kanri wa Tsuyoshi* [The people are weak; the bureaucrats are strong] (Tokyo: Kadokawa Shoten, 1971), 1–5. Hoshi's signs may have been like the Burma Shave ads in American cornfields. One British commentator on the Hoshi trial stated that the countryside would improve once Hoshi's signs were gone.

24. Hoshi, *Jinmin wa Yowashi*, 1, 86–90, 130–36.

25. Hoshi, *Jinmin wa yowashi*, 28–48; Hoshi Hajime, *Ahen Jiken* [The opium incident] (Tokyo: Hoshi Pharmaceutical Business School, 1926). This document was Hoshi's printed apology to his shareholders after his business went bankrupt.

26. Hoshi, *Jinmin wa Yowashi*, 42–44; Hoshi, *Ahen Jiken*.

27. Nitanosa, *Senso to Ahen*, 63–72, 126; Mantetsu Keizai Chosakai, Daigobu, *Chosen Ahen Mayaku Seido Chosa Hokoku*, 1932.

28. "Confession of Mr. Gibson, Englishman, Who Was First Officer Caught Smuggling at Rangoon," J. Slattery, December 28, 1929, PRO, FO 371/14768; Hoshi, *Ahen Jiken*, 26–28.

29. Hoshi, *Jinmin wa Yowashi*, 56–64.

30. Hoshi, *Jinmin wa Yowashi*, 64–72.

31. Bernard S. Silberman and H. D. Harootunian, eds., *Japan in Crisis: Essays on Taisho Democracy* (Princeton, N.J.: Princeton University Press, 1974).

32. Nitanosa, *Ahen to Senso; Asahi Shimbun*, March 20–30, 1919.

33. Hoshi, *Ahen Jiken*; Hoshi, *Jinmin wa Yowashi*. On the movement of opium from Vladivostok to China, see Alston to Curzon, January 27, 1922, FO 1105/504/10, *The Opium Trade*.

34. Hoshi, *Jinmin wa yowashi*; When he lost the election, Hoshi organized a study group to improve the political morality of Japanese people and to raise campaign monies. Goto's name was connected with this enterprise. Hoshi Hajime, *Senkyo Daigaku* [Election college] (Tokyo, 1924).

35. Hoshi, *Ahen Jiken*, 40–54; "Memorandum," PRO, FO 371/12527 108–12; "Opium Scandal," *Japan Chronicle*, May 17, 1925; P. D. Butler to Sir John Tilley, October 16, 1926, PRO, FO 371/11714.

36. *Sankyo Hachijunen Shi* [Eighty-year history of Sankyo] (Self-published, 1979); A. Morgan Young, *Japan in Recent Times* (Westport, Conn.: Greenwood, 1929); Japan, Foreign Ministry, "Dai Ju-ikkai Ahen I-inkai" [Eleventh Opium Committee Meeting], October 16, 1937, IMT document 3179, no. 607, Library of Congress Microfilm, WT series, shelf 5039, reel 81; *Gendai Nihon Jinbutsu Jiten* [Dictionary of modern Japanese notables] (Tokyo: Asahi Shimbun Sha, 1990), 1436.

37. Goto did an admirable job of eliminating the pamphlet. It is not in his personal papers at the National Diet Library nor is it mentioned in the four-volume biography of Goto by Tsurumi. The most recent study of Goto's life by Kitaoka Shinichi mentions briefly the role that it played in the fall of the Okuma cabinet. During the Washington Conference of 1921, the Chinese delegation purchased a copy and translated it, using it as evidence of Japanese treachery in their own land. *Menace to the Peace of the Far East* (Chinese People's Foreign Relation Society, 1921) was kindly sent to the authors by William O. Walker.

38. Sagataro Kaku, *Opium Policy in Japan* (Geneva: 1924).

CHAPTER FIVE

EUROPEANS

1 9 1 9 – 1 9 3 2

Recent restrictive measures in France, Germany, and Turkey make it practically impossible to obtain for other than legitimate needs any considerable quantities of narcotic drugs in Europe. . . . The situation in China has entirely changed. . . . European or Turkish [drugs] cannot be imported owing to the general depression and particularly to the decline of silver, so that Chinese interests are unable to pay prices which would be attractive to European producers. As a result the Far Eastern traffickers have turned to Chinese opium for their raw material and many factories have been established in China for the manufacture of narcotic drugs.

Elie Eliopoulos, narcotics trafficker[1]

Elie Eliopoulos once was described as having a Mephistophelean appearance. He was said to bear a resemblance to silent-screen star Conrad Veidt, an actor noted for his sinister roles. Yet Eliopoulos came from a privileged background. He had enjoyed an elite, cosmopolitan education as a youth; he spoke excellent French and English. Living in Paris in the late 1920s, when his business was at its height, he moved in fashionable circles; his Parisian friends included the owner of the exclusive Café Weber. In 1932, Harry Anslinger, the first head of the Federal

Bureau of Narcotics, called this man the preeminent "drug baron of Europe."[2]

ELIE ELIOPOULOS: DRUG ENTREPRENEUR

Eliopoulos operated between 1928 and 1931. His career flourished at a time when increasingly stringent international regulation began to take effect and shut down European sources of "white drugs" to the Far East. His career—successful though short-lived—reflects the changes taking place in the global market in reaction to the new restrictions. He thrived for a time, while many of his small-fry competitors failed, because he had the capital, acumen, and political connections to remain in the international narcotics business. He set out the story of his life in the business in a self-serving but usually accurate memoir that he dictated to American authorities in 1932, when he fell victim to the changing business milieu. The tale illustrates both the perils and the opportunities that confronted European drug traffickers in the late 1920s.

Born into a prominent trading family in the Greek port of Piraeus, he counted among his relatives several in the Greek diplomatic corps. As a young man, Eliopoulos pursued a variety of trading interests, mostly in the areas of military supply, with only modest success. In 1927, his fortunes changed when he met David Gourievidis, a Russian narcotics trafficker, who told Eliopoulos about opportunities in the Far East. A prudent businessman, Eliopoulos made two trips to China to assess the market before joining the venture. On the second journey, he met Jean Voyatzis, a fellow Greek who had been living in China for thirty years. Voyatzis was an established narcotics dealer in the Tianjin French concession. This early connection became the main axis of Eliopoulos's narcotics dealings. Between May 1928, when he entered the business, and 1931, when he left it, Eliopoulos estimated that he netted a $1 million to $1.5 million profit from the trade.[3]

Eliopoulos thrived because he could deliver a European product that was growing increasingly scarce. By 1928, it was becoming more difficult for illicit traders to make large purchases of narcotics from the West. British and American factories were closed to them, and Swiss and German manufacturers were beginning to feel the heat as their governments started cracking down on companies dealing with illicit traders. However, a few French factories, whose existence was tolerated by an indulgent government, continued to supply the illicit market. Eliopoulos established strong connections with two of these—the Comptoir des Alcaloides, owned by Paul Mechelaere, and the Société Industrielle de Chimie Organique, owned by Georges Devineau. His relations were close enough to these manufacturers that he often advanced them money to purchase crude opium, which was credited to him in the sale price.

In theory, French law prohibited uncertified foreign sales. Legislation that went into effect on January 1, 1929, restricted the ability of manufacturers to sell drugs at will on the free market. At first the new law made French narcotics manufacturers and traders apprehensive. In practice, however, they found they could circumvent the regulations easily by using licensed brokers who then assumed whatever small risk existed. Thus the French-based narcotics traffic continued, illicit but still robust, until August 1930, when the French government passed legislation that was genuinely restrictive by issuing narcotics trading licenses to only fifteen or sixteen reputable firms.

Eliopoulos had to be flexible. Until August 1930, he obtained his narcotics from French factories. After that date, he turned to Istanbul, where his old suppliers had opened a factory called ETKIM. In fact, Eliopoulos was able to carry forward a credit of 450 kilos of heroin he was owed by the Comptoir des Alcaloides to ETKIM. Eliopoulos shipped morphine and heroin to Voyatzis in Tianjin, where a network of Chinese and White Russians distributed the drugs locally. At the height of the business, Eliopoulos was sending an average of 300 kilos of white drugs per month to China, which sold for £70 per kilo. Voyatzis in turn would remit about £21,000 per month from Tianjin via American Express.

In order to maintain this level of success, Eliopoulos needed political protection. Early in his career, he struck a bargain with Inspector Martin of the Paris Prefecture of Police, who agreed to protect him, provided he did not sell drugs in France. Martin, who was responsible for overseeing narcotics enforcement throughout the country, was well placed to offer this kind of protection. At first, he received 5,000 francs per month for his services; later, as business flourished, the fee increased to 10,000 francs per month.[4] Martin protected Eliopoulos, even after French law changed in 1929. The relationship ended, however, in 1931 when an investigation exposed Eliopoulos, making the arrangement dangerous.

China was the primary market of the Eliopoulos venture, yet the trade with Voyatzis was not his only source of income. Contrary to Eliopoulos's profession "by the memory of his father, and all else that is holy, that he never sold drugs to America," he was a regular supplier of Jacob Polakiewitz (aka Jack Paull), then the largest exporter of narcotics to the United

States. Once when Martin showed Eliopoulos a photograph of Polakiewitz, whom the American government was trying to extradite from
France, Eliopoulos responded, "My God, that is my best customer."
Martin reassured Eliopoulos that he could rest easy; Polakiewitz would
not be troubled. Thus the relationship between the two drug dealers
continued to flourish. By early 1931, Polakiewitz's inventory consisted of
650 kilos of heroin and 650 kilos of morphine, all supplied by Eliopoulos.[5]

Eliopoulos's association with other drug traffickers could bring unexpected sources of revenue. For instance, the American government,
among others, had offered a reward for information leading to the interception of contraband narcotics. In 1930, a trafficker named Goldstein
forced Eliopoulos to sell him 100 kilos of heroin cheaply by threatening
to expose him if he did not. Eliopoulos complied, but when Goldstein
sent the drugs via ocean liner to America, Eliopoulos passed on this
information to Martin, who, in turn, told American authorities about
the shipment. Narcotics trafficker and police officer collected the reward. Eliopoulos's share amounted to 120,000 francs.[6]

Eliopoulos also made money by brokering deals among other traffickers. In October 1931, Polakiewitz was desperate for supplies. Eliopoulos knew that Gourievidis had 60 kilos of heroin for sale. Using fellow drug dealer Seya Moses to exchange the drugs for the money,
Eliopoulos arranged for the deal to be consummated in Berlin. When
the exchange was made, Moses turned the full $13,800 purchase price
over to Gourievidis, without first deducting Eliopoulos's 15 percent
commission. Seya Moses vividly recalled the recrimination that followed:
"In a letter Elie called me an idiot for not doing this, and said he lost
15,000 marks through my stupidity."[7]

Eliopoulos was an exemplary international drug dealer of this period.
If Harry Anslinger characterized him as the head of a dangerous narcotics "gang," it was no doubt because the word had a charged meaning
for Americans in the early 1930s. However, the term "gang," with its
overtones of violence and hoodlums, misrepresents Eliopoulos. He was
a quintessential entrepreneur, operating within a loosely defined community of independent narcotics dealers. Occasionally these men
formed long-term arrangements, as Eliopoulos did with Voyatzis. More
often, they cooperated on individual operations, advancing one another
money, brokering deals, buying and selling narcotics, and trading off
information for political protection and cash. They cheated one another
regularly, but, of course, had no redress through the legal system. Being

cheated did not mean that one trafficker injured his rival or even that he stopped doing business with him. For example, despite describing Gourievidis as "a despicable, double-crossing, thieving Jew" after being deprived of his 15 percent commission on the Berlin deal, Eliopoulos continued to do business with him. Had Elie's operation been more highly organized, he may have established his own means of enforcement.

Eliopoulos needed political protection to operate the supply and delivery aspects of his business, especially after January 1929, when his activities became illegal in France. It is here that he excelled. He readily paid Inspector Martin protection money, even after the fee doubled to 10,000 francs a month. Why not? Morphine and heroin could be purchased in Europe for £40 per kilo or less and sold in Tianjin at £70 per kilo. Monthly receipts of £21,000 yielded a gross profit of about £9,000 on the Tianjin business alone. In addition, the partnership with Martin occasionally produced direct revenue, as when they both collected the reward for exposing a rival trafficker. From Eliopoulos's perspective, political protection was a manageable cost in an extremely profitable business. Martin was simply one more person with whom he had a business arrangement.[8]

Eliopoulos's trafficking career came to an end when a rival leaked information about his activities to the French Sûreté, after which Inspector Martin could no longer protect him. He moved to Greece and apparently left the narcotics business altogether. Eliopoulos, with his multiple connections on both sides of the law and on two continents, represents the European drug trafficker in his most highly developed form. He was beginning to put together the kind of operation that his Asian competitors would refine: capital, political protection, a secure source of supply, and the ability to broker deals. He represents a transition from that more primitive variety of trader, the independent operator.

MR. GIBSON: DRUG SMUGGLER

Sailors have been smugglers as long as there have been goods that are available in one place and banned or taxed in another. The nature of the merchandise and its profitability vary according to time and place, but smuggling as an activity is a timeless appendage to the seagoing life. Narcotic drugs, as a high-value, low-bulk item, make ideal contraband. Sailors began to move them to China after 1907, when the prohibition of opium created a market there for morphine and heroin produced by

European and American pharmaceutical firms. Oceangoing cargo ships had numerous hiding places in public areas, such as behind a bulkhead in the engine room, where a sailor could secrete a load of drugs. In the unlikely event that a customs search would reveal the contraband, it could seldom be connected to a particular person.

A sailor who was even vaguely aware of world narcotics prices could buy drugs in a port where they were cheap and sell them where they were dear. Records of these foot soldiers in the smugglers' army are rare. In 1929, however, one came to light when the Rangoon police caught a British officer of the merchant fleet smuggling opium. He confessed, laying out his role in the international narcotics traffic. Throughout the long document, he is politely referred to as "Mr. Gibson," a drug smuggler perhaps, but a British ship's officer nonetheless.[9]

Gibson began his drug-smuggling career before the First World War when he was a junior officer. Chinese crew members taught him the craft. Eventually he decided to work alone, for if he had continued his association with members of his crew he would have found it impossible to maintain shipboard discipline. His early connections provided him with an introduction to Chinese clubs in ports throughout the world. A worn yellow paper with Chinese characters describing him as a trustworthy friend was his introduction to the sellers and buyers of drugs. Gibson always found the Chinese to be honorable business associates, claiming that he had never been cheated in a drug deal.

Gibson operated sometimes as an entrepreneur, buying and selling on his own, and sometimes as a contract courier, carrying drugs owned by others for a fixed percentage of its value. He always dealt in cash. He had heard of larger dealers such as Eliopoulos who relied on bank transfers, but he knew that he was not in that league. Gibson bought and sold drugs in port cities throughout the world. However, he most regularly bought opium in Calcutta and sold it in China. He once made a profit of 1,000 percent on a load of Indian opium he disposed of in Shanghai.[10]

Cocaine moved in the opposite direction. Gibson claimed there was no difficulty in obtaining supplies of the commodity in Japan. Hawkers came on board the ship with curios and porcelain, making enquiries of members of the ship's company as to whether they required cocaine as they sold their wares. Later they would deliver the goods without difficulty.[11] At the other end of the pipeline, Gibson emphatically declared that India was the best market in the world for cocaine. He found the people there prepared to pay a higher price for it than anywhere else, and the demand was practically unlimited.[12]

Unlike many other smugglers, Gibson never concealed drugs in ships' cargoes, preferring to use some public area of the vessel and then carry the contraband ashore in suitcases. His uniform was his shield. "In running drugs ashore, I traded on the fact that as a British ship's officer I was above suspicion and was not likely to be questioned or interfered with by anyone."[13]

His smuggler's tricks revolved around luggage. For instance, if he wanted to smuggle opium from Calcutta to Rangoon, he might send it ahead as advance luggage under an assumed name. Later he would go to a cheap hotel, register there under the false name and hand over his receipt to the hotel management, asking them to take delivery of the consignment in his place. The stuff would not be connected with him should an emergency arise.[14]

Gibson's arrest came when his two suitcases, each overloaded with eighty pounds of opium, drew the attention of a British policeman in Rangoon. He blamed this unfortunate disruption of his career on a piece of bad luck that would have a questionable impact on his future: "My being captured now with opium and being convicted will make it hard for me to get accepted with confidence by the Chinese; but it can be managed, I think."[15]

Gibson's career represents international narcotics trafficking in its most primitive form. Frequently broke and almost never dealing in sums of more than £100, Gibson was scarcely a major trafficker. He was tenuously connected to the larger world of smuggling through his affiliation with buyers and sellers of drugs in Chinese clubs in major ports. His supply was never secure. His smuggler's guile for breaching barriers never extended beyond his officer's uniform and a few suitcases, yet he had a reasonably successful career that lasted for nearly two decades before his arrest.

Gibson was a typical sailor/smuggler. As opium and then morphine, heroin, and cocaine became contraband items in the early twentieth century, sailors seized the opportunities presented to them by their itinerant lives to earn extra income as drug smugglers. As the Chinese market for narcotics expanded, men like Gibson provided an important early link between sources of supply and centers of consumption. Gibson's operation allowed him a certain amount of flexibility in the area of supply. He had to rely on his own good word and the reliability of friends, for he had no other way to enforce his will. He seldom had enough money to make banking a problem. His most vulnerable moments came during delivery. Indeed this is where his operation collapsed.[16]

DRUG SMUGGLING WORLDWIDE

International narcotics smuggling, which was barely organized above the level of Gibson's enterprise in the first two decades of the twentieth century, began to show signs of more complex development in the 1920s, as illustrated by Elie Eliopoulos's operation. Although the Chinese demand for refined opiates continued to grow, legal changes sponsored by the League of Nations made it increasingly difficult for smugglers to obtain supplies in Europe and ship their goods without detection past Chinese customs. These conditions created opportunities for entrepreneurs who could organize a business so that it would survive in a changing legal framework.

Early in the second decade of the twentieth century, drug smugglers were relatively free to purchase morphine and heroin in Europe to supply the newly illicit market in China. Because sales of these drugs were virtually unregulated before the League of Nations came into operation, there are few records of the transactions involved. Indeed, at that time, the European war commanded attention. For all it mattered to continental authorities, buyers of opiates might just as well have been purchasing French perfume or Swiss chocolates.

But once the war ended, British authorities, alarmed by the huge increase of British-manufactured morphine apparently headed to the China market, began to impose export controls on narcotic drugs. As we have seen, they passed the Dangerous Drugs Act in 1920. In 1923 pharmaceutical house T. Whiffen lost its license to manufacture morphine. Thus Britain dried up as a source for refined opiates, and smugglers had to look elsewhere. In the early 1920s, not satisfied with domestic reform, British authorities fed information about illicit narcotics activity to other European governments, pressuring them to impose stricter controls on the trade. Although drug traffickers were no longer able to buy morphine in Britain, they could still locate pharmaceutical firms on the continent that were willing to sell to them. Yet they could not be certain how long each country would continue to offer a friendly source of supply.

Shifting supply was only one problem facing drug traffickers in Europe over the course of the 1920s. Once they had obtained the opiates,

林公則徐拒毒遺訓

鴉片之毒，甚於洪水猛獸！

天下萬世之人，斷無有以鴉片爲不必禁者。⋯⋯此禍不除，十年後，無可用之兵，無可籌之餉。⋯⋯鴉片流毒內地，如癰疽流毒人身⋯⋯癰疽生則漸以成膿，鴉片來則漸以成寇。⋯⋯必須將鴉片烟銷解淨盡，乃爲杜絕病根

An anti-opium handbill depicting Commissioner Lin Zexu. The text reads: Words Passed Down to us from the Honorable Lin Zexu

Opium poison is like floods or wild beasts. Among all of the peoples of the world, there are none who would not prohibit it. If this calamity is not eliminated, ten years hence, we will not be able to use our army, we will not be able to supply our army. Opium spreads poison to the interior of the country just as an ulcer poisons the human body. When an ulcer appears, it gradually creates pus. When opium comes it eventually creates bandits. We must eradicate the smoking of opium, just as we would cut out a sick root. Luo Yunyan, *Zhonguo Yapian Wenti* [The Chinese opium problem] (Shanghai: Xinghua Baoshe, 1933).

Opium poppy showing the capsule. B.
Broomhall, *The Truth about Opium Smoking;
With Illustrations of the Manufacture of Opium,
etc.* (London: Hodder and Stoughton,
Paternoster Row, 1882).

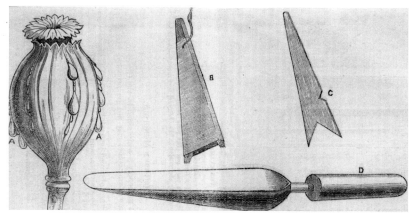

Opium poppy capsule shown with tools for extracting the latex. B. Broomhall,
The Truth about Opium Smoking; With Illustrations of the Manufacture of Opium, etc.
(London: Hodder and Stoughton, Paternoster Row, 1982).

The British East India Company commercialized the traffic in opium from their colony of India. It was packed in balls, three hundred or so to a chest. The processing plants were located in Patna and Ghuzapur. B. Broomhall, *The Truth about Opium Smoking; With Illustrations of the Manufacture of Opium, etc.* (London: Hodder and Stoughton, Paternoster Row, 1882).

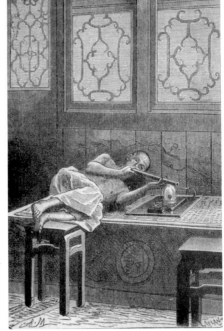

In spite of the prevailing image of the poverty-stricken opium smoker, many enjoyed their pipes in luxury. B. Broomhall, *Truth about Opium Smoking.*

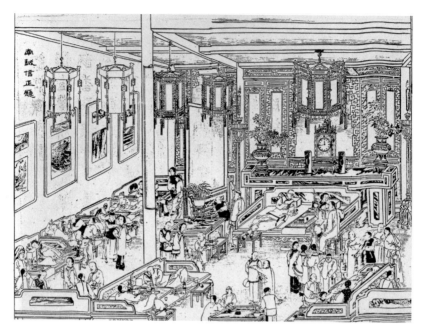

Shanghai opium dens were often ornate emporiums that were social gathering places. Source unknown.

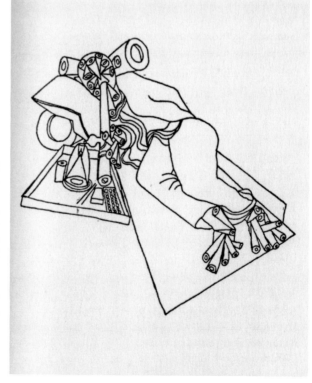

Opium smoking was not just a Chinese pastime. Jean Cocteau enjoyed the pipe and has left us with sketches of his experience. Jean Cocteau, *Opium: The Diary of a Cure,* Ernest Boyd, trans (London: Longmans, Green, 1932).

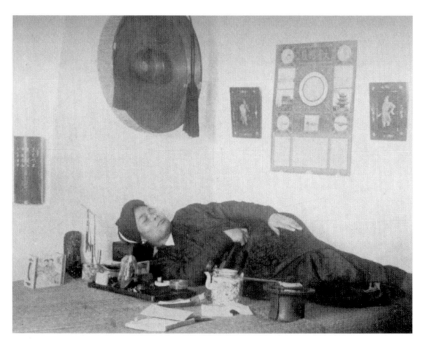

Opium reverie. Margaret Goldsmith, *The Trail of Opium: The Eleventh Plague* (London: Robert Hale, 1939).

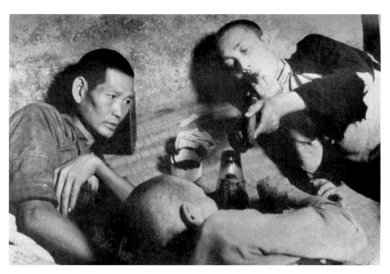

Opium smokers with pipe and lamp. Margaret Goldsmith, *The Trail of Opium: The Eleventh Plague* (London: Robert Hale, 1939).

The Yunnan opium scandal of 1916 tarnished the reputation of several men who were honored as heroes in this photo after they saved the Chinese republic from Yuan Shikai's attempt to make himself emperor of China. *Top right:* Brigade Commander Tang Jiyu; *bottom second from right:* General Ye Xiangshi; *third from right:* Member of Parliament, Zhang Yaozeng; *fourth from right:* Commander of the Army, Tang Jiyao. All were implicated in the smuggling scheme. Yu Enyang, *Yunnan Shouyi Yonghu Gunghe Shimo Ji* [A record of the righteous Yunnan leadership in protecting the republic] (Taibei: Wenhai Chubanshe, 1966).

Tang Shaoyi was the official who negotiated the 1906 opium import ban with the British empire. During the Second World War he sided with the Japanese. He was assassinated by Dai Li's undercover agents, who gained entry to his private residence by offering to sell him an antique vase. *Who's Who in China,* 5th ed. (Shanghai: China Weekly Review, 1936)

Shanghai gangster and Green Gang leader Du Yuesheng. *Who's Who in China,* 1936.

Shanghai gangster and Green Gang leader Zhang Xiaolin. *Who's Who in China,* 1936.

The "Young Marshall," Zhang Xueliang. He was himself an opium addict. But to avenge his father's assassination by the Japanese army and to keep control of his birthright, Manchuria, he launched an opium reform in the late 1920s. In 1936, he helped to kidnap Chiang Kai-shek. *Who's Who in China,* 1936.

Tang Yulin, aka "the toad general." He was the intelligence officer to Zhang Xueliang's father, Zhang Zuolin. During the early 1930s, he tried to establish his own narcotics empire, but he was put out of business by Japanese expansion. *Who's Who in China,* 1936.

T. V. Soong. As Chiang Kai-shek's brother-in-law, Soong was well placed to engage in opium smuggling of his own. *Who's Who in China,* 1936.

H. O. Tong. As a customs official in Shanghai and later Guangzhou, he was able to facilitate opium smuggling for friends such as T. V. Soong and Paul Crawley. *Who's Who in China,* 1936.

Yin Rugeng was educated in Japan. As Commissioner of the Hebei Demilitarized Zone during the 1930s, Yin was able to facilitate Sakata Shigemori's opium smuggling operation. He also had business ties to Zhang Xiaolin, the Green Gang boss. *Who's Who in China,* 1936.

they had to devise ways to ship them so that they were disguised as legal goods because Chinese customs presented still another obstacle. Smugglers relied either on packaging ruses or on bribing customs officials, and occasionally on a combination of both. Buyers in Europe needed confederates in the Far East to coordinate activities on the receiving end and to oversee distribution. Finally, smugglers needed means of communicating with one another, of transferring funds around the world, and of ensuring that business deals would be kept. Late in the decade, just as Mr. Gibson ran into problems, the Eliopoulos operation was growing to meet all of these challenges.

In the 1920s, the most important problem for European smugglers increasingly became securing a source of supply. In the early years of the decade, this was not so difficult. France, Germany, and Switzerland had thriving opiate industries. These nations allowed their pharmaceutical manufacturers sufficient room to deal in international markets. Even when Sir Malcolm Delevingne, the permanent undersecretary in the British Home Office, informed these governments of their nationals who were engaged in the drug traffic, they initially responded with studied indifference. In a 1927 survey of the seventy-five most notorious European drug suppliers compiled by the British government, fifteen are French, thirty-four are German, and twelve are Swiss.[17]

While a number of European pharmaceutical firms were willing to deal with smugglers, none was more compliant and successful at evading the growing web of regulation than the firm of Hoffmann La Roche. Based in Basel, with branch offices throughout Europe, the firm's name regularly appeared in the regulator's records as the source of contraband opiates seized in Asia. For instance, in 1924 Hong Kong customs officials seized a load of heroin from a Mr. Nakamura purchased from Hoffmann La Roche.[18] In 1923, H. R. Napp, a former manager of the London office, told an inspector of the Home Office that the company had no scruples and would send drugs from Switzerland under false descriptions, a practice they continued for years.[19] A later report described Hoffmann La Roche narcotics turning up in Hamburg labeled as "harmless chemicals" and in Dairen, China, labeled as "boot-nails."[20]

The name Hoffmann La Roche appears in British Foreign Office files on American drug trafficker J. W. Macdonald. Macdonald bought opiates from the firm and shipped them to Japanese companies in Osaka and Shanghai. As European governments in the 1920s began to crack down on drug traffickers who operated from their soil, Macdonald survived by moving periodically to friendlier locations. In 1924, when German authorities prosecuted and convicted Macdonald of smuggling, he claimed to be properly licensed in the Netherlands. Soon after the trial, he moved to Basel, Switzerland, where he continued to operate freely for several more years.[21]

Hoffmann La Roche's evasive business tactics mirrored those of Macdonald. When exports began to be more tightly controlled in Switzerland, the company referred questionable orders to its French office because as late as 1927 export certificates were not necessary in France. In 1928, when changed circumstances made exporting narcotics from western Europe more difficult, the company allegedly opened a narcotics factory in Turkey, which still had not signed the Opium Convention and did not regulate opiate manufacturers or shippers.[22]

Ports of entry in the Far East presented traffickers with another dilemma. Hong Kong and Shanghai had the relative advantages of being at the center of the large drug markets of southern and central China, respectively. However, their customs services were reputed to be more efficient and less corruptible than others, which posed increased risks for smugglers. Consequently, they often consigned drugs to other ports, such as the Manchurian city of Dairen or the Russian Far Eastern city of Vladivostok. The latter was particularly popular in the early 1920s because it was under the control of a tolerant "white" government. The Eric Moller Shipping Company in Shanghai was one European trafficker who took advantage of this route. Using the pretext of trading in fish, the company's vessels, *Minnie Moller* and *Nancy Moller,* sailed along the China coast moving narcotics through to the north. Sekito Senji from Japan, who got his supplies from the Hoshi Pharmaceutical Company and sold through the Yaguro Trading Company in Vladivostok, also favored this northern passage while it remained open.[23]

Northeastern China was an attractive port of entry. Japanese influence in Manchurian cities, which was strong even before that Chinese province became the puppet state of "Manchuquo," created a special advantage for Japanese smugglers, who were often the final link between European producers and Chinese consumers in those days before Japanese manufacturers took over the lucrative role of supply. Manchuria was connected to the vast drug market of North China by an efficient railway network. A. Grant Jones, the British consul in Harbin, Manchuria, described the workings of a Russo-Japanese combine of drug smugglers who operated in several Manchurian cities. They boasted that none of their goods came to any harm because most of the Japanese wharf police and members of the Chinese maritime customs at Dairen were on their payroll. Their cargo was brought up for examination and final release only when their men were on duty. They had similarly "squared" the Harbin police as well as their chief, who derived a substantial revenue from them.[24]

International narcotics traffickers of the 1920s were the first to face issues of communication and money transfer. In an age before reliable transcontinental telephone service, they preferred to contact their cohorts in telegraphic code. This allowed them to disguise the names of drugs and ports of consignment, but it required that both parties have copies of the code, which in itself created risks. When a smuggler was arrested, he was often carrying a telegraphic code book, which, like rolls of quarters for the pay phone in our own time, earmarked his occupation.

Traffickers needed banks to transfer large sums of money from buyers to sellers. Typically a buyer in the Far East would open a line of credit in favor of a European seller. Although this was an efficient means of making payments, it made smugglers vulnerable by exposing their transactions to the scrutiny of government officials. Sir Malcolm Delevingne tried to gather information about smugglers' financial activities by enlisting the cooperation of bank managers in China. In 1927, he distributed to British consuls in China the names of seventy-five European firms and individuals "known or suspected to be engaged in sending drugs to the Far East." He instructed the consuls to give copies to bank managers, who were then asked to report on any financial transactions involving the suspects. This was probably the first attempt to trace traffickers through their bank transfers, the forerunner of the contemporary focus in law enforcement on money laundering activities.[25]

Finally, drug traffickers had to ensure that they would not be cheated by those with whom they did business. This concern was a constant motif in their communications. Since trade was an illicit enterprise, they could not depend upon the legal system to mediate disputes. They relied, instead, upon trust, luck, and occasionally the threat of violence to ensure that bargains would be kept. An interesting illustration of the latter is a letter intercepted by the British Home Office from Charles Coy, a smuggler living in Kobe, Japan, to a Mr. Vietor, an American drug dealer.

Coy, who represented a Japanese syndicate, was trying to convince Vietor to buy European- and American-made morphine to ship to Japan. He indirectly warned Vietor about the consequences of cheating him by relating the fate of an earlier buyer. He claimed that some three years earlier a firm that was no longer in business undertook to supply morphine. They made three shipments of an excellent product, but then they shipped a substitute, drawing payment nevertheless. Trying to hide, the local representative slipped aboard a freight steamer headed to San Francisco. About one month after his arrival he disappeared and was never seen again. Later one of the principals of the firm met with a mysterious accident on a steamer trip and lost the use of his legs.[26] It is unclear whether this particular deal was ever consummated, but the message in Coy's letter is clear: Cheat us and you will suffer the consequences.

Y. MIYAGAWA: INTERNATIONAL DRUG TRAFFICKER

The changing business climate for drug traffickers relying on European suppliers is illustrated in the case of Y. Miyagawa.[27] Miyagawa was typical of many Japanese traffickers operating in the early 1920s who bought drugs in Europe for shipment to Japan, whence they would be smuggled into China. On November 5, 1923, City of London police arrested Miyagawa on a charge of illegally procuring 500 pounds of morphine. The morphine had been purchased for £9,000 from Swiss chemical dealer Bubeck and Dolder. Miyagawa intended to ship it to Japan through Marseilles, packing it in a larger load of tannic acid. He carried with him not only an invoice certifying that the cargo was entirely tannic acid but also a few blank invoice forms that Bubeck and Dolder had provided in case he needed to make any modifications in the official description before clearing customs in Japan.

Miyagawa had been buying narcotics from several legitimate European sources, including the respected German pharmaceutical firm C. H. Boehringer of Hamburg. In September and October 1923, he made purchases of £37,500 worth of heroin, which Boehringer's obligingly labeled as aspirin. His telegraphic code included references to several staff members at the company, among them the managing director, Albert Boehringer. Miyagawa bought drugs not only on his own account but on behalf of other Japanese firms. His correspondence shows that he was in close communication with other drug dealers, such as the aforementioned American, J. W. Macdonald.

In those early years of the 1920s, Miyagawa's business life in narcotics was relatively uncomplicated. He maintained close connections to legitimate suppliers who treated him not as an outlaw but as a valued customer. Firms like Boehringer's were only too happy to accommodate him despite his unusual packaging requests, even though there could be no question about the intended final destination of the narcotics that Miyagawa purchased in such large quantities. Boehringer's complicity in the China-bound opiate business was scarcely new. According to a British government report, the firm had been doing business with drug traffickers since the end of the war.[28]

The Miyagawa case led Delevingne and the British government to pressure Germany and Switzerland to comply with international regulations, citing it as evidence of these firms' involvement in the traffic. The German government replied with its opinion that there was no conclusive indication of any wrongdoing on the part of Boehringer's. The British responded testily that the German memorandum did "not appear to indicate a desire to cooperate heartily in the suppression of the smuggling operation."[29] It became clear, according to the British memo, that "the whole transaction was patently illegal and it is obvious that C. H. Boehringer well knew the real character of those huge consignments of narcotics. The amount of heroin actually seized, which was despatched by the firm equalled approximately twice as much as the total annual export of the drug from Great Britain."[30]

Delevingne reminded German officials that when the British government had discovered wrongdoing by T. Whiffen, one of their own nationals, it had suspended the firm's license to manufacture opiates. At that time, he pointed out, the drug traffickers immediately took their business to Germany, and "Messrs. Boehringer Sohn appear to have reaped the benefit of this action."[31] The British recommended that the German government follow its example in the Whiffen case by forcing Boehringer out of narcotics production. In the meantime, His Majesty's Government could no longer permit Boehringer to export its products to the United Kingdom.[32] The immediate result of this diplomatic controversy was slight. Three years later, Delevingne again complained that Boehringer was "up to the eyes in the illicit traffic." Even though the German government maintained that Boehringer's dealings were perfectly regular, nevertheless Delevingne saw "no evidence at all that they have changed their practices."[33]

The Miyagawa case illustrates the ease with which drug traffickers could work in most countries of continental Europe through most of the decade. German, Swiss, and French firms readily did business with smugglers, and shippers were happy to oblige them. Miyagawa ran into trouble only when he came within British jurisdiction. Delevingne set the police on international drug traffickers, and Miyagawa was one of the first big catches. This newfound British zeal toward controlling international trafficking was not immediately shared by continental governments. The latter were generally unconcerned as long as the narcotics in question were not consumed on their own territory, figuring that if the Chinese wanted to use heroin, then it was just as well for Switzerland or Germany rather than England to supply it. Indeed, in the early 1920s, the Swiss government agreed with its manufacturers' view that His Majesty's Government's attempt to restrict the international trade in narcotic drugs by continental firms was actually motivated by a desire to benefit British concerns rather than stop the trade altogether.[34]

Thus by the mid-1920s, Europe had become a crazy quilt of dangers as well as opportunities for drug traffickers. Britain was out of bounds as a supply and transit point, but the continent remained relatively safe. The center of the action in the European drug traffic had shifted from London to Hamburg and Basel. Yet even as Miyagawa began to serve time in a British prison and notorious traffickers like Macdonald continued to hustle narcotics from various cities in central Europe, the noose was tightening.

Despite foot-dragging by certain governments, the situation changed rapidly in Europe in the late 1920s. Enactment of the certificate system, universal enforcement of strictures against trafficking in western Europe by 1930, and the curtailment of output in European factories as a result of League of Nations initiatives reduced the legitimate opiate production of 1932 to less than half of what it had been in 1928. This crisis of supply forced a restructuring of the entire industry. As European pharmaceutical houses stopped dealing with them, traffickers needed to find new sources.

Elie Eliopoulos developed as the leading drug dealer of his era as a result of these changed circumstances in Europe. It was no coincidence that he began his drug business in Paris in 1928, for by that time enforcement in other European cities had toughened considerably. Even within the relatively tolerant confines of the French capital, the crisis of supply forced him to seek the political protection that Inspector Martin provided, at least for three years.

But Elie also came to feel the pinch of tightening European regulations. By the beginning of the 1930s, Eliopoulos's activities were being scrutinized, not just by the French Sûreté but by agents of the British Home Office, the American Federal Bureau of Narcotics, the Egyptian Central Narcotics Intelligence Bureau, and the League of Nations. Such regulations caused him to seek opportunities elsewhere. By the end of the decade, Elie, like his colleagues, began to look to Turkey.

THE TURKISH CONTRIBUTION

Turkey was the most significant nonadherent to the League's conventions. As the major supplier of the basic ingredients to the European pharmaceutical industry, the Turks had much to lose by a contraction of opiate manufacturing.[35] One American consul's comments demonstrate the dilemma that the Turkish government faced. He pointed out that raw opium, having been an important Turkish product, was feeling the economic effects of worldwide efforts to restrict traffic in narcotics. When the demand for this commodity fell, the price dropped from forty to about fourteen liras per kilogram. Suddenly, large stockpiles became a problem in Turkey. The logical solution was, of course, to convert them into opium derivatives for which international regulations had created a greater demand.[36]

In order to forestall a projected agricultural depression in its opium-growing regions, Turkey allowed a number of entrepreneurs to establish opiate-production factories in and around Istanbul. Japanese entrepreneurs established the first of these, opening the Oriental Products Company in 1928, which had an annual capacity of about 1,000 kilos. European manufacturers, escaping the restrictive measures of their own governments, soon followed suit, founding two more similar operations. By 1930, the largest of these factories was capable of producing 12,000 kilos per year. When compared to the total worldwide legitimate heroin production in 1930 of 4,088 kilos, the significance of the Turkish contribution to the illicit supply becomes clear.

The League of Nations and its members pressured the Turks by publicizing their unsavory role in the drug traffic, just as they had done with the companies Hoffmann La Roche and C. H. Boehringer. In response, Kemal Ataturk, the father of modern Turkey, dramatically closed these factories in 1931. Ataturk's decision to appease world opinion cost the Turkish peasantry dearly. Turkish opium production declined from 490 tons in 1931 to 96 tons in 1932. Although it recovered to average about 260 tons per year in the period from 1933 to 1939, the industry never regained the production level of 417 tons per year that it had averaged from 1926 to 1931.[37]

The last hurrah for legally produced European opiates intended for the illicit market took place in Sofia, Bulgaria. Between 1931 and 1933,

Bulgarian officials allowed several heroin factories to operate in the vicinity of that city. Although the precise output of these factories is unknown, it must have been considerable. According to a League of Nations official, Bulgaria imported enough acetic anhydride, a chemical essential to the manufacture of heroin but with few other uses, "to produce a quantity of heroin representing, in 1932, twice and, in 1933 four times the legitimate requirements of the entire world."[38] Once again, the publicity generated by this revelation induced the Bulgarian government to close these factories. Several continued to operate underground, however, for Bulgarian-produced heroin continued to appear in the illicit traffic throughout the decade, although in modest quantities.

After 1933, the narcotics supply line between European pharmaceutical manufacturers and Chinese consumers, which had functioned effectively since the early years of the twentieth century, was finally severed. Thereafter, Chinese addicts would find their sources closer to home. That did not mean that opiate production in Europe ceased but that it moved underground or shifted its location. As production beyond government-approved quotas became illicit, a few clandestine factories continued to function in and around Paris. For the most part, however, the traditional sources of supply in western Europe closed down as a result of League-sponsored legislation and new enforcement patterns.

GEORGES BAKLADJOGLOU: EUROPEAN TRAFFICKER

A lively if diminished narcotics business continued to thrive in southeastern Europe: Turkey, Greece, Bulgaria, and Albania. These countries had certain features that made them a natural locus for the industry. Opium was grown not only in Turkey but also in parts of Greece and Bulgaria. It provided an important source of livelihood for tens of thousands of peasant families, which tended to make government officials less than draconian in their enforcement efforts. The central governments exercised only minimal control over their borders and their miserably paid officials were chronically susceptible to bribery. Drugs produced in southeastern Europe were not easily transported to the traditional but distant markets in China. Nevertheless, the eastern seaboard of the United States was reachable through European ports. The American market for heroin, though quantitatively much smaller than that of China, was profitable. For entrepreneurs who could deliver the goods efficiently, the rewards could be attractive. A representative European trafficker of this stage was Georges Bakladjoglou, an ethnic Greek of Turkish nationality.

The American Federal Bureau of Narcotics placed an informer inside Bakladjoglou's operation, who reported regularly from January 1934 through November 1935. This man's numerous reports, contained in Bakladjoglou's recently declassified file in the American National Archives, provide an intimate picture of his business over a two-year period. At the age of fifty-eight, Bakladjoglou was an ancient in an occupation dominated by much younger men. He was "tall, stout, with chestnut hair" and had lived for many years in Turkey, where he had also reputedly been in the drug business. In 1933 he moved to Athens with his wife and three daughters to take up residence in a fashionable neighborhood, an address no doubt made possible by his success in the narcotics business.[39]

Bakladjoglou's legitimate business was a pharmacy in central Athens, which he owned with a partner. As the informer noted, however, he did not "take the least interest in the Pharmacy which shows that he uses it only as a blind."[40] By 1934, his narcotics business was extensive and varied. He usually purchased heroin from illicit factories in Bulgaria and Turkey. He bragged that he received most of his heroin from "hundreds" of small factories that "work in Turkey without the smallest danger." He explained that despite strict laws against them Turkish officials have decided that "one eye should be closed" to these primitive factories because they consume Turkish opium that became difficult to sell thanks to the competition of Yugoslavia and Bulgaria, which began selling considerable quantities of opium on the European market at prices much lower than the prices of Turkey.[41]

However, as a hedge against a sudden shift of Turkish enforcement policy, which would endanger his supply, Bakladjoglou also opened a heroin factory in Tirana, Albania. His partners were Italians, who supplied the raw material and actually ran the factory. Its capacity was considerable: two hundred kilos per month. Yet this operation never ran smoothly because Bakladjoglou faced his own enforcement problems. He had no recourse to the law, thus disputes with his partners, as well as certain technical problems, made the operation a continuing headache. He was forced out of Albania by his Italian partners less than a year after the factory opened, at which time he claimed that they cheated him out of sixty-five kilos of heroin.[42]

Bakladjoglou was both eclectic and imaginative about potential sources of supply. For example, one of the projects he discussed with the informer, who was himself a narcotics chemist, was the possibility of turning a half ton of codeine, a low-strength opiate, into heroin.[43] In order to impose a measure of control and safety over his drug empire, Bakladjoglou took different partners for different ventures. He dealt with Greeks, Bulgarians, Turks, or Italians, depending upon whether narcotics were to be purchased, financed, manufactured, or moved. He insisted on the principle that each partner had to have a financial stake in each venture's successful conclusion. Even his partner in the innocuous pharmacy that he used as a cover had to put up a token amount of capital. Principle notwithstanding, harmonious and enduring commercial relationships were not a feature of the drug traffic, especially for Bakladjoglou. He was regularly cheated by those with whom he did business. He complained most frequently about receiving heroin that was adulterated or of poor quality.

Bakladjoglou bribed government officials to facilitate border crossings and secure supplies. He paid off Albanian officials thoroughly enough to allow the plant in Tirana to function with no attempt at secrecy.[44] He boasted that his money reached customs men in Europe and America. Bribery was an ongoing and evolving commercial process. For instance, in March 1935, a revolution in Greece created both problems and opportunities for Bakladjoglou. On the one hand, the chief of police of Athens, who had been his main protector, lost his job. But on the other hand, the new government dismissed most of the officials who had been responsible for the suppression of smuggling, with the result that he could remark that "the illicit traffic has been remarkably extended."[45]

Bakladjoglou's main delivery system relied on Italian ocean liners that stopped at Mediterranean ports en route to New York City. He sent heroin in relatively small packages to limit his losses if any particular load were seized. Unlike European smugglers of the 1920s, he did not send his drugs as disguised cargo. Instead, he hired stewards working for an Italian steamer line as his couriers. These men picked up the heroin in one-kilo packages at ports such as Istanbul, Brindisi, or Naples. They were paid $30 per package to deliver the goods to New York harbor. Representatives of the buyers, who were responsible for getting the heroin ashore past customs agents, took delivery aboard ship. Bakladjoglou bragged that "he had buyers in New York who could take any quantity of goods, and that were it not for the difficulties in making shipments and deliveries he could do business with them in units of tons instead of kilos."[46] His buyers in New York had been Jews early in his career. By 1935, however, he was working with Italians, including "a member of one of the former Rum Running Organizations."[47]

Finance management concerned Bakladjoglou, as it did all major drug dealers. The file mentions several bank transfers of sums in the range of $50,000 from New York to Athens. Interestingly, Bakladjoglou did not receive the funds in his own name but had them sent to a partner. Furthermore, Bakladjoglou often dealt in cash, which presented special dangers to someone who bought and sold drugs in large quantities. Clearly, Bakladjoglou's aversion to bank transfers is one more indication of the increasing vigilance of law enforcement officials in Europe, as the movement of large sums of money in one's own name created too much exposure for European drug traffickers by the mid-1930s.

Bakladjoglou flourished in a period when Europe had ceased to be the center of the international narcotics traffic. His illicit operations thrived because he was able to find niches in southeastern Europe where officials allowed him to work, either because they perceived it to be in their national interest or because they were amenable to bribes. Furthermore, he showed great entrepreneurial skill in organizing a delivery system to move drugs in substantial amounts to the small but profitable American market. But in another sense, Bakladjoglou was a dinosaur. By the time his moment had arrived, the center of the world narcotics traffic had shifted from Europe to the Far East.

Elie Eliopoulos, more than any single man, represented the apogee of the European drug traffic. It had begun in earnest in the first decade of the twentieth century, when Chinese demand for refined opiates took off in the wake of their government's 1907 prohibition on importing smoking opium. European pharmaceutical firms showed neither moral scruples nor interest in the end use of their products. They were happy to meet this hunger for morphine and heroin. Although the trade's shadowy existence at this time is evidenced by occasional references to European drugs being consumed in China, it is only obliquely visible to the historian. Not until the early 1920s, in response to enforcement initiatives spearheaded by the British and then by the League of Nations, did European governments begin to join suppression efforts. And even then their efforts to recognize that a problem existed were tardy and often dilatory, thus creating an ever-changing checkerboard of safe havens and danger zones for traffickers.

As drug trafficking became more dangerous, it put a premium on those who could organize all facets of an integrated illicit business. What had begun as a relatively simple venture, open to virtually all comers, gradually became complex, dominated by the few who had a source of supply, financial and logistical sense, and above all, political protection. As a prototype, Mr. Gibson, the independent sailor/smuggler, was displaced by entrepreneurs like Miyagawa, and eventually by Eliopoulos. Finally, Bakladjoglou was, by 1934, an interesting historical footnote, smuggling modest amounts of drugs into America from his corner of southeastern Europe after the real action—supplying the China market—had shifted to the Far East itself.

Eliopoulos, in his 1932 statement to American authorities, analyzed the reasons for this shift, stating that the situation in China had entirely changed. Far Eastern traffickers, facing dwindling supplies of increasingly expensive European narcotics, turned to Chinese opium for their raw material, establishing factories in China. Initially Eliopoulos had scorned Chinese-produced opiates, which, like Chinese smoking opium, was regarded as inferior by consumers. However, he was certain that its quality would improve. Then, he predicted, "the Chinese, in a short time, will start exporting narcotic drugs to Europe and America, similar in quality to those made in Europe."[48]

Eliopoulos was right. As his words were being spoken, opiates produced within China flooded the local market, while the smallest trickle began to flow out toward America. The traffic came to be dominated by Asian men who would excel at putting together the kinds of complex organizations that Elie had only started to build.

NOTES

1. Report on Elie Eliopoulos, Narcotics Trafficker (hereafter Elie Report), box 4536, 800.114N16 ELIOPOULOS/27 RG 59, 2.

2. Elie Report, 16–17. It is necessary to read a second interview with Seya Moses, a confederate of Eliopoulos's, along with the Eliopoulos confession in order to sort out some of the self-serving lies that Elie naturally told. See 800.114N16 ELIOPOULOS/4, box 4536 (hereafter Moses Report), RG 59. See also "The Drug Barons of Europe," box 4, file 10, Harry Anslinger papers, Pattee Library Archives, Pennsylvania State University (hereafter HAP); "Copie de la Police rapport présenté par le Corps des Detectives de la Police Judiciaire Roumaine," 1933, PRO, FO 371/17172/87–93; "Eliopoulos, Voyatzis, Del Gratio etc. Gang," 1932, PRO, FO 371/16258/262–65; "Memorandum . . . Eliopoulos Case," 1932, PRO, FO 371/16251/228; "M. D. Perrins to D. Mackillop," April 8, 1932, PRO, FO 371/16251/246–49; and Alan A. Block, "European Drug Trafficking between the Great Wars:

Developing Illicit Markets and Criminal Syndicates," *Journal of Social History* 23 (Winter 1989): 315–37.

3. Elie Report, 5.
4. Elie Report, 4; Moses Report, 5.
5. Moses Report, 11.
6. Moses Report, 7.
7. Elie Report, 14. Eliopoulos's career had an interesting addendum. When George and Elie Eliopoulos fled from Greece to the United States in 1941 to avoid the Nazis, they were arrested on drug trafficking charges that stemmed from 1931. Despite assurances from the British and Greek governments that the brothers Eliopoulos had been out of the narcotics traffic for a decade, Harry Anslinger, U.S. commissioner of narcotics, insisted on prosecuting them. A judge dismissed all charges against them on technical grounds in 1942. Box 2978 (1940–44), 800.114N16 ELIOPOULOS, ELI/ 50–58, RG 59.
8. Elie report, 16–17. Mark Haller's data on the structure of American illicit enterprise at this time shows some interesting parallels to Eliopoulos and his colleagues: Mark H. Haller, "Illegal Enterprise: A Theoretical and Historical Interpretation," *Criminology* 28 (May 1990): 207–35.
9. See David Courtwright's interesting discussion of opium smuggling in turn-of-the-century America, *Dark Paradise: Opiate Addiction in America until 1940* (Cambridge, Mass.: Harvard University Press, 1982), 16–28; and his narrative of an American sailor/smuggler in *Addicts Who Survived: An Oral History of Narcotic Use in America*, ed. D. Courtwright, H. Joseph, and D. DesJarlais, (Knoxville: University of Tennessee Press, 1988), 225–30; "Notes of Conversations [between J. Slattery and Mr. Gibson, 1929]" [hereafter Gibson file], PRO, FO 371/14768/239–59.
10. Gibson File, 246–47.
11. Gibson File, 248.
12. Gibson File, 243.
13. Gibson File, 248.
14. Gibson File, 249.
15. Gibson File, 249.
16. To the extent that opiates and cocaine are proscribed and the laws are strictly enforced, we see throughout the world the tendency for drugs in their organic forms—opium and coca leaves—to be displaced in the market by their more potent and portable alkaloids: heroin and cocaine. Certainly observers in China noticed this. See "Report note no. 5, about China," box 4356, 800.114N16 ELIOPOULOS/ELI, RG 59; Yamauchi Saburo, "Mayaku to Senso; Nitchu Senso no Himitsu Heiki" [Narcotics and war; a secret weapon of the China war], *Jimbutsu Orai* [Who's who], October, 1956.
17. "Delevingne to Foreign Office," November 15, 1927, PRO, FO 371/12532/ 77–80.
18. "Delevingne to Foreign Office," January 18, 1924, PRO, FO 371/10340/ 68–69.
19. "Hoffmann La Roche [1923]," PRO, FO 371/9249/54.
20. November 9, 1927, PRO, FO 371/12533/361–66.

21. "Memorandum. MacDonald and Co. or Riehen, Basel," June 30, 1925, PRO, FO 371/10970/152–54, 163; Delevingne to Foreign Office, April 15, 1924, PRO, FO 371/10334/219–20; "undated and anon., probably from Delevingne," August 1923, PRO, FO 371/9248/142–44.

22. Delevingne to Foreign Office, November 9, 1927, PRO, FO 371/12533/361–66; "Delevingne to Mounsey," December 24, 1928, PRO, FO 371/13258/193.

23. D 441, SMP CID; Hoshi Nakaba, *Jinmin wa Yowashi*, 111–14.

24. "The Drug Traffic in Harbin [1928]," PRO, FO 371/13251/49; see also Dairen to British Embassy, July 9, 1925, PRO, FO 371/10970/177–80; "The Drug Traffic in Harbin," December 13, 1927, PRO, FO 371/13251/3–6; "Memorandum" [1928], PRO, FO 371/13251/12–13, 37–39. There are further reports of Japanese involvement in smuggling European drugs to China in "Memorandum" [1931], PRO, FO 371/15530/42–49; "Enclosure in Mr. Haag's Despatch no. 5," March 8, 1924, PRO, FO 371/10334/172–76; and Delevingne to Mounsey, June 20, 1925, PRO, FO 371/10970/124–26.

25. Delevingne to Foreign Office, November 15, 1927, PRO, FO 371/12532/77–80. On smugglers' use of banks, see Delevingne to Mounsey, Hongkong and Shanghai Banking Corporation, June 27, 1927, PRO, FO 371/12527/230–32; and PRO, FO 371/11715/158–69.

26. Chas. Coy to Mr. Vietor, June 30, 1923, PRO, FO 371/9248/173–74.

27. The details of the Miyagawa case were laid out in two British government reports: Eagleston to Foreign Office, November 8, 1923, PRO, FO 371/9248/215–17; and PRO, FO 371/9248/266–68.

28. Delevingne to Foreign Office, November 28, 1923, PRO, FO 371/9248/238.

29. D'Abernon to Streseman, August 11, 1924, PRO, FO 371/10335/123.

30. D'Abernon to Streseman, August 11, 1924, PRO, FO 371/10335/124.

31. Delevingne to Foreign Office, November 28, 1923, PRO, FO 371/9248/236.

32. D'Abernon to Streseman, August 11, 1924, PRO, FO 371/10335/126.

33. Delevingne to Mounsey, August 19, 1927, PRO, FO 371/12532/181.

34. Delevingne to Foreign Office, February 27, 1926, PRO, FO 371/11713/156.

35. In a typical defense of his country's situation, a Turkish observer to the League's 1925 opium conference wrote: "It is not necessary to emphasise the importance to Turkey of poppy growing and the opium trade. The immense fields of Asia Minor and the climatic conditions there are very favourable for cultivation of the poppy. . . . The annual production varies from 350 to 450 tons. The proportion of morphine contained in this opium is from 9 to 14 percent. A large number of foreign factories are dependent on opium imported from Turkey. . . . In Asia Minor the net return on a poppy field is far higher than that on a field of tobacco or any other crop. . . . It is natural, therefore, that the Turkish Government does not see the way in which so important a crop can be limited. Mehmed Sureya, "Memorandum on Poppy Growing and the Production of Raw Opium in the Republic of Turkey," December 9, 1924, LON, R791/40999.

36. Charles Allen, "Traffic in Narcotics," June 25, 1930, 800.114N16 DOLAN, JAMES S./54, RG 59.

37. On the Turkish production estimate, see John Anderson to Foreign Office, May 5, 1930, PRO, FO 371/14758/270. Almost immediately after the founding of the Oriental Products Company, its morphine began to appear in Shanghai, Delevingne to Mounsey, January 9, 1929, PRO, FO 371/13969/72; H.M.G. Consul, Constantinople to Foreign Office, October 1, 1930, PRO, FO 371/14759/355–57; H. Woods to Foreign Office, January 11, 1928, PRO, FO 371/13258/166–67; "Extract . . . Mulhouse," 1929, PRO, FO 371/13973/123–29. The British appraisal of the Turkish decision is interesting: "There is little doubt that this advance is due more than anything else to the iniquities so forcibly disclosed by Russell Pasha [of the Egyptian C.N.I.B.] at Geneva. In the face of those disclosures, Turkey felt that her claim to be one of the most civilised of modern Governments could not be maintained unless she took serious steps to clear her good name in this matter." "G. Clerk to A. Henderson," February 21, 1931, PRO, FO 371/15526/152; Reshat Saka, "Narcotic Drugs," Istanbul, 1948, box 8, file 3:25, HAP.
38. League of Nations, *The League of Nations and the Drug Traffic* (1934), box 10, file 14, HAP. See also Dalfour to Simon, August 19, 1934, PRO, FO 371/18203/209–12; "Illicit Drug Traffic," June 9, 1934, PRO, FO 371/18203/194–96; S. H. Harrison, "Illicit Trade in Narcotics [in Bulgaria]," July 15, 1932, PRO, FO 371/16253/10–16. An undated [1933?] and anonymous report in the Anslinger papers alleges that "Lazoff, a nephew of the Minister of War of Bulgaria, is still active in endeavoring to make the profits from narcotic factories [that] spell success for the Revolutionary movement." Box 8, file 9, HAP.
39. Report no. 1, July 25, 1935, Name file of narcotics traffickers, 1923–1954, lot 55 D607, box 1, RG 59. All succeeding references to Bakladjoglou are from this file.
40. Central Narcotics Intelligence Bureau, March 19, 1934.
41. "Paris, October 31, 1934."
42. "Paris, December 7, 1934."
43. "Paris, September 7, 1934."
44. "Paris, August 17, 1934."
45. "Paris, July 25, 1935," 8.
46. "Paris, September 7, 1934."
47. "Paris, August 20, 1935," and "September 7, 1934."
48. Eli Report, "Report Note 5 about China," 4.

CHAPTER SIX

WARLORDS

1916 – 1937

According to rumours in circulation Chiang Kai-shek will not inquire too closely into the case as he needs money for military expenses.

Tan Shaoliang, Shanghai Detective[1]

On August 25, 1916, the International Mixed Court for Shanghai found Li Zhengwu guilty of complicity in the case that the Shanghai press called the Yunnan opium scandal. The British assessor fined him $1,000 for his role in the operation.[2] As we saw in chapter two, Li was capable of profiting from duplicity, tipping off the police about the large opium shipment in the luggage of the delegates from Yunnan province, then offering to help them out of their difficulty, and then holding some of the opium to sell himself. In court he presented himself as an innocent bystander in the drama, guilty only of coming to the aid of a friend in difficult circumstances. At the time of his arrest, the Shanghai press described Li Zhengwu as a *Guomindang* leader, a general in the Zhabei army during the 1911 Revolution, and a compatriot of Shanghai's own recently martyred revolutionary, Chen Qimei. In fact, he was all of these things.

In spite of his trial and conviction in August, Li continued to work in local political circles. Several months after he paid his fine he organized a benefit theater production and raised money from his office at 155 Avenue Joffre in the French Settlement to help relieve the city of rowdy soldiers. Like many of China's large cities, in the wake of the rebellion of 1916 (already being called the Righteous Yunnan Uprising [*Yunnan Yiqi*]) Shanghai attracted discharged soldiers. They came to the city hoping for jobs in the new Chinese government being formed in the wake of the conflict. When the expected posts, like China's anticipated unification, did not materialize, they loafed on the streets causing trouble. To relieve the situation, Li raised money to compensate the soldiers, bought train tickets to send them to their homes, and organized a new army to go north to fight against Mongolian military activity.[3]

According to handbills that circulated through Shanghai early in 1917, however, Li privately squandered the money he publicly raised. The pamphlets claimed that he had been forced to leave his native Ningbo under threat of arrest just before the 1911 Revolution. Fleeing to Shanghai, he brought with him his own band of loafers and thugs, joining the ranks of Chen Qimei's revolutionary army from necessity rather than idealism. After the fighting finished, he used his position to engage in extortion and smuggling.[4]

Although someone in the Shanghai Municipal Police added a note at the bottom of the handbill stating that Li was not quite the rascal that the circular implied, his role in the Yunnan smuggling case indicates that he had his darker side. Indeed the leaders of the early *Guomindang*, out of political necessity, had to accommodate both idealistic patriots and gangsters in order to survive. Hoodlums supplied both street muscle and money that the *Guomindang* needed in those days of desperate struggle. To help fund the Yunnan Uprising, which the *Guomindang* supported, some groups used methods that were little more than extortion, including Chen Qimei's own Dare to Die Corps.[5]

This alliance with secret societies and gangs began as early as the turn of the century, when the party operated from underground. Yet it was the Yunnan Uprising that marked the introduction of opium into the political struggles. In chapter two, we saw that the rebellious army's choice of Yunnan for its base brought politics into an area already established as a primary source of opium supply. As the leaders of the uprising became heroes with larger political ambitions, some of them used their positions to transport opium across borders. The uprising coincided with the early years of international cooperation to control the traffic, which sent opium prices skyrocketing. The rewards of smuggling proved irresistible to some involved in the movement.

Yet the Yunnan scandal was only a beginning. In the late 1920s, once the *Guomindang* had reorganized and modernized itself and had established a credible claim to be China's government, political necessity pushed it into an alliance with a new breed of Shanghai gangsters who had themselves restructured to meet the changing narcotics market. Much more sophisticated than Li Zhengwu, they succeeded by putting together a solid organization combining police protection, military connections, and control of opium supplies. They perfected their structure during the early 1920s, the chaotic heyday of the warlords.

THE WARLORDS

The warlords sprang from the demise of Yuan Shikai, only months after the Yunnan Uprising. The 1916 conference that the Yunnan delegates were about to attend when their journey was interrupted was only the first of many attempts to reunify China. Instead, the country fractured into pieces, each fragment ruled over by a military governor. Foreign ministers continued to go to Beijing as though it were the sovereign capital, and dispatches still referred to a prime minister, usually the military leader who had captured the city for the moment. Yet one British diplomat privately admitted to feeling despondent about the outlook for the nation when he recalled that there had been "no less than seven Prime Ministers and acting Prime Ministers in Beijing during 1922, and four Foreign Ministers within the past six months."[6] China was mired in chronic civil war; militarists dominated the landscape. Political debate gave way to martial power.

Who were these warlords? The majority were officers from Yuan Shikai's *Beiyang* Army. During the early days of the republic, they had been assigned to various provinces as military governors. While Yuan lived, he kept these officers in line through bonds of loyalty, by treachery, or by force. Furthermore, the opium suppression campaign continued unabated during his presidency, for Yuan Shikai was an enemy of opium. Once he died, however, the military governors split into factions, larger ones fighting for control of the capital and smaller ones maneuvering inside the spaces created by the breakdown of the central government.[7] Narcotics provided a means to finance the expensive arms and ammunition required to survive as a warlord. Thus the Yunnan war and its related opium case provided the prelude to the decade that followed.

It was a violent decade. The contending warlord factions needed weapons to pursue their goals. Thus the 1920s saw an influx of gunrun-

ners along the China coast. Typical of the adventurers who swarmed
around the warlords was an American, Captain Lawrence Kearney, who
was caught in 1923 running arms to Lu Yungxiang in Zhejiang, just before Lu fought a month-long battle for control of the Shanghai opium
market. During this same period, the missionary stations scattered
throughout China provided mounting and dismal evidence of the recrudescence of opium growing in their areas. The same men and women
whose hopeful reports of only a decade earlier had convinced the British
government to curtail and finally to end its opium monopoly described
a rapidly deteriorating situation.[8]

By 1922, the only concrete result of the opium regulations was the
rise in the drug's price and the subsequent introduction of morphine
and heroin onto the market. "Where those [white] drugs are declining
in use," one source claimed, "the cause is the drop in opium [prices]
to a level where it is once again affordable." The reports were uniformly
the same; opium was enjoying a resurgence everywhere. If poppies were
not being grown in a certain location, as was the case in Guangdong
province, it was only because of an abundance of the crop coming from
a nearby province such as Yunnan. All reports pointed to local warlords
as the culprits.[9]

Warlords used creative methods to reintroduce and tax opium. Most
generals followed the examples set in the European colonies. They created monopolies, imposed land taxes on poppy fields, and issued licensing fees. General Tang Jiyao of Yunnan, whose cousin was involved in
the 1916 scandal in Shanghai, instituted such a measure in his province,
which soon became a major producer once again. A British observer,
although despondent over Yunnan's backsliding, admitted that the
province had a hard time finding a crop to substitute for opium, which
grew well in the tropical mountains.[10]

In coastal Fujian province (where in the early 1920s four generals
struggled for control) peasants were forced to plant poppies through
high-handed, even tyrannical, means. In the Hueian district, for instance, warlord troops and local gentry imposed an assessment of $16
per *mu* (6.6 *mu* = 1 acre) of land. Only by cultivating poppies could
farmers generate that kind of revenue. In Kien Ou a group of gentry,
merchants, and students petitioned both the central government and
the International Anti-Opium Association to come to their aid. They
claimed that their local magistrate was delivering poppy seeds to local
farmers and compelling them to plant them. Further south, Xiamen
became such a popular port for smuggling the drug that its money shops

boasted a huge cash surplus in spite of poor local industry and resources.[11]

DU YUESHENG, HUANG JINRONG, AND
ZHANG XIAOLIN

Spiraling warlord power struggles in the 1920s provided the background
to the formation in Shanghai of the narcotics conglomerate that eventually dominated China. Three men, Du Yuesheng, Huang Jinrong, and
Zhang Xiaolin, pulled together an organization that eclipsed Edward
Ezra's Opium Combine. The men belonged to the Green Gang, a secret
society that dominated the wharves and water transport along the Yangzi
River. In the 1920s and 1930s, they were known as Shanghai's three big
shots (daheng). Between the two world wars little got done in Shanghai
without their approval.[12]

The story of the relationship between Du Yuesheng and Chiang Kai-
shek is well known and has been told often. Du and his retainers helped
Chiang rid the Guomindang of its Communist and left-wing elements in
the Shanghai massacre of 1927, gaining, as a result, high-level political
backing that allowed Du's operation to dominate the China traffic by
the 1930s. But the Du-Chiang connection was the end product of years
of organization building on the part of the three big shots. Chiang was
the last of a string of warlords who benefited from connections with
the Shanghai group. Conversely, the narcotics organization built up in
Shanghai in the early years of the decade contained the seeds of the
combination that would prove so useful to the Guomindang after 1927.
It was underground, it was skilled at penetrating borders, and it had
access to vast quantities of capital. This combination would be co-opted
by Nationalist intelligence in the next decade, once the struggles in
China became international.[13]

In the early 1920s, the least known of the three big shots, Zhang Xiaolin, who had connections to the Beiyang warlords, supplied the crucial
link in putting together the combination of military connections with a
reliable opium supply that overcame other Shanghai rivals. Zhang Xiaolin, like his colleagues, was born poor. The son of a carpenter, he grew
up in the Zhejiang countryside. When he was twenty years old, he moved
to Hangzhou and apprenticed to the spinning trade. (He later claimed
to own a mill when he applied for a firearm license in the International
Settlement. The license was denied.) Since textiles held little appeal for
a man with a bad temper and little self-control, he joined the local mili-

tary academy, which suited him better. Nevertheless, he left the school before graduating to become a gambler and a thug, relying on his military contacts to keep him out of trouble. He might have remained a local bully had fate not intervened to bring him into a larger arena.[14]

Shortly after the 1911 Revolution, an internal struggle broke out among rival Green Gang leaders in Shanghai. One of the contenders, Li Yunqing, took brief refuge from the fray in Hangzhou, only a few hours away by train. At that time Zhang Xiaolin was running gambling operations in the area. The two men met and, when Li returned to Shanghai, Zhang followed. He established himself in a small way in the gambling rackets in the International Settlement, while maintaining his ties to Hangzhou. In Shanghai, he was introduced to Huang Jinrong, but Huang distrusted his rough manners, giving him little notice at the time. That would soon change.[15]

Huang Jinrong was a major presence in the Shanghai rackets of the 1910s and 1920s. Though overshadowed by Du and Zhang, he continued to be influential up to his death in 1951. Huang brought to the opium organization a second crucial link for success: police contacts. He was the son of a constable from Suzhou. His family came to Shanghai in the 1890s where they lived in an alley that was home to many police. His parents apprenticed him to a scroll mounter whose shop was located near the Temple of the City God. At that time in Shanghai, the temple was the home base of a successful criminal organization, the Five *Sheng* Gang, so named because the five bosses all had the character Sheng in their name. Instead of mastering his craft, Huang began hanging around with some of the gang's rowdies who frequented a local tea shop.[16]

In 1900, bored with picture mounting, he became a police detective in the French Settlement, but maintained ties with the underworld. These connections helped him solve several baffling cases. He became indispensable to the French police, whose protection allowed his underworld career to flourish. By the time Zhang met him, Huang controlled gambling and rackets in the French concession, and he owned theaters and bath houses throughout Shanghai. Both he and his wife trafficked in opium. Although well connected to both the Red and Green gangs, Huang himself never joined until quite late in the game. Nevertheless, he maintained his own group of followers.[17]

In the decade of the 1910s, Huang played a small role in the opium trade. At the time the traffic was dominated by the Big Eight-Leg Gang. Organized around Shen Xingshan, a detective with the International

Settlement's Shanghai Municipal Police, the gang came to prominence during the decade in which opium became illegal because they offered stability of supply and delivery in an uncertain market. They could do this because they had members placed within the Chinese river police, the International Settlement police, and the special opium detective squad that worked with Edward Ezra's Opium Combine to combat such smuggling. The Big Eight-Leg Gang put together a cartel of traders who paid them protection money for safe delivery. The value of their connections in the intensely competitive developing market of the decade was clearly demonstrated by the damage they did to a potential competitor in the Yunnan opium case of 1916.[18]

While the two policemen Shen Xingshan and Huang Jinrong were friends, their followers competed. Faced with well-placed competition from the International Settlement, Huang was able to control initially only 20 percent of the Shanghai opium traffic. He did this through the help of a young follower, Du Yuesheng, who aggressively maintained the Frenchtown gang's presence in the traffic. Du was born in the slum city of Pudong, across the river from Shanghai. Apprenticed to a fruit seller, he soon lost interest in the trade chosen for him and took to gambling. The contacts he made in the casinos and teahouses led Du to Huang, for whom he became an attendant. He ingratiated himself to Huang's wife when he traced down a stolen load of her opium. He then became a protector of opium shipments and did some stealing of his own, especially targeting the supplies of the Big Eight-Leg Gang. By the end of the decade he had opened his own opium shop under the guise of a jewelry store on rue Consulat in the French concession.[19]

The dominance of the Big Eight-Leg Gang marked the beginning phase of a complete restructuring of the Shanghai rackets in response to the new international supply and delivery situation. In the era when opium was legal, it remained the province of petty criminals. Thieves might steal it and sell it for a neat profit with little overhead. Some specialized in swimming out to the opium hulks and bringing the drug ashore. Once it became illegal, the price skyrocketed. Thus during the decade that saw Europe fall into world war and China face the consequences of revolution, the Chinese underworld moved aggressively into the traffic of the suddenly profitable commodity. It was this process that provided the background to the Yunnan opium scandal, for the Big Eight-Leg Gang had penetrated the Opium Combine detectives.[20]

In 1919, several events changed the balance in favor of Huang, Zhang, and Du in this reorganization. First was the fervor with which the anti-opium sentiment gripped the International Settlement. As the year opened, Shanghai officials burned opium with great ceremony on the Pudong wharf. It was a signal that the Big Eight-Leg Gang would have to make new arrangements to survive. Second was the success Du Yuesheng had stealing opium. With his connections to the French police, through his boss Huang, his nascent organization became the successor to the older gang.[21]

The third and most enduring event of 1919 was the entrance of Zhang Xiaolin into the group that would dominate Shanghai in the 1920s and 1930s. In 1919, Lu Yungxiang became the warlord from Hangzhou; his subordinate, He Fenglin, became Shanghai defense commissioner, the central government's military representative in the port. Zhang was a friend of He; thus he had contacts with local military authorities, which gave the French Settlement operation a wider range of protection. Zhang was able to negotiate between Huang and Du on the one side and the provincial military authorities on the other. The latter, like their Yunnan counterparts, wanted opium money to finance their stake in warlord politics.[22]

By 1924, the foundation was laid for a strong illicit opium operation. Over the next two years, two events shifted the balance away from Huang solidly into the hands of Du and Zhang. The first was a short, local skirmish: the Zhejiang-Jiangsu War of September 1924. Shanghai is situated between Zhejiang and Jiangsu, the two provinces that hug the China coast at the point where the Yangzi River enters the Pacific Ocean. Although Shanghai is located in Jiangsu, its economic and social ties are largely with Zhejiang. At the time, Shanghai had an autonomous administration with its own officials. Both Jiangsu and Zhejiang had their own military governors from the time of the 1911 Revolution. Shanghai had its defense commissioner stationed at the Longhua garrison next to the Shanghai arsenal.

In 1921 Lu Yungxiang officially became the military governor of Zhejiang and appointed his loyal subordinate, He Fenglin, as Shanghai defense commissioner. This should have given him tight control of the region; however General Xu Guoliang, commissioner of the Shanghai police, was himself connected to the military governor of Jiangsu province, Ji Xieyuan. The two warlords, Lu and Ji, were mutually hostile; indeed, they would have clashed sooner but for the foreign presence in Shanghai. Both extended their military influence into Shanghai through the police, but in numbers that effectively canceled each other out.[23]

Shanghai was attractive to these warlords because it could furnish two things they desired: weapons from the Jiangnan arsenal and opium revenue. When fighting broke out between the two sides late in 1924, both Lu and Ji publicly pointed to control of the arsenal as the cause of tension in the region. Indeed, as the war became a certainty, it delivered 50,000 rounds of 7.9 quick-firing ammunition and 4,000 rounds of shrapnel to the soldiers fighting for Lu. Although control of weapons was the immediate objective, the war's real prize was control of the opium traffic. Newspapers maintained a discreet silence on the issue, but a handbill attacking Lu that circulated just before the war claimed his vast wealth came from opium. It also accused him of the assassination of his Shanghai opponent, the police commissioner, General Xu.[24]

The Xu murder, which became the prelude to the Zhejiang-Jiangsu War, occurred on the evening of November 17, 1923. General Xu Guoliang had just finished relaxing at a public bath house across the street from Shanghai's entertainment center, the Great World. Casually dressed in plain padded silk trousers and jacket, he was just stepping into his car when two men approached him. One man tipped his hat as though to greet him, and then both men pulled guns and shot him. General Xu died two days later from his wounds. Both men ran after firing the fatal shots, but one tripped and was arrested by a Sikh patrolman. However, Settlement police turned him over to the Shanghai defense commissioner, He Fenglin, rather than Xu's own constabulary. This stroke of good fortune meant that the suspect was treated leniently.[25]

The Xu murder case revealed complex intertwining dramas just beneath its surface. Four possible motives were given for the crime by the Shanghai Municipal Police privately commenting on the case. The assassin claimed to be a minor member of the *Guomindang*, working on his own; his story became the official explanation. As the Chinese police commissioner, Xu had often harassed party meetings; the party retaliated by criticizing him when it could. During the Yunnan opium affair, for instance, *Guomindang* members accused Xu of playing the stooge for foreign interests by giving up sovereignty and allowing International Settlement police to prosecute the case.

Those with their ears close to the Shanghai streets, however, told a different story. During the last months of 1923, Lu Yungxiang and He Fenglin initiated an opium suppression bureau called the Wusong-Shanghai Investigation Bureau of All Prohibited Articles. Like so many others of its ilk, it was merely a front for a narcotics monopoly. The institution commissioned Du Yuesheng and Zhang Xiaolin to handle supply, while the Zhejiang warlord and his local agent set up several companies to market the drug. This group greeted the news that General Ji, the warlord in Jiangsu, was about to establish his own antismuggling office in the Shanghai constabulary with some apprehension.[26]

A third variation of the story claimed that supporters of Ji were trying, successfully, to alter a long-standing mutual arrangement with He and Lu to split opium revenues between the two factions. A last version, a variation on the *Guomindang* theme, completes the circle. Some Shanghai rumors, which proved to be accurate, had it that Lu, in collusion with Sun Yat-sen, hired professional assassin Wang Yazhao and his associates to kill Xu. Xu had always been an active antagonist of the party. In 1923, when he learned that Sun was in contact with the Soviet Union, police harassment of the party increased.[27]

These versions of Xu's assassination are by no means mutually exclusive. As the story of Li Zhengwu demonstrates, the boundary between gangs and the *Guomindang* blurred in spots. The martyred Chen Qimei had established ties to the Green Gang, including Li; after his death his nephews, Chen Lifu and Chen Guofu, became (and remained), friends of Du Yuesheng. (In the 1930s, these two brothers would form the powerful conservative C.C. Clique in the *Guomindang*.) Lu Yungxiang, in his attempt to survive in warlord China, allied himself to Sun Yat-sen, who was at the time reorganizing the *Guomindang*, with Soviet help, into a military force in the south. Therefore the death of General Xu eliminated a business rival for Du, a political rival for Lu and a hostile police officer for the Shanghai *Guomindang*.

The assassination should have left Lu Yungxiang secure in his hold on Shanghai. The fortunes of warlords were short-lived, however, and Lu was no exception. In September 1924 he went to war with his rival in Jiangsu and lost. He had to flee Shanghai. Although he returned briefly a year later, he was not able to reestablish himself in the area. Indeed, the death of Xu and the subsequent war ushered in an era of political instability. Between the years 1924 and 1927 Shanghai was occupied by four different generals.

In these chaotic condition, Du, Huang, and Zhang—the "three big shots"—consolidated their hold on the opium traffic. In such a business climate flexibility was essential to survival. Both Du Yuesheng and Zhang Xiaolin showed great resilience. They separated personal loyalties from commercial arrangements. They favored Lu (who controlled Zhang's native Hangzhou), providing sanctuary within the compound that they shared in the French Settlement for Lu's son and ex-defense commissioner He after the defeat of the Zhejiang armies. Yet they renegotiated a deal with his rival, Ji. When Ji fell from power they accommodated themselves to each warlord who came through Shanghai. Zhang Zongchang, the "dog meat general," for instance, arrived in town at the beginning of 1925. Du and Zhang, knowing his weakness for gambling and brothels, entertained him with an evening of mah-jongg while working out a deal with him. Warlords came and went, but Du and Zhang stayed and prospered. Early in 1925, they created the Sanxin Company as a vehicle for their growing organization.[28]

On the surface the three big shots were close business associates, and the Green Gang seemed to be a tightly coordinated organization through which they ran Shanghai from underground. In fact, neither was the case. The gang itself was a fraternity of members, each pledged to his own mentor. Each initiate, in turn, created his own cell once he had accrued sufficient seniority and influence. Joining the organization was like opening a franchise. The gang would provide protection and connections, but each individual had to make his own mark, establish a reputation, and attract a following. Du Yuesheng and Zhang Xiaolin were beholden to different elders of the Green Gang. Du, for all his power, still owed loyalty to Chen Shichang, who had introduced him to the gang.[29]

Therefore, even while Du was working for Huang, he was busy forming his own gang. Because he was an able diplomat, as well as a ruthless man, he managed to forge ties with rival International Settlement gangs. As Du's influence grew, Huang became suspicious. A distance grew between the two men, although publicly they remained close. Du was not above spreading rumors about Huang's personal life or meddling in the company finances.[30]

By 1924, Du and Zhang had become close friends. That year they built adjoining houses in a compound on the Rue Wagner in the French Settlement. They soon eclipsed their benefactor, Huang Jinrong, after a second event of 1924 weakened Huang's power. A weakness for theater and women caused the incident that marked his declining prestige. He fell in love with an actress, Lu Chunlan. He arranged for her to star in an opera at his own theater. One night as she was performing, she missed a line. No one in the audience had the nerve to make a noise except for Lu Xiaojia, the son of Lu Yungxiang, the warlord. Lu Xiaojia greeted the mistake with catcalls. Huang was so angry that he ordered his thugs to beat Lu black and blue. The next day, soldiers from the Shanghai garrison arrested Huang. He stayed in jail for seven days while Zhang and Du smoothed things over. The affair with Miss Lu and the public embarrassment that went with it marked the decline in Huang's influence and the rise of Du.[31]

Thus by 1925 the organization of Shanghai's illicit opium traffic began to take shape. Du and Zhang learned the need to diversify the sources of political protection from the 1924 skirmish between Lu and Ji. They strengthened their own ties to the French Settlement, where extraterritoriality shielded them from Chinese law. In 1925 they came to a formal agreement with consul-general M. Koechlin and his chief of police, Captain Fiori, both of whom received substantial monthly payments from the Sanxin Company in return for their support. According to International Settlement police information, the French authorities received $180,000 per month from Du's organization. The company, in turn, collected $3,000–$10,000 per month and an opium pipe fee of $.50 per day in opium protection fees from the various shops. Competition was no longer a serious problem, as anyone selling opium outside of the cartel was sure to be raided by the French police.[32]

Du's company acted as an opium wholesaler and distributor, as well as providing a measure of protection for the smaller, semi-independent gangs operating in their own territories around Shanghai and through China. For instance, one of many gangs was the Dongyang Gongsi (Eastern Sea Company), a group of twenty men led by Siau Koh Sheng and his deputy Liang Fah. The men worked from the Japanese wharf on North Yangzi Road. Like other such groups, they would deliver opium to Du's agent, one Mau Sang Sung, in Frenchtown, where he inspected and bought the cargo for the conglomerate, earning a commission on the transaction.

Du's ascendancy created a measure of stability among the gang groups because he acted as moderator in their disputes. Yet contending gangs still came into strife. The Dongyang Gongsi, for instance, nurtured a grudge against a rival gang that six years earlier had murdered their old boss, Liang Hong. Du gained influence over them because the smaller franchise gangs had to work with sympathetic police. The customs police were well rewarded for drug seizures, whereas after 1919 the International Settlement police force was not so well infiltrated with gang members as its French counterpart. Chinese river police proved more helpful in delivering the cargo from ship to middleman. Therefore, even though the gangs preferred to move opium overland, they found it safer to go by water. Du's influence with all of Shanghai's various police forces made him valuable to smaller gangs.[33]

Corrupt officials turned a blind eye not only to opium but to gambling as well. Du and Zhang opened what was at the time the largest casino in Shanghai, the Fusheng gambling house at 181 avenue Foch. As a concrete sign of his favored position in Frenchtown, Du was allowed to sit on the French council of ratepayers. By 1929, a British diplomat, commenting on the governance of the French concession, noted that "although M. Fiori was nominally head of the French police, the real power was in the hands of Mr. Du Yuesheng and his friends."

There was a saying in old Shanghai: "Huang Jinrong coveted money; Zhang Xiaolin loved to fight; Du Yuesheng understood people."[34] Although Zhang was the man who brought to the trio the useful introductions to *Beiyang* warlords, while Huang's French police connections gave the early monopoly a necessary safe haven, it was Du who gave these early lessons a wider scope as he set his sights on even larger endeavors. He stepped from warlord connections into national politics by becoming actively involved in labor relations and in Chiang Kai-shek's rise to power within the *Guomindang*.

In May 1925, British and Japanese authorities in the International Settlement fired on workers protesting conditions in foreign factories, killing three. During the strikes that followed Du got involved in labor politics, sending his Green Gang members to protect protesters. Around the same time he befriended the Chen brothers and other members of the Shanghai *Guomindang*. This provided him with a springboard into national politics.[35]

THE RISE OF CHIANG KAI-SHEK

During the warlord years of shifting alliances a new dimension to the violent politics of the age was added in 1923. Sun Yat-sen came to an agreement with agents from the Soviet Union, who helped reorganize the *Guomindang* and establish a power base in Guangdong. As a central figure in the Revolution of 1911, Sun acted as a magnet to those in China who yearned for a viable government. By 1925 Sun's reforms transformed the party into a disciplined body. Well-trained officers from the newly established Whampoa Military Academy began to form the base of an effective army under the leadership of Sun's protégé, Chiang Kai-shek. This new force became doubly effective by forging a working alliance with the young Chinese Communist Party. The maneuver brought angry peasants, like those in Fujian province, and workers in the cities, like those who had gone on strike in Shanghai in 1925, into the battle against the warlords. Yet this uneasy coalition between the *Guomindang* and radical revolutionaries quickly came to an end once Chiang Kai-shek rose to power.

In the early 1920s no one would have considered Chiang Kai-shek a rising star in the *Guomindang*. Born poor in Zhejiang province, Chiang, like so many in his day, had moved to Shanghai in his teens in search of a livelihood. There he lived a dissolute life, associated with members of the Green Gang, and perhaps joined the organization. More important, he met *Guomindang* party members who had been associated with the martyred hero, Chen Qimei. In the early 1920s he invested in a stock exchange with the Chen brothers. When the business failed, he went south to work with Sun Yat-sen. Once there he impressed Sun with his sincerity and was duly made head of the newly established Whampoa Military Academy. Despite many opponents and rivals in the party, Chiang's ties to graduates of this academy and to the Shanghai *Guomindang* gave him a solid power base.

In 1926 Nationalist armies commanded by Chiang Kai-shek, began the Northern Expedition to reunite China. By early spring of the next year, strategic areas of central China were in his control. Chiang felt secure enough to rid himself of the Communist allies that he had barely tolerated and never trusted. In executing his plan to purge the party, he sent two Whampoa Green Gang men to Shanghai to seek Du's help: Zhang Qun and Yang Hu. On April 12, 1927, Du's followers, along with those of Zhang Xiaolin, used weapons supplied by Yang Hu and began the systematic massacre of Communist Party workers in Shanghai. On the evening that the purge was to begin, Du invited the local Communist Party leader, Wang Shouhua, to his home for dinner. There Du's lieutenants waylaid Wang, who had considered Du an ally, and subsequently murdered him.[36]

By 1928 the Nationalists began to consolidate their hold on the lower Yangzi River region. Chiang Kai-shek formed a new government, moving the capital from Beijing (renamed Beiping) to Nanjing. Nationalist officials, including Chiang, publicly affirmed their anti-opium policy. Some, including Chiang, may actually have meant it. But the continuing problem of consolidating power in China—the desperate need for revenue—forced Chiang to acknowledge opium's significance. Colonel Joseph W. Stilwell, in his blunt summary of the situation in China in 1935, called opium the "chief prop of all power in China, both civil and military." He described a condition that had been developing since 1916 at least.[37]

OPIUM AND THE NATIONALISTS

To appease the Western powers, the League of Nations, and the anti-opium activists within their own party, the Nationalists covered their opium policies with the rhetoric of suppression, a ploy that had been used elsewhere by the warlords, by Japan, and by European nations in their own colonies. Nanjing passed its first opium suppression law in 1928, but little was actually done to end the trade except to attack those opium dealers who operated without Nanjing's approval. Instead, in the name of suppression, *Guomindang* officials, led by Chiang Kai-shek's brother-in-law, T. V. Soong, in 1932 developed a thinly disguised monopoly that came to full form by May 1935. The government, needing funds to fight Communists and other opponents, gradually centralized the opium trade. They created a special tax bureau and arranged to channel the funds through the Agriculture Bank. Xiao Juetian, who worked for the monopoly, described the situation. He claimed that in the early 1930s, He Chengjun and Xia Douyan independently dominated the Hankou traffic, thus controlling an important entrepôt on the Yangzi River. Chiang Kai-shek was able to replace them with his agents as he pursued his anti-Communist campaign. The local market temporarily collapsed and the price of opium dropped when the Chinese Communists came through the area on their historic Long March. Taking advantage of the situation, the Nationalist government established central warehouses and sold its opium to licensed brokers, cutting the old merchants out of the trade. Once established, and the area pacified, the price of opium regained its former level.[38]

Zeng Junchen, for one, profited by the new arrangement. From his previous career as a salt merchant in Sichuan province he had strong local connections in government and the military. He organized the Xinji Company and from 1935 to 1939 he and his investors prospered. He would collect the opium from the growing areas, ship it to Chongqing for processing, then reship it to Hankou. The profits were remarkable; one year his investors realized 800 percent on their investments. Yet taxes were heavy and unpredictable. He had to maintain his good relations with government officials and military leaders, especially in the finance and tax departments. Zeng made them shareholders in his company, giving them a direct interest in the continuing profitability of the enterprise. He also spent time and money entertaining them, a pattern he learned in the salt trade.[39]

Du Yuesheng, using the connections that accrued to him for services rendered in 1927, worked hard over the following years to secure his position in this network. Thus at the very moment when European traffickers were facing the onset of a crisis of narcotics supply and increased difficulties in delivery, Du carved out a comfortable niche in Shanghai that gradually extended deep into China. His connections with police assured smooth deliveries, and his eminent status in the gangs gave him the means to enforce his will without recourse to legal institutions. His forays into *Guomindang* politics would become the basis for securing a hold over supplies and safe deliveries.

Du, like Elie Eliopoulos, found government connections to be invaluable but at the same time problematic and uncertain. In 1931 the French consul-general with whom Du and Zhang had such close connections was recalled to his country. His replacement, M. Meyrier, began an anticorruption campaign. He brought in a new chief of police and started shutting down gambling and opium trafficking in Frenchtown. His British counterpart gave him credit for honesty in tackling a difficult task. However, it was also possible that his reforming zeal may have been caused by excessive demands for bribes beyond what Zhang and Du were willing to pay. Nevertheless, by the mid-1930s the Frenchtown haven was no longer essential to the operation because Du's strong ties with the Nationalist government, to which he was contributing $200,000 per month, obviated the need to hide behind treaties.[40]

By the 1930s, Du Yuesheng and his ally Zhang Xiaolin seemed to be fairly secure. Yet the relationship with Chiang Kai-shek was fraught with uncertainty. Although Du had influence with Chiang, bought by his substantial payments into the *Guomindang* war chests, nevertheless he was only one of the many factions in the *Guomindang* coalition. Chiang's own personality was aloof, his governing style, authoritarian and detached. He allowed rival factions to contend while keeping his distance.[41]

Still another worry for Du was Chiang Kai-shek's own apparent ambivalence about the traffic, at least in the early years of the 1930s. Chiang could turn on traffickers without warning, especially if he thought he were being cheated. In 1933 Chiang turned over a certain amount of officially confiscated opium and asked Du to process it over six months into medical-grade morphine. The proceeds were targeted to finance the Blue Shirts, one of the party's intelligence units. Du secretly augmented the supply with his own opium procured from connections in Tianjin and from Paul Yip. He set up the Yah Kee Company, a morphine and red pill factory in Nandao. The vested interests included the then mayor of Shanghai, Wu Tiecheng. At the end of the six-month deadline, Du asked for an extension, making the dubious claim that the product lacked demand.

Chiang Kai-shek personally disliked narcotics, especially morphine and heroin. When he discovered the deceit involved, he turned on Du. On November 17 of that year, the central military police launched a midnight raid on the establishment. Du, along with Zhang Xiaolin and Mayor Wu, flew to Nanchang to appease General Chiang and renegotiate their status. By December 2, the old operation was up and running again, but Du was shaken by the experience.[42]

Du had to find outlets for the immense wealth he was accumulating. Perhaps his supreme accomplishment of the 1930s was his transformation from Shanghai gangster into honored businessman, philanthropist, civic leader, and patriot. The change allowed him legitimate areas in which to invest his impressive capital, while enabling him to enforce his will more effectively by giving prestige to his gangster tactics. In 1931 he held a week-long celebration when he erected an ancestral temple at his natal village. He opened his own bank and eventually sat on the boards of numerous other Shanghai banks and businesses. As befitting a man worth over $40 million, he was Shanghai's leading philanthropist. He never forgot his origins; he generously supported hospitals, orphanages, schools, and a model farming community. In 1935 Du became managing director of the *China Press*, the *China Times*, the *China Evening News*, and the Shun Shih News Agency. In what even he must have appreciated as the supreme irony, when Chiang reorganized the opium eradication effort in 1933, Du joined the Shanghai Opium Suppression Board.[43]

Zhang Xiaolin maintained his ties to military and warlord circles, but never felt comfortable outside of the gangster world. In contrast to his partner, Du liked his political role. He was concerned with his public image. He played the part of the gentleman, which in China means supporting charities and acting as a public arbitrator. When the Japanese attacked Shanghai in 1932, Du became involved in negotiations through his position in the French Settlement and was active in organizing Shanghai citizens to help the Nineteenth Route Army as it fought this first skirmish of the China war unaided by Nanjing. Du was illiterate, yet he hired a personal reader and so had a working grasp of literature. In the 1930s he cured himself of his opium addiction. He required that his own followers be well dressed.[44]

Du Yuesheng developed the modern role of a narcotics trafficker to an unprecedented level. He perfected the patterns of opium control and trafficking that had been taking shape during the chaotic warlord years. As international sanctions created a crisis of supply and delivery, driving up the price of smuggled opium, a new kind of merchant had to be both heavily armed and alert to structural vulnerabilities in the official systems meant to suppress him. Those weaknesses usually came in the form of fiscal crises. The escalating costs of warfare forced even the most reluctant and high-minded politicians to turn to the opium business for revenues. The traffickers who succeeded entered into relationships with politicians who helped them suppress their competitors. Du's operation was the culmination of the Yunnan-style opium schemes of the 1910s and the relationships forged with warlords by his business partner, Zhang Xiaolin, in the early 1920s.

"Corruption" is an inadequate word to describe the relationship between Du and Chiang Kai-shek. Du became a political actor in the fullest sense of the word. Chiang recognized the power that Du held in Shanghai and accommodated him. Du provided Chiang not only with cash but with street thugs, political mediation, and intelligence. In return, Chiang allowed Du to become one of the wealthiest men in China and to assume the roles that money alone could not buy—civic leader and patriot.

It was, however, not an easy relationship. Chiang Kai-shek was puritanical by nature and by military discipline. He periodically tried to clean up the traffic, as happened in late 1933. He was hostile to morphine and heroin. Yet he needed money as he faced difficult challenges to the stability of his regime. The greatest of these, and the one that preoccupied him, was the Communist insurgency, which did not end with the white terror of April 1927. Decimated in the cities, party members retreated to rural base camps. From 1931 through 1935, Chiang fielded pacification forces in southeast China; after the Long March in 1935 he continued fighting Communists in the northwest. These campaigns required manpower and expensive equipment.

PACIFICATION FIRST, RESISTANCE SECOND

At the same time Chiang could not ignore Japanese army activity in China. Held in check by political parties at home during the 1920s, Japa-

nese military policy alternated between incremental territorial encroachment and outright invasion after the incident of September 18,
1931. On that evening officers in the Japanese Guandong Army stationed in Manchuria placed a bomb on the tracks of the Japanese-owned
South Manchurian Railway and thus fabricated an excuse to invade the
three northeastern provinces of China. In March 1932 they created the
puppet state of Manchukuo, from which they chipped away at China's
northern territory, incorporating Rehe in 1933, and creating Japanese-
dominated autonomous zones in North China proper in 1933 and
1935.[45]

Faced with internal disorder and foreign invasion, Chiang Kai-shek
chose to quell rebellion first. Using the slogan Pacification First, Resistance Second, he pushed *Guomindang* armies into continual engagement with Communist cadres, first in the southeast and later in the
northwest. As the decade wore on, this policy only caused further instability as dissension grew within his own ranks whenever otherwise loyal
subordinates (or those harboring personal ambitions) developed personal reasons to hate the Japanese more than the Communists. The
most famous case of insubordination against Chiang Kai-shek came at
the close of 1936, when Zhang Xueliang, originally of Manchuria, kid-
napped Chiang Kai-shek as he conducted an inspection of the troops
stationed at Xian. Zhang only released the Generalissimo after securing
his promise to put aside the crusade against Communists and fight the
Japanese. This incident is a milestone in Chinese history. It put the civil
war on hold, marking a turning point in China's reaction to Japanese
aggression.

Yet the Xian Incident was not the only attempt by *Guomindang* generals to change the official policy toward Japan. Less well known is the
attempted coup d'etat by the Nineteenth Route Army in Fujian province
at the end of 1933. The convoluted political rivalries in the province
before, during, and after the revolt involved Communists, anti-Japanese
patriots, and *Guomindang* factional politics. Entwined in the drama was
Paul Yip, Green Gang member, opium trafficker, and double agent. His
success in the area demonstrates the dynamics of mid-level Chinese drug
trafficking during the early 1930s.

UNREST IN FUJIAN PROVINCE

Fujian province is situated on the southern coast of China between Zhejiang to the north and Guangdong to the south. It is a mountainous,

rural area, yet the two principal cities, Fuzhou and Xiamen, are trading ports with long histories of foreign contact. Among the earliest of the treaty ports, Xiamen opened to modern commerce after the Treaty of Nanjing in 1842. Although dwarfed by the volume of Shanghai's trade, both cities supported foreign merchant communities with formal concession areas. Thus the people of Fujian had experience with outsiders living among them as merchants, as pirates, and as smugglers. They also had a predilection toward banditry and feuding. The rugged terrain and jagged coast were hospitable to roving bands of landless peasants who might turn to crime when nature proved fickle and tax collectors relentless. It was an area of enduring lineage ties with a history of clan warfare. Without a strong governing representative from the capital, Fujian province could easily break down into anarchy.[46]

In the early twentieth century just such conditions prevailed. The province experienced flooding in 1925 and alternating flood and drought in the 1930s that devastated farming communities. The warlord years took their toll as well. During the Zhejiang-Jiangsu War, for instance, armies supporting both sides camped in Fujian. Located as it is just south of the battleground, the fighting naturally spilled over into its territory. Fujian peasants suffered from the arbitrary nature of warlord policies. The military men who came and went whipsawed them with constantly changing opium policies. Peasants who faced forced plantings of opium because of heavy taxation in one season might the next year find officials uprooting poppy fields under orders of a new general seeking to increase the price of opium or an official notified of a sudden visit by an inspector from the capital.[47]

The resentment of Fujian's maltreated peasants became part of the overall strategy that made a success of the Northern Expedition in 1926. Fujian province had seen its share of Communist organizers working on behalf of the *Guomindang* before the White Terror of 1927. After that signal event, the rugged terrain of the area provided safe haven for many Communists who sought shelter from the Nationalist terror. Just over the southwest border in Jiangxi lay the major base camp area of the Chinese Communist Party, where Mao Zedong and Zhu De were in the process of perfecting the art of the protracted war. In the early 1930s Communist forces made incursions into Fujian. In April 1932 they reached Zhangzhou, only a hundred miles from Xiamen. In the north they moved down the Min River toward Yenping. Yet the Communist presence was not the only concern of provincial *Guomindang* officials.[48]

Many of the foreigners living in the province were Japanese. Only sixty miles off its coast sits the island of Taiwan, at the time a Japanese colony. Fujian was attractive to Japan for strategic reasons. Japanese merchants lived in the area while naval vessels of the Imperial Navy called at the ports regularly. There was also a portion of the provincial Chinese population that remained outside of Chinese control. These were the Formosans, Chinese who were Japanese subjects because they were born in Taiwan and therefore enjoyed extraterritorial rights.[49]

The strong Japanese presence provided a further obstacle to establishing public order in the province. The large Formosan community included many criminals. They used their legal immunity to engage in smuggling, often openly defying customs officials by claiming that they were exempt from all tariffs, a claim that was blatantly false. They smuggled everything: opium, of course, but also silver, sugar, paper, and anything else that might have a market in Fujian. Their shops sported signs advertising their exemption from Chinese control. They openly broke the law and when challenged would turn to the Japanese consular courts for protection. Formosan gangs periodically engaged in shoot-outs with Chinese police. In Xiamen, Chen Zhangfu, head of the Taiwan Association (Taiwan Gonghui) was known to be a smuggler and gangster.[50]

Such a mixture of foreign meddling, Communist insurgency, and common banditry became all the more volatile once Japanese aggression began in North China. In September 1931 the Japanese army occupied Manchukuo; in February of the next year, the fighting spread north of Shanghai. There Japanese troops ran into unexpectedly stiff resistance from the Chinese Nineteenth Route Army, which fought valiantly for over a month in the streets of Zhabei. In the end, the Japanese declared a unilateral withdrawal. News of the heroic resistance of the Nineteenth Route Army brought joy to the Chinese population in Fujian province. Although far from the action, many Fujianese could well identify with the plight of Manchurians and others in the north because of their own suffering at the hands of Japanese. The Chinese merchant associations in the cities organized anti-Japanese boycotts and students paraded in support of those armies still resisting in the north, while rumors circulated that Fujian would soon be occupied by Japanese troops.[51]

Yet in February 1932, General Zhang Zhen, the chairman of the Fujian provincial government, was in no position to fight the Japanese. His Forty-ninth Army had lost many men in battling Communists in the west. In just one year he saw his army of 800 officers and 9,600 men reduced to half. He was hard pressed to pay his troops; salaries were five months in arrears. In order to augment his forces, he recruited local bandit bands, euphemistically referred to as volunteers, into his army. One such group included the 2,000 men who made up the cohort of Chen Guohui. General Zhang encouraged poppy planting, taxing the fields for needed revenues. In May 1932, in order to combat the Communist threat to Zhangzhou, he acquired $200,000 in opium revenues. He allowed the volunteers who reinforced his armies the same privilege in the areas that they controlled. Thus the bandit Chen Guohui was allowed to collect poppy taxes, but his methods were so harsh as to bring complaints from the peasants.[52]

The citizens of Fujian province lived in the throes of the classic Chinese formula for disaster: internal rebellion, foreign calamity (*Neiluan, Waihuan*). Throughout 1932 and 1933, rumors predicted imminent Japanese occupation one month and equally certain Communist victory the next. In spring 1932, hoping to secure a definite solution on at least one front, the Nationalist government transferred the Nineteenth Route Army to Fujian. In keeping with Chiang Kai-shek's policy of pacification first, resistance second, the army, under the leadership of General Cai Tingkai, took to the field against the Communists. However, the Nineteenth Route Army, fresh from its costly victory in Shanghai, had a larger definition of pacification than anti-Communism.[53]

Three divisions of this force arrived during spring 1932. They incorporated the remnants of the Forty-ninth Army as well as the provincial volunteers into their own command. They began to establish order in the province. Fight Communists they did, but they also waged a moral campaign in the towns of Fujian, where years of banditry had left a legacy of gambling, prostitution, and opium use. In Zhangzhou, for instance, left in ruins after the brief Communist occupation, the Nineteenth Route Army began rebuilding. Posters soon lined the streets urging the townsmen to forego opium, give up gambling, boycott Japanese goods, and follow the army's own example of donating part of their salaries to Chinese resisting Japan in the north. They began a campaign to eradicate opium growing, reversing the trend of the previous administration. Their reforming zeal extended to the worst of the bandits who had been incorporated into their army. On December 23, 1932, they tried and executed the volunteer officer, Chen Guohui, in response to pleas from the citizenry.[54]

The Nineteenth Route Army defeated the Communists, forcing them back to their base camp stronghold over the border in Jiangsu province by May 1933. Yet the leadership of the army hated the Nationalists' policy of pacification first. After all, this force had faced terrible losses fighting the Japanese in Shanghai. It was also composed mostly of Guangdong men, and regional differences divided it from those holding power in Nanjing. The men surrounding Chiang Kai-shek tended to come from Zhejiang province or Shanghai. As the Nineteenth Route Army battled the Communists, it took steps to place its own members in key positions throughout the local government structure. By spring 1933 it became clear that it would be the Nineteenth Route Army, not Chinese Communists or Japanese, that would occupy Fujian province. By summer the area was all but autonomous.[55]

THE FUJIAN PEOPLE'S MOVEMENT AND OPIUM

The simmering differences finally erupted. On November 20, 1933, Fujian province, under the leadership of the Nineteenth Route Army, seceded from Nationalist China. Calling for a people's government, the leadership established what it called a democratic socialist state. Officers in the Fujian People's Movement had Guangdong connections and they arranged a truce with the leaders to the south of Fujian. They moved their troops north to do battle with the central government forces gathered in Zhejiang province.[56]

The Fujian forces were better trained and led, but they were outnumbered by Chiang's army. Lacking sufficient heavy armament for a long campaign, the Fujian People's Movement needed money if it was to succeed. In spite of their moral convictions, the movement's leaders turned to opium as a solution. From the moment they had set foot in Fujian province the Nineteenth Route Army had pursued a stringent policy of poppy eradication. Even at the beginning of the program, however, there had been rumors that their true motives were not so pure. They were, it was said, merely out to eliminate competition and ensure a good price for their own eventual monopoly. Those in the leadership protested against such claims. Hence they were most embarrassed when, on July 14, 1933, four months before the uprising began, one of their own naval ships fired on a Chinese maritime customs vessel. After a brief skirmish, the customs boat prevailed. Boarding the ship, customs men found a cargo of arms and opium. Nineteenth Route Army leaders claimed to know nothing about the incident.[57]

In fact, the opium monopoly rumors were true. Forced by rebellion to raise funds for arms, the Nineteenth Route Army had been negotiating for an opium monopoly since April 1933. To run the establishment, they turned to Ye Qinghe, aka Paul Yip, a Xiamen gangster who knew the smuggling business well. For $15,000 he purchased the monopoly rights for his Haifeng Company to sell opium, agreeing to pay taxes of $.50 per ounce of foreign opium, $.20 per ounce of Yunnan opium, and $.10 per ounce for native opium. All licensed dealers would pay $100 per month for a first-class license, $50 for a second class and $25 for a third-class license. Dens, of which there were four hundred in Xiamen alone, would pay extra fees of $.50 per lamp per day.[58]

Paul Yip was not a newcomer to the opium trade. He began his career in Shanghai in the days of legality as a member of the Chaozhou opium hongs. During the 1910s he and Edward Ezra made the transition from merchant to smuggler. They worked above ground consolidating control through their connections with the Opium Combine, while underground they set up a network to bring in opium from Persia using the swashbuckling ship's captain, Harry Yamazaki. In 1925, however, the partnership frayed when the operation came to light. Ezra provided evidence to the municipal authorities in the International Settlement, and Paul Yip spent eighteen months in jail.[59]

Shortly after serving his sentence, Yip made a move to Xiamen, only a few hundred miles north of Chaozhou. From there he resumed his smuggling activities. He had to compete with Formosan gangs who had the advantage of Japanese protection, but his ties to Du Yuesheng and the Shanghai Green Gang bolstered his own position and later saved his life. He was part of Du's network spreading from Shanghai throughout China. Paul Yip had the temperament of a born opium smuggler. He was quick to recognize opportunity where others saw only chaos in the shifting political alliances. He was willing to accommodate any side, and he was a violent man. Aside from his smuggling activities, he attracted the authorities' attention in 1935 when he came home one evening to find one of his mistresses in bed with his gardener. He shot them both.[60]

The Fujian People's Government lasted only two months. By January 17, 1934, the Nineteenth Route Army had been defeated by *Guomindang* forces because of internal treachery. The list of those who deserted the cause was long and complicated. It included the governor of Guangdong province, who had been brought over by Chiang Kai-shek's own secret service, as well as many defectors from within the leadership of the army itself. One division commander who defected was Tan Jixiu. His brigade of volunteers had been fighting along the Zhejiang-Fujian border in a desultory fashion. They also spent at least part of their time guarding the opium deliveries of fellow provincial Paul Yip.[61]

In February 1934, the Nanjing government began putting the province back under its control. This was not an easy process. In the first place, the Nineteenth Route Army was a distinguished military division of the republican regime. It would not do simply to treat those who took part in the rebellion as common traitors. A crucial part of the negotiations leading to the cease-fire was an amnesty for the rebels. One month after the rebellion ceased, however, it became clear that a few of the revolt's leaders would not be treated with the promised generosity. General Cai Tingkai and his closest cohorts felt obliged to flee, having been relieved of their command. As *Guomindang* officials filtered into the province to fill vacant posts, they completely reorganized the old Nineteenth Route Army, leaving pockets of discharged and disgruntled solders.[62]

The political disarray tempted seemingly loyal officers. In February General Du Jiyun, who had been sent to Fujian as chief of the Peace Preservation Bureau, began to plot his own uprising, hoping to feed off the discontent in the province. For financial backing he contacted a Japanese army agent named Genki, who agreed to provide him with a huge shipment of Persian opium said to be valued at over ¥100,000. The Japanese army hoped to use the political vacuum left in the wake of the revolt to destabilize the area. Over the first four years of the decade the Formosan population increased by 40,000 in Xiamen alone. Rumors circulated anew that Fujian would soon become an "autonomous area," a puppet regime that, like other regions in the north, was controlled by Japanese military forces.[63]

General Du's plot lasted no longer than a few weeks before his treachery came to the notice of the central government. In March he was recalled, tried for treason, and shot. He was replaced by General Chen Yi, former vice chair of the military, whose loyalty to Chiang Kai-shek seemed beyond question. (Chen Yi's loyalty to China was not so certain. He was friendly with Paul Yip; both men maintained close connections with influential Japanese in Fujian. In early spring 1935, he entertained Colonel (later General) Doihara Kenji, a Japanese officer noted for his espionage exploits throughout China. Several years later, during the Japanese occupation of Shanghai, Chen Yi became the puppet mayor of the town. He was assassinated by Dai Li's agents.) Thus in early 1934, after a false start, *Guomindang* government once again prevailed in Fujian province.[64]

Paul Yip survived these transitions, which must have been frustrating for a businessman. He had just been granted his opium monopoly by the Nineteenth Route Army only to see them replaced by the Nationalists. Yet he was able to adjust to the times. Paul Yip worked with the *Guomindang* opium suppression offices. Early in 1934 he reorganized his old firm into the Lutung Company (Egret Transport Company), which then became the official monopoly sales franchise for Fujian. He also established two subsidiary outfits: the Lutung Company (a pun on egret, this name means Land Transport Company) and the Haitung (Ocean Transport) Company, which delivered opium by land and sea.[65]

Presiding over a monopoly, of course, should be an ideal situation for any business. His *Guomindang* connections enabled Paul Yip to organize his company openly. Between 1935 and 1937 he moved opium from the Chinese interior with military protection from theft and official inspection. He was able to set up distribution networks, with centralized wholesalers in each county supplying retail shops in their areas. Yet the occasional *Guomindang* anti-opium decrees hindered his business. Initially the new laws caused the general price of Fujian opium to rise from $2 to $4 per ounce and he was able to handle large cargoes. In July 1935, for instance, the opium monopoly sold 136,468 ounces of opium. In June the Lutung Company delivered 213 chests of Yunnan opium at 450 catties per chest. In April the Haitung Company moved 117,600 ounces in 121 cases by sea from Shanghai. Business was booming.[66]

With monopoly privileges Paul Yip began by selling opium at $3.50 per ounce. Later, because of competition from smugglers and Formosans, he found he had to drop the price. Also, the Nationalists' ambivalent policies worked against his interests. In spite of the revenue they acquired from the trade, the Nationalists also insisted that the monopoly engage in some opium suppression activities. In 1936 all addicts were required to register. Few did. Fearing the threat of arbitrary cures rumored to bring with them certain death, opium users turned to unlicensed shops.[67]

Thus Paul Yip faced stiff competition from unlicensed smugglers. He met this problem by returning to smuggling and by taking control of the unlicensed business. He did this by dominating opium supplies. Through his connections to Cheng Wenshan, chief of the Opium Suppression Bureau, he siphoned off monopoly goods into the underground market, a practice that eventually got him into trouble. Yip also gained control of the Japanese connection. In 1934, after the fall of General Du, he secretly contacted Japanese opium monopoly officials in

Taiwan through Chen Zhangfu, the president of the Taiwan Association. Paul Yip went to Taibei, Taiwan, in October 1934 and arranged to take custody of the shipment of Persian opium originally promised to the unfortunate General Du.[68]

This Persian opium, which had been sitting in a Jilong warehouse for over four years, was a source of embarrassment for the Japanese government. Purchased in 1930, the Formosan monopoly planned to sell it in Taiwan after increasing the number of licensed addicts permitted in their own strictly regulated territory. The planned increase brought protests from their Taiwanese subjects, who at the time were pushing for home rule. The commotion then brought international embarrassment when news of the movement came to the attention of the League of Nations. The Taiwan monopoly quickly sold the opium to Yip.[69]

Paul Yip managed to live comfortably in the shadow area between the licit and illicit, communicating with both Chinese and Japanese. He kept his arrangements with the Fujian provincial authorities, yet he maintained cordial relations with Japanese in the area. He was Chinese, not Formosan, so he could not claim treaty protection. Yet his network was so extensive that when his Formosan competitors tried for a time to organize against him, even with the advantage of extraterritoriality, they finally had to join him instead. In 1936, in what looked like a victory for opium suppression, the Japanese government agreed to close down Formosan opium shops, a move that strengthened Yip's organization. In that year he reorganized his holdings once again into the larger Yumin Company. He married a Japanese woman and purchased Japanese citizenship for himself by donating $15,000 to the Japanese consul at Xiamen.[70]

Paul Yip's Fujian business came to an end in 1937. Evidence against his cohorts in the Fujian Opium Suppression Bureau, who had been routing government opium to the illegal market, surfaced in Nanjing. The Nationalists were not pleased by his unauthorized dealings. In June 1937, Yip went north to Fuzhou, hoping to expand into the morphine and heroin business. There he was arrested on drug smuggling charges. On the same evening police raided his mansion in the suburbs of Xiamen. The house had long been the meeting place for traffickers and gangsters in South China, seventeen of whom were arrested that night. The rooms of the villa, befitting the dwelling of an opium king, were fitted with ornate inlay panels that could be removed to hide drugs and drug-making apparatus.[71]

On July 12, 1937, even as Japanese and Chinese troops unsuccessfully tried to negotiate a new cease-fire agreement on the outskirts of Beijing, Paul Yip and those who helped him from within the Opium Suppression Bureau were brought to Nanjing and executed. At least that was what was reported in the newspapers. His family supported the story by arranging funeral services for him. Although several of his colleagues actually were shot, Paul Yip escaped punishment. He had been working all along with the Shanghai gangster Du Yuesheng, who in turn arranged a pardon for him. In 1938, Paul Yip turned up in Hong Kong working for Du's own organization.[72]

Paul Yip was a survivor. He rose far beyond his origins as a petty gangster. With his ties to the Shanghai gangs, the provincial Fujian government, and the Japanese, he not only dealt in narcotics, both openly and underground, but he traded information as well. Not quite so lucky or resourceful was special agent Zhang Chao. Zhang was the man whose careful investigation had yielded evidence about the irregularities taking place in the Fujian Opium Suppression Bureau that led to Yip's arrest. Even though Zhang worked for the local branch of Dai Li's secret police, his ties to the central government did not protect him in Fujian. He suffered the consequences of his diligence when General Chen Yi, the chairman of the Fujian provincial government, had him arrested and shot.[73]

In a larger sense, the story of the changing conditions in Fujian province demonstrates the qualities necessary to prosper in the evolving opium business of the 1930s. Paul Yip began with expertise in opium smuggling. He adapted to the new climate by grasping the traffic's political dimension. As Du Yuesheng had done on a larger scale in Shanghai, Paul Yip forged alliances with the political powers of Fujian. His task was complicated, however, by the rapid changes in the political landscape throughout the decade. It is a testimony to his acumen that his business thrived no matter who prevailed in local politics. Yet for all of his skills, Paul Yip would not have survived in the smaller arena without his ties to the larger Shanghai operation led by Du Yuesheng. Paul Yip became a middle-level manager in an operation that allowed him a measure of flexibility in his own territory. He understood the value of political connections, yet in the end it was his gangland connection that saved his skin. He learned, as did both Elie Eliopoulos in France and Du Yuesheng in Shanghai, that political connections, while necessary, could also prove fickle.

The chaotic period of warlord and civil war politics (1916–1937) created ideal conditions for the renaissance of the drug traffic in China and its consolidation in a few hands. Opium was the sustaining lifeblood of warlords, large and small. Even those with personal scruples about opiates, such as Chiang Kai-shek, could not afford to ignore the revenues that the drug traffic could generate. As Chiang consolidated his political power from 1927 onward, he found that it was essential for him to come to terms with gangsters like Du Yuesheng. Du provided Chiang with revenue, of course, but also with a variety of services, such as murdering Communists in Shanghai in 1927. The alliance between Du and Chiang at the national level was mirrored in scores of regional relationships, as illustrated by Paul Yip's accommodation to changing political powers in Fujian province. Those drug traffickers who succeeded were not only tough and shrewd but sophisticated enough to stay abreast of rapid changes in politics and to react accordingly. At the same time that this was happening in Nationalist China, Japanese soldiers of fortune, or *ronin*, were insinuating themselves into the drug traffic in the parts of China coming under Japanese control.

NOTES

1. "Report," November 30, 1933, D 5645 SMP CID.
2. "The Yunnan Opium Case," *North China Herald*, August 26, 1916; "Hung-zhun Yishi Zhi Yantu An" [The explosive news of the opium case], *Minguo Ribao* [Republican daily], August 18, 1916, 9.
3. "Report," November 3, 1916, IO 698, SMP CID; "Report," September 6, 1916, IO 562, SMP CID; "Report," August 6, 1916, IO 557, SMP CID; "Report," August 23, 1916, IO 530, SMP CID.
4. "Circular about Li Tsung-wu," April 16, 1917, IO 798, SMP CID.
5. Brian Martin, *The Shanghai Green Gang: Politics and Organized Crime, 1919–1937* (Berkeley: University of California Press, 1996), 80.
6. "China: Annual Report, 1922," PRO, FO 371/9216:2.
7. Ernest P. Young, *The Presidency of Yuan Shih-k'ai* (Ann Arbor: University of Michigan Press, 1977), 200–01.
8. "Exciting Story of Gun-running," *North China Herald*, July 14, 1923. Kearney also established a Chinese branch of the Ku Klux Klan, probably as a money-making scheme. "Report," June 27, 1924, IO 5645, SMP CID.
9. "China: Annual Report, 1922," PRO, FO 371/9216.
10. "Opium in Yunnan," *North China Herald*, April 23, 1921; "Opium in China," November 10, 1922, PRO, FO 3495/117/10.
11. Letter from Zhang Yaonan, *North China Herald*, February 2, 1924; "Appalling Tyranny in Fukien," *North China Herald*, February 16, 1924; "China Full of Opium," *North China Herald*, May 31, 1924; "Opium in China," Eastes to Alsten, September 22, 1922, PRO, FO 3548/504/10.
12. Shanghai also had representatives of the Red Gang, which dominated areas along the Yangzi River. Many authors writing about the Shanghai gangs treat

these bodies as monoliths, often implying that Huang or Du ran the entire operation as the central directors of a smoothly functioning corporate body. Often Huang Jinrong is described as the head of the Red and Green gangs. In fact, the gangs were filled with internal conflicts, and the three bigshots had their own falling out. Huang was familiar with members of both gangs but only joined the Green Gang later, as his own power waned. See Martin, *The Shanghai Green Gang.*

13. The story of Du and Chiang has been told many times. Jonathan Marshall pioneered this field in the article, "Opium and the Politics of Gangsterism in Nationalist China, 1927–1945," *Bulletin of Concerned Asian Scholars* (July–September 1977): 19–48. The most recent account can be found in Martin, *The Shanghai Green Gang,* and William Walker, *Opium and Foreign Policy* (Chapel Hill: University of North Carolina Press, 1991). A popular account is given in Sterling Seagrave, *The Soong Dynasty* (New York: Harper and Row, 1985).

14. Zhu Jianliang, "Zhang Xiaolin de Yisheng" [The Life of Zhang Xiaolin], *Jintai Zhongguo Banghui Neimu* [The inside story of modern Chinese gangs], (Peking: Masses Publishing Company, 1992), 1:422.

15. Shi Jun, "Shanghai Tan Daheng De Goujie He Douzheng" [The plots and conflicts of Shanghai's three bigshots], in *Wenshi Ziliao Xuanku* [Treasury of source materials] (Beijing: Zhongguo Wenshi Chubanshe, 1996), 20:326; Zhu, "Zhang Xiaolin de Yisheng," 423. This version of the story has Li going to Hangzhou to bring a famous actress to Shanghai. See also Zhang Jungu, *Du Yuesheng Zhuan* [Biography of Du Yuesheng] (Taibei: Zhuanji Wenxue Chubanshe, 1980), 1:142–43.

16. Zheng Xiwen, "Wo Dang Huang Jinrong Guanjia de Jianwen" [What I saw when I served as the watchman for Huang Jinrong's house], in *Jindai Zhongguo Banghui Neimu;* "Memo on Tu Yueh-sheng alias Tu Yuin," February 5, 1940, D 9319, SMP CID.

17. "Banghui Doumu Huang Jinrong" [Head of the gangs, Huang Jinrong], *Jiu Shanghai Fengyun Renwu* [People of Old Shanghai] (Shanghai: People's Publishing Company, 1989), 52–56.

18. Zhang, *Du Yuesheng Zhuan,* 1:121–24; Shi, "Shanghai Da Heng de Goujie he Douzheng"; Ping Jinya, "Jiu Shanghai de Yantu" [Opium in old Shanghai], in *Wenshi Ziliao Xuanji,* 631.

19. Zhang, *Du Yuesheng Zhuan,* 124–32.

20. Mei Zhen and Shao Pu, *Haishang Wenren Du Yuesheng* [Shanghai celebrity Du Yuesheng] (Zengzhou: Henan People's Publishing, 1987), 20–21.

21. Zhang, *Du Yuesheng Zhuan,* 136–37.

22. Zhang, *Du Yuesheng Zhuan,* 141.

23. "Imminent Prospects of War," *North China Herald,* August 30, 1924.

24. *North China Herald,* August 30, 1924.

25. The Chinese accounts all agree on the names of the two assassins: Zheng Yian and Zhu Shanyuan. The *North China Herald* gives the name Li Dahsung. Yu Likui, "Wang Yazhao Banghui Ansha Jituan de Neimu" [The real story about the Wang Yazhao assassin's organization], in *Anhuei Wenshih Ziliao Xuanji* [Selected source materials From Anhwei province] (Anhwei: An-

hwei Province Publishing, 1986), 116–17; *North China Herald*, November 17, 1923.

26. *North China Herald*, November 1924; "Report," May 2, 1924, IO 5374, SMP CID; "Report," April 4, 1924, IO 5374, SMP CID.

27. "Report," May 2, 1924, IO 5374, SMP CID. Although not directly involved in narcotics, Wang Yazhao's name appears from time to time in the documents up to 1936 when he himself was assassinated. According to most sources, he was an assassin with no political sympathies who got into the profession around 1911 through his association with the grandnephews of the Chinese statesman Li Hongzhang. Wang's own relatives, however, remember him as an ardent supporter of Sun Yat-sen and an opponent of Chiang Kai-shek. He went to Shanghai in the 1910s and befriended Lu Xiao-jia, the warlord's son, who introduced him to his father. See "Wang Yazhao," in *Hefei Wenshi Ziliao* [Source Materials from Hefei], 3:1986.

28. Du, *Shanghai Wenren*, 602–3; Mei and Shao, *Haishang Wenren*, 35.

29. "Zhang Rengui Yu Renhui" [Zhang Rengui and the benevolent society], in *Jiu Shanghai de Banghui: Shanghai Wenshi Ziliao Xuanji, no. 54* [The gangs of old Shanghai: Shanghai source materials, no. 54], 108–15.

30. Shi, "Shanghai San Da Heng de Goujie he Douzheng," 350–57.

31. Mei and Shao, *Haishang Wenren*, 27–30.

32. "Memo on Tu Yueh Sheng alias Tu Yuin," February 5, 1940, D 9319, SMP CID.

33. "Prevention of Opium Running," August 22, 1932, D 4009, SMP CID.

34. Mei and Shao, *Haishang Wenren*, 30.

35. "Memo on Mr Tu Yueh Sheng alias Tu Yuin," February 5, 1940, D 9319, SMP CID; for his role in labor politics, see Elizabeth J. Perry, *Shanghai on Strike* (Stanford, Calif.: Stanford University Press, 1993).

36. Mei and Shao, *Haishang Wenren Du Yuesheng*, 59–61; Yang Hu provided the guns; for a period of time before the massacre, the gang members trained under the eye of Ye Chaoshan.

37. Stillwell Report, 14.

38. Xiao Juetian, "Jiang Jieshi Jinyan de Neimu" [The inside story of Chiang Kai-shek's opium suppression], *Zhonghua Wenshi Ziliao Wenku*, 20:650–58.

39. Zeng Junchen, "Jingyung Deye Wunian Jilu" [Record of five years in a special industry enterprise], *Zhonghua Wenshi Ziliao Wenku*, 20:609–17.

40. Brenan to Ingram, November 1932, PRO, FO 371/17168; Du, *Shanghai Wenren*, 642–44; Nicholson Report, annex III, 5–6; Marshall, "Opium and Politics," 34; "Memo on Mr. Tu Yueh Sheng, alias Tu Yuin," February 5, 1940, D 9319, SMP CID.

41. Chiang's governing style is best described in Lloyd Eastman, *The Abortive Revolution* (Cambridge, Mass.: Harvard University Press, 1963). Chen Lifu claims to have been surprised after setting up an espionage unit to find that Dai Li also had a similar unit operating. See Chen Lifu, *The Storm Clouds Clear over China*.

42. "Report," November 25, 1933, D 5645, SMP CID; "Memo on Mr. Tu Yue Sheng alias Tu Yuin," February 5, 1940, D 9319, SMP CID.

43. M. R. Nicholson, "Reports," box 7208, 893.114NARCOTICS/2230, box 7209, 893.114NARCOTICS/2379, 2399, 2450, RG 59.

44. Mei and Shao, *Haishang Wenren*, 48.

45. Parks Coble, *Facing Japan: Chinese Politics and Japanese Imperialism, 1931–1937* (Cambridge, Mass.: Harvard University Press, 1991).

46. Cai Shaoqing, *Minguo Shiji de Tufei* [Local bandits of the republican period] (Beijing: Zhongguo Renmin Daxue Chubanshe, 1993), 233–25.

47. "Reformation of Changchow," *North China Herald*, February 4, 1922; "Fukien's Opium War," *North China Herald*, December 20, 1922; "Opium Revenue in Fukien," *North China Herald*, February 17, 1923.

48. "Monthly Report," April 1932, 893.00PRAMOY/56, RG 59; "Monthly Report," May 1932, 893.00PRAMOY/57, RG 59; "Monthly Report," September, 1933, 893.00PRFOOCHOW/69, RG 59.

49. "Formosan Smuggling Threatening Fukien," November 20, 1935, 893.114NARCOTICS/1415, RG 59.

50. "Monthly Report," August 1934, 893.00PRAMOY/84, RG 59; Nicholson, "Formosan Smugglers," November 20, 1935, box 7204, 893.114NARCOTICS/1415, RG 59.

51. "Monthly Reports," October 1931 through March 1932, 893.00PRAMOY/50–55, RG 59; "Monthly Report," June 1932, 893.00PRAMOY/58, RG 59.

52. "Monthly Report," February 1932, 893.00PRAMOY/54, RG 59; "Monthly Report," April 1932, 893.00PRAMOY/56, RG 59; "Summary of 1929," 893.00PRAMOY/85, RG 59.

53. "Monthly Reports," June–November 1932, 893.00PRAMOY/58–63, RG 59.

54. Cai, *Minguo Shiji de Tufei*, 247; "Monthly Report," June 1932, 893.00PRAMOY/58, RG 59; "Monthly Report," July 1932, 893.00PRAMOY/59, RG 59; "Monthly Report," December 1932, 893.00PRAMOY/64, RG 59.

55. "Monthly Report," March 1933, 893.00PRAMOY/67, RG 59.

56. "Report," February 7, 1934, D-5501, SMP CID.

57. Fuzhou to State, August 2, 1933, 893.114N16/535, RG 59.

58. "Monthly Reports," December 1933, January 1934, 893.00PRAMOY/76–77, RG 59.

59. *North China Herald*, January–July, 1925.

60. "Fukien Opium King," *North China Herald*, June 30, 1937.

61. "Report," D 5501, SMP CID.

62. "Monthly Report," March 1934, 893.00PRFOOCHOW/75, RG 59.

63. "Monthly Reports," February–March 1934, 893.00PRFOOCHOW/74–75, RG 59; M. R. Nicholson to Treasury, November 9, 1934, box 7283, 893.113NARCOTICS/927, RG 59.

64. "Monthly Report," January 1934, 893.00PRFOOCHOW/73, RG 59; "Monthly Report," March 1935, 893.00PRFOOCHOW/87. "Monthly Report," July 1937, 893.00PRFOOCHOW/114; For the Chen Yi case, see Frederic Wakeman Jr., *Shanghai Badlands: Wartime Terrorism and Urban Crime, 1937–1941* (New York: Cambridge University Press, 1996).

65. "Monthly Report," August 1934, 893.00PRAMOY/84, RG 59; "Monthly Report," September 1934, 893.00PRAMOY/85, RG 59.

66. "Monthly Reports," August–September 1935, 893.00PRAMOY/95–96, RG 59.

67. February 1935–January 1937, 893.00PRFOOCHOW/86–108, RG 59. The

U.S. Consul at Fuzhou likened the government's opium policy to Dr. Jekyl and Mr. Hyde.

68. M. R. Nicholson to Treasury, November 9, 1934, 893.114NARCOTICS/927, RG 59; "Six Poisons Attacking Amoy," March 16, 1936, 893.114NARCOTICS/1734, RG 59.

69. M. R. Nicholson to Treasury, November 9, 1934, 893.114NARCOTICS/927, RG 59.

70. M. R. Nicholson to Treasury, September 15, 1936, 893.114NARCOTICS/1729, RG 59.

71. "Fukien Opium King," *North China Herald*, June 30, 1937; "Monthly Report," June 1937, 893.00PRAMOY/118, RG 59; "Monthly Report," June 1937, 893.00PRFOOCHOW/113, RG 59.

72. Nicholson to Treasury, November 25, 1936, 893.114NARCOTICS/2393, RG 59.

73. Liu Zhennan, "Fujian Shenghui Jingcha Dewuzu Gaikuang" [A survey of the special service organization of the Fujian province party police bureau], *Juntung zai Fujian: Fujian Wenshi Ziliao, no.18* [The military statistics bureau in Fukien province: Fukien source materials, no. 18], 1988, 72.

CHAPTER SEVEN

SOLDIERS OF

FORTUNE

1927 – 1937

The number of Japanese heroin makers on the Chinese mainland increased like ants swarming around honey. The *Mantetsu* Director encouraged their industry and the *Guandong* Army protected it.

Yamauchi Saburo, heroin manufacturer[1]

In December 1928, Consul-General Hayashi of the Mukden, Manchuria, consulate wrote to his superiors in the Foreign Office in Tokyo in response to a general circular soliciting observations about Japanese soldiers of fortune active in China. His observations were bleak. He told his superiors that the activities of these *ronin*, or wave people, interfered with the prosecution of formal Japanese foreign policy by stirring up trouble with the Chinese population. Time and again, he said, his office had urged the Guandong (Japanese) police to control them, but to no effect. There was little he could do. If he were to extradite them, it would help Japan develop a better relationship with the local Chinese population. However, the jurisdictional situation in China was such that *ronin*, once threatened, escaped to areas outside of the consul's control.

The *ronin* would also complain about violation of their civil rights to their supporters in Japan, who included influential politicians and high-ranking army officers. The consul did not identify any one backer by name, but he urged the Tokyo authorities to try to sever the connections between influential individuals at home and the *ronin*. He also requested that the Guandong Civil Office chief Kinoshita Kenjiro be told about the threat the *ronin* posed.[2]

At the time, Consul-General Hayashi and his foreign minister, Tanaka Giichi (Tanaka was also prime minister at the time) were in the midst of damage control. Six months earlier Colonel Komoto Daisaku, acting independently of Tokyo authorities, murdered Zhang Zuolin, who, as the local warlord, represented Chinese government in the area. The act of insubordination was all the more blatant because Tanaka Giichi was himself a general who had joined the political party *Seiyukai* after a distinguished military career. In response to the incident, the Foreign Office kept a file of potential troublemakers covering from 1928 to 1932.

JAPANESE POLICIES IN TRANSITION

In a larger sense, Consul-General Hayashi was documenting a transition in Japanese politics taking place over those years, one in which Japanese soldiers of fortune and midlevel army officers were playing an increasing role. Japan had entered the modern age guided by the Meiji oligarchs, who controlled its government and foreign relations with a strong guiding hand. In the 1920s, however, as those elder statesmen died, a new generation of leaders came to the fore who used political parties as their avenue to power. Hara Kei of the *Seiyukai*, for instance, had made his peace with the elder statesmen, worked with them for more than a decade, and finally became prime minister in 1918. Thus political parties gave 1920s Japan the look of an emerging democracy, even though the cabinets continued to be chosen rather than elected.

In foreign policy, Japan participated in the prevailing internationalism of the early 1920s. Japan joined the League of Nations and the arms limitation conferences held during the decade. China policy too took a negotiated path of international cooperation rather than unilateral military action. This soft policy was opposed by men, primarily in the military, who felt that collective security and party government were eating away at the basis of Japanese culture and national strength. They saw Japanese interests in Asia being threatened by Western expansion and growing demonstrations of Chinese nationalism. Late in the 1920s this second group began to exert some influence. Since they could not act through formal government channels, they privately launched counterpolicies using the *ronin* as their agents. In doing so they set the stage for the militarism of the 1930s. It was at this juncture that Hayashi made his observations.

The political transition from oligarchy to party government to covert action against the parties was reflected in the structure of the Japanese narcotics industry as well. In the age of the oligarchs, Nitanosa and Hoshi had flourished through their contacts with Goto Shimpei. Hoshi's downfall came when political party members opened his monopoly to other players, ushering in a decade of open competition among Japanese traffickers in China. The 1920s saw narcotics manufacturing move into the hands of small operators on the Chinese mainland closer to the market. In the late 1920s military officers tapped the traffic's financial potential when furthering their political ends. The same *ronin* who played an active role in undermining the soft policy also had links to the narcotics industry. They were men who built careers in the shadows of China's civil war and thus were well placed as middlemen between army officers and traffickers.

POLITICIANS AND NARCOTICS

Narcotics traffickers were ready to adapt to any political change. Thus it is no surprise that even Hara Kei had his reputation stained by drugs. Hara Kei was prime minister from 1918 to 1921. He was known as a man skilled in compromise; he personally guided the *Seiyukai* from shaky beginnings at the turn of the century into a developed party with grass roots organization and support. During his tenure as prime minister he regularly appointed *Seiyukai* men to bureaucratic posts, hoping to extend party control into areas previously dominated by oligarchic supporters. The inevitable political friction between the two factions demanded that these appointees be as honest as possible. They often proved not to be immune to lucrative temptations.

Political scandals punctuated Hara's years in office. The Manchurian opium scandal, for example, became a subject of public interest in the spring of 1921. In February 1919, one of Hara's closest cronies, Koga Renzo, became the head of the Dairen Colonial Bureau. From this office Koga appointed his own protégé, Nakano Arimitsu, to the Guandong Civil Administration. In this position, Nakano was in charge of the opium monopoly. He found that he had stepped into a money pipeline.[3]

Koga began handing out opium franchises to friends, including one Kajii Sakari, a man variously described as a merchant, a journalist, and a soldier of fortune. Kajii was something of a China expert and had once acted as an escort for a group of *Seiyukai* Diet members visiting Manchuria. Kajii used his opium revenues to funnel funds to soldiers of fortune in North China, and through them to selected Chinese politicians and generals. Opium money could be used in this way to buy influence on the mainland.[4]

Opium money could also be useful at home. Nakano, at the request of Koga, had appointed a certain Kobata Teijiro to the Anti-Smoking Bureau of the *Kosai Zendo*, the organ responsible for opium licensing. Kobata channeled funds into the campaign chests of select *Seiyukai* candidates. Between June 1919 and September 1920 Kobata deposited more than ¥710,000 into an Osaka bank account under an assumed name to be redistributed for that purpose.

Kobata proved to be the weak link. Dairen police (Japanese) noted his movements and those of his friends. In 1921 they had enough evidence to arrest the ringleaders and expose the setup to the embarrassment of the *Seiyukai*. Publicly, army patriots claimed that politicians corrupted a drug licensing system set up to benefit Chinese addicts. Yet Koga's downfall resulted, not from his corruption of a pristine system but because personnel of the South Manchurian Railway and in the police force of the Guandong Leased Territory resented political upstarts encroaching on their territory. Therefore authorities vigorously investigated activities that under different circumstances would have been overlooked.[5]

Japanese democracy of the 1920s was inherently unstable, as were the political parties that served it. Hara Kei was assassinated in 1921. Thereafter the *Seiyukai* regrouped several times, finally finding a measure of stability in the leadership of General Tanaka Giichi. Smaller parties formed, dissolved, and reappeared, and in 1927 the *Minseito* became a second large party. Such conditions were not symptoms of a vibrant party system, nor did constant revelations of corruption in government that accompanied the political struggles convince the public at large of the strong moral fiber of most politicians. Indeed, many Japanese came to consider the entire constitutional apparatus as weak and corrupt. They scorned the cabinet for its willingness to adopt a soft, passive posture toward the Western powers, which could result in Japanese losses of hard-won gains on the Asian mainland.

Those who were most disaffected were younger members of Japan's

armed services. They were especially concerned with Japan's China policy. Middle-ranking army and navy officers considered that the national
interest had been betrayed by their government's agreement to arms
limitation treaties such as that signed in Washington D.C. in 1922 cutting Japanese naval strength to three-fifths of that allowed to Great Britain and America. Because they were so firmly convinced that they owed
loyalty to a higher power than the constitutional government of Japan,
namely, their emperor, they had no hesitation about acting outside of
the law. Using as agents the soldiers of fortune who roamed throughout
China in the war-torn 1920s and funding them in part by opium revenues, these dissident officers were able to initiate covert actions that
altered the plans of the civil government at home twice, in 1928 and in
1931.[6]

SOLDIERS OF FORTUNE

The *ronin*, or soldiers of fortune, were admittedly romantic characters
and often brave men. In the context of highly structured Japanese society, they were rebels. Unwilling or unable to fulfill the expectations of a
hierarchical society in Japan, they sought adventure and fortune in
China. Paradoxically, although they seemed to reject their society's values, they considered themselves to be quintessential Japanese. They
lived martial, adventurous lives, the embodiment of the true Japanese
spirit that they claimed was being eroded by corrupting Western in-
fluences: liberalism, capitalism, communism, jazz, and women who
smoked.

In the 1920s, they pointed to their own politicians' weaknesses, especially in foreign affairs, as a sign of this corruption. During that decade,
Japan, like many European nations, seemed committed to arms control
and collective security. Japan's martial spirit waned. The prestige of the
Japanese Imperial Army had sunk to such a low point in the early 1920s
that soldiers hesitated to wear their uniforms off base for fear of harassment. By the late 1920s Japan's internationalist foreign policy seemed
critically dangerous, coming as it did at a time of growing nationalism
in China.

In the 1920s, China was changing. Sun Yat-sen, the symbol of the 1911
Revolution, died early in 1925; the next year Chiang Kai-shek began his
Northern Expedition to unify the country. Chiang's successes derived
from aggressively patriotic rhetoric as much as guns. His agents appealed to the Chinese population through messages of antiforeignism.

At first the Soviet Union alone among the foreign powers supported the *Guomindang*. This, along with the early alliance between the *Guomindang* and the Chinese Communist Party, made Japanese who were concerned with China particularly sensitive about any intrusions on Japanese rights and interests in Asia just when many Chinese were challenging them.

Japanese living in China felt themselves to be under attack everywhere, especially after 1925. That year British and Japanese police in Shanghai shot at striking Chinese workers, which further incited antiforeign demonstrations. Chinese patriots advocated the boycott of foreign goods as a weapon the common people could use against imperial aggression. Although Japanese authorities pressured Chinese leaders to quell the protests, from 1925 through the outbreak of war in 1937 anti-Japanese boycotts reappeared whenever Sino-Japanese tensions neared the boiling point.

RENEWED CHINESE NATIONALISM

Chinese anti-opium groups joined forces with boycott movements. One such endeavor was initiated by Yan Yuheng in Manchuria in the 1930s. Yan was a member of the Y.M.C.A. in China who had connections with Chinese merchant and student groups. In 1930 he formed the Foreign Affairs Recovery Group, which used newspaper editorials, musical performances, and speeches to denounce the Japanese presence in Manchuria. Yan also allied himself with the Anti-Opium Association established in Shanghai in the early twenties.

Yan's activities included public meetings, such as one held on June 3, 1930, to commemorate the 1839 incident that caused the Opium War. Activists read one of Commissioner Lin Zexu's anti-opium memorials. They then celebrated Lin's earlier decisive action by publicly burning opium themselves. Yan gave many speeches throughout Manchuria in which he clarified the common goals of the anti-opium movement and the general boycott. "To boycott opium is to boycott the spread of foreign poison in our country," he said. He added a second message to arouse his listeners. Expressing the deep anger he felt whenever he saw refined opiates available in foreign shops, he called morphine "racial genocide" and a product that was making the Chinese government weak and unable to resist foreign aggression. His activities were so successful in the early thirties that the Japanese Guandong police department carefully kept a file on his associations.[7]

Yan, along with other Chinese patriots in the boycott movement, called for the recovery of Chinese rights lost through years of unequal treaties. His was a patriotic platform with a message endorsed by Western powers. Still, Japanese observers had reason to be cynical about Yan's motives. They noted that he was backed by the Chinese government of Zhang Xueliang, son of Zhang Zuolin, whose assassination in 1928 caused the Japanese government so much distress. They knew, as did most Manchurian residents, that the Zhang Zuolin government also derived revenues from opium. The Japanese police report noted that Yan established his group just at a time when the Chinese Eastern Railroad created tensions between the two countries. Thus they felt Yan's patriotism was mere fallout from the assassination of Zhang Zuolin.

The Chinese Eastern Railroad was created by Zhang Zuolin as a move to strengthen his power in the north. Zhang Zuolin had maintained a strong presence in the tumultuous warlord era through the 1910s and 1920s with the assistance of Japanese military advisers. By 1925 he extended his control into North China and briefly as far south as Shanghai. Although Zhang owed much to Japanese aid, his primary concern was survival. As the Northern Expedition proceeded, he seemed ready to make a warlord alliance to fight the *Guomindang*. At the same time, for strategic purposes and to cater to the nationalistic feelings of Manchurians, he began building the Chinese Eastern Railroad, which would compete directly with the Japanese South Manchurian Railway.[8]

THE JAPANESE POSTURE IN ASIA

Against this backdrop of renewed Chinese nationalism, Japanese living in China demanded a stronger foreign policy than they were getting from their home government. Tanaka Giichi seemed to be just the politician that Japanese in Manchuria desired. In 1925, Tanaka became the new president of the reorganized *Seiyukai* party. Tanaka was a career military officer and a protégé of the Meiji oligarchs. He had served in Manchuria, in Korea, and on the general staff. He advocated a strong independent role for Japan in the world, especially in Asia. Tanaka felt that Japanese control of Manchuria and Mongolia was essential to national well-being. Thus those Japanese advocating a stronger posture in Asia had cause to rejoice early in 1927 when Tanaka Giichi, as leader of the *Seiyukai* party, became prime minister.[9]

Tanaka immediately appointed Yamamoto Jotaro to be the director of the South Manchurian Railway. Yamamoto had served as the Shanghai branch office chief of Mitsui Shipping Company until he began his political career in 1915. He believed, as did Tanaka, that Manchuria and Mongolia should be developed into an industrial base for Japan separate from China. As soon as he got to Manchuria, he began negotiations with Zhang Zuolin to forestall the planned competitive railway. Through a combination of persuasion and threat he managed to bring Zhang around on the railway issue. He also began ambitious plans both to extend the South Manchurian Railway's lines and to expand its economic scope. Because of Yamamoto, Zhang seemed under control.[10]

But there were others in Manchuria who still considered Zhang Zuolin a potential liability, especially as it became obvious that he could not hold North China against the *Guomindang* forces. Chiang Kai-shek, who had halted the Northern Expedition a year before to purge the party of Communists and to consolidate his control, began to march north again. Some warlords read the writing on the wall and went over to the Nationalist side. Zhang Zuolin refused to budge. He remained in Beijing at the head of a fraying coalition.

Japanese feared the outbreak of disorders in areas that they tentatively controlled should the warlords lose. In response to the situation, the Japanese army moved into Shandong province in April of that same year, in order, they claimed, to protect national interests. In May, the army informed Zhang Zuolin that it would maintain order in Manchuria if he could not. This was a veiled threat that should any disorders arise in his absence, Zhang would lose his province to Japanese control. Thus in June 1928, Zhang returned to Manchuria to protect his stronghold. En route, saboteurs bombed his train as it passed over the tracks of the South Manchurian Railway. Zhang Zuolin died soon thereafter.

The assassination had not been sanctioned by Tanaka; indeed, it interfered with his own plans. It was the work of one Komoto Daisaku, a staff officer with the Guandong Army, who hoped that the mood set in Manchuria by the Tanaka policy would allow for the immediate Japanese occupation of the area. In 1928, he was not so much wrong as ahead of his time. The hoped-for operation would not begin until 1931.

The Zhang Zuolin affair ultimately brought down the Tanaka cabinet. It allowed Tanaka's political enemies at home to scrutinize the dealings of those close to him. As in the case with Hara Kei before him, revelations showed that Tanaka's political allies used the machinery of state to further their own goals and fill their bank accounts in the process. The findings demonstrated that the earlier opium scandal had not been an isolated affair.

Yamamoto Jotaro, for instance, brought his circle of friends with him to Manchuria. These friends, such as Yamazaki Takeshi, formed the core of a group, dubbed by one writer as the Manchurian interests movement, that agitated for a stronger Japanese presence in Manchuria. Their activities, which often bordered on banditry, were meant to counter the Chinese rights recovery agitation. Because they could not be funded by the government, even with a passively friendly Tanaka cabinet, they needed to look elsewhere for financial support. The benzolyne scandal, publicized only after the Tanaka cabinet fell, exposed one of their sources of funding.

This story has a modern ring to it; in today's world Yamamoto's cronies would be accused of creating designer drugs. In October 1927, an officer of the Department of Communications discovered upon inspection that a substance coming to Dairen from Germany, labeled as benzolyne, in fact contained 80 percent morphine. This substance entered Manchuria legally by parcel post. Enterprising middlemen then added acetyl chloride to separate the benzol from the morphine.[11]

Once they discovered the deception, Japanese officials restricted benzolyne in accordance with League of Nations guidelines to which Japan had recently subscribed. Nevertheless, a rider to the prohibition allowed anyone with orders already placed or in transit prior to the prohibition's enactment to bring the amount under contract into the port after December 1, 1927, when the new rule went into effect.

Around this same time General Kinoshita Kenjiro became the chief of the Guandong civil administration. One of Yamamoto's cohorts, Yamazaki Takeshi, acted as his right-hand man. For the next year Yamazaki used his position to create false permits acknowledging benzolyne orders made prior to October 1927 for his friends. In this way 8,000 kilos of the specially doctored benzolyne entered Manchuria. The profits went to support the Japanese soldiers of fortune whose activities increased in intensity between 1928 and 1931.[12]

Once the Tanaka cabinet, which had provided a brief period of strong foreign policy, became tainted with the assassination of Zhang Zuolin, it had to retreat from its aggressive stance. In 1929, after Tanaka resigned under pressure, Japanese diplomats returned to a more accommodating international posture. At the same time, Zhang Xueliang, the slain warlord's son, quite naturally became anti-Japanese. He allied himself with the *Guomindang* and gave official sanction to both anti-Japanese boycotts and an anti-opium campaign.

Under the circumstances of growing Chinese nationalism in Manchuria, it was possible for many Japanese to see the activities of the soldiers of fortune as sincere and patriotic. Both major Japanese parties were dragging their heels on the situation in China. Therefore, as the soldiers of fortune took Japan's foreign policy into their own hands, they could claim a higher form of patriotic morality. Their well-placed military connections gave them a kind of legitimacy, while the treaty situation in China provided them with the legal immunity of extraterritoriality that, as the Japanese consul lamented, made them uncontrollable. In the three years between the assassination of Zhang Zuolin and the creation of Manchukuo in 1931, they operated in an atmosphere of intensifying crisis.

It was easy for Japanese living in Manchuria to see the reforms of Zhang Xueliang as self-serving political maneuvers. Zhang was not the ideal anti-opium crusader. Like his father before him, he used opium and he understood the financial benefits that could accrue from the drug traffic. In 1925, for instance, when Manchurian troops briefly held control over Shanghai under Zhang Xueliang's command, they had tried to put into operation an opium monopoly scheme to pay for the military operations. However, Zhang Zuolin found it difficult to wrest the local opium trade from the well-established Green Gang, a lesson the Japanese would learn twelve years later when they occupied Shanghai. They gave up the attempt after the assassination of Zhang's commissioner and several others connected with the scheme.[13]

In 1929, however, filial piety and a strong fear that his patrimony in Manchuria would be wrested from him by the Japanese military, a fear born out in fact in 1932, convinced Zhang Xueliang to put his full support behind the anti-opium effort and full-scale boycott of Japanese goods, which included the activities of Yan Yuheng and the renewed building of the rival Chinese Eastern Railroad. Thus when Japanese police informers carefully noted that one Gao Ximing, known to be a crony of Zhang Xueliang rather than a passionate reformer, was among the speakers in Yen's anti-opium programs, they had good reason to suspect that the entire purpose of the campaign was anti-Japanese. Reform clearly hid a larger agenda.[14]

JAPANESE "NATIONAL WARRIORS"

Chinese movements that attacked both opium and foreigners, coupled with a government in Tokyo perceived to be weak, created an atmosphere in Manchuria in which many Japanese who felt threatened organized on their own for action. This provided a new outlet for the soldiers of fortune who had thrived during the years of civil strife following the Chinese revolution. The story of Sakaihara Masao demonstrates the connection between army and private policy. It shows the role that soldiers of fortune and opium played in Manchuria. Sakaihara, a Japanese Christian with a German wife, had amassed a sizable estate in Mukden province. In 1929 he discovered that Zhang Xueliang planned to build a narrow gauge rail line from Mukden to his martyred father's tomb, the tracks of which would run through Sakaihara's land. Sakaihara complained to the Japanese authorities, but found, in those times of accommodation, that his government would not aid him.

Sakaihara brought together a band of several hundred Japanese adventurers, whom he called "national warriors," to "fight those Chinese illegally trampling on Japanese rights." His group disrupted construction of the Chinese railway. Fearing a conflict could erupt from this effort, the Japanese Guandong Army sent a company of soldiers under the leadership of Tomiya Tetsuo. The presence of these troops not only insured that the Chinese rail construction ended permanently but also terminated Chinese control of the area in question. According to Yamauchi Saburo, a confessed heroin manufacturer, Japanese control transformed the area into a haven for the narcotics business.[15]

The atmosphere in Manchuria nurtured adventurers like the national warriors of Sakaihara. These soldiers of fortune enjoyed tacit support from the Japanese army. In return there were financial rewards for the adventurers. As unofficial agents, the *ronin* had several advantages. They were not as conspicuous as army personnel, and through their mercenary activities in China they had become familiar with the political terrain. They had access to useful information, and many had well-placed Chinese connections. Their unofficial actions continued Japanese expansion in China while the government at home pursued its official policy of international cooperation. Best of all, if and when they were caught, their actions could officially be denied.[16] The *ronin* became the agents of army officers pursuing a private foreign policy that remained unaccountable to the Japanese government as a constitutional body. Their activities continued, in part, because the narcotics trade provided them with a lucrative source of funding.

The activities of Abe Yoshinari demonstrate how soldiers of fortune fit into the dynamics of Japanese expansion in China. Abe showed up in Shandong province late in 1928, just when the Japanese were about to lose control of the area. Shandong province, situated just south of Manchuria, is important in the Chinese political landscape, not only for its strategic position, located as it is between the sea and Beijing, but because it is the birthplace of Confucius and Mencius. Shandong had been a German concession since 1897. In 1914 Japanese troops, as allies of Great Britain, occupied the province, laying claim to the German area. Japanese merchants moved to the province, protected by the Japanese army, which remained in formal control of the Shandong railway, and the important cities of Jinan and Qingdao until 1922. Even after the army officially left the territory, a strong Japanese presence remained.

Shandong was also an area in which Japanese opium merchants had prospered. When the Japanese occupation of Shandong began in 1915, the army established an opium monopoly bureau in the old German concession areas. In Shandong this agency operated even more loosely than it did in the Manchurian railway zone. The army authorized a local merchant, Liu Zeshan, to act as the local opium broker. Liu split his profits seventy/thirty with the Japanese army, wisely turning over the larger share to his military allies. During the years of occupation the army purchased real estate with profits from opium, using Chinese agents to obscure the transactions. After the Japanese army withdrew from Shandong, the opium trade fell into the hands of those Japanese merchants who remained. By 1931, one Japanese government official estimated that of the 2,000 Japanese residing in Jinan, the largest city in Shandong, half were involved in the trade.[17]

In 1925 the warlord Zhang Zongchang, known with little affection as the 'dog meat general,' became military governor of the province. Zhang, although not related to Zhang Zuolin, was allied with the Manchurian warlord. He was dependent on opium to finance his periodic wars. He was also beholden to Japanese soldiers of fortune, many of whom acted as his advisers. For instance, a certain Sado, a Japanese resident of Qingdao, owned a machine shop noted as a gathering place for other *ronin*, where men in Chinese army uniforms could be seen coming and going. Sado used his occupation as a front for opium sales that financed the even more important business of gunrunning. Sado worked for Zhang. Another resident of the port was a Japanese named Fujita, an ex-naval officer who helped Zhang establish an opium processing plant. Zhang stayed in Shandong until 1927, when the victories of Chiang Kai-shek's Nationalist army from the south forced him into retirement. He left Shandong for Japan, taking with him two of his forty concubines and a small fortune.[18]

In the vacuum left between the retreat of Zhang and the onset of a tentative Nationalist rule, the province became a magnet for adventur-

ers like Abe Yoshinari. Abe appeared on the scene, claiming to be the
secretly appointed emissary of Prime Minister Tanaka Giichi, charged
with the assignment of conducting talks with the Nationalist army about
withdrawal of troops. In this guise he began meeting with Chinese residents of the area. His activities came to the attention of the Ministry of
Foreign Affairs and provoked a written disavowal of any connections
from Tanaka himself.

Nevertheless, Abe was hard to control. He had previously been known
as a trafficker in arms and opium. Despite a break with previous partners, he still had connections in the business. Investigations revealed
that in 1928, only a few months after the assassination of Zhang Zuolin,
Abe was involved in a plot to assassinate Chiang Kai-shek, for which he
had received explosives from a General Yamaguchi Toya. The murder
did not take place.[19]

Considered as an individual, Abe was a misfit who was a minor embarrassment to his government. On a larger scale he was representative of
soldiers of fortune operating in the 1920s. As Japanese politicians formally relinquished territory on the Chinese mainland in a gesture of
internationalism, men like Abe maintained an informal presence in the
area. As a private citizen he gave active support to local Chinese army
commanders, while maintaining private connections to a particular Japanese officer. Although his assassination plot went nowhere, his willingness to entertain the proposal seriously enough for it to surface in a
Foreign Office file is typical of the behavior of many of his companions.
He was not the romantic patriot that *ronin* are often made out to be. He
was a man with a troubled personality who found a comfortable niche
in the shadows between illicit narcotics and arms trafficking and licit
mercenary activity. The conditions of the late 1920s in North China gave
him the opportunity to take foreign policy into his own hands.

SOLDIERS OF FORTUNE AND NARCOTICS

The role that soldiers of fortune played in the narcotics traffic is described by heroin maker Yamauchi Saburo. Yamauchi was a small-scale,
independent chemist who worked in Manchuria in the early 1930s. He
was one of a number of entrepreneurs who filled the vacuum left by the
demise of the Hoshi Pharmaceutical Company. These men located their
operations on the Asian mainland closer to the market. They often used
Japanese soldiers of fortune to deliver their product across borders. Following the trend of legitimate businesses, Japanese-owned morphine

and heroin factories began to spring up in Japanese concessions on the Chinese mainland where cheap labor and easier transportation increased their profits and made them more competitive. By the late 1920s, the Japanese product had all but pushed European brands out of China.[20]

In 1933 the American and British consular reports noted this trend. M. R. Nicholson stated that the manufacture and primary distribution of heroin in North China had become consolidated in Japanese hands over the years since 1929. His sources claimed that Japanese experts in production established themselves in the area and were able to produce a good product at a low price. As a result, heroin from Europe, which sold at £100–£125 per kilogram in 1926, dropped to £70 in 1929. At the same time heroin produced in China sold at £34 to £38 per kilogram. From the mid-1920s on, Japanese producers concentrated on heroin and found they could make improvements in its production. They hired young chemists who were sent to Europe to study alkaloids. By 1933 there were over forty narcotics factories in Manchuria. The market price of their product dropped so low it ended entirely the import of European heroin to China.[21]

Yamauchi Saburo left a record of his heroin business in his memoirs. In 1930 Yamauchi started out in Qingdao, Shandong province, where he worked in a heroin factory. In 1934 he relocated to Dairen, founding the South Manchuria Pharmaceutical Company, capitalized at ¥50,000. He did not have a factory but set up clandestine operations in an apple orchard where ten teams of three men worked at night distilling the heroin. Each group could produce ten kilos in an evening, which yielded gross profits of ¥5 million to ¥10 million each year.[22]

Nevertheless, expenses ate into his profits. Necessities like ether and alcohol he acquired cheaply enough through the Mitsubishi Company. More significant were the payments he made to his suppliers of crude morphine and the army officers who protected them. He claimed that some of his fellow heroin manufacturers (and we may assume that this also included Yamauchi) donated as much as ¥50,000 to local units of the Japanese Imperial Army, for which they received decorations presented in formal military ceremonies.[23]

Chemists like Yamauchi indeed produced a good cheap product. They improved the quality of the heroin by substituting acetone for ether in the distilling process, giving the resulting residue less bulk and producing a lower burning point in their heroin, which smokers appreciated. Japanese brand names, such as Tianjin LowBulk, advertised this trait.[24]

Yamauchi and other heroin makers used *ronin* as distributors. They found the soldiers of fortune to be independent and resourceful men. Yamauchi used one distributor who shipped heroin packed in cans of *nori* (the dark green seaweed product wrapped around sushi) from a popular department store in Dairen. In the early days of Yamauchi's career, heroin makers led precarious lives. If a factory were raided by the Chinese police, heroin makers would often set the facility on fire, causing the chemicals used in the process to explode, endangering both themselves and the police. At times heroin makers preyed on one another, raiding one another's operations and fighting over turf.[25]

Perhaps the quintessential soldier of fortune was Amakasu Masahiko. It was he who would eventually coordinate *ronin* activities. He was connected to the September 18, 1931, incident that created a Japanese-controlled state in Northeast China that was the culmination of four years of private foreign policy. Amakasu had been a member of the military elite. He graduated from the war college in 1906 and entered the *Kempei*, or military police, where he became a protégé of Tojo Hideki, later the leader of Japan's war cabinet. Amakasu's career took an uncommon turn in 1923, after the Great Taisho Earthquake destroyed Tokyo. Taking advantage of the chaos, he arrested and then strangled an anarchist, as well as the anarchist's wife and young nephew, for which he spent some time in prison and was relieved of his commission.[26]

This brutal act did not make Amakasu persona non grata in military circles. After his release from jail in 1929, he went to Manchuria and lived a life in the shadows until the end of the Second World War. He put together an organization of irregulars that eventually penetrated to the heart of China proper and acted as an informal spy network. Amakasu's organization was capable of any kind of mischief, yet he was intensely loyal to emperor and nation, to the extent that he shot himself rather than accept surrender at the war's end. Although no longer in the military after 1923, he kept close contacts with his old friends. His was a life of independent action and intrigue, yet he was amenable to tough military discipline. Indeed he respected Tojo Hideki, who had been his drill leader when he was an initiate at the military academy, because of the rigor and precision of the training he received. Amakasu was cultured and liked to dress well. In Manchuria he would often invite friends to his home where he would cook them a gourmet Chinese meal.[27]

From 1929 to 1931, not even his family knew precisely what he was doing. He traveled the length and breadth of Manchuria and often went to Tokyo to visit the head office of the Manchuria Railway Company's Asian Economic Research Bureau; indeed, there were hints that he was in their employ. In the fall of 1931, Amakasu told a friend that he had undertaken a new project. On September 18 of that year the friend discovered the nature of this task. That evening young officers in the Guandong Army abruptly ended the tense standoff with Zhang Xueliang in Manchuria by secretly placing a bomb on the tracks of the South Manchurian Railway. They blamed this sabotage of their own doing on Chinese bandits and used the incident as an excuse to create the puppet state of Manchukuo.

This incident had been planned well in advance, not by the general staff in Tokyo, but by a group of radical young officers in the Guandong army. Like Komoto Daisaku, who planned the Zhang Zuolin assassination, these officers, led by Colonel (later General) Ishiwara Kanji and Colonel (later General, then class A war criminal) Itagaki Seishiro, made their own decisive move because they felt that they were betrayed by a soft policy at home. They learned lessons from the Zhang Zuolin affair, however, and their actions were better planned. Immediate military action followed the bomb blast, and Manchuria was occupied by the Japanese army before the authorities in Tokyo had time to respond to international complaints. By February 1932, the state of Manchukuo replaced the three northeastern provinces of China, and the home government passed from the leadership of political party men into the hands of army sympathizers. In 1933, Japan left the League of Nations and incorporated the neighboring province of Rehe into Manchukuo.

Immediately after the initial incident, Amakasu moved to Harbin, a large city in the north close to the Soviet Union, where he and a group of trusted men staged incidents to be blamed on the Chinese, thereby insuring that the fighting would escalate. From this point on, Amakasu took charge of bringing the best of the *ronin* under his control. There came to be a saying among the residents of the three northeastern provinces that Manchuria belonged to the Guandong Army by day but to Amakasu by night.

A military action of the sort carried out by Itagaki Seishiro and Ishiwara Kanji required substantial funding. Five months before the incident occurred, the plotters sent representatives to Tokyo to visit high-ranking officers whom they knew to be sympathetic to their cause. The goal was to raise money needed for carrying out the extensive military action in Manchuria. The nature of the plot called for the utmost secrecy, of course, and little money was forthcoming from legitimate sources. Therefore the members turned to Fujita Osamu for a solution to their financial worries.

Fujita Osamu was born in Fukuoka prefecture in 1887. He attended Wasada University evening school. After graduation he became a reporter. When the First World War began, he followed the Japanese army to Shandong province where he made and lost a fortune selling heroin. He returned to Japan where he worked for various local papers. He used his newspaper connections and ties to Fukuoka nobility to expand his acquaintances into influential circles. In the 1920s his friends included Goto Shimpei, as well as notable political activists from both the political left and right. He also continued to traffic in narcotics. In 1925, for instance, he put together a deal with Zhang Zongchang in Shandong province.[28]

One problem that Fujita straightened out involved a major Japanese trading company. Facing bankruptcy because of the postwar business slump, the company bought a shipload of Indian opium, hoping to sell it in China, make a windfall profit, and so balance its books. Yet the company found it could do nothing in China without running afoul of the local gangs. It turned to Fujita, who successfully managed the transaction, receiving a commission of ¥300,000.

Yamauchi Saburo claimed that Fujita financed the establishment of Manchukuo. His contribution came about when the Manchurian conspirators were looking for money to finance the initial operation in summer 1931. The plot required secrecy; no money could be derived from the Japanese government without alerting the wrong people. To solve the problem, one of the conspirators, Colonel Itagaki Seishiro, contacted Colonel Hashimoto Kingoro, a fellow graduate of the military academy. Hashimoto was a Russian expert who had himself served in Manchuria. He was also an active ultranationalist distressed by decadent Japanese society. To that end he organized the Cherry Blossom Society, a group of young officers dedicated to reforming the Japanese government by violent means if necessary.

Itagaki met with Hashimoto in Tokyo two months before the September incident, and the two men shared ideas. Hashimoto assumed that action in Manchuria would create conditions favorable to reform at home; therefore he offered to help. Hashimoto first approached private contributors for funds with little success. The Cherry Blossom Society included Colonel (later General, then class A war criminal) Cho Isamu, who in 1938 would be instrumental in setting up the Japanese-run opium bureaucracy in occupied Shanghai. Cho, in turn, knew Fujita, as did his close friend and fellow society member, Colonel Shigeto Chiaki. They introduced Fujita to Hashimoto, after which Fujita contributed ¥50,000 to the cause, which Hashimoto handed over to the conspirators. It was enough to cover the expenses of the early operation on September 18, 1931. It is no exaggeration to agree with Yamauchi and say that Fujita's opium profits financed the Japanese takeover of Manchuria. After the initial occupation, Manchurian coffers fell under the control of the Japanese army.[29]

Increased control of heroin manufacturers occurred naturally after the creation of Manchukuo. In spite of the fiction that Japanese maintained for foreign consumption—that the new state was independent and sovereign—Manchukuo was perhaps the most perfect example of a puppet state that has ever existed. Its government had Chinese or Manchurians in charge of each bureau, just as it had its Manchurian emperor. But vice ministers, Japanese to a man, actually ran the affairs of state. This government immediately established an Opium Monopoly Bureau, which began the process of bringing narcotics producers in the three northeastern provinces under control. Yamauchi felt the effects of this move.

HEROIN PRODUCTION IN MANCHURIA AND NORTH CHINA

The years from 1929 to 1936 saw an increasing systematization of heroin manufacture in Manchuria and North China. Competition was intense, and the entrepreneurs required political protection. Those who did not have the proper connections did not survive. A 1936 report describes only six narcotics factories in Tianjin, where there had once been seventeen. Fires and explosions got rid of some, and a Japanese government crackdown eliminated the rest. The six remaining factories were in the hands of experienced chemists.[30]

As the 1930s wore on, heroin manufacturers and distributors increasingly came under the control of the army, especially the *Kempeitai*, or military police, and the Special Service Section, or army intelligence. The survivors accommodated themselves to the army, assuring themselves and their distributors safe passage along railways and across borders. Over the years the entire industry was systematized. Japanese acted as the chemists and wholesalers, while Koreans or Chinese ran the retail shops.[31]

Japanese flooded into Manchukuo. Bureaucrats came from Japan to set up the machinery of a new country whose purpose was to enhance Japan's own industrial and military capability. Along with them came a host of new soldiers of fortune, Japanese down on their luck who hoped to make a better life in the new land. One man who appeared in Manchukuo soon after its establishment was Nitanosa Otozo. Part of the Japanese drive toward Manchurian economic development was their renewal of the opium growing program. Thus in the early 1930s, after ten years of obscurity, Nitanosa once again reigned as the opium king. This time it was not bureaucrats who called on his expertise but the army. Earlier when he had traveled to Korea to advise on poppy planting conditions, he found the soil to be inferior. At that time he noted that Manchurian soil contained the proper combination of loam and sand. The Korean experiment had never produced morphine-rich poppies, and given the international pressures of the day, it had been abandoned. In 1934, however, Nitanosa found just the right growing conditions in the county of Andong in Fengtien province of Manchuria.

Nitanosa's trip to Manchuria, one of three he would make during the Japanese occupation of China, was the adventure of a lifetime. In 1934, the Manchurian countryside was not yet pacified, nor was transportation convenient or comfortable beyond the railway lines. It was the first time that Nitanosa, the farmer, had been on a horse, not an experience he remembered fondly. The journey, filled with rumors of rebels, had to be made with a military guard. On the way, however, Nitanosa befriended Miyazawa Shuji, a twenty-eight-year-old agent of the newly established Manchukuo Opium Monopoly Bureau. Soon after Nitanosa returned to his poppy farm in Osaka, Miyazawa joined him and became his apprentice. In 1936, Miyazawa returned to Manchukuo with a letter of commendation from his mentor, and himself became the poppy expert of the expanding Japanese empire. He worked in Jehol and later in Mongolia, where extensive poppy fields continued to blossom as Japanese armies fanned out into North China. [32]

The development of the opium industry in Manchukuo was no longer constrained by Japanese concerns about international opinion. Once Japan was out of the League of Nations, Japanese army personnel could ignore the Narcotics Advisory Board regulations with impunity. In 1934, one year after Japan left the League, supervised poppy plantings began in Manchuria. Increasingly during the 1930s, and especially after 1936, foreign observers reported that Japanese army officials used the idealistic rhetoric of opium control to eliminate independent competitors, not opium use.

One notorious competitor was the "toad general," Tang Yulin. Tang had been the head of the Rehe provincial committee before the creation of Manchukuo. He was a comrade-in-arms to Zhang Zuolin from the early days when they were little more than bandits, and later he became the head of his secret police. After the death of Chang, Tang took over the local administration of the Rehe province, a strategic area southwest of Manchuria and north of Beijing. In this capacity he dominated the opium and heroin traffic of the area.

At one point, early in his operation, he ran into conflict with the anti-opium boycott sponsored by Zhang Xueliang. In 1929, overzealous Mukden police raided the local residence of Tang while undertaking a roundup of known opium dens in that city. A standoff ensued, and for several weeks police guards sealed off the building before an amicable settlement could be reached. Until 1932, Tang ran his own heroin factories, reportedly established under Japanese supervision. After that date, however, he lost his concession to a Japanese syndicate, the Itahara (probably the Sakata) group.[33]

Zhang Xueliang did not give up on the idea of an opium monopoly either. In 1932, as his Manchurian army staged the last efforts to regain Chinese control of the provinces being incorporated into the Japanese puppet state of Manchukuo, Zhang Xueliang raised money to pay his troops from the licensed sale of opium in those districts of North China still under his control. Revenues came to his hands through an institution located in Beijing called the Northeastern Fund Raising Society, which sold opium in fifty- and one-hundred-ounce packages. In this venture Zhang Xueliang relied on the expertise of his father's old colleague, Tang Yulin.[34]

The defeat of Zhang Xueliang and the fall of operators like Tang Yulin was the first step in the rationalization of the industry. The increasing control of the soldiers of fortune by Amakasu strengthened that tendency. After 1936, when the control faction, as it came to be known, gained a clear ascendancy over the radical officers who had the ties to *ronin*, narcotics organization tightened further. In September of that year, for example, ten months before war with China broke out, Japanese and Korean adventurers in Beijing organized themselves with the help of the Japanese garrison stationed there. They created the East Asia

Club, to which they each paid 5 percent of their profits. The club funneled their monies to the local Japanese garrison and in return received
protection for its members. This garrison was the same one that later
became involved in a shooting skirmish in the area of the Marco Polo
Bridge outside of the city, an incident that escalated into the Second
World War when the Chinese chose to resist.[35]

In spite of the rhetoric of the rousing nationalist speeches by men
like Yan Yuheng and in spite of the obvious benefits narcotics monies
brought to the furthering of the aims of army officers, the Japanese
military and government never set out on a program of institutionalized
genocide. Military officers at the highest level were uncomfortable with
narcotics and explained that their monopoly only sold opium as a policy
of compassion aimed at gradually reducing the number of addicts. Yet
despite this official policy, narcotics money provided middle-level officers in North China the seed capital to underwrite foreign policy ventures forbidden by official sanction. The actions of field-level officers
created conditions that proved beneficial to senior officers. It was the
field level officers who turned to narcotic funds as an expedient. The
narcotics traffickers adapted to the times.

The soldiers of fortune and field officers who employed them were
motivated by extreme, idealistic patriotism. Furthermore, their decisions to use the plentiful opium monies to further political ends were
made in an atmosphere in which ethical choices about narcotics were
muddied. The wealth from the traffic was clearly being appropriated by
other powerful groups in China. Japanese in Manchuria understood that
anti-opium movements such as that of Zhang Xueliang, not to mention
the opium monopoly created by the Nationalist government in Nanjing,
were politically driven; thus the choice to use such funds was hardly
troubling. Whatever one's personal stance on opium might be, the traffic generated profits that could not be ignored, especially if one needed
to finance a shadow foreign policy.[36]

As a result, however, on both the Chinese and Japanese sides the narcotics business became more consolidated. Moreover the profits were
increasingly channeled into the legitimate economy of China through
Japanese colonial banks as well as through Chinese government financial institutions. Once war broke out between the two sides, the pattern
was set. Traffickers and soldiers of fortune would both still be serving
field-level officers, but they would be furthering wartime goals rather
than advancing private policies.

NOTES

1. Yamauchi Saburo, "Mayaku to Senso; Nitchu Senso no Himitsu Heiki" [Narcotics and war; a secret weapon of the China War], *Jinbutsu Orai* [Affairs of notable men], October 1956.

2. Consul General to Tanaka Giichi, December 10, 1928, "China *Ronin*," shelf no. 5039, microfilm reel no. 117, Japan, Ministry of Foreign Affairs, 1868–1945, Archives, S series.

3. Oi Shizuo, *Ahen Jiken no Shinso* [The facts about the opium incident] (Tokyo: privately issued, 1923), 4.

4. Oi Shizuo, *Ahen Jiken no Shinso; Asahi Shimbun*, July 12–14, 1921, February 20, 1922; H. Gurney to Earl Curson, March 25, 1921, PRO, FO 371/6594.

5. Imai Seiichi, *Taisho Demokurashi*; Harada, *Mantetsu*, 104–10.

6. Jonathan Marshall, Peter Dale Scott, and Jane Hunter, *The Iran Contra Connection: Secret Teams and Covert Operations in the Reagan Era* (Boston: South End, 1987), use the term "private foreign policy" to describe Oliver North and the covert actions of the intelligence community. It could be as easily applied to this case. Ivan Morris, *Nationalism and the Right Wing in Japan: A Study of Post War Trends* (London: Oxford University Press, 1960), claims right-wing organizations became subcontracting groups to those in power.

7. Kantocho Keimukyoku Koto Keisatsuke [Kwantung office police department upper division police bureau], "Joshiki Sokushin Kai Kyotoku Kai Hainichi Undo Taiyo" [The aims of the anti-Japanese movement of the practical progressive club and the eradicate poison club], 1931, document 2589, Toyo Bunku [East Asia Collection], Tokyo, Japan.

8. Gavin McCormack, *Chang Tso-lin in Northeast China, 1911–1928: China, Japan, and the Manchurian Idea* (Stanford, Calif.: Stanford University Press, 1977), 223–27.

9. William Fitch Morton, *Tanaka Giichi and Japan's China Policy* (New York: St. Martin's, 1980); Nobuya Bamba, *Japanese Diplomacy in Dilemma: New Light on Japan's China Policy, 1924–1929* (Vancouver: University of British Columbia Press, 1972).

10. Morton, *Tanaka Giichi and Japan's China Policy*; McCormack, *Chang Tso-lin in Northeast China, 1911–1928*, 230–33.

11. The chemistry described in the benzolyne scandal article is not accurate. What is described would produce heroin, however, presumably as intended. Authors' conversation with William Miles, associate professor of chemistry, Lafayette College, Easton, Pa. The Shanghai Municipal Police found a similar case during these same years involving the following procedure. "The basic material of the whole process is a benzoyl derivative of morphine, actually benzoyl-morphine-hydrochloride. . . . The mechanism of the process is quite simple. The treatment of the solution with caustic soda results in the elimination of the benzoyl group with the reformation of morphine, which remains in solution as the soluble sodium compound of morphine. The addition of an ammonium salt or even of bicarbonate of soda will then result in the precipitation of free morphine which is separated and then treated with dilute hydrochloric acid in order to form the soluble hydrochloride of morphine." The source of this altered drug was also Germany.

"J.G.C. Walker to Shanghai Municipal Council," May 21, 1928, D 309, SMP CID.

12. Mokuda Katsuji, "Bakurosareta Manshu Gigoku" [Manchurian scandals disclosed], *Waga Kan* [My view], 78 (May 1930).

13. League of Nations, "Prospectus of an Opium Company at Shanghai," May 22, 1926.

14. Kantocho Keimukyoku Koto Keisatsuke, "Joshiki Sokushin Kai Kyotoku Kai Hai-nichi Undo Taiyo," 61.

15. Yamauchi Saburo, "Mayaku to Senso," 174–75.

16. Amakasu Masahiko always knew that if he were caught, his ties to the army would be denied. When he worked in Harbin after the Manchurian incident in 1931, he was prepared to take his own life should he run into unexpected difficulties. In this he shows more honor, or perhaps more understanding of the nature of his situation, than Oliver North, who turned on his superiors during his defense. Tsunoda Fusako, *Amakasu Tai-i* [Captain Amakasu] (Tokyo: Chuo Bunku, 1974).

17. Eguchi Keiichi, *Nitchu Ahen Senso*, 35–36; Nitanosa, *Senso to Ahen*. When the Japanese army withdrew from Shandong, Liu got involved in a banking scheme, but before it got off the ground, he absconded to Shanghai with the investor's money. *Zoku: Gendai Shi Shiryo, Manshu* no. 32 (Tokyo: Misuzu Shobo, 1986).

18. "Report," December 9, 1931, Records of the Foreign Office, Consulate General, Tsingtao; Nitanosa, *Senso to Ahen*, 108.

19. Japan, Ministry of Foreign Affairs, S series no. 5039, reel 117, "China Ronin."

20. Nitanosa, *Senso to Ahen*, 94–100.

21. "Activities of Philippe Shifman . . . Report," May 8, 1933, box 4539, 893.114NARCOTICS/497, RG 59; "Article by One Marcus Mervine . . . Narcotic Trade," April 16, 1937, box 7207, 893.114NARCOTICS/1943, RG 59; Yamauchi, "Mayaku to Senso."

22. Yamauchi, "Mayaku to Senso."

23. Yamauchi, "Mayaku to Senso."

24. Yamauchi, "Mayaku to Senso."

25. Yamauchi, "Mayaku to Senso."

26. Tsunoda, *Amakasu Tai-i.*

27. Tsunoda, *Amakasu Tai-i*; Yatsugi Kazuo, *Kishi Nobosuke no Kaiso* [Recollections of Kishi Nobosuke] (Tokyo: Bungei Shuso, 1976), 28–29.

28. Fujise Kazuya, *Showa Rikugun Ahen Boryoku no Taizei* [The opium crimes of the Showa army] (Tokyo: Yamanote Shobo Shinsha, 1992), 110–11.

29. Hashimoto Kingoro, *Hashimoto Taisa no Shuki* [The memoirs of Colonel Hashimoto] (Tokyo: Misuzu Shobo, 1963), 107.

30. M. R. Nicholson, "Report on Tientsin Narcotic Situation," September 30, 1936, box 7206, 893.114 NARCOTICS/1745, RG 59.

31. Yamauchi, "Mayaku to Senso."

32. Nitanosa, *Ahen to Senso*, 142–52.

33. Shanghai to Treasury Department, May 9, 1936, document 9517, exhibit 391, International Military Tribune [IMT], National Diet Library, Tokyo;

American Consulate General, Mukden to American Minister, "Tang Yulin's opium," May 13, 1931, box 7201, 893.114NARCOTICS/255, RG 59; "Conditions in Jehol, Conversation with Mr. Upton close," August 30, 1932, box 7201, 893.114NARCOTICS/405, RG 59.

34. "Prospectus of the Shanghai Tat Seng Company," May 22, 1926, LON. Trying to take over the Shanghai operation was a dangerous business. One of Chang's representatives was murdered during a conference with the Shanghai interests; Nelson T. Johnson to Secretary of State, July 6, 1932, 893.114NARCOTICS/369, RG 59.

35. M. R. Nicholson to Treasury, January 13, 1937, document 9519, Exhibit 399, IMT.

36. Frederic Wakeman Jr. raises the larger issue of the lack of clarity of choice in wartime China in *Shanghai Badlands*. It is an important point to keep in mind when trying to understand the motivations of seemingly idealistic people who became involved in the narcotics traffic. Charging them with outright cynicism is too simple.

CHAPTER EIGHT

SPIES

1937 – 1945

More than the Japanese wartime mobilization, that of the Chinese has real results. This means that as far as Japan is concerned, war, politics and economics are separate. For China, they are all one body. Therefore the Chinese attack with military might, and they also attack with ideas and economics.

Kodama Yoshio[1]

On March 17, 1939, Kodama Yoshio left snow-covered Tokyo for more springlike weather in Shanghai. As he was driven from the airfield to his hotel in the International Settlement, he observed the many signs of war along the way. He described battle-scarred bunkers scattered here and there among creeks flowing with red water; in their midst, a white wooden marker commemorated a fallen war hero. In one field young boys dressed in rags harvested bullet casings. In another, uniformed soldiers tended cattle to supply their army. He was moved to write the following poem:

> A field of recent battle,
> Dressed in uniform
> They tend springtime cows.[2]

Kodama Yoshio rode to the Astor House Hotel with Shanghai's Japanese vice consul Iwaii Kazuo. (At ¥12 a day, meals not included, he found the hotel expensive, yet comfortable, with a view of the Japanese flag out his window.) During the next few days he met with top officials of the Japanese occupation. Yet two years before, on the eve of the first battles of the Second World War, this same man had only just finished serving time in prison for attempting to destroy a military transmitter in conjunction with an ultranationalist coup d'etat attempt. Like many of his fellow idealists, he hoped to establish an egalitarian Japanese state free of Western corruption.[3]

Upon his release in 1937, he found that right-wing idealists of his ilk had been eclipsed by equally right-wing militarists. If he wished to remain politically active, and he did, he had to accommodate men who would rather control the very Japanese capitalists and politicians that he had set out to destroy. Kodama secretly nurtured his earlier distrust (or at least so he claimed in his postwar memoirs) as he worked for the Japanese military throughout the war in East Asia. During the war he accumulated wealth and political influence that survived long after the war ended. His fortune and his power came from his ability to trade opium for information and military supplies.

THE STRUGGLE FOR CONTROL OF THE NARCOTICS INDUSTRY

Kodama's career illustrates a transition taking place in the narcotics industry during the 1930s. In the first half of the decade both the Japanese militarists and the Nationalist government of Chiang Kai-shek in Nanjing consolidated domestic political power and expanded their territory. During those years narcotics traffickers adapted to the opportunities created by increasing international tensions in Asia. Traffickers and politicians worked out the details of mutually beneficial relationships. In the process, the profits from opium became integrated into the governing structures on both sides, despite official rhetoric about the evils of drugs and bureaucratic organizations geared toward prohibition.

These systems were disrupted, in July 1937, when Chinese and Japanese soldiers collided along the fluid North China border. The result was war. The environment changed once the shooting began, and the traffickers had to scramble to find their places under the new conditions. Those who succeeded found that opiates could fit into the military needs of both Chinese and Japanese commanders. Kodama, like his Chi-

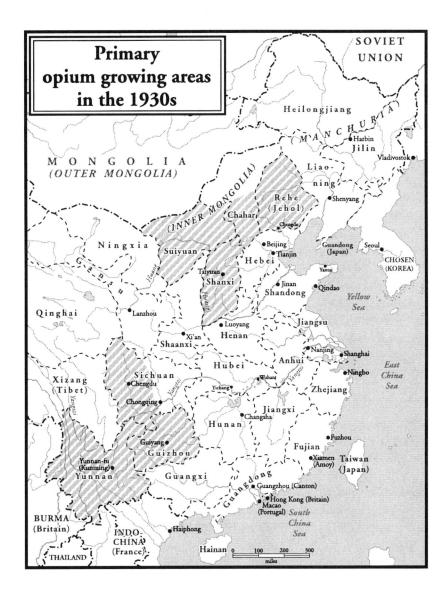

Primary opium growing areas in the 1930s

SOVIET UNION

Heilongjiang

MANCHURIA

Harbin
Jilin

Vladivostok

MONGOLIA
(OUTER MONGOLIA)

Liao-ning

Shenyang

(INNER MONGOLIA)

Chahar

Rehe
(Jehol)

Chengde

Ningxia

Suiyuan

Beijing

Tianjin

Guandong
(Japan)

Seoul

CHOSEN
(KOREA)

Gansu

Taiyuan

Shanxi

Hebei

Jinan

Shandong

Yantai

Qingdao

Yellow
Sea

Qinghai

Lanzhou

Luoyang

Henan

Jiangsu

Xi'an

Shaanxi

Nanjing

Shanghai

Xizang
(Tibet)

Sichuan

Chengdu

Hubei

Wuhan

Anhui

Ningbo

East
China
Sea

Chongqing

Yichang

Zhejiang

Yangzi

Jiangxi

Changsha

Hunan

Fuzhou

Guiyang

Guizhou

Fujian

Xiamen
(Amoy)

Taiwan
(Japan)

Yunnan-fu
(Kunming)

Yunnan

Guangxi

Guangdong

Guangzhou (Canton)

BURMA
(Britain)

INDO-CHINA
(France)

THAILAND

Haiphong

Hainan

Hong Kong (Britain)
Macao
(Portugal)

South
China
Sea

0   100   200   300
miles

nese counterpart, Dai Li, thrived in this new environment, making the transition from poverty, to soldier of fortune, to military spy, and finally to a man of political influence.

Yet it would be too simple to claim that Chinese and Japanese military commanders of the 1930s envisioned narcotics within the war's strategic scope. Men closer to logistics and operations, often the same men who had used opium monies while pursuing private foreign policies earlier in the decade, were the ones who continued to appreciate its tactical application. Opium revenues financed armies of both nations even as national leaders continued to mouth prohibitionist sentiments. Control of opium continued to be a goal of rival factions within each side throughout the war. Despite policy statements eschewing the opium traffic, it was the bone and sinews of the war effort on both sides.

The Second World War began in Asia outside Beiping[4] on July 7, 1937. On that evening someone fired at Japanese soldiers patrolling near the Marco Polo Bridge. At the time it seemed likely that the incident would result in yet another excuse for the Japanese army to continue its policy of incremental territorial encroachment into North China. However, two events of the previous year, the Young Officers' Insurrection of February 26, 1936, and the Xian Incident of December 12, 1936, insured that events at the Marco Polo Bridge would instead lead to full-scale war. Both incidents were caused by factional strife.

TWO PIVOTAL INCIDENTS

On the Japanese side, the February 26 incident consolidated the political power of central military planners, allowing them to set policy in pursuit of a national defense state that would channel the productive capacity of the country and colonies toward military ends. It also gave them ascendancy over their erstwhile allies, the ultranationalists. In the 1920s idealistic young officers in the services, along with civilian ultranationalist groups, worked with military officers to fight the political party governments they considered so weak. Once the party-based government had been eclipsed and Manchukuo became a reality, the alliance disintegrated and tensions between these right-wing factions increased.

On February 26, 1936, young officers of the Tokyo-based First Division attempted to topple the government. Calling for a Showa restoration, they surrounded the imperial palace, held the emperor hostage, murdered the finance minister, and attempted to take the life of the prime minister as well. For three days Japan functioned under martial law. Ultimately the army itself broke the siege. Army authorities arrested thirteen young officers, tried them in secret, and executed them without ceremony.

Although this was a case of the military disciplining its own, in the uncertain atmosphere created by these right-wing extremists since at least 1928, those in the military who advocated strict social control and preparation for total war gained the upper hand. After 1936, it was this element of the government alone that seemed to be decisive enough to carry out policy. These were men who advocated a unified national defense state and a pan-Asian league. They were not given to compromise in Asian affairs.[5]

The February 26 incident affected the balance between right-wing factions. After the failure of the coup, the army tightened its hold on the reigns of government. This began the political ascendancy of officers such as Tojo Hideki. Once in power, control militarists began to purge their former allies, ultranationalist officers such as Hashimoto Kingoro, who often found themselves transferred to postings where they could do little harm. Like the idealists, the soldiers of fortune, with their peculiar blend of patriotism, opportunism, and independence, found their activities under increasing supervision. Survival required adaptation to new conditions. Once the conflict began in earnest many found their calling in espionage.[6]

The second event to change the dynamics of Chinese-Japanese interaction was the Xian incident of December 1936. During the early 1930s, General Chiang Kai-shek doggedly pursued his policy of pacification first and resistance second, choosing to eliminate all domestic rivals, especially the Chinese Communist Party, before moving against Japan. This choice had its consequences. Given the relentless and occasionally ferocious Japanese advance in North China in the early 1930s, coupled with the repression with which Chiang chose to answer his critics, the policy eventually alienated even close supporters. We have seen how the Nineteenth Route Army had rebelled in Fujian province in 1933 under just such conditions. In 1936, Zhang Xueliang became equally disillusioned.

By 1936 the Chinese Communists were reduced in number to a mere 10,000 and were locked in the Yan'an base camp area, where they found a safe haven after the Long March. They braced themselves to fight yet another campaign against Nationalist forces, this time led by Zhang Xueliang. This new area in Northwest China was close to Japanese-held territory. Zhang Xueliang was Manchurian; his father, the warlord

Zhang Zuolin, had been killed by a Japanese bomb in 1928. Although Zhang Xueliang was an effete ex-playboy and ex-opium addict who had shown little effort in defending Manchuria against invasion in 1932, he had strong reasons to dislike Japan. Like many others in the *Guomindang* camp, he wondered why Chinese were fighting each other. He worked out an ad hoc truce with the Communists.

On December 12, 1936, Chiang Kai-shek flew to Xian to inspect the new anti-Communist front. The next morning Zhang Xueliang took him captive. For a week Chiang Kai-shek's fate remained uncertain. However, given the crisis caused by the Japanese invasion and an unexpected show of anxiety about the situation from the general public, Zhang Xueliang and the Communist leader Zhou Enlai agreed to release Chiang once he had promised to put aside the civil war and establish a united front with the Communists to fight against the Japanese.

The Xian incident put an end to the Chinese policy of accommodation and negotiation with the Japanese in the north, while the February 26 incident increased the political power of those Japanese militarists whose social vision was founded on the preparation for war. Therefore when shooting erupted between Japanese and Chinese forces around the Marco Polo Bridge on July 7, 1937, the event expanded into full-scale invasion.

THE CHINA WAR

In the early days of the war Japanese victory seemed certain. Through 1937 and 1938 the Japanese Imperial Army swept south along the coast of China, delivering a series of stunning defeats to the Chinese armies. Beijing fell in August 1937; Shanghai, November 1937; Nanjing, December 1937; Xuzhow, May 1938; and Wuhan and Guangzhou, October 1938. In December 1937 the Nanjing government retreated to Wuhan; in October 1938 it relocated once again to the protection of the mountainous western provinces of Sichuan and Yunnan. Chongqing became the wartime capital of Nationalist China, and the government vowed to fight on to victory. The Communists held their own in Northwest China. Thus, after 1938 the China war that initially seemed destined to be short developed into a stalemate.

Once the China theater became a war of attrition, espionage grew in importance. Leading up to the outbreak of hostilities, both Japanese *ronin* and Chinese gangsters had consolidated power bases in China. For funds, these adventurers and their clients had turned to the lucrative opium and heroin traffic. Once war began, opium continued to play a role. As espionage organizations on both sides became further consolidated and rationalized, so did the wartime traffic in narcotic drugs.[7]

Japanese espionage had become particularly complex by 1937. The elite military police unit, the *Kempetai*, is perhaps best known in the West. It was a stepping stone to power in the Japanese army; Tojo Hideki made his mark in the *Kempeitai*, and it was to this organization that Yamauchi the heroin-maker made his contributions. For traditional espionage work, each Japanese army had its Special Service Agency (*Tokumu Kikan*), the first having been established in Harbin at the end of the First World War. After the creation of Manchukuo, new Special Service Agencies appeared. One, aimed at intelligence and propaganda inside Inner Mongolia, became important to Japanese expansion in that area. The Japanese command formed a second in North China to counter the perceived threat caused by *Guomindang* espionage units in the area in the early 1930s. These units were semi-independent until 1938, when they were reorganized into the Special Service Bureau (*Tokumu Bu*).[8]

After the February 26 coup attempt in 1936, reorganization efforts aimed at creating a national defense state began in earnest. In the autumn of that year, general staff officer Ishiwara Kanji produced a five-year plan for national defense. After the China War began, national coordination of resources and personnel became a priority. Thus in October 1937 a cabinet planning board was formed, followed in April 1938 by the National Mobilization Law. The government directed by the military established schemes during this period to harness the productive powers of the private sector; they went so far as to reorganize the semi-private South Manchurian Railway Company to keep its directors from any temptation to place more importance on profits than patriotism. Large infusions of Japanese capital began moving into China.[9] Within the growth of this complex military, commercial, and espionage network, men like Kodama were able to build personal empires even as they served their country.[10]

In 1939 Kodama described Shanghai as a city plagued by terrorist organizations. He was referring to the bands of agents working for the Chinese Nationalist Military Statistics Bureau run out of Chongqing by Dai Li. These Chinese men, whom Dai Li called his students, carried out spectacular assassinations of Chinese who collaborated with Japan. Compared to its Japanese counterparts, by 1936, the Chinese *Guomindang* espionage apparatus was centralized and professional. Created for anti-Communist activity, it should have easily turned its resources toward the Japanese invasion after the Xian incident created a united front between the two sides. In fact, the beginning of hostilities in 1937 found the Military Statistics Bureau totally unprepared. Nevertheless, the bureau quickly recovered and the organization benefited from the wartime opportunity to grow and strengthen, without ever letting go of its original anti-Communist purpose.[11]

In the early 1930s Chen Lifu formally directed information gathering for the *Guomindang*. Chen, together with his brother Chen Guofu, formed the core of the powerful C.C. Clique within the party. He had impeccable Shanghai credentials and connections. His uncle, Chen Qimei, was a local hero of the 1911 Revolution who had been assassinated by Yuan Shikai in 1916. Chen Lifu was educated in the best schools in Shanghai and studied engineering in the United States. He counted Du Yuesheng among his friends. In 1926 he became Chiang Kai-shek's secretary, eventually becoming secretary-general of the *Guomindang*. He was also head of the second (special affairs) section of the organization department of the Military Affairs Committee.[12]

DAI LI

Working under Chen Lifu in the second section was Dai Li, the man who would become the eminence grise of the *Guomindang*. He was born in the Zhejiang countryside in 1896. In his youth he circulated among petty gangster circles in Shanghai, where he and ten friends supported themselves by selling information to the *Guomindang* general, Hu Zengnan. In 1926 he enrolled in the Whampoa Military Academy, although he did not graduate. Instead he and his friends began gathering information informally for Chiang Kai-shek. These men formed the core of the second section (special service section) of the Military Affairs Committee, which later was reorganized and renamed the Military Statistics Bureau (*Jun Tong Ju*).

In the early 1930s Dai Li was not so powerful as he would become later. Between 1932 and 1936 he slowly expanded his control over *Guomindang* espionage and police organizations. He worked for the Military Affairs Committee, but he also joined the Fu Xing Society when it was formed and ran its second section. Better known as the Blue Shirts, the organization consisted of about three hundred Whampoa Military Academy graduates whose goal was to infuse a martial purity into the corrupt Chinese society. The society, modeled after its European fascist namesakes, engaged in propaganda and anti-Communist activities. The claim by Japanese commanders in the north that these Blue Shirts formed a terrorist organization aimed at destroying their treaty rights in China could not have been further from the truth. Dai Li's victims in North China, as well as in Shanghai, included Communists and any other group openly critical of Chiang Kai-shek.[13]

In the early 1930s, Dai Li expanded his own power base within the Nationalist espionage establishment. In doing so, he came into opposition with the C.C. Clique, especially Chen Lifu, for whom he worked. The elite Chen Lifu despised peasant Dai Li, who looked like a horse and suffered from rhinitis. Chen was born with connections, which he used. But he lacked Dai Li's cunning and in the end was no match for him. Dai Li proved his worth to Chiang Kai-shek through spectacular espionage feats, including the 1933 infiltration of the Nineteenth Route Army's short-lived government in Fujian province, the collapse of which brought Paul Yip's Persian opium to Du Yuesheng's morphine factory as an extra bonus. Eventually, his influence eclipsed Chen Lifu. By 1938 Chen formally stepped out of espionage but ran a civilian intelligence unit even while serving as minister of education.[14]

In the early years of Dai Li's espionage career, he worked from an office in Nanjing where he lived a spartan life. But he kept rooms in Shanghai, where he savored the pleasures that the city had to offer on his frequent trips there. He knew Du Yuesheng and his organization protected Du's opium concerns. In 1933, when Chiang Kai-shek raided Du's Nandao morphine factory, Dai Li helped smooth things over and protect the most important members of the gang. He offered this service at the same time that the *Guomindang* opium monopoly grew more efficient.[15]

Dai Li spread his influence by patiently placing his agents inside other Nationalist law enforcement agencies in the Shanghai-Nanking area, including the Opium Suppression Bureau. As his operation grew, it intertwined with narcotics on several levels: his personal ties to Du, his people in the bureau, and the opium monies that went from the monopoly through the Agricultural Bank into his operating budget. In the beginning he worked in the shadow of Du Yuesheng, at least as far as Shanghai and opium were concerned. By the end of the Second World War, however, the roles would be reversed.[16]

By the time of the Xian Incident (after which Dai Li also incorporated several of Zhang Xueliang's lieutenants) in 1936, Dai Li's organization numbered 3,000 agents. After 1941, when Americans joined the war, he became more powerful still as his bureau teamed up with American naval intelligence. Dai Li and his Military Statistics Bureau carried a lot of weight with American naval officers from the beginning because they had managed to learn in advance of the planned Japanese invasion of Pearl Harbor. Dai Li sent this information to American authorities through his people attached to the Chinese embassy in Washington, but it was ignored. After the event, however, Dai Li's stock soared with the Americans. Together with Milton Miles, he headed the Sino-American Cooperation Organization, which worked in both intelligence and military procurement. From 1942 on Dai Li increased the number of his agents, and with American cooperation set up listening posts behind enemy lines that transmitted weather and intelligence information back to headquarters in Chongqing. Dai Li also dunned the Americans for more sophisticated apparatus, especially American electronic and radio equipment. Milton Miles complained that he had to listen to many speeches "showing the need for more stuffs."[17]

Wartime espionage work allowed Dai Li to continue to expand his influence into other Nationalist-affiliated organizations. He brought under his control agencies that at first glance would not seem related to espionage. Transportation networks are a good example. He acquired control of transport by placing his agents in shipping or trucking agencies when he could. For instance, T. L. Soong, the younger brother of Finance Minister T. V. Soong and brother-in-law of Chiang Kai-shek, set up the South Western Transport Company in 1937 to move goods and strategic supplies through South China and later along the Burma Road. In the beginning, T. L. Soong hired dependents of his friends and classmates. Eventually, however, more and more of his personnel came from the Military Statistics Bureau. The South Western Transport Company often included opium smuggled among its cargo.[18]

Dai Li also became director of goods transportation control. After the fall of Changsha in 1938, the local garrison commander was executed for his failure to hold back the Japanese army. This unlucky general had also occupied the post of director of goods transportation control, using his garrison to supervise trade along the Yangzi River. After his death Dai Li took the position. During these same years Dai Li used the war to spread his influence into Du Yuesheng's own territory, the Green Gang, as many of its members worked for the Military Statistics Bureau.[19]

Control of transportation was valuable to Dai Li. It ensured the efficiency of his operations. He needed to supply the listening posts behind enemy lines, and indeed he did this well. He was able to staff and equip the stations with American and Chinese personnel and even to travel with Milton Miles deep into enemy territory. It also provided vehicles for opium operations, from which his bureau profited. Likewise control of the Green Gang assured Dai Li that he would have the loyalty of people who could be potentially formidable adversaries. The usefulness of such coordination was demonstrated in Chun'an, Zhejiang province. Located in an area that remained outside of Japanese control, the town maintained a Sino-American Cooperative Organization listening post. It also had a branch of the trading company run by Du Yuesheng and Dai Li, the Tongji Gongsi, which bought up war supplies from Shanghai.[20]

Dai Li was a peasant who mingled among the elite. But his rough origins shone through in his managerial style. He ran his agency with an iron fist and a hot temper. He paid and fed his agents well, but he also subjected them to harsh and arbitrary discipline. He demanded they remain single, yet he was himself a womanizer who loved luxury. As his power increased during the war years, he established several villas in the unoccupied area, which he filled with antiques and luxury items brought to him in part by the South West Transport Company. (After his death, the wives of his fellow administrators looted his estate.) In his Chongqing villa, where he lived with a film star named Butterfly, he built a garish garden that his snobbish acquaintances ridiculed behind his back. He always maintained that his three most precious treasures were his students (the name he gave to his agents), his guns, and his cars.[21]

Before the Japanese invasion, the agents of the Military Statistics Bureau worked against all groups or individuals opposing Chiang Kai-shek, many of whom resided in the safety of concession areas. For this reason they carried out their work through kidnapping and assassination in order to avoid extradition legalities with foreign police. The experience that the Military Statistics Bureau gained working under such conditions in the early 1930s was put to effective use against the Japanese army and its collaborators after July 1937.[22]

When the war began, the Japanese espionage apparatus was not so centrally concentrated as that of the *Guomindang*. Indeed it was quite diffuse. As mentioned earlier, economic organizations were created to consolidate national productive capability. Often these included their own espionage components. For example, in 1939, Colonel Iwakuro Hideo brought together representatives from Mitsui, Mitsubishi, and other commercial enterprises to form the Showa Trading Corporation, which entered the business of military procurements. The organization included a research bureau and its own second section, which, in fact, engaged in espionage. Ogishi Yoriyoshi, a military academy graduate who ran the second section, had earlier been actively sympathetic to the February 26, 1936, rebellion.[23]

KODAMA YOSHIO

Among the men employed by the Showa Trading Company to travel throughout Asia in search of strategic supplies, Kodama Yoshio had a career that exemplifies the transition from ultranationalist to spy. Like Dai Li, he was born into poverty. As a young man, he worked in steel mills and became involved in labor union movements, although he remained staunchly anti-Communist all of his life. Kodama's sense of the injustice of the prevailing system, coupled with his deep feelings of Japanese pride, led him into ultranationalist circles. In the late 1920s he made his reputation and received his first prison term, by handing a letter of protest to the emperor. He returned to jail several times; his 1933 sentence came when he was implicated in a plot to bomb a Tokyo power station.[24]

Young Kodama, the radical activist, claimed he did not admire the military. Writing in 1949, he blamed the nation's descent into the China conflict, and ultimately the Pacific War, on the victory of the militarists over the ultranationalists in February 1936. Yet he decried the political naivete and lack of organization of his fellow idealists and their consequent need to rely on sympathizers in the armed forces, a combination that made them easy pawns of those with expansionist motives. This later condemnation of the military is ironic, for Kodama made a fortune during the war through his military contacts.[25]

Finding the atmosphere in Japan too restrictive for his temperament, Kodama gave in to his wanderlust after his release from prison in 1937. He went to Manchuria and from there roamed through the mainland, where his connections with other ultranationalists allowed him to travel extensively. When he reached Shanghai, he met Vice Consul Iwaii Kazuo. Iwaii was a graduate of the East Asian Language Academy, who was fluent in Chinese and thus suited to be a translator and information officer attached to the foreign service. Iwaii in turn introduced Kodama to important military personnel. These contacts arranged for his first important assignment. In 1938, he was sent to Hong Kong as a bodyguard assigned to escort Wang Jingwei to Nanjing.[26]

Wang Jingwei was important to the Japanese military command. Although he was a high-ranking member of the *Guomindang* who had been active in the Chinese revolution since the early 1900s, he had never risen any higher than the second tier of offices in the Nationalist organization. Yet Wang Jingwei was ambitious. Overshadowed as he was by Chiang Kai-shek, he defected to Japan. In 1939 he formally became the leader of occupied China, although, as usual, the Japanese military retained control. A defector of Wang's level was, of course, a prime target for Dai Li's assassination squads. Indeed, he just missed being shot in Hanoi during his travels. In agreeing to become Wang's bodyguard, Kodama was ready to assume an important and dangerous position.[27]

Kodama did not get to carry out his assignment. He went to Hong Kong only to discover that Wang had changed his route in midjourney, going directly from Hanoi to Nanjing. Nevertheless, during this assignment Kodama gained the acquaintance of high-ranking army and naval personnel, including Okada Yoshimasa of the army general staff. While Kodama was in Hong Kong, he undertook the purchase of German arms and ammunition for a Tokyo arms company and thereafter began working for the Showa Trading Company.[28]

In December 1941, he branched out on his own, forming the Kodama Agency [*Kodama Kikan*], which worked for the Japanese navy. It was through this agency that Kodama made his fortune trading opium for tungsten. Because the war quickly exhausted the logistical capabilities of the Japanese army, the search for strategic materials became an important component of espionage. Coincidentally, as we shall see, as both sides were purposely undermining the other's currency, opium soon became more than contraband; it was a measure of real value. Thus it became an instrument of exchange in areas where the debased currency had lost value. The Showa Trading Company bought narcotics from the authorities specifically to use in trades, while its intelligence division worked on opening new sources of strategic supply.[29]

The contacts Kodama gained in this phase of his career allowed him to begin a new life after the war as a behind-the-scenes political fixer. He continued in that role until his implication in the Lockheed scandal of 1976 ended his career and made him a household name in Japan. Because of Kodama's later notoriety, his agency has become the best known wartime spy organization. During the war, however, Kodama's group had several important counterparts. Kodama owed some of his success to a man who was laying the groundwork for his own operation as Kodama languished in prison in the early 1930s. Sakata Shigemori was a pioneer in the strategic use of opium in North China. It was not

Sakata Shigemori's smuggling routes

SOVIET UNION

Heilongjiang

MANCHURIA

Harbin
Jilin

Vladivostok

MONGOLIA
(OUTER MONGOLIA)

(INNER MONGOLIA)

Liao-
ning

Shenyang

Rehe
(Jehol)

Chahar

Chengde

Ningxia

Suiyuan

Beijing
Tianjin

Guandong
(Japan)

Seoul

CHOSEN
(KOREA)

Hebei

Taiyuan

Shanxi

Yantai

Jinan
Shandong

Qindao

Yellow
Sea

Qinghai

Lanzhou

Luoyang

Jiangsu

Xi'an
Shaanxi

Henan

Anhui

Nanjing

Shanghai

Hubei

Wuhan

Ningbo

East
China
Sea

Xizang
(Tibet)

Sichuan
Chengdu

Yichang

Zhejiang

Chongqing

Jiangxi

Changsha

Hunan

Fuzhou

Guiyang

Guizhou

Fujian

Yunnan-fu
(Kunming)

Yunnan

Guangxi

Xiamen
(Amoy)

Taiwan
(Japan)

Guangdong

Guangzhou (Canton)

Hong Kong (Britain)
Macao
(Portugal)

South
China
Sea

BURMA
(Britain)

INDO-
CHINA
(France)

Haiphong

Hainan

THAILAND

0   100   200   300
miles

Sakata's opium
smuggling route,
1934-1936

Sakata's opium
and currency
smuggling route,
1939-1945

used as a form of genocide, as Chinese propaganda of the time declared, but as a tool to weaken the Chinese economy.

OPIUM STRATEGY

Sakata Shigemori was the quintessential China *ronin*. He was born in Wakayama prefecture. In the 1920s he went to China to study language; in 1927 he enrolled in Beijing University and he studied transportation. Not content with schoolbook Mandarin (he once saw a professor of Chinese from a prestigious Japanese university unable to communicate with a rickshaw driver), he studied the coarse language of the streets as well as regional dialects. He understood the importance of customs and body language, those cultural idiosyncrasies that could give away an impostor. He became so proficient that he could pass as native Chinese. He had several Chinese personas, including Tian Cheng, a name derived from the second and third *kanji* of his Japanese name, and Tian Cheng-fu, a dealer in curios. He never enlisted in the Japanese military, but he was, at times, on the payroll of the general staff of the Japanese Guandong Army and worked with the various special service agencies.[30]

Obviously Sakata was well-positioned for a career in espionage. He would later serve his country through operations such as one in Hong Kong in 1940, when he tried to woo leaders of the Red Gang to the Japanese side against the British. During the same time he tried to negotiate a truce with *Guomindang* leaders using mutual anti-Communist feelings as a negotiating point. He was able to conduct these later operations because of the contacts he made among the Chinese gangs when he worked as a drug trafficker in North China. Sakata's goal in this earlier operation was to gain control of the Tianjin opium market to undercut a source of the Chinese government's financial support.[31]

Tianjin was the center of narcotics trafficking in North China. It served this function not only because of its convenient location central to inland transport but also because it had a quiltlike pattern of concession areas—British, French, Japanese, Italian—each one giving consular protection to its residents based on treaty privilege. In the early 1930s, Japanese traffickers were strong newcomers in the Tianjin narcotics trade, in which Europeans like Elie Eliopoulos were losing ground. In these same years, the Chinese monopoly was also extending its authority into the local market. After 1933, when Manchukuo expanded to incorporate neighboring Jehol province, Japanese smugglers could enter this market with a competitive product. Foreign opium, considered the best, was hard to acquire because of League of Nations measures. The Chinese monopoly relied on Yunnan, Sichuan, and Suiyuan opium, considered to be far inferior to that from Rehe.[32]

Tianjin was the city where entrepreneurial Japanese heroin traffickers such as Yamauchi Saburo made such an impressive entrance into the market in the late 1920s. As Yamauchi's experience demonstrates, the Japanese army increasingly coopted private enterprises in the early 1930s. This process began when field officers perceived a threat from Dai Li's spy organizations operating in the area, which they knew were also financed by opium monies. Their concern increased in 1935, when they saw Chinese financial reforms strengthen the economy of the region.

In 1934 Lieutenant Sakai Shigeru, chief of staff to General Umetsu Yoshijiro in North China, together with Colonel Iwakuro Hideo, later of the Showa Trading Company, began discussing the financial and strategic importance of opium with one of his intelligence officers, Okada Yoshimasa (the same Okada who worked with Kodama). Together these men put together an opium trafficking scheme. Okada knew Sakata from 1927, when they both were in Beiping. He seemed to be the right man for the job.[33]

In 1934, Sakata was working as a translator for the South Manchurian Railway Company. Officers in the Guandong Army arranged to introduce him to Yin Rugeng, a petty warlord and Japanese protégé who was building a power base in the area between Beiping and Manchukuo. Sakata set up a transport and construction company. Soon his trucks began running opium from Chengde in Rehe province through the Great Wall at Gubeikou to Beiping and Tianjin. Both Manchukuo customs officials, controlled by the Japanese, and their Chinese counterparts, paid off by Yin, ignored Sakata's trucks, which could make one trip a day on roads improved by his company engineers.[34]

Okada rode along with Sakata on a cold February day and later described the trip. They traveled out of Beiping in the morning, stopping to look at a Llamist temple in the northern suburbs. Sakata told him that Sun Jiyuan, a warlord who supported the *Guomindang*, stockpiled his Suiyuan opium there before running it to Tianjin. Once each morning, he was told, the customs agents at each checkpoint turned their backs to allow this competitor, one with a markedly inferior product, to move his goods through the barrier. By noon the two men had reached Gubeikou. Sakata pointed out Yin's armed soldiers at a checkpoint. After a signal the truck moved through easily, stopping only long enough to drop off one or two sacks of flour. The trip Okada described included nothing of the adventure or risk commonly associated with opium smuggling. Indeed, the routinizing of the process indicates how deeply and successfully narcotics trafficking had become imbedded in the Sino-Japanese commerce in North China at this period.[35]

Sakata did well with his trucking company, so well that he attracted the envious attention of his superiors in the Manchukuo bureaucracy. Just before the China war broke out, he retired, handing the organization over to his old employers, the South Manchurian Railway. He then switched his base of operations to Shanghai and he began working to infiltrate the Green Gang. He became friendly with Huang Jinrong and made several contacts who would later prove useful to him. These included Xu Caicheng, a friend of the underworld boss Du Yuesheng, and Xie Wenda, a Green Gang member and a graduate of the Whampoa Military Academy.[36]

These contacts became especially useful when staff officers in North China chose Sakata's organization to spread counterfeit currency through China in order to destroy the effectiveness of the 1935 currency reform. Okada remembered that on the trip to Rehe, Sakata would sometimes bring along passengers and sometimes silver coins. By carrying silver out of China, he was participating in a speculation spree that was sweeping the treaty ports at the time. In the early 1930s, China's silver currency was worth more as bullion than as coins. Silver began to drain out of China. In 1934 alone China lost $260,000,000 of silver, most of it leaving from foreign banks in the treaty ports. In November 1935, with advice from international specialists, the government nationalized silver and issued paper currency, the *fabi*.[37]

The currency reform occurred just as the Chinese opium monopoly was undergoing restructuring. The old organization had been loose and ineffectual except as an instrument to funnel some of the opium money into the hands of the government. The new monopoly did little more to end the trade or cure addiction, but it tightened the reigns on the traffic, increased the scope of government sales, and generated more revenues. Japanese military authorities in China knew that the opium monopoly financed terrorist organizations. They interpreted the currency reform as Western attempts to prop up a failing government in China. Therefore they saw both as threatening.[38]

The opium and currency reforms were no doubt the source of Kodama's later perception that China was fighting an economic war. He was wrong, however, in his critical assessment of Japan's piecemeal response. The Japanese high command understood the Chinese monetary reform as strengthening the *Guomindang*'s ties to Great Britain and the United States. It was inevitable that it should see the reform not merely as an attempt to handle a financial crisis but as the creation of an anti-Japanese alliance. It responded accordingly. Sakai Shigeru and Okada Yoshimasa (who earlier tried to undermine the Tianjin opium market) began plotting an attack on currency. This time, however, the scope of the operation was much larger.

In 1937, just before the China War began, the Japanese army brought together a group of engineers to the Army Scientific Institute, which was located on the agricultural campus of Meiji University outside of Tokyo. These men worked long hours to perfect plates, paper, and ink and finally created a duplicate of the Chinese *fabi*. Their creation was so complete in detail that the forgers themselves could not tell the difference between the real and the fake. The men of the forgery unit became so good at their jobs that as the war progressed they turned their hands to other fakeries such as Russian passports and labels for a British brand of canned salmon that could be booby-trapped with a time bomb.[39]

Once the money was ready, it needed an instrument to bring it to the market. Once again Okada turned to his friend Sakata. In 1939, Yamamoto Kenzo, the chief engineer of the counterfeiting project, came to Shanghai with a trunk full of the shiny new bills. He met Sakata and passed over the contents to him for a trial under fire. Sakata looked at the new bills and saw in their crispness a fatal flaw. He crumpled them up with mud, salt, and butter, making them look as though they had been long in circulation. Then he took the money out for a trial run. First he went to a gold shop. The owner should have been able to spot a fake, but Sakata managed to purchase an ounce of gold. Then he went to the Wing On Department Store and bought linen handkerchiefs. Finally, in the ultimate test, he took the currency to a Shanghai casino. The money changers accepted it. Only then was he certain that the money would circulate.[40]

Sakata set up two Chinese trading companies, the Chengda Gongsi, which Xie Wenta managed and the Huaxin Gongsi, which Xu Caicheng ran. At first their goal was simply to flood unoccupied China with currency and inflate prices. As the war progressed, however, their motives changed. With the army starved for strategic supplies, Sakata moved into logistics. He began purchasing war materials from *Guomindang*-occupied territory, especially rice, salt, and nonferrous metals. He also supplied opium to the army, which used it to pay for information gathering. One soldier remembers the intelligence officers in his unit at Yichang, near the border of Chinese-held territory, being given an ounce of opium once a month to use when paying informants.[41]

This time Sakata's operation received more appreciation than his previous caper. In 1940 he went to Tokyo to meet Tojo Hideki in the general's office. Tojo, usually a severely formal man, chatted with Sakata in a friendly manner, sitting on the front of his desk and holding in his hand the ounce of gold that Sakata had purchased from the Shanghai money shop. Sakata also prudently banked some of the profits for himself. When the war ended, Sakata returned to Tokyo with a small fortune that he used to buy a building on the Ginza and establish an import-export company. Kodama Yoshio introduced him to some of the more important underworld figures in Japan. Had he lived beyond 1950, he may have become as politically powerful as Kodama.[42]

Sakata and Kodama were important behind-the-scenes players in the Pacific War; military procurement and covert operations merged in their careers. They made out well by combining patriotism, idealism, and the pursuit of personal wealth. Functionally, they were soldiers of fortune in the purest form, although technically they were called *gun-zoku*—civilian employees of the Japanese army. And as they helped the military strategists, their personal fortunes grew.

For both men, narcotics was a secondary pursuit; but not for another civilian employee of the Japanese army, Satomi Hajime. In 1939, the Satomi Agency (*Satomi Kikan*) slipped into the vacuum left in Shanghai by the departure of Du Yuesheng. Eventually it operated a monopoly that sold opium in Shanghai by franchise and funneled the profits directly into an account in the Bank of Taiwan belonging to the Special Service Bureau attached to the Japanese army in Shanghai. But the agency did not immediately find it easy to control the port's opium trade. Indeed the first two years of Japanese occupation were a period of trial and error.[43]

During the first year of the China War, as coastal cities fell to Japanese forces, field officers had to fill the political vacuum left by retreating Chinese officials. At first there was no general plan for governing occupied territory, and those on the spot had to improvise. At the same time, they urgently needed money. Shanghai, where the Special Service Bureau took charge of establishing order, was an example of this early situation. Given its importance to the international opium trade, the city presented a special set of challenges, as well as rewards, to the victors.

THE OCCUPATION OF SHANGHAI AND THE NARCOTICS CONSORTIUM

The battle for Shanghai began in August 1937. As the fighting began, Chinese gangster Du Yuesheng provided aid and support for those on the front lines, just as he had during the battle of February 1932. (When the Chinese defense failed in November, he once again pocketed donations made for the fighting men.) As Japanese forces moved into the city, Du left for Hong Kong, leaving behind several trusted retainers to look after his assets and interests as best they could in the circumstances. (At least one source mentions that Sakata Shigemori moved his operation into Du's mansion at this time.)[44]

When Du left Shanghai, he created a crisis in the local opium market. Suddenly it found itself cut short of supplies and, more important, organization. The turmoil accompanying the transition in leadership can be seen in the market price of narcotics. As hostilities began, the price of opium went from $3.50 per ounce to $16.00 per ounce. Heroin and morphine jumped to $100.00 per ounce. Immediately after the war began, Persian opium reportedly sold for $40.00 per ounce. The Japanese commanders, desperate to meet the needs of addicts simply to keep order in a town so long accustomed to an adequate supply, began looking for someone to take Du's place.[45]

The Green Gang had never been a monolith. It functioned as a federation of related gang groups (today we would call them crews); Du Yuesheng's genius lay in his ability to negotiate and ameliorate hostilities among the groups as well as between gang members and outsiders. Not all Green Gang members followed Du to safer havens. Some stayed behind at Du's bidding to watch over his affairs, but others remained out of preference, coming to separate arrangements with the Japanese regime.

One of Du's associates who worked with the Japanese was Zhang Xiaolin. Zhang, it will be remembered, came to prominence in the Shanghai rackets because of his ties to the old *Beiyang* warlords, many of whom had looked to Japan for support in their battles against the *Guomindang*. He also had business ties with Yin Rugeng, the Japanese sympathizer in the north who was so helpful to Sakata's trucking route. On top of this, Zhang had been nursing a grudge against Chiang Kai-shek since 1933 because the Generalissimo refused Zhang's son a banking job after his return from a year's study in France. When Shanghai fell, therefore, Zhang stayed behind and actively helped the occupiers, presumably enjoying the company of Sakata Shigemori, who moved into Du Yuesheng's residence next door. He was duly labeled a traitor (*han jian*), and in 1940 he was assassinated by Dai Li's hit squads.[46]

Yet Zhang did not take over the narcotics consortium. Instead, during the first months of the occupation of Shanghai, those who stepped forward were previously small actors in the world of opium. One such man was Wang Shaocheng, who operated out of the Pingan Hotel on avenue Edward VII in the French Settlement. Wang owned one of the smallest of the opium firms before the war. Alone he had little influence in Shanghai and no personal source for the drug. Since supply was a problem, he had to rely on his Japanese benefactors for his stocks. He served as an intermediary between Japanese authorities and opium merchants during the interim as the Japanese tightened their control of the area.

In 1938 two men associated with the Special Service Bureau came to Shanghai to coordinate the opium monopoly: Colonel Kusamoto Sanetake and Colonel Cho Isamu. Both men were graduates of the Japanese Military Academy and the prestigious War College. Kusamoto was an abstemious man of few words who avoided raucous gatherings and kept mostly to himself. He had been assigned to Shanghai in 1936 as a staff officer in the China section. In the autumn of 1937, after the escalating hostilities extended to Shanghai and a Special Service Bureau had been created for that theater, Kusamoto became its head. In this position he began work with Cho, a man who in temperament was his exact opposite.

Cho had an outgoing personality. He loved sake, geisha, and singing. He was an expert in the martial arts, and, as we will remember, he had been active in the Cherry Blossom Society. In 1936 Cho had been assigned to Hankou. When hostilities began in 1937, he was transferred to Shanghai as a staff officer in the intelligence section. He had good contacts with *ronin*; as a result, he was able to provide good information to the Japanese expeditionary army during the battle for Shanghai.[47]

Kusamoto and Cho immediately set to work to bring the opium organization into Japanese hands. Yet they met with unexpected troubles. Shanghai had long supported a large population of addicts and devotees to narcotics whose cravings would not disappear simply because of war. However, taking over the distribution and supply system was not to be accomplished overnight. Du Yuesheng's influence remained in Shanghai and was not easily dislodged. Also supplies were not readily available to the Japanese authorities in Shanghai. In spite of the quantities of Japanese opium available from Rehe, the central army found it difficult to procure. In the early days of the war, before a systematic occupation policy came out of Tokyo, the Japanese army occupied China piecemeal. Indeed, the rivalries among Japanese armies there were echoes of recent warlord politics. Thus the Japanese North China Expeditionary Army proved to be reluctant to ship supplies to the Central China Army, hoping to eventually administer the entire operation themselves. Like the Green Gang and the *Guomindang*, the Japanese armed services were riddled with factions. This posed an immediate problem for the army officers in Shanghai, with its population of addicts suddenly deprived of narcotics.

In October 1937, needing help to solve this problem, Cho Isamu sent a telegram to his old compatriot from the Cherry Blossom Society, Fujita Osamu. "I want you to come to Shanghai quickly," it said. Fujita had spent the early years of the decade in Tokyo, where he kept company with ultranationalists and with men who served in the *Kempeitai*. Once summoned, Fujita went to Shanghai and contacted Wang Shaocheng, whom he had known from his early days in the Shantung narcotics traffic. Wang appreciated the possibilities that Fujita's connections with the Japanese army presented and the two men soon made a deal.[48]

Fujita arranged to import 120,000 kilos of Iranian opium for which he would pay US$6,000 per chest, one third of which he received in advance. He met with Cho a second time and obtained from him the required opium import permit issued by Kusamoto from the Special Service Bureau. Once these arrangements were made, Fujita went to the headquarters of Mitsui Shipping Company. Mitsui had held the monopoly privilege of supplying the Guandong Army in Manchuria with opium purchased in Iran. It had a standing arrangement with Amin and Company, an opium firm whose owner was well-placed in the Iranian government.[49]

The Mitsui representative in Iran could not arrange for the entire 200,000 catties; however, he did procure 1,400 chests and 120 catties (160 pounds), which were sent off to Shanghai in two shipments. One arrived in April 1938, and the second in January 1939. Somewhere in the Shanghai dealings, in the transfers between Mitsui, Fujita, Wang, and the Special Service Bureau, there seemed to be a discrepancy between the amounts contracted for and the amount delivered. It is possible that Fujita kept for himself as many as 550 chests of opium, which, at $6,000 a chest, represented a lot of money. It was the last narcotics venture for Fujita, however. He fell out of favor with the military and, Yamauchi tells us, at one point feared for his life. In 1938 he was replaced in Shanghai by Satomi Hajime, a man who had worked for Itagaki Seishiro in North China during the 1930s. Unlike Fujita, he remained in good standing with the military commanders.[50]

Cho Isamu also did not last long in Shanghai. Hoping to create a new Manchurian-style state in the city, he proposed a Taiwanese Chinese, Wang Zehui, to head a provisional government for Shanghai. Wang spoke excellent Japanese but only broken Chinese. Even the personnel in the Japanese navy and the Foreign Office recognized that such a government head would be a travesty. Cho was persuasive, however, and when the puppet government was finally formed, his candidate, although not head of the city, did become the head of the industrial section. Cho himself did not remain in Shanghai. Early in 1938 he was transferred to command the 74th Brigade of the Korean army. When he left Shanghai, he gave a banquet at one of the city's exclusive restaurants for eighty *ronin*. He continued to live the high life even at his post in the north of Korea, no doubt funded with some of Fujita's opium profits.[51]

In early 1938 Satomi Hajime moved from Tianjin to Shanghai to take the place of Fujita. Satomi was born in Fukuoka in 1897. In 1916 he went to Shanghai to attend the East Asian Language Academy, where he studied Chinese. After a brief tenure at the school he rambled through North China, ending up as a reporter for a Japanese-language paper in Tianjin. In the late 1920s he began working for the South Manchurian Railway Company. He went to Nanjing, where he made influential friends in the *Guomindang* and among wealthy Hong Kong merchants. These connections allowed him to consolidate the Shanghai opium trade when he took over from Fujita in spring 1938.

Satomi was not new to the drug traffic. After the Manchurian incident he became a public relations agent for the new government, taking over a Chinese-language paper in Mukden. As the paper's editor, he used the company as a cover to bring opium from Manchuria to Tianjin, where the money earned funded intelligence and insurgency operations in that city. He began a friendship with a Chinese salt merchant named Sheng Wenyi at that time. Sheng was a nephew of Sheng Xuanhuai, one of China's pioneer industrialists. Thus Sheng was well-connected with the Chinese elite. More important, Sheng was an opium addict who had ties to the Green Gang. This gave Satomi the entree he would need to find suitable merchants to open opium shops under the new system.[52]

Satomi had friends among the control faction in Manchuria. From the beginning of Manchukuo, he had worked with Tojo, Doihara, Itagaki, and Kishi Nobusuke. He was reportedly a financial source for the covert operations of Amakasu Masahiko as well. Satomi was also not so greedy as Fujita, turning 80 percent of his earnings over to the military authorities. Satomi was a chain smoker who spoke colloquial Chinese with a smoker's gravely voice. He was attractive to women. He lived in a luxury apartment across from Pierce Garden in the International Settlement, which at any given time of the day might be filled with all sorts of characters, adventurers, and piles of money. He began selling the Iranian opium imported by Mitsui, using his Chinese name, Li Ming.

Satomi's career in Shanghai coincided with the creation of the puppet Chinese government in the occupied coastal zone, nominally under the control of Wang Jingwei. The goal of this new government was to coordinate the increasingly complex empire and to harmonize military regions. Wang reigned over a government laced with Japanese military advisers, modeled after Manchukuo and complete with organizations claiming to be dedicated to pan-Asian economic development. One government agency created through this program was the Ko-A-In (Asian Development Agency).

The Ko-A-In began operation in September 1939. It had political, economic, and propaganda branches and served as a conduit for policy made by the Japanese military. With its headquarters in Tokyo, its various branch office functions were distributed to the army and the navy. These became the police, the tax office, and, of course, the opium supply agency for the areas they served. Satomi Hajime described the operations of the Shanghai branch of the Ko-A-In.

Satomi worked directly for Colonel Kusamoto Sanetake. The Persian opium in question was stored at the time in special military warehouses. Satomi sold it to Chinese merchants for whom he arranged special permits. These Chinese deposited money in Satomi's account in the Bank of Taiwan. Satomi, in turn, rendered an accounting to Kusumoto twice a month. Once the Ko-A-In was established under the auspices of the Chinese puppet government, Satomi's contact, Kusumoto, became its Shanghai liaison officer. To handle the specific functions of opium business, they created a bureau called the Kosai Zendo under the Ko-A In. Originally the Kosai Zendo had been a Chinese benevolent society co-opted by Japanese in Manchuria twenty years earlier. Satomi became the vice chairman of the entire organization. (As in Manchukuo, Chinese held the top positions, but had no authority. As vice chairman, Satomi was in charge.)

During the war years, according to Satomi, opium came from two sources: Manchurian and Mongolian fields, where it was cultivated under the supervision of Nitanosa's student, and from Persia, where it was brought in by the Mitsui Bussan Company. The main office of the Ko-A-In headquarters in Tokyo controlled supplies and determined where opium should be delivered. Prices reflected the cost of raw opium, a premium for the Mongolian government, and an 8 percent handling fee for the Ko-A-In. As with other scarce war material, there was never enough opium to satisfy the Chinese market.[53]

Chinese opium traffickers continued to target the Shanghai market as well as they could under the new conditions. An opium combine from Shantou successfully smuggled some quantities of the drug into the concession areas, which remained under foreign control until the war in the Pacific broke out in 1941. The Chinese maritime customs noted a spectacular increase in confiscations at the time, although many of their leads came from Japanese sources who were anxious to stamp out competition.[54]

Du Yuesheng continued to exert as much influence as he could in Shanghai from his suite at the Gloucester Hotel in Hong Kong. Agents watching the narcotics situation from the International Settlement, such as M. R. Nicholson, the American treasury attaché, assumed that Du continued to control the Shanghai market, as have historians of the opium trade ever since. Yet Du could not manage the traffic in Shanghai as effectively once he was away from familiar ground. And given the changing situation, he had to make choices.[55]

When Shanghai first fell, Du was inclined to stay in the safety of the concession areas. He left late in 1937 but settled in Hong Kong, thereby distancing himself from the Nationalist government fighting the Japanese. He maintained his connections with the *Guomindang* by allowing his gang members to work as agents with Dai Li's Military Statistics Bureau. Early into the war, he had no way of knowing which direction events would take. Of the men he left behind to tend to his affairs in his absence, several maintained contacts with the Japanese, especially Xu Caicheng, who also worked with Sakata. While living in Hong Kong, Du met with representatives of the Japanese-sponsored Wang Jingwei government several times, and rumors circulated that he had gone over to the Japanese side. Later, when events forced his retreat to Chongqing, he was willing to meet secretly with members of anti-Chiang Kai-shek factions as well.[56]

Du left Shanghai with considerable assets. But maintaining the scale of his Shanghai operation required substantial monthly expenditures, and his influence to a certain extent depended on maintaining his lavish living style.[37] Establishing a new operation in Hong Kong proved to be even more costly. Du's wealth and influence came from the protection he provided for others who trafficked in opium directly. He could do this because of the network of influence he had built up over the years, not only with Chiang Kai-shek but with other influential Shanghai residents who came to his side through bribery, favors, or intimidation. Once he settled in Hong Kong, his web of connections dissolved, causing him problems. Reestablishing broken ties and currying favor with new power brokers all cost money. In 1938 Du tried to procure the drug on his own. He put together a group of dealers from Guangzhou who commissioned him to buy opium, handing him 30 million dollars of the grossly inflated *fabi*. But supplies were hard to come by, and he had to turn to Dai Li for assistance.

Dai Li knew the value of opium in funding underground operations. Retreat from the China coast pushed the *Guomindang* into Szechuan and Yunnan, an area once only nominally under their control. This southwestern part of China was a principal opium-growing region and had supplied Du through his connections with the local gang, the Baoge Hui. After 1937 Dai Li controlled this area and its opium income. He agreed to supply Du with the required opium, but he stalled on the delivery for over a year.

In the end Dai Li never made the promised delivery. If he were to ship the opium abroad, he required the proper international certificates. Such permits had to be issued through the Chinese Ministry of Finance. At the time, the office was controlled by Dai Li's rivals within the *Guomindang*, T. V. Soong and H. H. Kung. Thus the deliveries were delayed. In 1941 Du went to Chongqing to try and handle the problem. While he was there, the Japanese attacked Pearl Harbor and a month later Hong Kong fell. Du remained in Chongqing, and the problem of delivering the promised opium disappeared.[58]

Du lived the last years of the Second World War in a private villa in Chongqing, playing mah-jongg with friends. During those years his relationship with Chiang Kai-shek was distant. But he maintained business ties with Dai Li in spite of the earlier impasse. After the summer of 1943, Dai Li seized an opportunity to attack H. H. Kung, the powerful rival who had stopped the previous opium deal. Agents in the Anti-Smuggling Office, supervised by Dai since 1942, caught one of H. H. Kung's minions smuggling goods, including opium, into Chongqing using his position in the Central Bank of China. Dai Li brought the information directly to Chiang Kai-shek, who executed the unlucky traf-

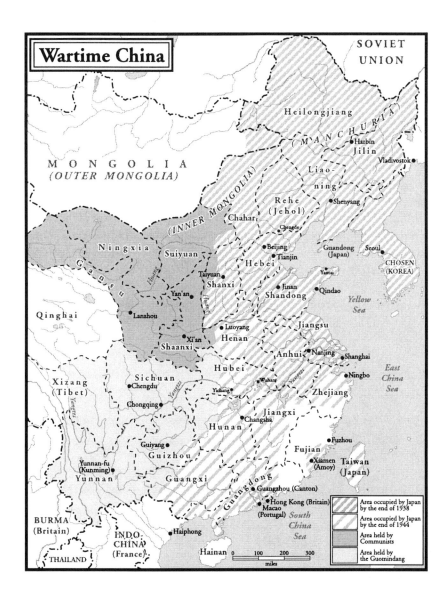

Wartime China

SOVIET UNION

Heilongjiang

MANCHURIA

Harbin

Jilin

Vladivostok

MONGOLIA
(OUTER MONGOLIA)

(INNER MONGOLIA)

Liao-ning

Shenyang

Rehe
(Jehol)

Chahar

Chengde

Ningxia

Suiyuan

Gansu

Huang

Taiyuan

Shanxi

Yan'an

Lanzhou

Beijing

Tianjin

Hebei

Jinan

Shandong

Yantai

Qingdao

Guandong
(Japan)

Seoul

CHOSEN
(KOREA)

Yellow
Sea

Qinghai

Xi'an

Shaanxi

Luoyang

Henan

Jiangsu

Xizang
(Tibet)

Sichuan

Chengdu

Chongqing

Yichang

Wuhan

Hubei

Yangzi

Anhui

Nanjing

Shanghai

Ningbo

Zhejiang

East
China
Sea

Jiangxi

Changsha

Hunan

Guiyang

Guizhou

Yunnan-fu
(Kunming)

Yunnan

Guangxi

Fuzhou

Fujian

Xiamen
(Amoy)

Taiwan
(Japan)

Guangdong

Guangzhou (Canton)

Hong Kong (Britain)

Macao
(Portugal)

South
China
Sea

BURMA
(Britain)

INDO-CHINA
(France)

Haiphong

THAILAND

Hainan

	Area occupied by Japan by the end of 1938
	Area occupied by Japan by the end of 1944
	Area held by Communists
	Area held by the Guomindang

0   100   200   300
miles

ficker. Du and Dai opened several companies to engage in smuggling of their own. These including the Tongji Company, which had branches close to enemy-occupied territory. Through the agency of the ubiquitous Xu Caicheng they acquired supplies from Shanghai that they resold for a substantial profit. They made contacts with Sakata's organization, as well as the Kodama Agency. Dai Li's control of transportation and inspection paid off in furthering this business.[59]

Dai Li, Kodama, and Sakata all played a double game, doing business with each other as they fulfilled their respective roles in the war. By 1943 both sides were so desperate for supplies that their cooperation looked less like collaboration or betrayal than desperate procurement measures. Dai Li remained loyal to Chiang Kai-shek, but he must have recognized kindred spirits in Sakata and Kodama. Sakata had, after all, tried to negotiate a truce with the *Guomindang* in 1940. All three men were anti-Communist, and all were growing wealthy from their patriotism. Although not flagging in his efforts to press the war, Dai Li used the company to pass counterfeit Japanese war-zone currency printed by his organization in Chongqing on machines supplied by Americans.[60]

AFTER THE WAR

When the war ended, Du returned to his mansion in the French Settlement of Shanghai. On the surface of things, he seemed to resume his old life. Yet in the postwar years he was, compared to his past life, almost reclusive. No longer was his home the scene of banquets, parties, and decision making. The war made him less open and receptive to all who came his way. Shanghai itself had changed. His friend and colleague Zhang Xiaolin was gone. Communists were regaining their prestige among labor groups. As the civil war rekindled, Dai Li became more important to Chiang Kai-shek than Du, who slowly lost his influence with the government in Nanjing. Du's loss of political clout was most glaringly demonstrated in 1948, when his son was arrested.

Dai Li emerged from the war with his power enhanced. Because of Du's wartime exile away from his power base, Dai was able to gather into his own hands much of the economic strength that opium could bring. Dai developed important connections with members of Du's old gang. He maintained contacts with members of the American intelligence services with whom he had worked during the war in the Pacific. As the last phase of the Chinese Communist revolution began late in 1945, his

Military Statistics Bureau became more important to Chiang Kai-shek than ever.

At the end of the war, Dai Li, Du Yuesheng, and Milton Miles showed up in the town of Chun'an, Zhejiang province, where an important listening post had been operating through the war. At that time the three men met with groups of agents of the Military Statistics Bureau and Shanghai hoodlums brought to the town by Xu Caicheng. Even as the war against Japan came to its close, the men who had prospered from the course of battle were preparing for the coming Chinese civil war. Unfortunately for their plans, none of the men at the meeting would carry on at the front of the coming battle. Milton Miles, for one, returned to Chongqing suffering from the strain of war. He was soon relieved of his duties. He spent the early 1950s on the periphery of the espionage establishment.[61]

Dai Li spent the last year of his life establishing agents behind Communist lines and recruiting collaborators into his organization, yet he did not live to apply his talents to the cold war. He had always claimed that he would be killed by Chiang Kai-shek. The plane crash that killed him was attributed variously to the Communists, the OSS, and Sun Yat-sen's ghost. In fact, Dai Li died in the stubborn pursuit of a woman.[62]

In March 1946, Dai Li was in Beijing overseeing anti-Communist operations in the area. On the evening of March 17, he loaded a plane with extra fuel and took off for Chongqing, where he wanted to foil a rival's bid to become commissioner of police. He planned to stop first in Shanghai to persuade Butterfly's inconvenient husband to agree to a divorce. He also changed pilots at the last minute, opting for a man with less flying experience but with contacts for a moneymaking scheme involving American currency. The weather in the Shanghai-Nanjing area was rainy and treacherous, yet he insisted on making the landing. It was an ill-fated decision. The plane missed the runway and crashed, bursting into an inferno of burning fuel.[63]

If he had not died, Dai Li might have emerged as a force to be reckoned with during the cold war. Instead, the Military Statistics Bureau split into factions as his three subordinates struggled to control the organization. Thus it was Dai Li's Japanese alter egos, Sakata Shigemori and Kodama Yoshio, who carried the threads of the system developed by so many capable hands into the postwar world. Both men left Shanghai shortly after the surrender, bringing with them a vast amount of treasure in cash and precious metals. Both served time in Sugamo Prison as class A war criminals.

Released from prison, Sakata went to work for American intelligence. He returned to prison in 1949 after he was implicated in a scheme to smuggle opium into Japan to raise money for Chiang Kai-shek's retreating armies. He died shortly thereafter, leaving Kodama Yoshio to become a shadowy fixer for conservative Japanese politicians. Satomi Hajime also returned to Japan after the war, bringing his own fortune in gold and precious stones and buying a house in Kyoto. Although he was not as active as his two colleagues, he donated some of his money to Chinese soldiers on Taiwan.[64]

The war did for all goods what international sanctions had done for opium; it made them difficult to get and inflated their value. Opium shared space with all kinds of goods being smuggled back and forth between the areas held by the contending armies. In Central China, for instance, salt became scarce as the Japanese army blockaded the resource. Sending much of it back to Japan, they carefully parceled out portions of salt to their supporters, whereas other Chinese caught with salt were shot immediately. Salt became as important as opium.[65]

Opium was especially valuable to the Chinese and Japanese military establishments because both were critically dependent on profits generated by its trade. Opium was more than a scarce commodity. It became a necessary tool in pursuing the war. So much was this the case that even the Chinese Communists in Yen'an, in spite of their rhetoric, found that they had to resort to the traffic during the critical years of the war.[66] It would be convenient for us to picture evil Japanese militarists and calculating Chinese generals using opium as a weapon in a well-stocked arsenal and part of a master plan. But the lines were not so neatly drawn. The war in Asia was chaotic. It was fought in an area that had been at the center of global narcotics consumption and production. Traffickers provided funds and expertise to both sides. But their reward, given the scope of the conflict, was often the destruction of their base. Du Yuesheng's own experience demonstrates how fragile was the relationship between trafficker and politician. In the early 1930s he seemed indestructible. By the end of the war his operation had been co-opted by Dai Li. After the Communist victory in 1949, he retired to Hong Kong. Meanwhile, a new generation of traffickers found opportunities created by the onset of the cold war. The links among espionage, military procurement, and narcotics that were established in Central China during the war by agents of Dai Li, Sakata, and Kodama created patterns that would continue into the postwar world, albeit in the hands of different players.

Until the Communist victory in 1949, China remained the center of the drug traffic. Thereafter, America emerged into the world spotlight by default. The American market, minuscule by Chinese standards, had developed in a peculiar way, not only because of its small size but also because of the different enforcement patterns that prevailed there.

NOTES

1. Kodama Yoshio, *Gokuchu, Gokugai* [In prison, out of prison] (Tokyo: Ajia Shonensha, 1942), 183.
2. Kodama, *Gokuchu, Gokugai*, 164–66.
3. Takamori Hisaakira, *Miezaru Seifu: Kodama Yoshio to Sono Kuro no Jinmyaku* [The invisible government: Kodama Yoshio and his black network] (Tokyo: Shiraishi Shoten, 1976), 43–45.
4. From 1927 to 1949 the capital of China was located in Nanjing and during the war years, 1938–45, in Chongqing. During this period, "Beijing," meaning the northern capital, became "Beiping," meaning northern peace.
5. See Ben-Ami Shellony, *Revolt in Japan* (Princeton, N.J.: Princeton University Press, 1973).
6. Hashimoto himself was moved from staff officer to the reserves. Oe Shino, *Tenno no Guntai* [The emperor's army] *Showa no Rekishi* [History of the Showa period] (Tokyo: Shogaku Kan, 1988), 3:249–50. At the end of the war, however, he spent time in Sugamo Prison as a class A war prisoner. Kodama Yoshio describes the smouldering animosity lingering in the atmosphere of the prison, in which men of different military factions had to live together as prisoners of war. Kodama Yoshio, *Sugamo Diary* (Tokyo: Radio Press, 1960), 257.
7. In both Chinese and Japanese espionage organizations, the character *te* or *toku* "special" appears. In both cases opium is also called "special goods" using the same character.
8. Yoga Hiroshi, "Kitashi, Mokyo no Tokumu Kikan" [The special service organs of north China and Mongolian border region], *Kokuho* [National defense] (January 1972), 122–35.
9. Perhaps the most concise description of mobilization efforts in English is found in W. G. Beasley, *The Rise of Modern Japan* (New York: St. Martin's, 1990), 187–99.
10. Yoga, "Kitashi, Mokyo no Tokumu Kikan," 122–35.
11. Shen Zui, "Wo Suo Zhidaode Dai Li" [The Dai Li that I knew], in *Wenshi Ziliao Xuanzhuan* [Selected historical resources] (Beijing: Zhonghua Shuchu, 1961), 22:77–78. We call the Military Statistics Bureau more professional in that Dai Li and his officers did not treat espionage as a stepping-stone to higher command but as a career in itself, expanding personal power from within the agency.
12. Shen, "Wo Suo Zhidao de Dai Li," 65–66; Chen Lifu, *Storm Clouds Clear over China* (Palo Alto, Calif.: Hoover Institution on War, Revolution, and Peace, 1994), 64–66. Chen Lifu is still alive at this writing and has even published

a book of personal philosophy, which these authors have seen for sale in the New Age section of the Barnes and Noble bookstore in Berkeley, California; Chen Lifu has a rosier memory of the split. He claims that when he learned that there was a rival intelligence agency, he asked Chiang about it. Later, like the dutiful first wife accommodating a powerful concubine, he worked with Dai Li in the reorganized agency.

13. Shen, "Wo Suo Zhidao de Dai Li," 69.

14. Shen, "Wo Suo Zhidao de Dai Li," 64–66, 83–85; Hu Xiaohua, "Cong Fenyungdui dao Biedongjun" [From brave troops to special commando unit], *Wenshih Ziliao Xuanji* [Selection from historical source materials] (Beijing: Zhongguo Wenshi Ziliao Chubanshe, 1989), 19:185–94.

15. Shen, "Wo Suo Zhidao de Dai Li," 75–76.

16. Shen, "Wo Suo Zhidao de Dai Li," 66.

17. Everything written in Chinese about Dai Li mentions this event, but we have yet to see it mentioned in English. The Milton Miles papers leave out any mention of it, saying only that Milton Miles was impressed that Dai Li knew he did not eat chicken when they first met. See Shen Yuan, "Dai Li Tieshi" [Dai Li's iron deeds], in *Wenshi Ziliao Xuanji* [Selection from historical source materials] (Beijing: Zhongguo Wenshi Ziliao Chubanshe, 1989), 19:178–83; Shen, "Wo Suo Zhidao de Dai Li," 117; Zhou Lang, *Dai Li Waizhuan* [Unofficial biography of Dai Li] (Hong Kong: Starite Book, 1989), 1:1193–1214; Zhang Weihan, "Dai Li yu Juntongju" [Dai Li and the military statistics bureau], in *Zhejiang Wenshi Ziliao Xuanji* [Historical sources for Zhejiang province] (Zhejiang Renmin Chubanshe, 1982), 104–07; Miles to Wright, April 5, 1944, Office of Naval Intelligence, Records of Naval Group China and V. Adm. Milton E. Miles, box 4, RG 38.

18. The travels are detailed in the Milton Miles's papers and are described in Milton Miles, *A Different Kind of War: The Little-Known Story of the Combined Guerrilla Forces Created in China by the U.S. Navy and the Chinese during World War II* (Garden City, N.Y.: Doubleday, 1967); a less sanguine view of the partnership is found in Michael Schaller, *The U.S. Crusade in China, 1938–1945* (New York: Columbia University Press, 1979).

19. Guo Yu, "Song Ziliang Yu Xinan Yunlunchu" [T. L. Soong and the South West Transport Company], *Guangdong Wenshi Ziliao* [Source materials of Canton province], vol. 11 (Guangzhou: Chinese People's Political Consultative Committee of Guangdong Province, 1963); Zhang, "Dai Li yu Juntongju," 112–14.

20. Liu Peifang, "Dai Li, Du Yuesheng Lai Chun Huadong Diandi" [A bit of activity when Dai Li and Du Yuesheng came to Chun], in *Chunan Wenshi Ziliao* (Zhejiang: 1986), 2:84–85.

21. Shen, "Wo Suo Zhidao de Dai Li," 163–64, 175–76, 205–07. He was never a good shot, nor did he ever acquire skill at martial arts, although he thought of himself as a hero in a martial arts novel.

22. Shen, "Wo Suo Zhidao de Dai Li," 61–74.

23. Yamamoto Tsuneo, *Ahen to Taiho: Rikugun Showa Tsusho no Nananen* [Opium and cannon: nine years in the army's Showa trading company] (Tokyo: PMC Publishing, 1986), 42–44, remembers thinking that this man was a danger-

ous revolutionary and feeling a kind of dreadful awe when he saw him as part of the company business.

24. Takemori, *Miezaru Seifu,* 45–48. Kodama himself remembers the time he spent in prison as one of personal spiritual growth; Kodama Yoshio, *I Was Defeated* (Tokyo: Radio Press, 1951), 45–48.

25. Kodama Yoshio, "Akusei, Jusei, Ransei" [Evil government, the sound of guns, the world in chaos], *Fuun* [Wind and clouds] (Tokyo: Nihon Oyobi Nihonjin Sha, 1972) 2:109–22.

26. Kodama, "Akusei, Jusei, Ransei," 119–28.

27. Kodama, "Akusei, Jusei, Ransei," 146–56.

28. Kodama, "Akusei, Jusei, Ransei," 146–56.

29. Kodama, "Akusei, Jusei, Ransei," 143–49; Yamamoto, *Ahen to Taiho,* 34.

30. Takasugi Shingo, "Akuma no Boryaku" [The devil's strategy], pt. 2, *Sunday Mainichi,* December 9, 1984.

31. Okada Yoshimasa, "Ahen Senso to Watakushi no Taiken" [The opium war and my own experience], *Zoku: Gendaishi Shiryo Geppo* [Continued: modern history materials monthly report], June 1986.

32. Elie Eliopoulos describes the Japanese success at taking over the Tianjin market, Box 4536. 800.114N16ELIOPOULOS/27, RG 59; "Akuma no Boryaku", pt. 3, December 23, 1984.

33. Okada, "Ahen Senso to Watakushi."

34. Okada, "Ahen Senso to Watakushi."

35. Okada, "Ahen Senso to Watakushi."

36. Okada Yoshimasa, "Chukoku Shihei Gizo Jiken no Zembo" [The complete picture of the Chinese currency counterfeiting caper], *Rekishi To Jimbutsu* 110 (October 1980).

37. Earnest Hauser, *Shanghai: City for Sale,* 222–29; Arthur Young, *China and the Helping Hand* (Cambridge, Mass.: Harvard University Press, 1963); Nan Wei Cheng, "U.S. Silver Purchase Legislation, June, 1934," the *Chinese Mercury,* January 1937.

38. Takamatsu Shigeru, "Watakushi Wa Teikoku Rikugun de Gizo Shihei o Tsukuru" [I made counterfeit currency for the Imperial Army], *Gendai,* September 1967.

39. Takamatsu, "Watakushi Wa Teikoku Rikugun de Gizo Shihei o Tsukuru."

40. Takamatsu, "Watakushi Wa Teikoku Rikugun de Gizo Shihei o Tsukuru."

41. Takamatsu, "Watakushi Wa Teikoku Rikugun de Gizo Shihei o Tsukuru"; Yamamoto Kenzo, Mise Hohei Kosoko No.

42. "Akuma no Boryaku," pt. 2, December 9, 1984.

43. Satomi Hajime, "Satomi Hajime Sensei Kojutsu Sho" [Satomi Hajime's oral deposition]; Eguchi Keiichi, *Shiryo: Nitchu Sensoki Ahen Seisaku* [Sources: opium policy during the China Japan war] (Tokyo: Iwanami Shoten, 1985), 623–26; "Kokkin o Okasu Gun Meirei," *Shukan Yomiyuri,* (June 5, 1955), 4–13.

44. "Akuma no Boryaku," pt. 2, December 9, 1984.

45. "Wang Feng-shih, Shanghai's New Opium King," June 17, 1938, box 7209, 893.114NARCOTICS/2308, RG 59.

46. Yu Yunjiu, "Wo Suo Zhidao de Zhang Xiaolin" [The Zhang Xiaolin that I

knew], *Jindai Zhungguo Banghui Neimu* [The inside story of modern Chinese gangs] (Beijing: Masses Publishing, 1992), 427–30; "Akuma no Boryaku," pt. 2, December 9, 1984.

47. Hata Ikuhiko, *Showa Shi no Gunjintachi* [Soldiers in Showa history] (Tokyo: Bungei Shunju, 1982), 113–19.

48. American intelligence sources describe Wang as a petty trafficker, one of the least important of Du's associates. Japanese sources talk of his importance. Clearly the Japanese connection, while it lasted for him, worked to his professional advantage. Fujise, *Showa Rikugun Ahen Boryoku no Taizai,* 116, 126.

49. Fujise, *Showa Rikugun Ahen Boryoku no Taizai,* 119–27; "Kokkin o Okasu Gun Meirei," *Shukan Yomiyuri.*

50. Fujise, *Showa Rikugun Ahen Boryaku no Taizai,* 129–32; "Kokkin o Okasu Gun Meirei," *Shukan Yomiyuri.*

51. Fujise, *Showa Rikugun Ahen Boryaku no Taizai,* 172; "Kokkin o Okasu Gun Meirei," *Shukan Yomiyuri.*

52. Fujise, *Showa Rikugun Ahen Boryaku no Taizai,* 61–62, 132; "Kokkin o Okasu Gun Meirei," *Shukan Yomiyuri.*

53. Satomi Hajime, "Satomi Hajime Sensei Kojutsu Sho."

54. "Narcotic Situation in Shanghai," June 21, 1938, 893.114NARCOTICS/2287, RG 59.

55. Nicholson to Treasury, October 21, 1938, 893.114NARCOTICS/2379, RG 59.

56. Fan Shaozeng, "Guanyu Du Yuesheng" [About Du Yuesheng], Wenshi Ziliao Xuanji; Quanguo Zhengxie, 1982, 84:187–91. Du himself spent the war outside of Shanghai, but he wanted his trusted deputies to remain. One such underling panicked when the *Kempei* began keeping him under surveilence. He fled to Hong Kong but received a cold reception from Tu. A second bookkeeper fled only when told he was about to be arrested, but seeing Tu's displeasure in Hong Kong, he returned. When he was arrested and tortured, the intervention of Xu Caicheng secured his early release and probably saved his life.

57. At the peak of his powers, Du kept a house with his three wives on Rue Wagner in the French concession, where he entertained lavishly. His staff included three secretaries at $300 per month, four honorary secretaries, $500. His head bodyguard earned $150 per month; an assistant, $100, sixteen other guards got $80 per month, including men stationed at the gate and behind the house. He had thirteen chauffeurs and maintenance men at $50 and $30 each. His kitchen staff was substantial, as he entertained extensively. The head chef earned $10. per month, the kitchen staff $80. Servants, tea servers, and door guards got $50, maids, $20 month. Huang the bookkeeper received $200 per month. Du had a second houshold on Rue Lafayette where a fourth wife resided. He owned a steamer, a villa in Suzhou and in Hangzhou, a mountain retreat, plus his family temple, all of which required upkeep. Huang calculated his worth at 5.7 million just before he left for Hong Kong. He made money on the war, especialy as the ubiquitous Xu Caicheng managed to send cloth and other goods from

Shanghai into the war areas where they were sold at a profit. Yet when he returned to Shanghai after the war his spending habits altered considerably and he became comparatively austere. Huang Guodong, "Dumen Huajiu" [Old talk from Du's house], in *Jiu Shanghai de Banghui* [Gangs of old Shanghai] *Shanghai Wenshi Ziliao Xuanji* [Selected source materials of Shanghai], 54:252. Sakata, we are told, took a fortune with him to Tokyo at war's end, some of which belonged to Shanghai gang members, and invested the funds in an import/export company on the Ginza.

58. Fan, "Guanyu Du Yuesheng," 187–91. Luck once again intervened on Tu's behalf. He kept a shrine to the fox god. Perhaps that is why the course of history so often seemed to work in his favor.

59. Zhang, "Dai Li yu Juntongju," 112–14; 115–16. This incident had many consequences. H. H. Kung was enraged and his wife complained to her sister, Mme. Chiang Kai-shek. As rumors flew through the wartime capital about Dai Li's character, Milton Miles found he had to engage in some damage control. RG 38, Office of Naval Intelligence, Records of Naval Group China and V. Adm. Milton E. Miles. Box 39, September 20, 1943; Huang, "Du Men Huajiu," 253.

60. Zhang, "Dai Li yu Juntongju,"112–13.

61. Liu, "Dai Li, Du Yuesheng Lai Chun." The best discussion of Dai Li's relationship with U.S. intelligence is Jonathan Marshall, "Opium, Tungsten, and the Search for National Security, 1940–1952" in *Drug Control Policy*, ed. William O. Walker, (University Park: Pennsylvania State University Press, 1991), 89–116.

62. On the rumors about Dai Li's death, see Schaller, *The U.S. Crusade in China*, 249.

63. Shen, "Wo Suo Zhidao de Dai Li," 198–208; Zhao Xin, "Dai Li Shuaisi Qianhou" [The events surrounding Dai Li's death crash], Wenshi Ziliao Xuanpian (Beijing: 1988), 35.

64. Morris, *Nationalism and the Right Wing in Japan*, 46; "Kokkin o Okasu Gun Meirei."

65. "Akuma no Boryaku," pt. 2, December 9, 1984.

66. Chen Yung-fa, "The Blooming Poppy under the Red Sun: The Yenan Way and the Opium Trade," in *New Perspectives on the Chinese Communist Revolution*, ed. Tony Saich and Hans van de Ben (Armonk, N.Y.: Sharpe, 1995), 263–98.

CHAPTER NINE

AMERICANS

1920 – 1945

The Italians stepped on the H much more than the Jews, and they charged more money . . . But gradually it [heroin] got weaker, and weaker, and weaker . . . In the thirties I was skin popping. I didn't start mainlining until the stuff got really bad, during the war.

Al, heroin addict[1]

April 17, 1933, was an unfortunate day for the Ezra family.[2] Agents from the Federal Bureau of Narcotics arrested Edith Mercer in San Francisco for selling a small amount of morphine to an informer. In hopes of gaining leniency, Mercer agreed to lead the men to her supplier, identified only by her street name, "Jew Annie." After Mercer purchased several packets of the drug from Annie using marked money, agents followed Annie and watched her buy morphine from her supplier, Florence Moore. When Moore was arrested, she immediately confessed to being one of several runners who sold morphine for Earl King.

The next day the agents hid in Florence Moore's apartment where they observed her meeting with King and his associate, Julius Stern, who supplied her with an ounce of morphine. Stern led the agents to Amelia Cuneo, who was, at the time, in possession of twenty-seven ounces of the drug. When arrested, Cuneo claimed that it belonged to John Rose and agreed to let the men watch as she gave it to him. Rose claimed that the drugs actually belonged to Judah Ezra, a resident of Shanghai temporarily living in San Francisco. On May 13, four weeks after Edith Mercer's apprehension, Ezra was arrested while in possession of thirty ounces of morphine. Shortly thereafter, agents also arrested Isaac Ezra, Judah's twin brother, and charged both of them with running a narcotics importation and distribution ring.

The brothers' arrest was a melancholy end to a rich and powerful family that had once dominated the legitimate opium business in prewar Shanghai. Judah and Isaac's father, Isaac Ezra Sr., along with their elder brother, Edward Ezra, had once headed Shanghai's powerful Opium Combine. In 1911, the Ezra family profited enormously from the Chinese opium prohibition. After Isaac Sr. divided the spoils among his children, his eldest son, Edward, shrewdly invested his share of the proceeds in real estate. He also maintained his ties to the opium traffic. Along with Paul Yip, he continued to supply the illicit Shanghai market until Yip's arrest in 1925. He became even wealthier than his father.

The younger sons, including Isaac Jr. and Judah, dissipated their patrimony. By the mid-1920s, the twins were broke and had been disowned by their elder brother for stealing some of his money. They reverted to the family business of dealing in drugs, now an illegal activity in Shanghai. Beginning in 1927, Judah smuggled narcotics from Europe to Shanghai under cover of a silk importing company. Isaac, meanwhile, married and settled in San Francisco. By 1931 European narcotics were growing scarce, which caused a dearth of opiates on the West Coast. The brothers responded to the situation by importing directly from Shanghai to San Francisco.[3]

Using a phony wood oil importing company as a business front, between 1931 and 1933 the brothers' agents in Shanghai purchased opium, cocaine, morphine, and heroin, packed the drugs in secret compartments hidden inside the walls of wood oil drums, and then shipped the goods to San Francisco aboard Japanese freighters. The Ezras paid for their consignments through bank transfers to the Dahlong Tea Company of Shanghai, another fictitious firm. In San Francisco, Judah placed an order with the McCoy Label Company for tags that would disguise the illicit Chinese morphine and heroin as high-quality French pharmaceuticals, since American drug addicts at this time were extremely brand-conscious consumers who preferred French opiates. Meanwhile Isaac and an associate rented a warehouse in which the narcotics were removed from the wood oil drums and sold to distributors.

The Ezra brothers distributed narcotics along the West Coast through John Rose, Leong Chung, and "Black Tony" Parmagini. The San Francisco district attorney estimated that the total street value of the drugs that moved through this system was $1.5 million.

When they were arrested, the Ezra brothers tried to offer information for leniency, as had Edith Mercer and their other distributors. Judah disclosed the location of 500 ounces of morphine, and both brothers cooperated with federal narcotics agents by naming all of their associates in Shanghai and in California. Despite their guilty pleas and cooperation, Judah and Isaac Ezra both received prison sentences of twelve years and fines of $12,000 each, with minor defendants receiving lesser sentences.

CHANGES IN THE GLOBAL NARCOTICS MARKET

The Ezra case dramatically highlighted a reversal in the flow of the global narcotics market. As recently as the late 1920s, Judah Ezra, like Elie Eliopoulos, had been in the business of smuggling European pharmaceuticals into China. One of the Ezras' unwitting accomplices in Shanghai, when told of their activities, expressed amazement: "I always hear and see in the papers that people are being caught for smuggling drugs into China, but I never heard that drugs are smuggled *out* of China." By 1933, this incredulity may have seemed a bit naïve to those in the business, but it is an accurate reflection of how the informed public on both sides of the Pacific reacted to the Ezra case. Shanghai, once the great consumer of European opiates, became the prime producer and exporter to the illicit world drug markets. The United States was a small, secondary market that had previously been supplied from Europe. But now it began to receive a substantial part of its supply from the Far East.

On January 9, 1932, Paul Crawley was arrested in Shanghai, further demonstrating the shifting direction of the traffic. Crawley, who operated from Shanghai, might have continued his trade had he not mistreated his wife. Lucy Fontaine Ivanoff Crawley met Paul in Harbin, Manchuria, in 1922. She was a cabaret dancer and he was a young man from California claiming to be involved with the film industry there.[4] Situated at the northern terminus of the Manchurian rail network, Harbin in those days was a meeting ground of White Russians, Japanese

soldiers, Chinese patriots, warlords' agents, and adventurers of every nationality. It was, as a result, a transfer point for arms and opium.

Paul was a charming, aggressively daring individual who could do
business in Russian, Mandarin, and Japanese. He thrived in Harbin. In
the late twenties he moved his operation to Shanghai. He, Lucy, and
their two children lived at 41 Verdun Terrace in the French Settlement.
She began working at the Del Monte Cabaret while he established an
import/export business. He brought American pianos, slot machines,
and arms into China, sending heroin to California in return. Lucy
helped him in his operations by packing drugs into tins for export. He
operated safely in Shanghai because he had a wide net of influential
connections. Most important among these was one H. O. Tong, a Shanghai customs agent and friend of T. V. Soong, brother-in-law to Chiang
Kai-shek.

Thus Crawley had a connection to the Shanghai syndicate that provided the kind of protection so valuable to traffickers. In 1931, however,
his relationship with Lucy began to unravel. He beat her and sexually
abused their daughter. Lucy found out from an acquaintance that he
was having an affair with a Eurasian woman named Hilda. Fearing for
her life, Lucy sought protection from the American consulate but received no help until she mentioned the source of her husband's wealth.
On October 26, 1931, just before she left Paul, he beat her all night and
wounded her with a knife. She was given shelter by P. S. Cox of the
Shanghai Municipal Police and his wife, who tended to her wounds. Her
information about Crawley's business activities led Settlement police to
arrest her husband.[5]

Lucy knew intimate details of Paul's operation. She revealed his
sources of narcotics, including Zih Lau-sai [Shanghai pronunciation],
son of Zhu Baosan, a prominent Shanghai financier who worked out of
his father's old residence at 832 Avenue Joffre. Paul relied on sailors and
marines to transport his goods to California. One of his better personnel
recruiters was Jim, a Chinese bartender at the Chang Kee Bar on Avenue
Foch, a favorite hangout for American marines on leave in Shanghai.
Lucy knew Paul's telegraphic codes and his American contacts. Especially valuable was a Mr. Short, code for William Sloat of the Merchant
Inn, 44 California Street, San Francisco. Paul also had an enforcer in
the United States, one Mickey O'Brian, said to be a perfect killer.[6]

Lucy risked her life by becoming an informant. Paul at first tried to
circulate the rumor that she was mad. A friend who gave her shelter
hired a doctor who certified her sanity. Lucy was followed and threat-

ened with the abduction of her children. Several Shanghai women gave her shelter, including Lama King who disappeared not long after Lucy left. Lucy was not lonely, however. She had several admirers, including a certain detective with the Shanghai Municipal Police. In spite of the danger, her information landed Paul in jail. Japan's February 1932 war in Shanghai put an abrupt end to Paul's slot machine business, which the faithful Hilda had continued to run for him during his incarceration.[7]

Paul Crawley's operation, like the Ezra brothers', thrived for a few years by taking advantage of the new American market for Chinese opiates. Yet the fate of the Ezra brothers and Paul Crawley revealed the different relationships between drug dealers and public officials in China and in America. By 1933, Du Yuesheng thrived because of his alliance with Chiang Kai-chek, the Chen brothers, and T. V. Soong. He became the apex of a narcotics federation that had representatives as far away as San Francisco. Agents like Crawley developed the market through China and then worldwide. In Manchukuo, Tianjin, and other Japanese concessions in China, Japanese civil and military authorities allowed the narcotics business to flourish under their sponsorship. China was disintegrating and civil war remained endemic, which made it possible for drug dealers to centralize and expand their operations. By contrast, in the politically stable United States of the 1930s and 1940s, narcotics remained a small-scale business in which consolidation was impossible.

Narcotics did, however, provide an opportunity for some ambitious souls. At the time of the Ezra and Crawley arrests, Harry J. Anslinger, the tough new head of the Federal Bureau of Narcotics, was beginning to make a career out of highly publicized drug busts. He had the resources and the incentive to pursue international narcotics cases that local police did not. Anslinger operated within a legal and moral framework that considered narcotic drug use to be an evil scourge. When Judah and Isaac Ezra received twelve-year prison sentences, they must have been shocked to discover that their captors regarded drug trafficking as a serious offense, not a minor peccadillo. Anslinger and his colleagues made war against drug dealers. As a result, drug trafficking in America differed drastically from drug trafficking in the Far East.

OPIUM IN AMERICA

Opium had not always been vilified by Americans. In the nineteenth century it was commonly regarded as a wonder drug.[8] Usually consumed as laudanum—a potent mixture of alcohol and opium—it soothed rumbling stomachs, alleviated chronic pain, brought sleep to the sleepless, and repose to the anxious. Injected morphine appeared just prior to the Civil War (1861–1865). Given the extraordinarily high number of casualties and the excruciating pain of battlefield injuries, military doctors on both sides resorted to indiscriminate shots of morphine. As a result, so many troops returned home with cases of drug addiction that for many years it was referred to as "the soldiers' disease." But morphine addiction was so widespread that the large number of Civil War veterans affected by it was surpassed by the number of middle-aged women who had begun taking morphine under doctors' supervision. By the 1890s, a maximum of 300,000 Americans—mostly female and mostly middle-aged—were addicted to opiates, a per capita rate that was about twice as high as it is today. However, drug addicts of that era were pitied, not feared. One's life and property were little threatened by an elderly, debilitated gentlewoman, whatever the nature of her chemical dependence.

Chinese immigrants, however, were perceived as distinctly more dangerous. They had moved to the United States in the late nineteenth century, bringing their opium with them. Elderly gentlewomen who had acquired an addiction in the course of medical therapy might be forgiven or even accommodated. But opium-smoking Chinese ("They take our jobs, and they take our women!") were another matter. They were not pitied but despised. Although they were the most visible, the Chinese were not the only persons of color who were associated with the recreational use of drugs. In the 1880s and 1890s southern newspapers increasingly reported cocaine use by black men, usually in exaggerated and lurid terms: "Cocaine-Crazed Negroes on Crime Spree!" By 1900, narcotic drug use had become fairly common among white urban youth gangs and the criminal underworld. Thus by the turn of the century the public had become alarmed about drug use.[9]

There is an irony here. The actual number of drug addicts in America peaked in the 1890s and then declined. By 1930, they numbered no more than 150,000, and perhaps as few as 75,000. In any case, addicts constituted a much smaller percentage of the population than they had forty years earlier. Yet the hysteria about drug addicts had grown as their number decreased. Clearly this alarm was the result of who the addicts were and the kind of drugs they were taking. An old lady quietly drifting off to sleep on laudanum was pitiful but harmless. Cocaine-sniffing black men, opium-smoking Chinese, and dope-taking young hoodlums brought home the danger of narcotic drugs in the most tangible way.

ANTIDRUG EFFORTS

As the reality and the image of drug addiction changed, so did the laws controlling it. The first antidrug statute in America, a local ordinance banning opium smoking, passed in Carson City, Nevada, in 1875. As Chinese immigrants fanned out in Western towns and then began to move eastward, local and state laws directed against opium smoking appeared in their wake. Despite an intense xenophobic reaction to the Chinese throughout the nineteenth century, it was not until 1909 that the importation of smoking opium was actually banned by federal law.

At first, the federal government had been reluctant to regulate the traffic or sale of narcotic drugs. The first piece of federal legislation, the Pure Food and Drug Act (1906), required the accurate labeling of narcotics in patent medicines. But it was not until 1914 that Congress passed the Harrison Act, which for the first time brought pharmaceuticals such as morphine, heroin, and cocaine—as well as smoking opium—under federal control. One consequence of the Harrison Act was to dry up addicts' legitimate sources of drugs and make them even more dependent on illegal suppliers. This reinforced a trend already under way to link drug users to the criminal underground. During the 1920s these demographic and legal changes continued. Although the number of drug users declined, the typical user was increasingly a young, white, urban, male delinquent or a person of color. Public opinion and the legal system treated the drug addict with little compassion. In the Prohibition Era, America was in high moral dudgeon. If alcohol users were to be denied their drug by the federal government, many Americans wanted to know why opiate and cocaine users should be treated any differently. Harry J. Anslinger emerged from this milieu as a man who promised to make unceasing war on drugs, on drug sellers, and on drug addicts. For over three decades he reigned as America's first drug czar.

HARRY J. ANSLINGER

Harry Anslinger was born in Altoona, Pennsylvania, in 1892, the son of a Swiss immigrant who worked on the Pennsylvania Railroad.[10] As a young adult, Harry was both hardworking and lucky. He dropped out of school after eighth grade to help support his family by joining his father at the "Pennsy." Nevertheless, he continued his education in a variety of ways, and he attended Pennsylvania State College from 1913 to 1915. On the railroad, Anslinger held different jobs. When he was assigned to the intelligence unit, Anslinger solved an important case of fraud that saved his employer $50,000, for which he was promoted to captain of the Pennsylvania Railroad police. Equally talented in both detective work and administration, he followed his former railroad boss to the state government in Harrisburg in 1916, where he oversaw a reorganization of the Pennsylvania State Police. All of this happened before he turned twenty-five. After the war, Anslinger won a place in the U.S. diplomatic service in The Hague, in part because of his proficiency in German, his family language.

In 1918, at the end of World War I, the German kaiser fled to Holland. At the time it was not clear whether his government-in-exile would be restored to Germany by the victorious allies. The American government wanted more information about the kaiser and his advisers. Anslinger, using his excellent German, was able to penetrate the kaiser's entourage and bring valuable information back to senior American diplomats. On the basis of this postwar triumph and a critical posting to Berlin, young Anslinger's diplomatic career seemed to be taking off. But eventually Anslinger, like most junior diplomats, had to take a remote assignment in the backwoods of Venezuela, where he pined for the bright lights and diplomatic action of Europe. Several impassioned entreaties for transfer finally (in 1926) resulted in a posting to the Bahamas, which for decades had been a sleepy British outpost in the Caribbean. However, prohibition had transformed the Bahamas into a staging area for alcohol smugglers. Liquor was imported legally from England and then smuggled into America. Local officials usually looked the other way, and Bahamian citizens grew rich in the booze business.

Anslinger changed that. He negotiated the "Anslinger Accord" with British officials, an agreement that effectively curbed liquor traffic routed through the Bahamas. Andrew W. Mellon, secretary of the treasury, was responsible for overseeing the Prohibition Bureau. He arranged to "borrow" Anslinger from the State Department and asked the rising young diplomat to negotiate similar accords with Canada, Cuba, and France. In 1926–27 Anslinger concluded these treaties, which were bright spots in a service that was rife with corruption and failure. For his accomplishments, Anslinger was promoted to assistant commissioner of prohibition in the Narcotics Division in 1929.

A year later, Anslinger was the recipient of yet another double stroke of good luck. Congress, fretting about the drug problem in America, established a separate Federal Bureau of Narcotics (FBN). At the same time, personal and professional scandals tainted Levi G. Nutt, the deputy commissioner in charge of narcotics, the obvious choice to head the new Federal Bureau of Narcotics. Anslinger prevailed over a field of a dozen strong candidates and at thirty-eight years of age became the director of the Federal Bureau of Narcotics, a position he held for thirty-two years.

At six feet, 190 pounds, and balding, Anslinger looked and acted less like a polished federal bureaucrat than a tough beat cop. He was a rule enforcer, not a philosopher, and he saw no moral shadings in the world of narcotics. In Anslinger's view, drug addicts were not unfortunate souls who had fallen prey to a disease, but criminals who had broken the law. Consistent with his belief that drug users were "criminals first and addicts afterwards," Anslinger once urged judges to "jail [narcotics] offenders, then throw away the key."[11] As far as Anslinger was concerned, they could suffer the excruciating pain of heroin withdrawal in the cold comfort of their jail cells. Drug sellers were even less deserving of public sympathy than addicts. Anslinger characterized drug dealers as "murderers," a rhetorical device that became a standard part of the popular image of the trade. Anslinger's character and background assured that this would be more than posturing. His experience in investigative work and diplomacy, and specifically his successes in negotiating bilateral agreements directed against liquor smuggling, pointed him toward the international side of the narcotics traffic. Following the same logic as Sir Malcom Delevingne, he reasoned that if the domestic demand for drugs were to be reduced, the international supply must be choked off.

Prior to Anslinger's arrival, enforcement of narcotics laws had been haphazard at best. Thanks to legal ambiguity and enforcement laxity, the supply of opiates had not been a serious problem for American addicts until the mid-1920s. Morphine and its more potent sister drug, heroin, were often available legally, either through prescriptions written by compliant "dope doctors," or, for a few years after the First World War, in municipal clinics. Addicts who had difficulty procuring drugs legally could turn to street peddlers who secured their supply either by stealing from the stocks of pharmaceutical companies or by obtaining them from associates who received American opiates exported to Canada and Mexico, and then smuggled back into the United States. However, both licit and illicit sources closed down by the mid-1920s, when

federal court cases shuttered the clinics and federal legislation proscribed heroin in 1924. Of greatest consequence for the traffic, however,
was the Miller-Jones Act of 1922, which constrained pharmaceutical
companies from continuing their dubious exports to Canada and Mexico. Catering to the needs of America's addicts was a promising business
opportunity for traffickers who could find a source of supply.[12]

ILLICIT ENTERPRISE

Into this vacuum stepped the greatest American illicit entrepreneur of
the 1920s—and maybe of all time—Arnold Rothstein, aka "The Brain."
Rothstein was the wayward son of an orthodox Jewish family who, in the
1920s, was known primarily as a gambler and a financial backer of criminal enterprise. He had a close relationship with the corrupt Democratic
politicians of New York's Tammany Hall, which meant that his gambling
houses and other activities in Manhattan operated with official protection. By the mid-1920s, Rothstein had already experienced considerable
success in smuggling. Using Waxey Gordon (Irving Wexler) as a business
associate, he had pioneered the business of buying liquor in Europe and
moving it into the United States during the first years of Prohibition.
The sudden dearth of American-produced opiates led Rothstein and his
associates to look once again to Europe as a source of supply.[13]

By the mid-1920s, Rothstein was sufficiently wealthy and discreet to
stay in the background. His associates did the actual smuggling, while
Rothstein financed and supported them. For example, Sidney Stajer,
Rothstein's personal secretary, was discovered trafficking in European
narcotics in 1927. In 1926 Rothstein posted bail for Charles Webber and
William Vachuda, who were arrested in New York with 1,220 pounds of
heroin, morphine, and cocaine that they had purchased in Europe and
brought to America aboard the transatlantic liner *Arabic.*

Federal prosecutors claimed that Webber, Vachuda, and their associates had smuggled more than two tons of narcotics into the country in
a period of six months. Although this claim is dubious, it is clear from
the seizure record that drugs were pouring into the country in substantial quantities in the late 1920s. Jill Jonnes, in her superb history of drug
use in America, notes that in 1926 United States Customs had confiscated 449 pounds of opium, 42 pounds of morphine, $3^{1}/_{2}$ pounds of
heroin, and 10 pounds of cocaine. By 1928 those figures rose to 2,354
pounds of opium, 91 pounds of morphine, 27 pounds of heroin, and 30
pounds of cocaine.[14]

Rothstein may have been involved in small-scale local narcotics dealing earlier in his career, but by 1926 he was certainly the leading figure in the Euro-American traffic. He did not have a personal monopoly, however; to the contrary, Rothstein financed many smugglers. At the height of his power, his role in the New York underworld was strikingly similar to that of his Shanghai contemporary, Du Yuesheng. He brokered deals and arranged protection instead of engaging in smuggling himself. Like Du, he believed in diversity. Narcotics was only one of his many lucrative occupations; indeed, most of his income came from bankrolling bootleggers and from gambling.[15]

Rothstein was murdered on November 4, 1928. True to the underworld code, he refused to tell police the name of his assailant as he lay dying. The crime was never solved, largely because his Tammany Hall cronies did not want Rothstein's financial dealings exposed in a public trial. One guess is that he was killed by his one-time employee and partner, Legs Diamond (John T. Nolan), over a narcotics deal gone bad. Ferdinand Pecora, who was a New York City judge at the time, recalls hearing that the culprit was a bookmaker named George McManus who was angry about questionable gambling losses.[16]

In spite of Rothstein's death, the transatlantic pipeline bringing European drugs to America, which he had done so much to establish, continued to operate unabated. In 1930 suspicions that federal narcotics authorities were complacent or even complicit in the traffic surfaced when it was revealed that Levi Nutt's son-in-law had maintained significant business dealings with Arnold Rothstein. Nutt was forced to step aside, making way for Harry Anslinger to become commissioner of the newly established Federal Bureau of Narcotics, which was freed of its earlier ties to the tainted Prohibition Bureau.

ANSLINGER AND INTERNATIONAL NARCOTICS ENFORCEMENT

Anslinger brought both zeal and cunning to his mission. In particular, he understood the importance of foreign intelligence gathering and of coordinating his efforts with those in other agencies trying to accomplish parallel objectives. Anslinger forged a close working relationship with Stuart J. Fuller, the State Department's expert on international narcotics diplomacy. Between 1932, when Fuller assumed his post, and 1941, they worked closely, sharing intelligence and coordinating policy decisions. With the retirement of Sir Malcolm Delevingne, Anslinger became the driving force behind the League of Nations Opium Advisory Committee in the late 1930s. He also established, in 1931, a highly successful secret network of chief narcotics officers in key countries. In 1936, Fuller explained the workings of this network to a colleague as a direct exchange of police intelligence about the illicit traffic in narcotic drugs provided by the narcotics bureaus of twenty-three countries.[17]

Anslinger's most important contribution to international narcotics enforcement, however, was his creation of a filigreed global intelligence network of both American government officials and paid informants. From the earliest years of his tenure, Anslinger relied on the reports of American officials in key stations. The best example was M. R. Nicholson, the U.S. Treasury attaché in Shanghai during the 1930s. Nicholson's voluminous information came from a large ring of Chinese informants. His nearly daily reports kept Anslinger apprised of the vagaries of the Chinese drug traffic in punctilious detail.

In addition to consular officials, Anslinger decided that he needed international intelligence from his own employees. Immediately after his appointment in 1930, Anslinger hired several Treasury agents to work abroad. One of these was Charles Dyar, Harvard graduate and cerebral sleuth nicknamed "The Sphinx." Dyar's efforts paid off immediately in two key seizures in 1930 and 1931. One involved 20,000 pounds of morphine cubes coming from Turkey on the *SS Alesia*; the second involved a ton of opiates from Hamburg on the *SS Milwaukee*. In both cases, Dyar paid informants substantial sums—$20,000 in the first case, $8,800 in the second—for the crucial intelligence. From the 1930s through the 1950s, Anslinger often dispatched his closest lieutenants, like Charles "Charlie Cigars" Siragusa, George H. White, and Garland H. Williams, to important hot spots in the international drug traffic.[18]

Particularly in the careers of these three men, the roles of Anslinger's Federal Bureau of Narcotics, the wartime Office of Strategic Services, and the postwar Central Intelligence Agency often overlapped. Anslinger's friendship with the founder of the OSS, William J. "Wild Bill" Donovan, dated to the 1920s. Anslinger agreed to transfer Siragusa, White, and Williams to Donovan during the war. In the postwar period, these three, and others, shuttled between the Federal Bureau of Narcotics and other government intelligence agencies. The cooperation between the FBN and the CIA continued in the postwar years. Indeed, as John C. McWilliams has recently revealed, FBN personnel—especially George White—worked with the CIA in its LSD experiments in the 1950s. The CIA was hoping to discover a "truth serum" that it could use to elicit cold war secrets from unwilling subjects. The agency used its safehouses and hired prostitutes to lure unwitting subjects into situations in which they would be given LSD. The experiments proved that the psychotropic drug disoriented subjects in different ways, but it did not necessarily compel them to tell the truth.[19]

Finally, Anslinger relied on informants and undercover agents. The *Alesia* and *Milwaukee* seizures convinced him that the best source of information about narcotics smuggling came from smugglers and their close associates. Drugs were so small relative to their worth that a valuable shipment could easily be hidden in personal luggage or even on the person of an international traveler. Random searches by customs agents, no matter how skilled, rarely yielded significant results. Successful drug busts were more likely to result from tips supplied by insiders who were paid for their information. Thus, in an extraordinarily important and far-reaching decision, Anslinger plunged the bureau into the murky business of employing smugglers to catch smugglers.

Why did smugglers sometimes become informants and what were their concerns? In a conversation with Treasury agent Nicholson, who was trying to recruit him, veteran drug smuggler F. V. Schihman gave one reason. He pointed out emphatically that he was not a "squealer." Rather, he was looking to get even with some people who had cheated him in the past and at the same time make some reward money.

There is no certainty that Schihman turned informer, but other drug dealers did. Agent M. R. Nicholson was at the center of these efforts in the Far East. But using informants brought the agents into the same dark shadowlands as the traffickers they sought to control. At times their identities blurred. Nicholson, for instance, in spite of an impeccable reputation, terrified Lucy Fontaine Crawley. When Shanghai officials offered her his protection from her abusive husband, she refused because she considered Nicholson to be in league with Paul Crawley.[20]

Monetary rewards caused some traffickers to become informants. The amounts involved were often substantial. In 1940, for instance, the Federal Bureau of Narcotics offered a reward of $1,000 for information on the whereabouts of a minor drug dealer.[21] In 1934 Anslinger offered to help a suspected drug smuggler have his name removed from the international "black list" if he gave him the location of Sam Bernstein, a major drug dealer who was then at large.[22] The willingness of authorities to pay for information bred new employment opportunities for the professional informant, whose connections occasionally turned him into an extortionist. In 1931 an American consul stationed in Turkey reported that Mr. Lorenzetti, a local informant, was living off illicit traders in narcotics. He would first intimidate the trader into paying him the amount of the reward he would receive for denouncing the shipment. If paid, he would transmit the necessary information to the League of Nations or to Charles Dyar, U.S. Treasury agent in Paris, too late to permit any confiscation of the goods. If the trader did not pay, the information went forward in time to permit the seizure.[23]

The rewards of the Federal Bureau of Narcotics' policy of relying on informants were significant, but so were the risks. For one thing, the bureau's integrity was compromised by employing persons whose connection to the narcotics traffic was ongoing. One such informer was a thirty-nine-year-old American, Thomas Robert Hoag. In 1935 he was arrested in Hamburg, Germany, and was charged with complicity in smuggling 108 kilos of crude opium destined for the United States. Hoag was well known to European and American authorities as a member of one of the major smuggling syndicates based in Paris. Although drug charges were eventually dropped for lack of sufficient evidence, Hoag was convicted on a currency charge for which he received an eighteen-month prison sentence. When he was released in 1937, he was broke, had no employment prospects, and had nothing to sell but information. He was hired for an assignment by Al Scharff, a Treasury representative in Paris, to ferret out information from his former business associates at Fr100 a day. But Hoag found that "they would have nothing to do with me . . . due, no doubt, to the fact that I had been convicted in Hamburg and served a sentence there." His fellow smugglers knew that as a recent convict, Hoag may well have been "turned" by the authorities and that it was dangerous to associate with him.[24]

According to Hoag, he finally accepted an assignment by boarding the *SS Duchess of Bedford* in Liverpool on June 18 to spy on a former accomplice, Victor Walleck. As Hoag reported it, he spent the entire trip to Montreal trying unsuccessfully to get information out of Walleck, but Walleck kept his business to himself. Although he claimed to be acting on behalf of his American employers, Hoag was probably trying to insinuate himself back into the drug trade. Scharff, meanwhile, disowned Hoag ("a diseased mind") and had him arrested when the ship docked in Montreal. According to Scharff, Hoag had acted as a double agent, informing at least one prominent French narcotics dealer that Scharff was trying to engineer his arrest. Hoag's case illustrates the difficulty of relying on informers, whose close ties to drug dealers made them suspect and unreliable.[25]

If Hoag caused Anslinger some discomfort, Captain Cecil Herbert Attfield caused him acute pain.[26] Attfield was a British infantry officer who had drifted into gunrunning after the First World War. In 1924 he and two associates, one of them his father, were convicted in England of selling machine guns to the Soviet Union without an export permit. Attfield paid a heavy fine and served fifteen months in prison. Upon his release he was hired as an undercover agent by the U.S. Prohibition Bureau. His greatest triumph came in 1929, when his detective work in the Bahamas led to the indictment of a British liquor dealer on charges of complicity in a smuggling scheme.

When the Federal Bureau of Narcotics was carved out of the old Narcotics Division of the Prohibition Bureau in 1930, Attfield went along, apparently at Anslinger's invitation. Attfield was dispatched to Hong Kong in 1930 to supply Anslinger with information on the narcotics traffic there. He was a paradigm of indiscretion. When opening a bank account, Attfield announced to the bank clerk that he was an undercover narcotics agent of the U.S. Treasury Department. Within hours, local British and American authorities who had not been informed of his mission discovered his identity. Attfield became embroiled in several acrimonious public controversies and made himself persona non grata within months of his arrival in Hong Kong. Stuart Fuller of the State Department wrote a withering memo declaring that Attfield's work consisted mostly of general information that was already known to both the State Department and the Treasury Department before Attfield ever left for China. Any details were usually inaccurate. He seemed to have a childlike faith in the honesty of his informers and a preconceived notion that everyone else was a liar.

Despite Attfield's ineptitude, Anslinger continued to express confidence in him and in 1933 sent him to Prague. Once again, Anslinger had not told the American consul of Attfield's identity or mission. Nevertheless, Attfield once again blew his cover by telling a telegraph clerk (!) that he was an undercover narcotics agent. The American consul in Prague expressed incredulity and dismay, but Anslinger once again protected Attfield. Attfield's connection to the Federal Bureau of Narcotics was finally severed in summer 1933, when he proposed that he be given $2,500 to invest in a drug smuggling venture. Despite being fired by Anslinger, Attfield raised the money, bought into the ring, and was arrested for smuggling 108 kilos of hashish into Egypt in 1934. He asserted that he was operating as an American government agent. But no one would substantiate his claim, and he was convicted, fined, and sentenced to nine months in prison. Barred from entering the United States, Attfield wrote a plaintive letter to President Roosevelt in 1935, enumerating his many accomplishments as an undercover narcotics agent and decrying critics, like Fuller, who had questioned his competence.

Attfield's career represents an Anslinger blunder in his first years in office. The British officer's conviction as a gunrunner did not deter the Prohibition Bureau from hiring him originally, nor did it deter Anslinger from taking Attfield with him to the Federal Bureau of Narcotics. Anslinger did not inform State Department personnel of Attfield's presence in their jurisdictions. Indeed, Anslinger did not even inform M. R. Nicholson, the Treasury attaché in Shanghai, that he had sent Attfield to China. Only Attfield's bumbling incompetence revealed his identity to other American officials, both in China and in Czechoslovakia.

Attfield's judgment was so badly flawed that he asked the Treasury Department to stake him to a partnership in a smuggling ring. When he was rejected and fired, he bought into the deal anyway. Unlike his contemporary Charles Dyar, Attfield was not a smooth operative, silently gliding around the globe in search of narcotics intelligence. To the contrary, he was a loud-mouthed braggart of limited wit and even more limited discretion, whose actions caused embarrassments for Anslinger and the American government and opened rifts between the Departments of State and Treasury. The wonder is not that he was finally fired in 1933 but that he lasted for over six years and that he enjoyed Anslinger's confidence for at least the last three.

What accounts for his longevity? Attfield claimed that his wife was Anslinger's secretary. Perhaps this personal connection clouded Anslinger's judgment. Or perhaps Attfield's success in the Bahamas in 1929 gave Anslinger reason to believe that Attfield could repeat his coup as a narcotics agent. In any case, Attfield left dirty footprints around the globe and compromised the FBN's early efforts at international intelligence gathering.

Fortunately for the reputation of the Federal Bureau of Narcotics, in the 1930s Attfield's bizarre career was anomalous. Anslinger learned from this early near disaster to exercise greater caution in his selection of secret agents. For the most part, his intelligence network was extremely effective. As a result, the changing enforcement climate made the 1930s a much more difficult time for drug smugglers than the previous decade. It became virtually impossible for them to procure legal narcotics in Europe. After 1930, smugglers had to rely on illegal sources of supply, either in Europe or in the Far East, which greatly increased the risks. Furthermore, smugglers were much more likely to encounter dangers in moving narcotics into the United States, since they could never be certain whether a disgruntled associate, for reasons of profit or revenge, had tipped off authorities to their shipments. Finally, if they were caught, smugglers were likely to encounter effective government prosecutions and face long prison sentences if convicted.

By the 1930s drug users in America were perceived to be dangerous social misfits, although their numbers were dwindling. Anslinger skillfully cultivated and reinforced this image, arguing that the Federal Bureau of Narcotics was vital to eliminating the narcotics threat to America. To a considerable extent Anslinger made good on his promise both to harass drug addicts and to prosecute international smugglers who supplied them.

This combination of changing world market conditions and enforcement climate affected the flow of drugs into America. Beginning in 1926, the Treasury Department issued an annual report on the drug traffic in the country. Until 1929 the reports made no mention of efforts to interdict drugs coming into the country. This was not because the international drug traffic did not exist but because the Prohibition Bureau's Narcotics Division ignored it, either because of ineptitude or corruption. In any case, the 1929 edition of *The Traffic in Opium and Other Dangerous Drugs* admitted that this was a mistake. It pointed out that well-organized groups of traffickers smuggled narcotic drugs, principally morphine, cocaine, and heroin into the United States largely through the port of New York, from which point they were distributed to the interior. Further, it proved difficult to apprehend the leaders of these groups because they operated through a system of agents who, in turn, sold only in large quantities to smaller dealers. These smaller traffickers, when apprehended, steadfastly refused to divulge their source of supply. The 1929 report announced that the new Federal Bureau of Narcotics would follow a different policy by directing concentrated investigations on the illicit traffickers operating on a large scale.[27]

THE RESULT OF ANSLINGER'S POLICIES
The Federal Bureau of Narcotics new focus on international traffickers paid dividends almost immediately. In 1930 narcotics agents seized 612 kilos of morphine and heroin that were smuggled into New York on board the luxury liner *Ile de France*. This enormous quantity of drugs had been carelessly shipped by the smuggler Jacob Bloom and his associates,

Sam Bernstein and Jacob Polakiewitz. These three had been among the most important smugglers who exported drugs from Europe to America in the 1920s. Assistant U.S. Attorney Henry Gerson explained how the gang had moved drugs from Paris to New York over a three-year period. They had agents in Paris who placed orders with their own contacts in Turkey. The drugs would then be delivered in powder form or in cubes in boxes to a Paris hotel, where the morphine would be packed into specially made trunks. Payment, made in cash in the United States, traveled across the ocean by cable to a Paris bank, where it could be withdrawn. When the trunks arrived in New York, forged customs labels pasted onto the trunks indicated that they had been inspected and marked by customs authorities, thus making the border crossing simple.[28]

Yet the very simplicity of the system that prevailed in the 1920s made traffickers of the time grow lax just when American government officials increased their vigilance. The *Ile de France* shipment was discovered through just such carelessness. A trunk filled with narcotics went through customs along with the luggage of Sir Duncan Orr-Lewis, an English baronet and friend of the Prince of Wales. On arriving in New York, Sir Duncan noticed an unfamiliar trunk among his consignment of luggage. He notified the authorities, who opened the trunk and discovered that it contained narcotics. Two men posing as aides to Sir Duncan later arrived to claim the trunk and led authorities to Jacob Bloom, who later implicated Bernstein and Polakiewitz.

Bloom's inattention to the finer points of the smuggler's craft was doubtless engendered by a decade of lax enforcement. Since the early 1920s, international narcotics smugglers had little to fear from importing drugs into the United States. Through the *Ile de France* seizure, Bloom not only lost a substantial capital investment but he was also sentenced to prison for eight years. The incident became a cautionary tale for smugglers in two ways. First, Bloom's lost opiates represented an outlay of $144,000, a sum equivalent to several million dollars in 1990s currency. From 1930 on, no American importer was willing to take that kind of financial risk. Henceforth drugs were imported in much smaller lots. Through the remainder of the decade, narcotics agents never intercepted a single load of more than 120 kilos, and most seizures were of much smaller quantities. Second, Bloom's long prison sentence signaled to smugglers that the price of failure was high. Whereas drug smugglers convicted in Europe and Asia could expect imprisonment for two years

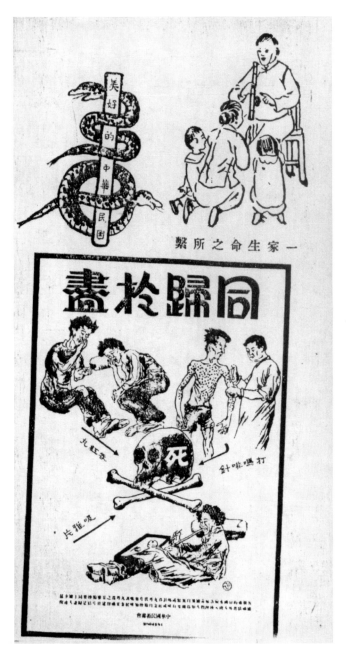

An anti-opium poster from the 1930s. *Top left:* The snakes are strangling an ancestor plaque that reads, "The Beautiful Republic of China." *Top right:* The text reads, "The entire families' lives are involved." *Bottom:* The heading reads, "All come to the same end." The central skull reads, "Death." The top left arrow reads, "Swallowing red pills." The top right arrow reads, "Injecting morphine." The bottom arrow reads, "Smoking opium." Luo, *The Chinese Opium Problem.*

Dai Li, head of the Military Statistics Bureau. Records of Naval Group China and V. Adm. M. E. Miles, box 39, RG 38.

Hu Die, or Miss Butterfly Wu, China's movie queen of 1935. She worked for the Star Motion Picture Company. She was also Dai Li's lover. Dai Li died in a plane crash en route to visiting Hu Die. *Who's Who in China*, 1936.

Factory in the Japanese concession of Hankou that housed an opium shop. Margaret Goldsmith, *The Trail of Opium: The Eleventh Plague* (London: Robert Hale, 1939).

Hiding places for opium (Under the Eaves). Margaret Goldsmith, *The Trail of Opium: The Eleventh Plague* (London: Robert Hale, 1939).

Hiding places for opium (inside hollowed-out bricks of a Chinese stove). Margaret Goldsmith, *The Trail of Opium: The Eleventh Plague* (London: Robert Hale, 1939).

The Sakata group. Sakata Shigemori is seated in the center of the photograph. "Akuma no Boryaku" [The devil's strategy]. *Sunday Mainichi*, December 9, 1984.

Kodama Yoshio at the time of
the Lockhead scandal.
UPI/Corbis-Bettman.

Harry Anslinger of the
Federal Bureau of
Narcotics. Walter
Bennett/*Time* Magazine,
March 21, 1955.

SMUGGLING FILE

Lucy Ivanoff alias L. J. Ivanova alias Julia Ivanova alias Mrs. Paul S. Crawley. Photo taken October 1931 when she applied to Public Safety Bureau for visa to visit Harbin. Visa was refused as she failed to comply with Regulations requiring registration once a year. One maisorff - Russian employed in Chinese Bureau of Public Safety (Passport Dept.) is attempting to assist Mrs. Crawley in obtaining visa. Implicated with Crawley in placing opium and diamonds aboard U. S. S. Chatmont August 12, 1931.

Lucy Ivanoff Crawley. Shanghai Municipal Police, Criminal Investigation Division, file D 3057.

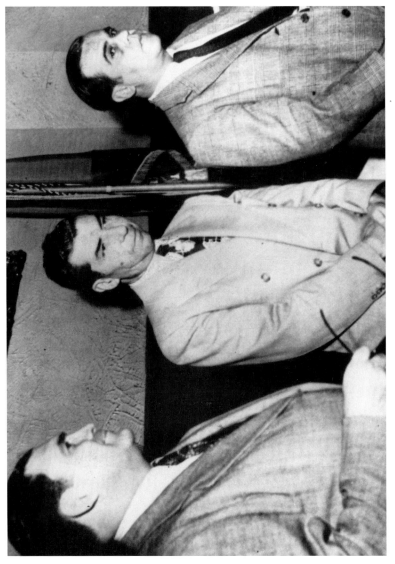

Charles "Lucky" Luciano, *center*, in Cuba. UPI/Corbis-Bettman.

or less, Bloom's sentence was typical of the much harsher fate awaiting them in America.

Anslinger's international enforcement policies drastically affected the structure of the drug importing business. One importer could not afford to become so big that he attracted the bureau's concentrated attention. Given Anslinger's intelligence resources in the supply areas of Europe and China and within the drug smuggling fraternity, any attempt to buy and ship narcotics in large lots was likely to lead to the smugglers' apprehension and conviction. The result was a reduction of the American-bound international traffic as a whole, and its fragmentation into the hands of many smaller dealers. This structural shift occurred so quickly that in 1932 the Federal Bureau of Narcotics noted the change. In a report the bureau pointed out how the general condition of the illicit traffic was in marked contrast to that of only a few years earlier, when seizures in a single year amounted to as much as three and a half tons, mostly of morphine. The report concluded that "the stream of illicit traffic at present flowing to the United States is a rivulet as compared to the river which was emptying into the country for a long period of years."[29]

Thus the crisis of supply, felt so strongly in Asia, had its counterpart in the United States as well. In the 1930s it became both expensive and dangerous to obtain drugs in Europe. With the closing of the Bulgarian factories in 1933, the last legal source of supply dried up. Clandestine factories, especially in Turkey, the Balkans, and Paris, continued to produce illicit heroin throughout the decade, but drugs were increasingly difficult to procure. Although Europe was shutting down, Shanghai, the great drug emporium of the East, remained open for business. The Ezra brothers and Paul Crawley were among the first to import Asian drugs to the American market. By 1933 China and Japan had become the major exporters of opiates to the American illicit market, a position that they held throughout the decade.

Yet this new reality posed a dilemma for American drug importers. For over a decade they had found their sources of supply in Europe. Since they had no connections to Asian sources, they had to rely on persons whose trustworthiness was questionable. Their lack of fixed connections increased the risks for drug smugglers. For example, when the Katzenberg ring went to China to buy drugs in 1935, their contact, Joe Schwartz, turned out to be a Federal Bureau of Narcotics informer who eventually exposed the entire operation.

YASHA ''JACK'' KATZENBERG

In the 1930s, with Europe closing down as a source, smugglers began to look to China, and especially to Shanghai, as a source of supply for the American market. Despite the pioneering failure of the Ezra brothers, other smugglers were not deterred by their unhappy fate. To the contrary, international smugglers were migrating in force to Shanghai even as Judah and Isaac Ezra were being convicted in an American court. Yasha "Jack" Katzenberg was one such migrant. He was convicted in 1938 of participating in an international smuggling ring that had operated between China and the United States from 1935 to 1937. In order to try to influence his sentence, Katzenberg dictated a long statement that detailed his life as an illicit entrepreneur in the 1920s and 1930s.[30]

Born into a Jewish family in Rumania in 1891, he emigrated to America in 1916. After failing in a series of "straight" jobs after his arrival, Katzenberg began to work in the liquor business in Prohibition-era New York City. From 1921 through 1932, he worked successively as a courier, a retail supplier, a wholesaler, and then as an international buyer for an importing syndicate. Although he participated in several partnerships over that period, his most regular partner was Jake Lvovsky. By 1928 he was near the top of the business. In the last few years of Prohibition, his associates included nearly all of the most prominent bootleggers of that era: Joe Adonis, Charlie Solomon, Benjamin "Bugsy" Siegel, Meyer Lansky, Salvatore "Lucky" Luciano, and Louis "Lepke" Buchalter. In the 1930s, and particularly after 1933, Katzenberg's international business ventures shifted from illicit alcohol to narcotic drugs.

It is worth noting several characteristics of Katzenberg's business life as a liquor dealer, since they later appeared in his career as a drug trafficker. First, his business associations were constantly changing. Entire partnerships came together and dissolved quickly; even within ongoing organizations, personnel constantly turned over. Katzenberg and his associates were not functionaries in a hierarchically structured gang but independent businessmen who brought resources or expertise to separate business ventures. Like his partners in the liquor business, Katzenberg was involved in other illegal businesses—in his case, bookmaking.

Second, Katzenberg and his associates cheated one another regularly. This was such a fact of life in the liquor business that being cheated did not necessarily preclude further business dealings with the cheater. In 1928, when Katzenberg returned from Rumania with his bride, his partners threw an elaborate dinner party for him. On that evening, Katzenberg recounted, he received a telephone call during dinner, informing him that the warehouse where he had stored the liquors had been robbed and all the goods hijacked. He immediately went to the scene of the crime, where he learned that the job had been done by Jerry Sullivan. The next day he met Jerry Sullivan at Lindy's restaurant. Sullivan guaranteed him protection against further hijacking in return for partnership. The two men remained business associates for about a year.

Third, violence and the threat of violence was only occasionally used to ruin a competitor but was regularly used to make him accept a business proposition. In 1924 Katzenberg and his organization were coerced into buying their alcohol from Dutch Goldberg. Shortly thereafter they were forced to merge with a more powerful organization headed by Bugsy Siegel and Meyer Lansky. However, the circumstances of threat under which the merger took place did not affect the smooth operation of the new organization. The two "divisions" coordinated their efforts but functioned separately, with the Lansky-Siegel group handling the wholesale supply side and Katzenberg's group taking care of retail distribution.

Fourth, ethnicity was not a particularly important factor in determining Katzenberg's partners. Although his closest associates were Jewish, he readily did business with the Italians and the Irish. The various organizations in which he participated functioned less like a neighborhood street gang than a limited business partnership. Never once in his detailed discussion of his dealings did Katzenberg mention the term "mafia" or even suggest that ethnicity mattered in the liquor business.

All of these facets of the liquor traffic were replicated in the relationships among narcotics dealers. This new, multiethnic organization represents what Albert Fried has called the rationalization of criminal entreprises carried out by the likes of the Lansky/Luciano partnership in New York and the Capone/Guzik syndicate in Chicago. Giving a more personal coloring to the same events, Joe Bonanno has accused these same key actors, especially Luciano and Capone, of causing the decline of the "Sicilian Tradition" by placing profits before honor and loyalty. It is important to note here that the rationalization of American gangs coincided with the ban on alcohol. The Volstead Act reproduced in the United States the same conditions and business opportunities that the opium eradication movement created in China.[31]

With the end of Prohibition in sight by 1931, Katzenberg and his associates decided to move into the narcotics business. He had previously run into the ubiquitous drug dealer Jacob Polakiewitz when he was buying liquor in Europe. Now, as Katzenberg sought new business opportunities, he agreed to buy twenty kilos of heroin from Polakiewitz for $350 each. Polakiewitz, playing the role of mentor to the apprentice drug smuggler, instructed Katzenberg in the fine art of packing heroin inside heavy objects to make its weight less obvious. Only when he reached New York did Katzenberg discover that Polakiewitz had sold him adulterated goods. A wiser Katzenberg returned to Europe and bought forty kilos of morphine from Paul Carbone for $12,000. Alas, this shipment was "knocked off" by American customs officials who felt that the bribes that they had been offered were insufficient. Still another narcotics deal came to a bad end when Katzenberg discovered that twenty kilos of heroin that he had obtained from the French supplier, Louis Lyon, was talcum powder.

Europe was a natural place for Katzenberg to begin looking for narcotics. Even after legal drugs were no longer available there in the 1930s, illegal factories in Turkey, eastern Europe, and France continued to be an important, although reduced, source of drugs for smugglers supplying the American market. Certainly the most important French supplier during the 1930s was the wealthy and well-connected Louis Lyon, whose elegant Paris restaurant served as the headquarters of his drug business. Lyon was finally arrested on drug charges in 1938. The main issue during his trial was why he had not been brought to court earlier.[32]

In 1935, a factory owned by Lyon in rue St. Honoré in Paris blew up. An investigation revealed that the factory had been used to produce heroin. An American Treasury agent stationed in Paris complained that "Lyon was not tried after the explosion and everything indicates he was given police protection." Indeed, down to 1938, and even through his trial, the agent noted, the French Sûreté appeared to be protecting Lyon. Why? French newspapers speculated that high government officials, including M. Marx Dormoy, the former socialist minister of the interior, had close ties to Lyon. Dormoy testified at the trial that he knew Lyon but he denied any improper relationship. Certainly Lyon had helped the government, informing on Elie Eliopoulos in the 1930s, and probably on other drug dealers as well.[33]

The complete details of Lyon's government connections never emerged at the trial, but it was clear that he could not have operated without political protection at the highest levels. What did Lyon give his protectors? Undoubtedly he fed them information about his rivals, and perhaps he shared with them a percentage of his profits, just as Eliopoulos had paid off Inspector Martin between 1928 and 1931.

What did emerge at the trial was a glimpse of Lyon's operation. In addition to the ill-fated factory in Paris, Lyon received heroin from factories in the French province of Alsace, in Turkey, and even in China. The raw opium for his French factories came through Marseille. Over the years, sixty tons had been allegedly diverted by local gangster Paul Carbone for Lyon's use. The American agent who reported on Lyon's trial claimed that Lyon was one of the largest exporters of heroin to the United States. Although the complicity of the French officials was never proven, the evidence on the drug charges was sufficient to convict Lyon. By American standards he received a comparatively light sentence of two years in prison.

Failing to buy narcotics in Europe, Katzenberg finally found a connection in China. An old acquaintance, Joe Schwartz, approached Katzenberg and told him that he had a source of supply in Shanghai, a Greek named Janis Tsounias. Katzenberg accepted the offer. He constructed an organization based on his former associates in the liquor trade that moved 649 kilos of heroin and morphine from Tianjin to New York City between 1935 and 1937. Katzenberg provided a detailed description of his system. His group stationed an agent, one Sammy Gross, in China. Gross periodically bought narcotics from Tsounias, whose source of supply was a narcotics manufacturer in the Japanese concession of Tianjin. The heroin was packed in steamer trunks and sent to Marseille, where a bribed American Express agent shipped it in bond to Cherbourg, where it was rerouted to New York City. A courier was recruited in New York to travel to Shanghai and accompany the trunks back to New York. American customs officials were bribed to pass the trunks through without inspection. Katzenberg's group sold the narcotics to wholesalers in New York who distributed them throughout the country. This brief account makes it sound like an efficient and profitable smuggling ring. It was anything but. As Katzenberg's account shows, the organization was plagued with problems at virtually every stage of the operation. Katzenberg, the harried chief executive officer, was continually making adjustments and responding to crises.

In China, Katzenberg's main concern was his relationship to Janis Tsounias, his supplier. Tsounias began by charging Katzenberg a commission of $50 per kilo—on top of the purchase price of $250—on each kilo of heroin he bought for him. In addition, Tsounias was given "title" to six kilos of heroin in the shipment. If it made it to New York, he was given a purchase price of $600 per kilo. In this way Katzenberg ensured that Tsounias had a stake in the shipment's reaching its destination.

Tsounias adjusted his commission depending on what the traffic would bear. At the height of the gang's success, Tsounias raised his commission by $50 per kilo. When business slackened, he agreed to take a straight cut of 20 percent of the profits in lieu of other fees. Besides Tsounias, the gang had to deal with Nick Negro, an assistant manager at the Cathay Hotel who was paid $500 to oversee the packing of heroin into steamer trunks, and a Greek restaurateur who received money transfers through his account for a commission of 2 percent.

In France, Katzenberg's agent, Nathan Gross (no relation to Sammy), oversaw the transfer of the heroin-laden trunks from Marseille to Cherbourg. Nathan's connection was an American Express agent who was willing to forward the trunks in bond for an indeterminate sum. When the American Express connection disappeared, Katzenberg was able to bribe a French customs agent in Marseille to serve the same role. Once the narcotics entered New York harbor, they had to be cleared by American customs. Katzenberg bribed two customs agents—Hoffman and MacAdam—$4,000 per shipment to pass through the trunks filled with heroin. Hoffman and MacAdam posed a thorny problem for Katzenberg. They constantly demanded more money, and they hijacked his last shipment and sold it to rival narcotics dealers.

Finally, Katzenberg had to deal with his customers in New York. He sold his first shipment of heroin to Louis Kravitz and Harry Koch, who paid him $40 an ounce. However, Kravitz was connected to Lepke Buchalter, who then muscled into Katzenberg's operation. Lepke became a full partner, occasionally providing capital, but always taking at least one-third of the profits. Kravitz was able to force Katzenberg to reduce the selling price of the drug to $31 and then to $22 an ounce. Lepke, although not an active partner, was the biggest name associated with the enterprise. When federal agents closed in on the ring, they went after him. By offering reduced sentences to lesser members of the gang, they were able to elicit testimony that resulted in Lepke's conviction on a narcotics charge, and he was sentenced to twelve years in prison.

In addition to problems along the supply line, Katzenberg had other difficulties. Finding cash was one. Katzenberg recited the businessman's lament when he complained, "You see we never had any money [as] it was tied up in merchandise, and as soon as we received any money we had to send it to China so if Lvovsky or myself needed $300 or $500 we would take it from these moneys and send China less." He raised capital from business associates (including one elderly courier); he received credit from his supplier, Tsounias; and very occasionally he was able to divert enough profit from one load to fund expenses for the next. But the overwhelming impression left by Katzenberg's memoir is of an entrepreneur beset by nagging cash flow problems.

Katzenberg also had to deal with threats from disgruntled partners and possible informers. At one point Nathan Gross, his European contact, felt that he had been wronged and was not paid his fair share of the profits. Gross said "that he would even go so far as high-jacking or squealing to right this wrong." Eventually Gross appealed to Lepke for mediation and was awarded $500, a judgment that Katzenberg was forced to accept.

A more dangerous threat came in the form of Joe Schwartz, his original China contact, who turned up once again in Shanghai in 1937. Schwartz, a veteran of the narcotics traffic, was connected to a drug dealer who had recently been arrested by U.S. authorities. Thus his arrival in Shanghai was suspicious. Tsounias "thinks Schwartz is coming with the aid of either the American authorities or from the League of Nations." Indeed, Schwartz sniffed out Katzenberg, who was then in China, and tried to insinuate himself into his current deal. Katzenberg prudently kept his distance. Katzenberg never discovered, even after his conviction, that Schwartz had been an informer since 1936, supplying details of the operation to American Treasury agent M. R. Nicholson.

The endless double-crossing among drug dealers, informants, and the authorities surprised even the veteran Nicholson. He later ruminated on the situation, confessing that he found it hard to believe that Schwartz (code name Sahib) had deliberately double-crossed the agency, yet he had much to explain. It was true that he had entered into negotiations with the Katzenberg crowd before he consented to work with Treasury and he gave some inkling of what was about to happen. Yet he failed to be completely forthcoming with what he knew. Nicholson assumed that Sahib had trouble with the Shanghai group, who may have double-crossed him by eliminating him after first contacts were made with Tsounias and his Chinese sources of supply. However, Nicholson suspected possible treachery by a man who could very well have been turning a double trick to his own advantage. In such a case, Nicholson vowed, "I shall have my own way of dealing with him which I think he will fully understand."[34]

Finally, Katzenberg and his partners cheated one another when they thought they could get away with it. On at least two occasions, Katzenberg stole ten kilos from a load of Chinese heroin, lying to his New York partners that their Asian associates were to blame. On the last trip,

Katzenberg convinced his associates to send him rather than Sammy Gross to China. He casually commented that "I wanted to get out of the business and if they gave me a large sum of money I would have gone to Rumania and never come back." Did his partners intuit Katzenberg's larcenous intent? Perhaps so, because they entrusted him with only a modest amount of cash and forced him to collect the balance of their investment by wire in China.

There was money to be earned in the drug traffic, but it was hard to make a decent living at it. Katzenberg bought heroin at about $300 per kilo in China and sold it at about $1,100 per kilo in New York. While that brought him a substantial gross profit, he had heavy expenses. Customs men cost $4,000 per trip, and even an assistant hotel manager in Shanghai came in for a $500 cut. When Lepke muscled in for a share of the profits, Katzenberg could offer only 33 percent, pleading that his many expenses had to be taken out of the remainder. And when the customs men hijacked his last load, Katzenberg was broke. He had lost everything and soon found himself facing a heavy jail sentence. Katzenberg's sorry experience, even before his arrest and conviction, was a poignant example of the tribulations faced by American drug smugglers.

SMUGGLING DRUGS INTO THE UNITED STATES

The records of arrests, interrogations, and trials show a pattern of drug smuggling into the United States from the 1930s through the 1950s that was fragmented into many small streams rather than a single large river. There was no single individual or even group of individuals who dominated the international narcotics traffic into the United States. Nor was there a single modus operandi for smugglers. Narcotic drugs crossed the border in astoundingly different ways. All this drug smuggling activity is remarkable for the sheer number of people involved, their inventiveness and variety, and the modest quantities of drugs they smuggled.[35]

One of Louis Lyon's main business contacts, for instance, was Carlos Fernandez Bacula, a dapper and polished Peruvian diplomat who was part of the European-American drug traffic from 1928 through 1931.[36] From 1926 to 1930 Bacula was an official in the Peruvian embassy in Vienna. In 1930 he was transferred to Oslo, where he served for less than a year before a revolution at home deposed the ruling faction and cost Bacula his job. The most important asset that Bacula brought to drug smuggling was his diplomatic passport, which allowed him to pass his luggage through customs without inspection. Even after being severed from the Peruvian diplomatic service, he somehow managed to have his diplomatic passport renewed, presumably by bribing his former colleagues.

Bacula first carried a load of 120 kilos of heroin from Europe to America in 1928 for Joseph Raskin, at that time a major European drug dealer. Later Bacula worked with Louis Lyon in Europe and with the Newman brothers and Wilhelm Kofler in America. In 1930 and 1931 Bacula and Lyon made six trips to the United States, Canada, and Cuba. According to Anslinger, Bacula smuggled approximately 250 kilos of narcotics under cover of his diplomatic passport on each trip. If Anslinger is even close to the truth, Bacula was responsible for moving nearly 1,500 kilos of drugs into North America between 1928 and 1931. He smuggled more narcotics across the Atlantic than anyone else during the last glory years of the Euro-American traffic. Bacula continued to operate in Europe until 1938, but after 1931 Anslinger made it too dangerous for him to bring drugs into North America. Bacula was finally arrested on drug charges in Vienna on a complaint by the French. He was tried and convicted in both Austria and France and served consecutive prison terms in the two countries from 1939 to 1943.

Latin America's importance in the drug traffic to the United States in those days was less as a producer of cocaine and more as a staging area for North American smugglers. Drug control regulations in Latin America were often poorly enforced or were overlooked altogether for persons connected to influential politicians. Narcotics were legally imported from European pharmaceutical firms and then sold to American smugglers.

Cuba was a center of international smuggling in the 1920s. Because it lies only ninety miles from southern Florida, it played an especially important role in the liquor traffic to the United States. Drugs were often shipped along with loads of alcohol as a simple "add-on." They were conveyed in weighted bags that could easily be jettisoned if the smugglers were approached by a Coast Guard cutter. An American undercover agent in Cuba in 1925 represented himself as a drug dealer and approached a pharmaceutical firm in Havana that was reputed to be a source of smuggled drugs.[37] The "druggist" welcomed him and introduced the agent to his political protectors, who included the former president of the city council and a deputy leader of a prominent political party, who was a personal friend of the current president of

Cuba, Santiago Rey. The agent was astounded not only by the easy availability of narcotic drugs but by the apparent eagerness of drug dealers
to show off their political connections.

Other agents' reports corroborated the impression that Havana was
a wide-open city where businessmen and politicians provided a ready
source of supply for drug dealers in the 1920s. American smugglers
quickly appreciated Cuba's advantages. Drugs were readily available;
politicians could be easily bought; and smugglers had to move their
cargo across a relatively short stretch of blue ocean. Furthermore, the
economics of the drug traffic through Cuba were most favorable. Opium
that was purchased for $25 in Havana could be sold for $60 in New York
City. Cuba continued to be a source of illicit drugs entering the United
States throughout the 1920s and 1930s.

As war in Europe and Asia disrupted traditional sources of narcotics
to the American market, Mexico filled the void. Anslinger estimated that
by 1941, Mexico was producing annually five tons of opium, most of
which was converted into morphine and heroin for the American market.[38] As early as 1939, the largest Mexican supplier was a fifty-year-old
woman, Ignacia Jasso Gonzalez, better known as "La Nacha," or "Pug-
Nose." La Nacha operated a drug store in Juarez, directly across the Rio
Grande from El Paso, Texas, openly selling opium, marijuana, heroin,
and cocaine to American customers who crossed the border. That was
simply the retail part of a vertically integrated business, which included
poppy fields in Sinaloa and an opiate factory in Guadalajara. She operated with impunity and the obvious protection of Mexican government
officials until 1942. In June of that year, Federal Bureau of Narcotics
agents lured two of her runners to San Antonio, Texas, where they arranged to buy fifty-five ounces of morphine. The runners were arrested
and American officials made a case that led to the indictment of La
Nacha. Anslinger used his contacts in the State Department to put heavy
pressure on Mexican officials to extradite her. Even then, La Nacha had
clout. "So, these Treasury men think they are very smart," she said when
told of the American requests. "But they are so dumb. They will never
put me in an American prison. I will fight extradition!" She was pro-
phetic. In an apparent compromise, Mexican officials refused to extradite La Nacha, but they did convict and sentence her to two years in a
Mexican prison, where she achieved local fame as a renowned tortilla
maker.

La Nacha's case is important not only as an indicator of the changing
flow of drugs during the war years but as an adumbration of the delicate

issue of extradition. European and American authorities regularly extradited drug dealers to one another, even during wartime. But Latin American countries were considerably more reticent to do so. Latinos did not see drug dealing to "yanquis" as a moral evil but as a business opportunity. Surrendering their citizens to the severity of North American justice for turning a peso in the drug business was not attractive to Latin American governments in the past, nor is it today.

Compared to the vast market for illegal drugs in and around China, the American market from the 1920s through the early 1950s was minuscule and declining. Fewer than 5 percent (perhaps as few as 1 percent) of the world's drug addicts were American. The United States did not shape the international narcotics market. It was a tiny and rather unimportant outlet.

Against this background, the Ezra case takes on special significance as a place where several historical vectors converged. First, China came to America. The flow of worldwide narcotics was reversed as Chinese-produced heroin and morphine were delivered into the veins of American addicts. An old and honorable Shanghai family, whose fortune had been made when dealing in drugs was legal in China, came to a bad end at a time and place when it was not.

Second, the Ezra brothers ran into agents of Harry Anslinger's Federal Bureau of Narcotics. They were tough and effective "narcs" who built a case against the international importers through careful detective work. The Ezra brothers' sentence, twelve years, also represented a new severity in Anslinger's war on drug dealers, especially in comparison to the mild sentences meted out to drug traffickers in Europe and the Far East.

Third, the shock of the Ezra case, and the *Ile de France* seizure the year before forced smugglers to rethink their business. In America it was impossible to buy political protection, as Du Yuesheng had done in China or as Louis Lyon had done in France. Anslinger was not only incorruptible but his intelligence network was extremely effective. Drug dealers who grew too big created exposure that eventually attracted Anslinger's attention.

Fourth, informants placed major drug dealers in great jeopardy. All of the minor members of the Ezras' distribution ring readily agreed to testify against the brothers in exchange for leniency. Likewise, when the entrepreneurial Jack Katzenberg attempted to establish a modest smuggling operation between China and New York, he was foiled by Federal Bureau of Narcotics informer Joe Schwartz.

All of this meant that the drug traffic in America was structured quite differently than it was in the Far East or even in France. Without political protection, drug smugglers could not expand and consolidate their business. In comparison to Du Yuesheng and other Asian dealers, American drug smugglers were small-time operators in a business that was, as Jack Katzenberg discovered, only marginally profitable and very risky. It was tough to be an addict and even tougher to be a successful drug dealer in Anslinger's America.

America seemed to have the narcotics problem contained in the 1950s. Drug addicts were rare, depraved creatures who might surface in stories like Nelson Algren's *Man with the Golden Arm*, but they did not haunt middle America. When Anslinger retired from his post in 1962 at age seventy, he had every reason to feel satisfied with his work. What Anslinger could not anticipate was the coming storm of the 1960s, when America's youth rediscovered drugs. LSD, marijuana, methamphetamine, and even heroin and cocaine became vehicles to explore "inner space." An entire generation extolled the virtues of mind-altering substances, seeing in them a way to reach truths never before imagined. Marijuana growers in Mexico, opium growers in Southeast Asia, and even a few coca growers in Latin America rejoiced at this newfound opportunity to serve America's youth.

NOTES

1. Quoted in David Courtwright, Don Des Jarlais, and Herman Joseph, *Addicts Who Survived: An Oral History of Narcotic Use in America, 1923–1965* (Knoxville: University of Tennessee Press, 1988), 98.

2. Information on the Ezra case is drawn from two State Department files in the United States National Archives: 800.114N16, EZRA, JUDAH, and "Name Files of Suspected Narcotics Traffickers, 1923–1954," lot 55 607D, EZRA, JUDAH, box 5, RG 59. We are grateful to our friend and colleague William O. Walker III who made us aware of the existence of this latter class of documents.

3. Judah Ezra was a gambler, and not an honest one. As mentioned in chapter 2, in 1918, his involvement in the Shanghai baseball scandal led to the elimination of his brother from the prestigious Shanghai Municipal Council.

4. Actually Paul had come to Harbin to escape from his involvement in the Goldenberg murder. He murdered the Shanghai film distributor, stole the Asian copy of the film *Way Down East*, and sold it to a Japanese distributor. "Interview with Lucy Ivanoff," November 12, 1931, D 3057 SMP CID.

5. D 3057, SMP CID.

6. D 3057 SMP CID.

7. D 3057, SMP CID.

8. The material for this section on the history of drugs in America is drawn from the following sources: David Courtwright, *Dark Paradise: Opiate Addiction in America before 1940* (Cambridge, Mass.: Harvard University Press, 1982); David Musto, *American Disease;* H. Wayne Morgan, *Yesterday's Addicts: American Society and Drug Abuse, 1865–1920* (Norman: University of Oklahoma Press, 1974); John Frisch, *Another Slavery: A Synoptic View of Opiate Dependence* (unpublished manuscript, 1979); and Jill Jonnes, *Hep-Cats, Narcs, and Pipe Dreams: A History of America's Romance with Illegal Drugs* (New York: Scribner's, 1996).

9. For an example of anti-Chinese, anti-opium polemics, see H. H. Kane, M.D., *Opium Smoking in America and China* (New York: Putnam's, 1882).

10. The background information on Anslinger is drawn from John McWilliams, *The Protectors* (Newark: University of Delaware Press, 1991).

11. Quoted in McWilliams, *Protectors*, p. 78.

12. Musto, *American Disease*, 140–200; Jonnes, *Hep-Cats, Narcs, and Pipe Dreams*, 72–86.

13. Jonnes, *Hep-Cats, Narcs and Pipe Dreams*, 72–86; Albert Fried, *Rise and Fall of the Jewish Gangster in America* (New York: Columbia University Press, 1993), 95–98.

14. Jonnes, *Hep-Cats, Narcs, and Pipe Dreams*, 78.

15. Fried, *Rise and Fall of the Jewish Gangster in America.*

16. Hon Ferdinand Pecora, interviewed by Donald Shaughnessy, typescript, October 1961, "The Reminiscences of Hon Ferdinand Pecora," Oral History Project, no. 451, Columbia University, 13:556.

17. Fuller to Nicholson, January 10, 1936, Name File, lot 55 D607, SCHWARZ, JOSEF, box 6, RG 59.

18. Jonnes, *Hep-Cats, Narcs, and Pipe Dreams*, 78.

19. McWilliams, *Protectors*, 167; details of the LSD experiments and their side effects on American society can be found in Jay Stevens, *Storming Heaven; LSD and the American Dream* (New York: Harper and Row, 1987); Martin Lee and Bruce Shlain, *Acid Dreams* (New York: Grove Weidenfeld, 1985); John Marks, *The Search for the Manchurian Candidate: the CIA and Mind Control* (New York: New York Times Books, 1979).

20. "Interview with Lucy Fontaine Crawley," October 26, 1931, D 3057, SMP CID.

21. Hull to Gray (telegram), March 1, 1940, Name File, lot 55 D607, BECKMAN, RALPH, box 2, RG 59.

22. H. Charles Spruks, "Memorandum," October 23, 1934, Name File, lot 55 D607, FEINBERG, HERMAN, box 5, RG 59.

23. Charles Allen to Secretary of State, Constantinople, December 31, 1930, 800.114N16, LORENZETTI, MARIO F./1, RG 59.

24. Name File, lot 55 607D, HOAG, THOMAS R., box 7, RG 59.

25. Name File, lot 55 607D, HOAG, THOMAS R., box 7, RG 59.

26. Name File, lot 55 607D, ATTFIELD, CAPT. CECIL HERBERT, box 1, RG 59.

27. Federal Bureau of Narcotics, *Traffic in Opium and Other Dangerous Drugs for 1929* (Washington, D.C.: Government Printing Office, 1930), 4–5.

28. Name File, lot 55 D607, BLOOM, JACOB, box 2, RG 59; see also 800.114N16, POLAKIEWITZ, JACOB, RG 59.

29. *Traffic . . . 1932*, 12.

30. Name File, lot 55 607D, KATZENBERG, JACK, box 8, RG 59. See also the files on his collaborators in the same group of documents: Jacob Lvovsky (box 9), Louis Buchalter (box 2), and Janis Tsounias (box 14), RG 59.

31. Fried, *Rise and Fall of the Jewish Gangster in America*; Bonanno, *Man of Honor*, 288–91, Humbert S. Nelli, *The Business of Crime: Italians and Syndicate Crime in the United States* (New York: Oxford University Press, 1976).

32. Name file, lot 55 D607, LYON, LOUIS, box 9, RG 59.

33. Name file, lot 55 D607, LYON, LOUIS, box 9, RG 59.

34. Telegram dated February 7, 1938, Name File, lot 55 D607, SCHWARZ, JOSEF, box 6, RG 59.

35. At our insistence, the U.S. State Department declassified a series of over two hundred files of suspected narcotics traffickers who operated between 1923 and 1954. We were the first historians to use these files, which reveal rich and detailed portraits of drug smugglers at work.

36. Name File, lot 55 D607, BACULA, CARLOS FERNANDEZ, box 1, RG 59.

37. Coast Guard central files, box 64, files 1002–04. We are indebted to Mark Haller, who shared this data with us.

38. "Extradition of Ignacia Jasso Gonzales (La Nacha) from Mexico," August 4, 1942, Name File, lot 55 D607, GONZALES, IGNACIA JASSO, box 6, RG 59.

CHAPTER TEN

COMMUNISTS

1 9 4 9 – 1 9 5 4

The policy prohibiting opium and narcotics is a thorough
extermination. Among the four areas of concern—prohibition of
planting, prohibition of selling, prohibition of transport and prohibition
of consumption—we will take sales and transport bans as a focus. We
will be lenient towards past offenses, but strict in present and future
cases; we will be lenient towards those who confess, but strict with
those who resist. Petty criminals, casual offenders and accomplices will
be treated leniently. Big criminals, kingpins and habitual offenders will
be handled severely. The general spirit is to severely investigate and
leniently carry out. To combine punishment with education. To use
struggle to reform the majority.

Li Xiannian, mayor of Wuhan[1]

Wuhan was liberated on May 16, 1949, four and a half months before
the final battles of the Communist victory on the Chinese mainland. The new city officials inherited a commercial port that had been
a lively opium market for more than a century. It was also a town that
had seen its share of opium reform. As early as 1837, Commissioner
Lin Zexu had initiated an opium reform in the area. Again in 1908 the
governor of the province promoted the Qing dynasty's short-lived

opium ban. In the 1920s and 1930s local warlords established monopolies as a source of income, a practice continued by the Nationalists. Thus when the Communists took over, they found a city of addicts with over 4,000 people engaged in the business of transporting and selling narcotics alone.[2]

After liberation, residents like Zhao Dianzhi became the immediate focus of Communist investigation. Zhao was a natural target; he was an opium merchant as well as a leading capitalist. He began his career as a humble rice merchant. His luck changed at the time of the 1911 Revolution, which began in Wuhan. The chaos of the fighting allowed the clever Zhao to buy all sorts of goods cheaply. He prospered when order returned by selling to the new Republican Army. He invested his newfound wealth by expanding into the cotton, leather, and, of course, the opium trades. In 1919, he opened the Datong Inn, where he developed useful connections by offering *Beiyang* warlords both opportunities to invest and a congenial place to dine and gamble. His connections paid off in the 1920s when he became head of the regional anti-opium bureau. He also joined the Wuhan Chamber of Commerce. During the *Guomindang* years Zhao opened a new restaurant, where he continued to court the favor of the new regime. He maintained alliances with police and city officials, and in 1933 he stepped into a new level of respectability when he opened the Commercial Bank.[3]

THE COMMUNIST ANTI-OPIUM PROGRAM

Wuhan had become a transshipping entrepôt for opium traveling north as well as a market for the drug. Wang Siji was one resident who prospered from manufacturing opium and morphine in Kunming and Yunnan and then selling through Wuhan. Such enterprises became targets for the new Communist authorities. On June 8, 1949, the Wuhan garrison and the Wuhan people's general police bureau issued a bulletin prohibiting the transportation and sale of opium and narcotics. This early sanction, and others like it in other liberated areas, was reinforced at the national level on February 24, 1950, only five months after total victory on October 1. On that day, Zhou Enlai signed a government administrative council order, "Concerning the Strict Elimination of Opium Poison," formally launching the Chinese Communist anti-opium campaign. Wording of the order indicated the political concerns of the new regime, even as it listed the causes of China's opium problems. It began by pointing out that for more than a century imperialist nations had forced opium on China. It continued by citing the role of reactionary rulers of the country before liberation, of the dissipated and decadent lifestyle of the bureaucrats, the warlords, the feudal compradores, and the Japanese invaders.[4]

Patriotic language had been used many times in China's struggle with the drug traffic, with few results. This case proved to be different, for over the next two years the Communist regime carried out an effective and thorough antinarcotics program. It did so by combining legal restrictions with mass movements to educate people against drugs. The communist cadres could arouse the fervor of the people because they identified drug manufacture, sales, and use with national enemies. The eradication of drugs became a revolutionary action.

The central government followed the February order by immediately involving local government bureaus and people's organizations. These bodies began the process of spreading anti-opium propaganda and practical information about giving up narcotics. In the spring various regional military committees created their own anti-opium orders, beginning in Southwest China. Throughout the nation basic preliminary measures included the registration of addicts and the establishment of opium recovery hospices. Regional police offices oversaw programs to eliminate both poppy cultivation and the processing and sale of opiates. The Wuhan authorities, for instance, created the Wuhan Anti-Opium Anti-Poison Committee in April 1950.[5]

After two years passed, the initial campaigns were considered to be insufficient. The bureaucratic and legal apparatus was in place, but without mass participation they continued to be inadequate. Therefore, in April 1952 the central government issued a "Directive Concerning the Quelling of the Popularity of Poisonous Commodities." The order renewed the government's commitment to the drive against narcotics just as the country was pursuing the Three Antis and Five Antis campaigns. These larger campaigns were well-orchestrated mass movements to rid China of the failings of its rulers and business managers. The Three Antis targeted government corruption as well as waste and oppressive bureaucratic attitudes, while the Five Antis focused on bribery, tax evasion, theft of state property, cheating on government contracts, and theft of state secrets, all crimes of the bourgeoisie. The campaigns featured mass rallies and self-criticism that became prominent features of Chinese political movements in the following decades.[6]

In handling narcotics offenders, the guidelines offered a two-pronged formula: strict punishment along with reeducation. The central government instructed local authorities to punish few, reform many; punish large dealers, be lenient with small operators; be strict with present offenders and lenient with past abusers; be harsh with those who hide their vice and go easy on those who confess. Those who were caught transporting or manufacturing drugs or who had a counterrevolutionary background were singled out for harsh punishment.[7]

At the end of May 1952, the Wuhan People's Political Committee and leaders of important metropolitan organizations held a consultative meeting to develop a strategy to involve the masses in the attack on narcotics use in their city. At the end of the day the mayor gave a closing speech highlighting the focus of the drive. In July the city government reiterated the importance of anti-opium work as second only to increasing productivity. At the same time the police prepared to concentrate their efforts on narcotics offenders. In August, 210 small action units of four to six people undertook to arrest one narcotics law violator each. Vowing to fight a war of annihilation against the opium evil, they successfully brought in 206 criminals; four others left town.[8]

Simply arresting these criminals was not considered thorough enough to make the desired impact on the entire population. The offenders themselves were cavalier. In court they denied their crimes, resisted officers, or quibbled with the judge. Some taunted the officials, suggesting that they try opium themselves or insinuating that the Communist government needed money and was planning to sell the confiscated goods. To make an impression, each ward leader, street leader, and unit leader undertook to explain personally to those under their charge the Chinese government's commitment to total opium eradication between August 14 and August 18. On August 16 the city publicly burned 300 *jin* of confiscated opium. At the same time, mass meetings were held at different locations through the city. At a meeting in Sun Yat-sen Park, 4,700 activists held a rally for citizens and ranking city officials. Later there were public meetings at which the families of addicts described the hardships they had endured for the assembled crowds.[9]

COMMUNISTS AND OPIUM REVENUES

The mass movements indicated that the Communists were serious about solving the opium problem. Their anti-opium policy emanated from deep conviction; however, their determination must be appreciated within the political context of the period. Opium was easily identified with Nationalist and imperialist enemies, and therefore useful in conjunction with patriotic campaigns. Nevertheless, the taunts of the opium sellers in the Wuhan courtroom that Communists needed opium revenues hit a raw nerve. In spite of the Communists' antipathy to opium, the party itself had briefly trafficked in the drug.

Chen Yungfa, a scholar with Academia Sinica who has scrutinized the economy of the North China Communist base camp area, has uncovered significant notations of "special products" in the trade statistics for the Shaan-Gan-Ning border region. He has determined that during the desperate war years from 1941 to 1946 the Communist leaders, like other warlords, turned to opium revenues to fund their protracted war.[10]

In October 1935 the remnants of the Red Army came to the Shanganning border area of North China to escape Chiang Kai-shek's extermination campaigns. The region was bleak and inhospitable; a sparse farming population eked out a miserable livelihood. The addition of a bedraggled army imposed a terrible burden on the meager productive capacity of the area. Initially the Communists funded their operations through confiscating landlord properties. The early years of the truce between the *Guomindang* and Communists that followed the Xian Incident of December 1936 gave the Communists a short respite when aid came through from the Soviet Union and other money came in from patriotic students who gathered at the base camp to fight the Japanese invaders. But by 1940 the area was again blockaded by both the Japanese enemy and the Nationalists to the south with whom the uneasy truce of 1936 was wearing thin.

In spite of difficulties, in 1940 the Communist Party launched a separate currency for the areas they controlled and called it the *bianbi*. This currency immediately suffered inflation against the *Guomindang fabi*, which was also severely inflated. To meet the crisis, the party resorted to printing more currency and to trading outside of the base camp area. One commodity they could export was locally produced salt. But salt was difficult to transport and, as we have seen earlier, the Japanese army blockaded it from the salt-deprived Central China region and treated anyone caught carrying it as an enemy agent. Trafficking in salt then, became even more dangerous than trafficking in opium.[11]

According to Chen, there was a "special product" that balanced the books during those difficult years. It was sold by the chest, had to be smuggled, and was sold in special shops. He concludes (with good reason) that the product was opium. The Chinese Communists did not allow opium smoking in the area they controlled. However, they did allow poppy cultivation using confiscated seeds or seeds that peasants had hidden away. In 1942 peasants were permitted, even encouraged, to plant poppies, although they were forbidden to market the crop to anyone but government agencies. Despite these plantings, however, the Communists obtained most of the opium they sold from regions just outside their control. They sold it in both Japanese- and Nationalist-controlled areas. The policy was so fruitful that by 1944 the *bianbi* stabilized. Communist opium sales proved crucial through the crisis years of 1941–44 and may have continued through 1946.

THE MECHANICS OF THE ANTI-OPIUM CAMPAIGN

The Communists regarded these measures as emergency actions that ran counter to their long-term plans for the nation. Within several months of victory in October 1949, Zhou Enlai made his anti-opium proclamation. Immediately thereafter each province and large city of China set up its own administrative machinery to carry out his directive. Fujian province provides a good example of how the campaign worked. Located on the coast directly across the straits from Taiwan, where the *Guomindang* remained in control, Fujian was a primary focus of anti-opium activity. It had been the location of an active opium trade since the beginning of the nineteenth century. In the 1830s there were at least twenty opium smuggling vessels working in Fujian waters. In the 1920s, warlord policies had encouraged poppies as a taxable cash crop. In the 1930s and 1940s both the *Guomindang* and the Japanese had operated monopolies, and men like Paul Yip grew rich catering to both. Thus liberation found Fujian rich in poppy fields, manufacturers, traders, and smokers.

In April 1950 the Provincial People's Government issued its own "Strict Elimination of Opium" order. In July it created the Fujian Provincial Committee to Eliminate Opium Poison. In September, the poppy planting season, the committee sent inspectors to villages to encourage compliance with the directive. In spring of the next year, the committee dispatched inspectors on follow-up visits to uproot poppy sprouts. This activity coincided with land reform. To underscore the seriousness of the directive, in the first year's campaign, the Public Safety Office arrested 198 opium criminals, closed 133 smoking houses, and seized 5,165 ounces of opium. Yet this was a small beginning.[12]

After the central government's second directive against opium in 1952, the provincial authorities directed their concern toward the apparent feeling among some segments of the public that opium smoking was a fashionable and harmless pastime. To this end, they launched a two-pronged attack. On the one hand, opium criminals would be arrested and some, at least, dealt with harshly. More important, they began a widespread campaign to educate people about the horrors of drug use. The ongoing Three Antis campaign helped the anti-opium initiative by bringing to light the names of several corrupt cadres who accepted bribes from opium criminals. The movement began with the public arrest of the owners of three of the largest opium companies and the seizure of 3,122 *jin* of opium and 123 ounces of morphine.

At the same time, the province organized an opium eradication headquarters, from which mass movements originated. Over 10,000 activists went into the countryside and cities to explain the evils of narcotics use. They arranged meetings at which family members of addicts would denounce their relatives and describe the hardships that drug use had brought to the clan. Sound trucks and stage plays reiterated the message, reminding people that opium use was brought to China by imperialists and feudal reactionary elements in the old society. In Fujian province, authorities targeted eight regions, including both the cities of Fuzhou and Xiamen and surrounding counties, deemed to have the strongest history of narcotics use. The movement began on a small scale in Fujian and intensified after 1952.[13]

Tianjin, a city steeped in drug use, was a different matter. Opium elimination began there even earlier than in the rest of China. Tianjin was liberated on January 15, 1949, and anti-opium work commenced early that August with a temporary prohibition law. Tianjin authorities concentrated their efforts on eliminating large-scale narcotics dealers. In 1950 the head of the municipal police became chairman of the Tianjin Eliminate Opium, Eliminate Poison Committee. He began investigations of men who had made fortunes selling narcotics in the city over the years. By July 1951 his committee had enough evidence to arrest and bring to trial several notorious dealers, including Shi Ziwen. Shi, also known as the narcotics king, had been in the business since the war with Japan. He continued his business using morphine brought to the mainland through Hong Kong. Smuggling techniques were often ingenious. They included false-bottomed suitcases, drugs wrapped in asphalt sheeting, and packets of morphine carried in the body cavities of couriers (referred to by the police as the anus brigade). Shi was tried and convicted in 1951.

In 1952, Tianjin authorities used the Three Antis campaign to target government workers who aided people like Shi, especially in the postal service and railway system. They also used mass movements to encourage addicts to give up their habits and to refrain from restarting. The national policy of punishment and reeducation, in combination with larger political movements, had a nearly miraculous effect. China was free of drugs for the first time in hundreds of years.[14]

A DRUG-FREE CHINA

Why did this movement work? One reason is that the combination of revolutionary isolationism with the outbreak of the Korean war effectively cut China off from the rest of the world at the moment the campaign got under way. With the borders hermetically sealed through ideology and international blockade, traffickers found it increasingly difficult to deliver their product. But tight border control can only offer a temporary cure for the problem. The Communists succeeded because they had perfected the technique of mass action.

Two American criminologists, Michael White and William Ludsetich, studied heroin prices and police enforcement strategies. They came to the conclusion that user harassment is more effective than seller harassment in curbing voluntary exchange crimes like narcotics use. Along the same lines, recent studies of drug programs in the United States have concluded that those that teach new social skills and use role-playing techniques are most effective. If we project these two findings onto the population at large, we come close to the kind of program that the Communists employed in the early 1950s. Bringing the stories of addicts' lives into the streets for all to see and hear, blaming a foreign criminal during the heightened national feelings in time of war, and indicting people who trafficked as class enemies created an environment in which traffickers found no market for their product. Narcotics use in China was suppressed quickly and effectively.[15]

But this success must be counted in decades, not centuries. In the 1980s, along with economic liberalization, came a resurgence of opium and heroin use in China. Although nowhere close to the prerevolutionary statistics, the current numbers are worrisome to Chinese authorities. In 1988, 239 kilograms of opium and 166 kilograms of heroin were confiscated. By 1991 the amounts had risen to 2,026 and 1,959 kilograms, respectively. Reintroduction of narcotics came from traffickers who began to use China as a transshipping route to the West after they found their usual routes becoming more treacherous as a result of increased international pressure in the early 1980s. The resurgence began in the border regions among minorities who had earlier experience of opium consumption. At least that is the official explanation. We cannot help but add that the revolutionary fervor that stimulated opium prohibition in the 1950s had burned itself out during the years of the Great Proletarian Cultural Revolution. With the opening of China's borders to trade with the West, hedonism blossomed in China once again. Chinese youth, in addition to embracing Western-inspired fashions and rock 'n' roll, also rediscovered the pleasures of the rite of their ancestors: opium.[16]

NOTES

1. Quoted in Chen Shouqian, "Wuhan Jindu Yundong" [The opium prohibition movement in Wuhan], in *Jinchang, Jindu: Jianguo Chuqi de Lishi Wenti* [Prohibit prostitution, prohibit poison: historical problems from the early period of national construction], ed. Ma Weigang (Beijing: Jingguan Jiaoyu Chubanshe), 234.
2. Chen, "Wuhan Jindu Yundong," 235.
3. Chen, "Wuhan Jindu Yundong," 230; for a sketch of Zhao's life, see Shao Shunjin, "Wuhan Yantu Tawang, Zhao Dianzhi," in *Zhonghua Wenshi Ziliao Wenku*, 20:621–27.
4. Ma, *Jinchang, Jindu*, 1–3.
5. Ma, *Jinchang, Jindu*, 1–3.
6. Ma, *Jinchang, Jindu*, 1–3.
7. Ma, *Jinchang, Jindu*, 1–3.
8. Chen, "Wuhan Jindu Yundong," 235–36.
9. Chen, "Wuhan Jindu Yundong," 236–38.
10. Ch'en, "The Blooming Poppy under the Red Sun."
11. "Akuma no Boryaku," pt. 2, *Sandae Mainichi*, December 9, 1984.
12. Ma, *Jinchang, Jindu*, 3–6.
13. Chen Xuncheng et al., "Fujian Jinyan Jindu Douzheng Jianji" [A short record of the struggle in Fujian province to eliminate opium and eliminate poison], in *Jinchang, Jindu*, 218–27.
14. Xiang Baosheng, "Jiu Tianjin de Yanduji 1952 Nian de Jindu Yundong" [Opium in old Tianjin and the 1952 eliminate opium movement], in *Jinchang, Jindu*, 336–62.
15. Michael White and William Ludsetich, "Heroin: Price Elasticity and Enforcement Strategies," *Economic Inquiry* 21, no. 4 (October 1983): 557–63; see for example Phyllis L. Ellickson and Robert M. Bell, "Drug Prevention in Junior High: A Multi-Site Longitudinal Test," *Science*, March 16, 1990; David Van Biema, "Just Say Life Skills: A New School Antidrug Program Outstrips D.A.R.E.," *Time*, November 11, 1996; both critics and apologists of D.A.R.E. agree that the program does enhance popular perceptions of the police. The same could be said for the early Chinese mass movements.

See "School Board Might Find DARE a Habit It Can Kick," *Chapel Hill News,*
May 8, 1997.

16. Cheng Yin, ed., *Baise Youling: Zhongguo Dupin Neimu* [White ghost: the inside
story of Chinese narcotics] (Beijing: Guangming Ribao Chubanshe, 1993),
1–12.

CONCLUSION

THE MYTH OF CONSPIRACY
1945 – 1997

A shot of morphine will cut off your descendents!
Opium is racial death!
Opium is the agent of national death!
Narcotics are the genocidal weapon of Imperialism!

Anti-Opium League, 1931[1]

I believe genocide has always been on the minds of many white
politicians and others who create the game rules. They're probably
thinking, "give minorities drugs and we can keep them at a level they
belong—impoverished."

Marcia Jones Cross, "Drugs, Genocide,"
Chicago Defender, October 25, 1989[2]

On October 23, 1996, Jack Blum testified at a special hearing of the
Senate Select Committee on Intelligence. The committee called
him as an expert witness to respond to serious allegations made by *San
Jose Mercury News* reporter Gary Webb in an exposé entitled "Dark Alli-

ance" that appeared in mid-August. Webb charged that through the 1980s there had been close connections between the Central Intelligence Agency, certain Contra leaders fighting the Sandinista government in Nicaragua, and American cocaine traffickers, specifically Freeway Ricky Ross. The article drew attention to the business relationship between Ross, a crack trafficker in south-central Los Angeles, and his suppliers, Danilo Blandon and Norman Meneses. At the time both men were members of the Nicaraguan Democratic Force, the Contras. Blandon and his arms supplier, Ronald J. Lister, both bragged about their CIA connections. According to the Webb article, they worked openly until 1986; only after Congress finally voted funds to support the effort against the Sandinistas were they arrested.[3]

"Dark Alliance" caused an immediate uproar in the black community. Activist and comedian Dick Gregory, radio host Joe Madison, and other prominent black leaders made widespread public appeals for official investigations into the charges. On September 23, 1996, they protested outside of the Drug Enforcement Agency, surrounding the building with scene-of-the-crime tape to call attention to their demands. They were arrested while trying to enter the building to see DEA administrator Thomas Constantine. Two days later, Democratic Congressional representative Maxine Waters used the occasion of the House discussion to approve intelligence funding for the coming fiscal year to make an impassioned appeal to Congress for investigations into the relationship between the war in Central America and the crack cocaine epidemic in African-American communities.[4]

Other opinion makers were skeptical. The mainstream media, after some initial coverage, downplayed the claim. By November, leading newspapers, including the *New York Times* and the *Washington Post*, criticized Webb and the *Mercury News*. Those papers claimed that highly placed CIA agents denied any knowledge of Contra ties to narcotics. In the wake of such attention, Jerry Ceppos, editor of the *Mercury News*, undertook an internal review of the series. After an interval of silence, he took an unprecedented step when he publicly announced on May 12, 1997, in his own paper, that the series was flawed.[5]

In the midst of the initial public debate, the Senate Intelligence Committee convened a special October 24 session to look into the matter. Jack Blum was one of the best witnesses that the committee could have called. He had been special counsel to the Senate Foreign Relations Committee from January 1987 to May 1989. As such, he had been in charge of the investigations into government wrongdoing during the

Iran-Contra affair. He, more than most people, was familiar with the events discussed by Gary Webb in "Dark Alliance." Nor was it his first time in the Senate hearing room. As he told the story of his earlier experiences, a boisterous crowd cheered him on from the gallery.[6]

Jack Blum's testimony before the committee satisfied neither side of the debate. He assessed the role of government agencies in the American narcotics problem in terms of how the question is worded. If the question is, Did the CIA conspire to sell drugs to African-Americans? then the answer must be no. However, if the question is, Did well-placed people in the government turn a blind eye to the illegal activities of their allies in the Nicaraguan war, allowing them to compensate themselves while avoiding the embarrassment that the arrest of high-ranking Contras would bring? then the answer is yes.[7]

Jack Blum described a situation in which American intelligence and law enforcement allowed powerful people in friendly nations and organizations to flout the law and enrich themselves. He discussed the many times that his own investigations had to end because he could not get clearance from high-level sources to continue. He told of reports that CIA people screened all of the DEA's informants, sat in on witness interviews and trial preparations, or intervened in pending cases to help their friends. Ironically, the profits did not go to the Contras in the field but helped finance the lavish lifestyle of a few leaders in Miami. His own investigators ran into problems with the Justice Department, which went out of its way to discredit his findings in the press.[8]

Chronic narcotic drug use is most noticeable when it appears in a community in distress. In Jack Blum's analysis of the recent American situation, cocaine from South America flooded the entire American market from the early 1980s on. In African-American neighborhoods, customers ran out of money quickly, and a large number of them went into the trafficking business. The ensuing turf war brought violence in its wake, destabilizing poor neighborhoods. In the face of eroding job opportunities and a decline in public assistance, escalating violence and the volatile nature of crack made a bad situation worse. The assumption that the condition was a result of a plot was an easy one for anyone experiencing it to make.

Black Americans are not alone in reaching the conclusion that a conspiracy against them is at work. In China in the 1930s, violence connected with the narcotics trade was dwarfed by endemic civil war and invasion. Yet when anti-opium organizations saw the coincidence of eroding public order and national wealth, followed by Japanese expansion and increased activity in the narcotics traffic, they were quick to blame the Japanese invaders, using the same language of genocide and conspiracy that black American activists have adopted in recent times. We cannot simply dismiss these sentiments as foolish or paranoid notions, for in both cases observers described accurately the desperate conditions they witnessed. In the American ghettoes of the 1980s and China of the 1930s there was a coincidence of social disintegration and increased addiction. More important, in both cases the charge of genocide served a purpose in mobilizing a community under siege to identify and fight against a common enemy and to make the considerable effort to give up habit-forming drugs.[9]

What looked like genocide and conspiracy at the highest levels, however, in fact was political compromise in pursuit of larger goals. What we found in Asia in the 1930s was not a high-level plot; rather, it was a kind of bureaucratic schizophrenia. The Chinese and Japanese governments both formally denounced opium; *Guomindang* reforms after 1936 and Japanese reforms in Taiwan and Manchuria in the 1930s went forward. But their announced policies conflicted with the field operations and covert actions of their own armed forces. In fact, the limited success of both reforms, coupled with the international sanctions to which they were tied, increased the efficiency of the political economy of the narcotics traffic at the ground level. Thus strategists on both sides found it difficult not to use opium or heroin in pursuing a larger policy. The result was not so much high-level conspiracy as denial.

Conspiracy takes coordination by a tight group of leaders who enjoy a shared set of strategic goals. In our research we found leadership both in governments and among the traffickers to be less static and focused. As individuals pursued long-term goals, they engaged in factional rivalries to enrich themselves and realize their ambitions. They undercut each other as they jockeyed for position. Politicians who used narcotics for tactical purposes often turned to traffickers for money or information, but their alliances with drug dealers were as fluid as those among the traffickers themselves. Such conditions did not, and do not, foster successful conspiracies.

What looked like conspiracy to the victims of narcotics abuse was, in fact, the operation of the political economy that emerged when narcotic drugs were outlawed by international sanction. Increasingly efficient regulation created both problems and opportunities for traffickers. In order to survive in the changed conditions, they needed to find official protection, especially in their supply, delivery, and, more recently, their investment operations. The international instability of the 1920s and 1930s gave shape to an industry that thrives in conditions of conflict and turmoil. The industry that was born in the interwar period and became moribund during the Second World War revived in the 1950s.

This is not to deny that individuals, bureaus, and proxies of the American government have been involved with drugs and traffickers as the United States assumed the lead in fighting the cold war. The CIA experiments with LSD, the alliance and breakup with Manuel Noriega, and the policies in Afghanistan that turned the area into the Golden Crescent are only a few examples of American agencies' relationships with drug dealers and users. The difference is whether we interpret them as continual—built into the American power structure, manipulated by a few power brokers, and therefore conspiracy—or as episodic reiterations of historical patterns.

Those who see an American government conspiracy point to one specific moment in the postwar world as the origin and prototype of all that followed. In 1946 New York State prison officials released Salvatore "Lucky" Luciano from Dannemora Prison. The prevailing wisdom about Luciano is summarized in Alfred W. McCoy's influential book, *The Politics of Heroin in Southeast Asia:* "In 1946 American military intelligence made one final gift to the Mafia—they released Luciano from prison and deported him to Italy, thereby freeing the greatest criminal talent of his generation to rebuild the heroin trade."[10] However, McCoy misrepresents a crucial fact: Luciano's sentence was commuted by Governor Dewey, not by military intelligence. Furthermore, McCoy's sources for his allegation that Luciano reconstructed the postwar heroin trade are either books or statements by agents of the Federal Bureau of Narcotics who, as we shall see, had a vested interest in portraying Luciano as an all-controlling villain. The reality, however, was rather different.

Luciano was born in Sicily in 1897. He emigrated with his mother and father to New York City in 1904, although he never became an American citizen. The wayward son of industrious and honest parents, Salvatore dropped out of school after fifth grade. After two years' work in a factory, where he made seven dollars a week, young Luciano declared if he had to be a "crumb," he would rather be dead.[11] It was his last honest job.

Luciano bumped along as a criminal adolescent, accumulating arrests for, among other things, heroin possession, once in 1916 and again in 1923. Prohibition proved to be a godsend for Luciano, as it was for other young hoodlums of his generation. His ruthlessness and street smarts catapulted him to success in the illegal alcohol trade. He climbed steadily within New York crime circles throughout the 1920s. His big breaks came between 1929 and 1931. Lucky got his nickname on a grim October night in 1929. A rival narcotics dealer cut his throat and left him suspended by his thumbs from the rafters of a Staten Island warehouse. Luciano survived by struggling free from his bonds and crawling to Highland Boulevard. When the police questioned him, he claimed that he had no idea who had tortured him or why. His admiring underworld colleagues bestowed the name "Lucky" on him in recognition of both his good fortune and his unwillingness to share information with the authorities.

Luciano's ascent to the top of the New York City criminal underground began in 1931. On April 15 of that year, Joseph "Joe the Boss" Masseria, Luciano's superior, was gunned down in a Coney Island restaurant. Luciano claimed that he had been in the men's room washing his hands and had missed all the action. In the wake of Masseria's killing, Luciano organized a group of younger generation gangsters who challenged the older Sicilians for leadership. Luciano's older rival was Salvatore Maranzaro, who in the summer seemed to be consolidating power. Then, on September 10, 1931, Maranzaro was shot dead in his office. Some forty to fifty of his associates around the country were slain within a few days. It was widely assumed, although never proven, that Luciano had coordinated the killings. By 1931, Luciano had a secure power base. He was the most important criminal entrepreneur in New York City.

Luciano's business ventures were widespread. Certainly they included narcotics distribution, although there is no evidence that he was significantly involved in international smuggling. Lucky brought organization and rationalization to his businesses, which included prostitution. By the mid-1930s, his extensive control of brothels in New York made him a tempting target for Thomas Dewey, then a New York State special prosecutor. In 1936 Dewey successfully prosecuted Luciano on a charge of forced prostitution, which yielded the remarkably stiff prison sentence of thirty to fifty years. Luciano seemed destined to spend the remainder of his prime years in the cold confines of Dannemora Prison in upstate New York. Then, once again, he got lucky.

In 1942, shortly after America had joined the Allied war effort, a naval intelligence officer named R. Charles Haffenden solicited Luciano's assistance in the war effort. What Haffenden wanted from Luciano was never entirely clear. Haffenden himself refused to discuss the matter on the specific instructions of the U.S. Navy. Luciano's attorney, Moses Polakoff, claimed in a letter to the New York Parole Division that his client had furnished military authorities with information about Sicily that was helpful in the American invasion of that Italian island.[12] Murray Gurfein, who had been on Dewey's prosecutorial staff and later served in the Office of Strategic Services (OSS), remembered the request rather differently: "The Navy," Gurfein said, "felt that the many sinkings of United States' ships along the Atlantic coast indicated that the U-boats were not returning to home bases but were being refueled and resupplied offshore." Gurfein went on to suggest that Joseph Socks Lanza, because of his experience in the Fulton fish market, "might be able to make contacts and help find out how the U-boats were being refueled and supplied, and if so, where, and by whom."[13] Gurfein hoped that Luciano would motivate his underworld friends to supply some useful information. Nevertheless, the War Department, the Department of the Navy, and the OSS all denied authorizing contact with Luciano or profiting from whatever information he might have furnished. Even Luciano himself made contradictory statements about his wartime contributions.[14]

The issue surfaced again in 1945–46, when the New York State Parole Division met to consider a recommendation to Governor Thomas Dewey to commute Luciano's sentence. Eventually the Parole Division recommended commutation, with its chair, Frederick Moran, downplaying Luciano's dubious war service and stressing the "routine grounds" on which the decision was made.[15] Dewey himself made mention of it at the time of the commutation: "Upon the entry of the United States into the war, Luciano's aid was sought by the Armed Services in inducing others to provide information concerning possible enemy attack. It appears that he cooperated in such effort, although the actual value of the information procured is not clear."[16] Of far greater importance, according to both Moran and Dewey, was that Luciano had already served ten years of hard time of an unusually severe sentence, that his prison behavior had been exemplary, and that he was an alien whose deportation would save the taxpayers the expense of further incarceration. Accordingly, in January 1946, Luciano's sentence was commuted and the gangster was deported to Italy.

Despite the denials of Moran and Dewey, the commutation raised suspicions that it was a payoff for Luciano's wartime cooperation. Regardless of appearances, Luciano's State Department file does not offer any conclusive evidence either that Luciano made much of a contribution to the war effort or that Dewey was particularly influenced by it.[17] In 1954, still plagued by rumors of a Luciano deal, Dewey asked New York State Commissioner of Investigations William B. Herlands to look into the allegations. The Herlands Report was concluded in 1954 after the committee had taken testimony from various participants in the affair. The report, which was not made public, mirrored earlier judgments: Luciano had cooperated with Naval Intelligence during the war, but his assistance had been of dubious value, and in any case Luciano's commutation was justified on other grounds.[18]

Luciano did not stay long in Italy. By October 1946 he turned up in Cuba, which was still the booming center of illicit enterprise in the Caribbean. By February 1947 Anslinger was surprised to learn that Luciano was so close to his cronies and suspected that he was trying to revive his narcotics business. Luciano claimed that he "wanted to buy a piece of the [legal] gambling rackets at the Gran Casino Nacional and the Oriental Race Track."[19] Anslinger was not convinced. He notified the Cuban government that he would halt all exports of legal narcotics to Cuba so long as Luciano remained on the island. This heavy-handed maneuver worked. Cuban secret police picked up Luciano, and he was again deported to Italy on March 20, 1947.

Anslinger was still not satisfied. He was in close contact with Italian officials who shared his concern that Luciano might get back into the narcotics business. Luciano was arrested immediately upon his return to Italy in April 1947, released, and rearrested in 1949, when a man suspected of being a Luciano associate was found in possession of a load of heroin.[20] When he was not in jail, Luciano was continually watched by agents of the Italian Ministry of the Interior. In 1951, Giuseppe Dosi of that ministry stated in a memo to Anslinger that "in spite of the strict and continual surveillance of which he [Luciano] is the object, nothing has been found against him."[21] Furthermore, Anslinger occasionally despatched his Italian-speaking lieutenant, Charles Siragusa, to check on Luciano personally and to keep the heat on the Italian authorities. The only "evidence" Siragusa could cite of Luciano's continued participation in the narcotics traffic was that he was visited by a stream of known gangsters and that he received large amounts of money from American friends that supported his lavish lifestyle.[22]

On the basis of this paper-thin evidence, Siragusa testified in 1951 before the Senate Crime Investigating Committee, chaired by Estes Kefauver, that Luciano "still ruled the narcotics traffic in the United States, operating from Sicily."[23] That continued to be the Federal Bureau of

Narcotics line. In 1952, when leaders of a major narcotics importing ring were indicted in San Francisco, the bureau's district supervisor George Cunningham, claimed that "Luciano controlled all of the narcotics smuggling from Italy," although "he kept very much 'in the background.'"[24] At the same time, the vigilant Dosi in Italy told the United Nations that he had kept Luciano "constantly under surveillance, but has been unable to pin anything on him."[25]

The recently declassified file on Luciano in the State Department supports Dosi's interpretation of Luciano's activities. In none of the correspondence between Anslinger and his agents, or between Anslinger and Dosi, is there any evidence that Luciano was actively engaged in the international narcotics business. Indeed, given his periodic incarceration and constant surveillance, it is impossible to believe that Luciano could have been the executive of a major international narcotics smuggling operation. Drug smuggling is a business that needs constant communication and attention to detail. The occasional visits of subordinates would not have given Luciano sufficient information and control to run a smuggling operation. Luciano may have had a role as adviser and mediator among drug dealers, but that does not mean that he established and controlled the entire transatlantic operation.

Why would Anslinger and his subordinates have so grossly misrepresented Luciano's role? Anslinger was keenly attuned to shifts in the political winds, especially in Congress, the source of his funding. The Kefauver Committee (1951) created in the public mind the idea of the "mafia" as a tightly run Sicilian brotherhood that controlled all aspects of illicit enterprise in the United States.[26] Luciano was a notorious gangster whose early release from prison left a residue of suspicion that he had cut a deal with public officials. Anslinger was probably correct in believing that Luciano would have liked to reenter the narcotics business if circumstances had permitted. Ironically, it was largely because of Anslinger's attention that Luciano was unable to do so. Anslinger must have known that he had Luciano locked up so tightly in Italy that he could never effectively control a vast international smuggling ring. Drugs that entered postwar America (in the early 1950s they came in a trickle rather than the flood that came later) came from many and varied sources, just as they had before the war. But to say that did not make for dramatic publicity. The Federal Bureau of Narcotics needed monstrous villains for public consumption, and Luciano, the archetypal *mafioso*, filled that role. In the public eye, he became Mr. Big, craftily manipulating the international heroin traffic from his apartment in Italy, safely outside Anslinger's jurisdiction. At most, Luciano was remotely connected to the less well-known smugglers who actually moved drugs from Europe to America after the war, the most important of whom used Marseille as their transhipping point.

Harry Anslinger needed a super villain to maintain his position in the American bureaucracy. He used the myth of Luciano, the "drug king-pin," to maintain funding for his Federal Bureau of Narcotics and to protect it from periodic criticism. More important, in the early 1950s Anslinger ushered his vision of narcotics control policy through Congress. Anslinger, like many before him going back to Lin Zexu and the Daoguang emperor, favored interdiction over legalization, supply-side solutions over demand reduction, enforcement over treatment. In 1951 he saw his recommendations realized when the Boggs Act, which included provisions for mandatory sentencing, passed through Congress. The provisions were reinforced in the Narcotics Control Act of 1956.[27]

Harry Anslinger and his bureau were using narcotics in the same way that Chinese patriots of the 1930s and present-day black leaders used it. He manipulated public fears of the crime and disorder associated with narcotics to pursue a cause. One of Anslinger's ploys to maintain the status and funding of the FBN was to bring the cold war into the crusade against hard drugs. To that end, his bureau undertook a campaign against Communist China beginning in the early 1950s and continuing to his retirement in 1962. He accused the Chinese government of flooding the free world with narcotics. He brought his claims before Congress and the United Nations, and he published them wherever he could in the American press. A good example of this attack can be found in the page-long editorial entitled "Mr. Attlee's Friends, the Chinese Commies, Are the World's Leading Dope Smugglers" that appeared in *The Saturday Evening Post* on November 13, 1954. The article began by criticizing Clement Attlee of the British Labour Party, who toured mainland China and then reported that drug use had disappeared in that country. The article cited the United Nations Commission on Narcotic Drugs and its American representative, Harry Anslinger, as proof that "Red China is the chief supplier of illicit dope . . . to pushers the whole world over." The profits were used, the article claimed, to finance Communist activities in Asia and to pay for strategic war material. It finished by chiding Mr. Attlee for relying on "I was told" information.[28]

As we have seen, Attlee's hearsay evidence was sounder than Anslinger's. While the Americans were conducting their Red Scare, the new government in mainland China was carrying out its effective anti-opium campaign. It succeeded because political stability brought to the Chinese mainland the same conditions that had helped keep the American narcotics traffic to a trickle in the prewar years. More important, the Communist leadership effectively employed the same technique that African-American community activists are trying to use in self-defense and that Harry Anslinger manipulated to expand his bureau's program. They turned the message and mechanics of opium eradication and elimination of addiction into a tool of their larger political agenda.

The myth of the international narcotics conspiracy is powerful. It is compelling to ascribe the depredations of narcotics use to a plot between a shadowy government agency and a syndicate or an individual trafficker who is conveniently outside the law's reach. The obscurity that necessarily cloaks traffickers and their political partners makes it easy to believe this myth. Furthermore, the rhetoric of mythmaking has served the social and political agendas of groups and individuals as diverse as Chinese nationalists, African-American community activists, and the head of the Federal Bureau of Narcotics. But the reality is more prosaic.

Drug traffickers are entrepreneurs. In the early years of the twentieth century, when their business became illegal, they sought the assistance of political figures who could help them solve specific problems of supply, delivery, finance, and contract enforcement. These problems are vexing for ordinary businessmen working in normal circumstances, but they become acute for entrepreneurs operating in an illegal environment. Their efforts to solve these problems and stabilize their business met with varying degrees of success. Generally, they flourished in times and places of political instability, where politicians needed money, intelligence, and other resources that traffickers could offer. These alliances were often productive in the short term, but they rarely lasted. Both drug traffickers and their political allies were consummate opportunists, and opportunities appeared or disappeared with changing circumstances, which not even the most powerful among them could entirely control. As long as there is a demand for drugs and the drugs in demand are illegal, traffickers will seek out and establish alliances with politicians. These alliances are not conspiracies but are the political economy of the international narcotics traffic.

NOTES

1. Kantocho Keimukyoku Koto Keisatsu ka [High level police department of the Kuantung police affairs bureau], *Joshiki Shoku-shin-kai Kyo-doku-kai Hai-*

Nichi Yundo Taiyo [A general survey of the anti-Japanese activities of the society to promote common sense and the anti-opium society], 1931, document 2589, Toyo Bunko, Tokyo.

2. Marcia Jones Cross, "Drugs, Genocide," *Chicago Defender*, October 25, 1989.

3. Gary Webb, "Dark Alliance," *San Jose Mercury News*, August 18–25, 1996. The series featured a page on the World Wide Web, which gave it a wider audience; "Dark Alliance," August 18, 1996, HTTP://www.sjmercury.com/drugs/day1main.htm, October 9, 1996.

4. "Democracy Now," Pacifica Radio Archives PZ0827.157, September 24, 1996; "Ex-Fed Links US to Dope Deal," *New York Daily News*, September 24, 1996; "Four Arrested Outside of DEA," *Washington Post*, September 24, 1996; Congress, House, Maxine Waters on Central Intelligence Agency and Crack Cocaine to House Select Intelligence Committee, Conference report on HR 3259, 104th Cong., 2d sess. *Congressional Record* , 142, no. 134, (September 25, 1996).

5. Jerry Ceppos, "Epilogue: Dark Alliance," May 12, 1997, HTTP://cgi.sjmercury.com/drugs/column051197.htm, June 6, 1997; "Expose on Crack Was Flawed, Paper Says," *New York Times*, May 13, 1997.

6. "Democracy Now," Pacifica Radio Archives PZ0287.179, October 24, 1996.

7. "Democracy Now," Pacifica Radio Archives PZ0287.179, October 24, 1996.

8. Jack Blum, "Commentary: Former Senate Special Counsel Discusses Controversy," October 23, 1996, HTTP://cgi.sjmercury.com/drugs/postscript/update1023.htm, June 6, 1997.

9. Patricia A. Turner, *I Heard It on the Grapevine: Rumor in African American Culture* (Berkeley: University of California Press, 1993), describes the role of rumor in the black community as a useful tool of resistance rather than a pathological preoccupation. Certainly the usefulness of the charge of genocide in the Chinese case is equally clear.

10. Alfred W. McCoy, *The Politics of Heroin* (New York: Lawrence Hill Books, 1991), 23–24.

11. Hickman Powell, *Ninety Times Guilty* (New York: Arno, 1974), 70.

12. Albert Deutsch, "Dewey Owes People the Facts in Strange Case of Luciano," February 25, 1947, Name File . . . , Lot 55 D607, LUCANIA, SALVATORE [Lucky Luciano], box 9 (hereafter Luciano file), RG 59.

13. Rodney Campbell, *The Luciano Project* (New York: McGraw Hill, 1977), 35.

14. Campbell, *Luciano Project*, 281.

15. Campbell, *Luciano Project*, 246.

16. Campbell, *Luciano Project*, 247.

17. Luciano file.

18. Campbell, *Luciano Project*, 259–82.

19. Luciano file, Joseph A. Fortier (U.S. Treasury agent, Havana) to Commissioner of Customs, March 27, 1947, 3.

20. "Luciano Facing Exile to Sicily after Rome Narcotics Inquiry," *New York Herald Tribune*, July 9, 1949, Luciano file.

21. Memorandum by Ministry of the Interior, Italian Central Office for the International Criminal Police, Rome, March 8, 1951, p. 1, Luciano file.

22. Siragusa to Anslinger, May 12, 1951, Luciano file.

23. "Luciano Rules U.S. Narcotics from Sicily Senators Hear," *New York Times,* June 28, 1951, Luciano file.

24. "Luciano Is Linked to Heroin Arrests," *New York Times,* March 9, 1952, Luciano file.

25. "Italy Tells UN It Can't Get Dope on Lucky," *New York Post,* May 6, 1952, Luciano file.

26. Pino Arlacchi, *Mafia Business: The Mafia Ethic and the Spirit of Capitalism* (London: Verso, 1987), argues that the mafia as a formal organization never existed in Italy either. He calls the mafia a way of behaving and, agreeing with Joe Bonanno, a tradition.

27. Douglas Clark Kinder, "Bureaucratic Cold Warrior: Harry J. Anslinger and Illicit Narcotics Traffic," *Pacific Historical Review* (1981), 50:169–91.

28. "Mao's Dope Industry," *America,* June 19, 1954; "Dope from Red China," *Time,* March 21, 1955; "Mr. Attlee's Friends, the Chinese Commies, Are the World's Leading Dope Smugglers," *Saturday Evening Post,* November 13, 1954.

BIBLIOGRAPHY

Abadinsky, Howard. *Organized Crime.* Boston: Allyn and Bacon, 1981.

Adler, Patricia. *Wheeling and Dealing: An Ethnography of an Upper Level Drug Dealing Community.* New York: Columbia University Press, 1989.

Akimoto Shunkichi. *Manchurian Scene.* Tokyo: Taisho Eibunsha, 1933.

Arlacchi, Pino. *Mafia Business: The Mafia Ethic and the Spirit of Capitalism.* London: Verso, 1987.

Assam Opium Enquiry Committee. *Assam Congress Opium Committee Report.* N.p., 1925.

Bamba, Nobuya. *Japanese Diplomacy in Dilemma: New Light on Japan's China Policy, 1924–1929.* Vancouver: University of British Columbia Press, 1977.

Beasley, W. G. *The Meiji Restoration.* Stanford, Calif.: Stanford University Press, 1972.

———. *The Rise of Modern Japan.* New York: St. Martin's, 1990.

Beeching, Jack. *The Chinese Opium Wars.* London: Hutchenson of London, 1975.

Bendiner, Elmer. *A Time for Angels: The Tragicomic History of the League of Nations.* New York: Knopf, 1975.

Block, Alan. "European Drug Trafficking between the Great Wars: Developing Illicit Markets and Criminal Syndicates." *Journal of Social History* 23 (Winter 1989): 315–37.

Block, Alan, and William Chambliss. *Organizing Crime*. New York: Elsevier, 1981.

Bruun, Kettil, Lynn Pan, and Ingemar Rexed. *The Gentlemen's Club: International Control of Drugs and Alcohol*. Chicago: University of Chicago Press, 1975.

Broomhall, B. *The Truth about Opium Smoking*. London: Hodder and Stoughton, Paternoster Row, 1882.

Cai Shaoqing. *Minguo Shiqi de Tufei* [Bandits in the republican era]. Beijing: Zhungguo Renmin Daxue Chubanshe, 1993.

Campbell, Rodney. *The Luciano Project*. New York: McGraw-Hill, 1977.

Ch'en, Jerome. *Yuan Shih-k'ai*. Stanford, Calif.: Stanford University Press, 1972.

Ch'en Li-fu. *Storm Clouds Clear over China*. Palo Alto, Calif.: Hoover Institution on War, Revolution, and Peace, 1994.

Ch'en Yung-fa. "The Blooming Poppy under the Red Sun: The Yenan Way and the Opium Trade." In *New Perspectives on the Chinese Communist Revolution*, edited by Tony Saich and Hans van de Ven, 263–98. Armonk, N.Y.: Sharpe, 1995.

Ch'i, Hsi-sheng. *Warlord Politics in China, 1916–1928*. Stanford, Calif.: Stanford University Press, 1976.

China: Inspector General of Customs. *Opium: Historical Notes or the Poppy in China*. Special Series, no. 13. Shanghai: Kelly and Walsh, 1889.

Chinese People's Foreign Relations Society. *Menace to the Peace of the Far East*. N.p., 1921.

Clubb, O. Edmund. *Twentieth Century China*. New York: Columbia University Press, 1964.

Coble, Parks. *Facing Japan: Chinese Politics and Japanese Imperialism, 1931–1937*. Cambridge, Mass.: Harvard University Press, 1991.

Collis, Maurice. *Foreign Mud*. New York: Knopf, 1946.

Courtwright, David. *Dark Paradise: Opiate Addiction in America before 1940*. Cambridge, Mass.: Harvard University Press, 1982.

Courtwright, David, Don Des Jarlais, and Herman Joseph. *Addicts Who Survived: An Oral History of Narcotic Use in America, 1923–1965*. Knoxville: University of Tennessee Press, 1988.

De Quincey, Thomas. *Confessions of an English Opium-Eater and Other Writings*. New York: Oxford University Press, 1985.

Du Yingmo. *Shanghai Wenren Du Yuesheng* [Du Yuesheng, a Shanghai VIP]. Taipei: Mingwang Chubanshe, 1987.

Eguchi Keiichi. *Nitchu Ahen Senso* [The Japanese-Chinese opium war]. Tokyo: Iwaname Shoten, 1989.

Ellickson, Phyllis L. and Robert M. Bell. "Drug Prevention in Junior High: A Multi-Site Longitudinal Test," *Science*. March 16, 1990.

Fay, Peter Ward. *The Opium War, 1840–1842.* Chapel Hill: University of North Carolina Press, 1975.

Fogel, Joshua, trans. *A Life along the South Manchurian Railway: The Memoirs of Ito Takeo.* Armonk, N.Y.: Sharpe, 1988.

Foster, Arnold. *Municipal Ethics.* Shanghai: Kelly and Walsh, 1914.

Friman, H. Richard. *Narco-Diplomacy: Exporting the U.S. War on Drugs.* Ithaca, N.Y.: Cornell University Press, 1996.

Frisch, John. "Another Slavery: A Synoptic View of Opiate Dependence." Unpublished manuscript, 1979.

Fujise Kazuya. *Showa Rikugun Ahen Boryaku no Taizai* [The opium crimes of the Showa army]. Tokyo: Yamanote Shobo Shinsha, 1992.

Gardner, Brian. *The East India Company: A History.* London: Granada. 1971.

Gendai Nihon Jinbutsu Jiten. [Dictionary of modern Japanese notables]. Tokyo: Asahi Shimbun Sha, 1990.

Giles, Herbert. "The Opium Edict and Alcohol in China." *Nineteenth Century* 370 (December 1907): 987–1002.

Greenberg, Michael. *British Trade and the Opening of China, 1800–42.* Cambridge: Cambridge University Press, 1951.

Haller, Mark H. "Illegal Enterprise: A Theoretical and Historical Interpretation." *Criminology* 28 (May 1990): 207–35.

Harada Katsumasa. *Mantetsu* [South Manchurian Railway]. Tokyo: Iwanami Shoten, 1981.

Hashimoto Kingoro. *Hashimoto Taisa no Shuki* [The memoirs of Colonel Hashimoto]. Tokyo: Misuzu Shobo, 1963.

Hata Ikuhiko. *Showa Shi no Gunjintachi* [Army men in Showa history]. Tokyo: Bungei Shunju, 1982.

Hauser, Ernest. *Shanghai: City for Sale.* New York: Harcourt, Brace, 1940.

Hoshi Hajime. *Ahen Jiken* [The opium incident]. Tokyo: Hoshi Pharmaceutical Business School, 1926.

———. *Senkyo Daigaku* [Election college]. Tokyo: N.p., 1924.

Hoshi Shinichi. *Jinmin wa Yowashi; Kanri wa Tsuyoshi* [The people are weak; the bureaucrats are strong]. Tokyo: Kadokawa Shoten, 1971.

Hosie, Sir Alexander. *On the Trail of the Opium Poppy.* Vol. 2. London: George Philip, 1914.

Imai Seiichi. *Taisho Demokurashi* [Taisho democracy]. *Nihon no Rekishi* [Japanese history]. Vol. 23. Tokyo: Chuko Bunko, 1990.

Ingles, Brian. *The Opium War.* London: Hodder and Stoughton, 1976.

Jennings, John M. *The Opium Empire: Japanese Imperialism and Drug Trafficking in Asia, 1895–1945.* Westport, Conn.: Praeger, 1997.

Jiu Shanghai Fengyun Renwu [People of old Shanghai]. Shanghai: People's Publishing Company, 1989.

Johnson, D. Bruce. "Righteousness before Revenue: The Forgotten Moral Crusade against the Indo-Chinese Opium Trade." *Journal of Drug Issues,* Fall 1975, 304–26.

Jonnes, Jill. *Hep-cats, Narcs, and Pipe Dreams: A History of America's Romance with Illegal Drugs.* New York: Scribner's, 1996.

Kaku, Sagataro. *Opium Policy in Japan.* Geneva: N.p., 1924.

Kane, H. H. *Opium Smoking in America and China.* New York: Putnam, 1882.

Kinder, Douglas Clark. "Bureaucratic Cold Warrior: Harry J. Anslinger and Illicit Narcotics Traffic." *Pacific Historical Review* (1981) 50:169–91.

Kitaoka Shinichi. *Goto Shimpei: Gaiko to Bijyon* [Goto Shimpei: foreign policy and vision]. Tokyo: Chuo Koron Sha, 1988.

Kodama Yoshio. "Akusei, Jusei, Ransei" [Evil government, the sound of guns, the world in chaos]. *Fuun* [Wind and clouds]. Vol. 2. Tokyo: Nihon Oyobi Nihonjinsha, 1972.

———. *Gokuchu; Gokugai* [In prison; out of prison]. Tokyo: Ajia Shonensha, 1942.

———. *Sugamo Diary.* Tokyo: Radio Press, 1960.

———. *Unmei no Mon* [Gate of fate]. Tokyo: Rokumeisha, 1950.

———. *Ware Yaburetari* [I was defeated]. Tokyo: Tokyo Shuppansha, 1949.

"Kokkin o Okasu Gun Meirei" [Military orders to violate national prohibitions]. *Shukan Yomiyori* [Weekly Yomiyori], June 5, 1955, 4–13.

Lamley, Harry J. "Lineage Feuding in Southern Fujian and Eastern Guangdong under Qing Rule." In *Violence in China: Essays in Culture and Counterculture,* edited by Jonathan Lipman and Steven Harrell. Albany: State University of New York Press, 1990.

Lee, Martin A., and Bruce Shlain. *Acid Dreams.* New York: Grove Weidenfeld, 1985.

Lowes, Peter D. *The Genesis of International Narcotics Control.* Geneva: Droz, 1966.

Ma Weigang, ed. *Jin Chang Jin Du: Jianguo Chuqi de Lishi Huigu* [Eliminate prostitution, eliminate narcotics: historical review of the founding of the country]. Beijing: Jinguan Jiaoyu Chubanshe, 1993.

Marks, John. *The Search for the Manchurian Candidate: The CIA and Mind Control.* New York: New York Times Books, 1979.

Marshall, Jonathan, Peter Dale Scott, and Jane Hunter. *The Iran Contra Connection: Secret Teams and Covert Operations in the Reagan Era.* Boston: South End, 1987.

———. "Opium and the Politics of Gangsterism in Nationalist China, 1927–1945." *Bulletin of Concerned Asian Scholars* 8, no. 3 (July–September 1977): 19–48.

Martin, Brian. *The Shanghai Green Gang: Politics and Organized Crime, 1919–1937.* Berkeley: University of California Press, 1996.

McCormack, Gavin. *Chang Tso-lin in Northeast China, 1911–1928: China, Japan, and the Manchurian Idea.* Stanford, Calif.: Stanford University Press, 1977.

McCoy, Alfred. *The Politics of Heroin: CIA Complicity in the Global Drug Trade.* New York: Lawrence Hill Books, 1991.

McWilliams, John. *The Protectors.* Newark: University of Delaware Press, 1991.

Mei Jun and Shao Pu, eds. *Haishang Wenren Du Yuesheng* [World renowned VIP Du Yuesheng]. Henan Peoples Publishing Co. 1987.

Meyers, Ramon H., and Mark R. Peatie. *The Japanese Colonial Experience.* Princeton, N.J.: Princeton University Press, 1984.

Miles, Milton. *A Different Kind of War: The Little Known Story of the Combined Guerrilla Forces Created in China by the U.S. Navy and the Chinese during World War II.* Garden City, N.Y.: Doubleday, 1967.

Minami Mantetsu Kabushiki Kaisha, Keizai Chosakai, Daigobu [Manchuria railway economic investigation bureau, section five]. *Chosen Ahen Mayaku Seido Chosa Hokoku* [Report on an investigation of opium and narcotics in Korea]. Mimeographed report, 1932. Washington, D.C.: Library of Congress.

Mokuda Katsuji. "Bakurosareta Manshu Gigoku" [Manchurian scandals disclosed], *Waga Kan* [My view], May 1930, 78.

Morgan, H. Wayne. *Yesterday's Addicts: American Society and Drug Abuse, 1865–1920.* Norman: University of Oklahoma Press, 1974.

Morris, Ivan. *The Right Wing in Japan.* London: Oxford University Press, 1960.

Morse, H. B. *The Chronicles of the East India Company Trading to China, 1635–1834.* London: Oxford University Press, 1926.

Morton, William Fitch. *Tanaka Giichi and Japan's China Policy.* New York: St. Martin's, 1980.

"Mr. Attlee's Friends, the Chinese Commies, Are the World's Leading Dope Smugglers." *Saturday Evening Post,* November 13, 1954.

Murphy, Rhodes. *Shanghai: Key to Modern China.* Cambridge, Mass.: Harvard University Press, 1953.

Musto, David. *The American Disease: The Origins of Narcotic Control.* New Haven, Conn.: Yale University Press, 1973.

Newman, R. K. "Opium Smoking in Late Imperial China: A Reconsideration." *Modern Asian Studies* 29, no. 4 (1995): 765–94.

Nisbet, Charles T., and Firouz Vakil. "Some Estimates of Price and Expenditure Elasticities of Demand for Marijuana among U.C.L.A. Students." *The Review of Economics and Statistics* 54 (1972): 473–75.

Nitanosa Nakaba. *Senso to Nihon Ahen Shi; Ahen O Nitanosa Otozo no Shogai* [War

and the history of opium in Japan; the life and times of Nitanosa Otozo].
Tokyo: Subaru Shobo, 1977.

Northedge, F. S. *The League of Nations: Its Life and Times, 1920–1946*. New York:
Holmes and Meier, 1986.

Oe Shino. *Tenno no Guntai* [The emperor's army]. Vol. 3, *Showa no Rekishi* [History of the Showa period]. Tokyo: Shogaku Kan, 1988.

Oi Shizuo. *Ahen Jiken no Shinso* [The facts about the opium incident]. Tokyo:
Privately published, 1923.

Okada Yoshimasa. "Ahen Senso to Watakushi no Taiken" [The opium war and
my own experience]. *Zoku, Gendaishi Shiryo Geppo* [Continued. modern
history materials monthly report]. June 1986.

———. "Chukoku Shihei Gizo Jiken no Zembo" [The complete picture of the
Chinese currency counterfeiting caper]. *Rekishi To Jimbutsu* 110 (October
1980).

Okura Sho [Ministry of Finance]. *Meiji Taisho Zaisei Shi* [Financial history of
the Meiji and Taisho years, 1868–1925]. *Gaichi Zaisei* [Overseas finance].
Tokyo: Keizai Orai Sha, 1958.

Owen, David Edward. *British Opium Policy in India and China*. Hamden, Conn.:
Archon Books, 1968.

Parssinen, Terry M. *Secret Passion, Secret Remedies; Narcotic Drugs in British Society,
1820–1930*. Philadelphia: Institute for Study of Human Issues, 1983.

Perrine, Daniel M. *The Chemistry of Mind-Altering Drugs: History, Pharmacology, and
Cultural Context*. Washington, D.C.: American Chemical Society, 1996.

Perry, Elizabeth. *Shanghai on Strike*. Stanford, Calif.: Stanford University Press,
1993.

Powell, Hickman. *Ninety Times Guilty*. New York: Arno, 1974.

Reins, Thomas. "Reform, Nationalism, and Internationalism: The Opium Suppression Movement in China and the Anglo-American Influence, 1900–
1908." *Modern Asian Studies* 25 (February 1991): 101–42.

Renborg, Bertil. *International Drug Control*. New York: Kraus Reprint, 1972.

———. "The Grand Old Men of the League of Nations," *Bulletin on Narcotics*
16, no. 4 (October–December 1964): 1–11.

Ryu Meishu. *Taiwan Tochi to Ahen Mondai* [Control of Taiwan and the opium
problem]. Tokyo: Yamakawa Publishing, 1983.

Sato Saburo. "Kindai Nihon ni Okeru Ahen no Mondai." *Kindai Nitchu Koshoshi
no Kenkyu* [Studies in modern Sino-Japanese diplomatic history]. Tokyo:
Yoshikawa Kobunkan, 1984.

Scott, Peter Dale, and Jonathan Marshall. *Cocaine Politics*. Berkeley: University of
California Press, 1991.

"School Board Might Find DARE a Habit It Can Kick." *Chapel Hill News*. May 8,
1997.

Seagrave, Sterling. *The Soong Dynasty*. New York: Harper and Row, 1985.

Shellony, Ben-Ami. *Revolt in Japan*. Princeton, N.J.: Princeton University Press, 1973.

Shimada Toshihiko. *Kantogun: Zai Man Rikugun no Dokuso* [The Kwantung army: the independent actions of the army in Manchuria]. Tokyo: Chuo Koronsha, 1965.

Silberman, Bernard, and H. D. Harootunian, eds. *Japan in Crisis: Essays on Taisho Japan*. Princeton, N.J.: Princeton University Press, 1974.

Spence, Jonathan D. "Opium Smoking in Ch'ing China." In *Conflict and Control in Late Imperial China*, edited by Frederic Wakeman Jr. and Carolyn Grant, 143–73. Berkeley: University of California Press, 1975.

Stelle, C. *Americans and the Chinese Opium Trade in the Nineteenth Century*. Chicago: University of Chicago Libraries, 1941.

Stevens, Jay. *Storming Heaven: LSD and the American Dream*. New York: Harper and Row, 1987.

Szasz, Thomas. *Ceremonial Chemistry: The Ritual Persecution of Drugs, Addicts, and Pushers*. New York: Anchor Press, 1974.

Takamatsu Shigeru. "Watakushi Wa Teikoku Rikugun de Gizo Shihei of Tsukuru" [I made counterfeit currency for the Imperial Army]. *Gendai*. September 1967.

Takasugi Shingo. "Akuma no Boryaku" [The devil's invasion]. Pts. 1–5. *Sandae Mainichi* [Sunday Mainichi]. December 2, 1984; December 9, 1984; December 16, 1984; December 23, 1984.

Takemori, Hisaakira. *Miezaru Seifu: Kodama Yoshio to Sono Kuro no Jinmyaku* [The invisible government: Kodama Yoshio and his black network]. Tokyo: Shiraishi Shoten. 1976.

Tan, Chung. *China and the Brave New World*. Bombay: Allied Publishers, 1978.

Taylor, Arnold. *American Diplomacy and the Narcotics Traffic, 1900–1939: A Study in International Humanitarian Reform*. Durham, N.C.: Duke University Press, 1973.

Trocki, Carl A. *Opium and Empire: Chinese Society in Colonial Singapore, 1800–1910*. Ithaca, N.Y.: Cornell University Press, 1990.

———. "The Rise of Singapore's Great Opium Syndicate, 1840–86." *Journal of Southeast Asian Studies* 18 (1987): 58–80.

Tsunoda Fusako. *Amakasu Tai-i* [Captain Amakasu]. Tokyo: Chuo Bunko, 1974.

United States Treasury Department. *Traffic in Opium and Other Dangerous Drugs*. Washington, D.C.: Government Printing Office, 1931–38.

Van Biema, David. "Just Say Life Skills: A New School Antidrug Program Outstrips D.A.R.E.," *Time*. November 11, 1996.

Van Creveld, Martin. *The Transformation of War*. New York: Free Press, 1991.

van Ours, Jan C. "The Price Elasticity of Hard Drugs: The Case of Opium in the

Dutch East Indies, 1923–1938." *Journal of Political Economy* 103 (April 1995): 261–79.

Wakeman, Frederic, Jr. *Policing Shanghai, 1927–1947.* Berkeley: University of California Press, 1995.

———. *The Shanghai Badlands: Wartime Terrorism and Urban Crime, 1937–1941.* Cambridge: University of Cambridge Press, 1996.

———. *Strangers at the Gate: Social Disorder in South China, 1839–1861.* Berkeley: University of California Press, 1966.

Walker, William O. *Opium and Foreign Policy.* Chapel Hill: University of North Carolina Press, 1991.

Walters, F. P. *A History of the League of Nations.* London: Oxford University Press, 1969.

Warren, Samuel. *The Opium Question.* 3d ed. London: J. Ridgeway, 1840.

White, Michale D., and William A Luksetich. "Heroin: Price Elasticity and Enforcement Strategies." *Economic Inquiry* 21 (October 1983): 557–63.

Yamamoto Tsuneo. *Ahen To Taiho: Rikugun Showa Tsusho no Nananen* [Opium and guns: nine years in the army's Showa trading company]. Tokyo: PMC Publishing, 1986.

Yamauchi Saburo. "Mayaku to Senso; Nitchu Senso no Himitsu Heiki" [Narcotics and war; A secret weapon of the China war]. *Jimbutsu Orai* [Affairs of eminent men]. October 1956.

Yan, Zhengyun. *Zhungguo de Fanzui Wenti Yu Shehui Bienchien de Guanxi* [Crime in relation to social change in China]. Beijing: Beijing University Press, 1986.

Yatsugi Kasuo. *Kishi Nobosuke no Kaiso* [Recollections of Kishi Nobosuke]. Tokyo: Bungei Shuso, 1976.

Yoga Hiroshi. "Kita-shi, Mokyo no Tokumu Kikan" [The Special Service Organs of north China and Mongolian border region]." *Kokuho* [National defense], January 1972, 187–99.

Young, A. Morgan. *Japan in Recent Times.* Westport, Conn.: Greenwood, 1929.

Young, Arthur. *China and the Helping Hand.* Cambridge, Mass.: Harvard University Press, 1963.

Young, Ernest P. *The Presidency of Yuan shih-k'ai.* Ann Arbor: University of Michigan Press, 1977.

Yu Enyang. *Yunnan Shouyi Yonghu Gunghe Shimo Ji* [A record of the righteous Yunnan leadership in protecting the republic]. 1917. Reprint, Taipei: Wenhai Chubanshe, 1966.

Zhang Jungu, *Du Yuesheng Zhuan* [Biography of Du Yuesheng]. 4 vols. Taipei: Zhuanji Wenxue Chubanshe, 1967.

NEWSPAPERS AND PERIODICALS

Asahi Shimbun. Tokyo, Japan.

Canton Register. Guangdong, China.

Minguo Ribao [Republican Times]. Shanghai, China.

New York Times. New York, United States.

New York Herald Tribune. New York, United States.

North China Herald. Shanghai, China.

Shen Pao. Shanghai, China.

PUBLISHED DOCUMENT COLLECTIONS

Eguchi Keiichi, ed. *Shiryo: Nitchu Senso ki Ahen Seisaku* [Source materials: the China war era opium policy]. Tokyo: Iwanami Shoten, 1985.

Great Britain, Foreign Office. *The Opium Trade, 1910–1941.* Wilmington, Del.: Scholarly Resources, 1974.

Jindai Zhongguo Banghui Neimu [The inside story of modern Chinese gangs]. Beijing: Masses Publishing Company, 1992.

Zhonghua Wenshi Ziliao Wenku [A treasury of Chinese source materials]. Vol 20. Beijing: Zhongguo Wenshi Chubanshe, 1996.

Zhou Yumin, and Shao Yong, eds. *Zhongguo Banghui Shi* [History of Chinese gangs]. Shanghai: Shanghai People's Publishing, 1993.

Zoku: Gendaishi Shiryo [Continuing: modern history source materials]. Tokyo: Misuzu Shobo, 1986.

ARCHIVAL SOURCES

Harry Anslinger Papers. Pattee Library Archives. Pennsylvania State University. University Park, Pennsylvania.

International Military Tribunal Records. National Diet Library. Tokyo, Japan.

League of Nations Archive. Geneva, Swtzerland.

Papers of Naval Group China and Vice Admiral M. E. Miles. Office of Naval Intelligence. Record Group 38. National Archives. College Park, Maryland.

Records of the British Foreign Office. Public Records Office. London, England.

Records of the Internal Affairs of China. United States Department of State. Record Group 59. National Archives. Washington, D.C.

Records of the Japanese Foreign Ministry, 1868–1945. Microfilm WT series. Library of Congress, Washington, D.C.

Shanghai Municipal Police, Criminal Investigation Department. National Archives. College Park, Maryland.

Wenshih Ziliao [Source materials]. Center for Chinese Studies Library. Berkeley, California.

INDEX

In this text all Chinese words are rendered in pinyin except for names for which the non-standard spellings have become commonplace: Chiang Kai-shek; Sun Yat-sen; T. V. Soong; T. L. Soong; and H. H. Kung.

ABOUT THE AUTHORS

Kathryn Meyer received her B.A. from the University of Vermont and her Ph.D. from Temple University. She has taught East Asian history at Temple University–Japan, Ohio Wesleyan University, and Lafayette College, where she is assistant professor of history. In 1990, she was awarded a National Endowment for the Humanities fellowship that supported research for this book. She lives in Easton, Pennsylvania.

Terry Parssinen received his B.A. in History from Grinnell College and his M.A. and Ph.D. in the History of Ideas program from Brandeis University. He has taught at Grinnell College, Temple University, the University of Maryland, College Park, and he is presently professor of history at the University of Tampa. His previous book is entitled *Secret Passions, Secret Remedies: Narcotic Drugs in British Society, 1820–1930* (ISHI Publications, 1983).